The Political Power of the Business Corporation

The Political Power of the Business Corporation

Stephen Wilks

Professor of Politics, The University of Exeter, UK

Edward Elgar
Cheltenham, UK • Northampton, MA, USA

© Stephen Wilks 2013

All rights reserved. No part of this publication may be reproduced, stored in a retrieval system or transmitted in any form or by any means, electronic, mechanical or photocopying, recording, or otherwise without the prior permission of the publisher.

Published by
Edward Elgar Publishing Limited
The Lypiatts
15 Lansdown Road
Cheltenham
Glos GL50 2JA
UK

Edward Elgar Publishing, Inc.
William Pratt House
9 Dewey Court
Northampton
Massachusetts 01060
USA

A catalogue record for this book
is available from the British Library

Library of Congress Control Number: 2012951745

This book is available electronically in the ElgarOnline.com
Social and Political Science Subject Collection, E-ISBN 978 1 84980 732 6

MIX
Paper from responsible sources
FSC
www.fsc.org
FSC® C018575

ISBN 978 1 84980 730 2 (cased)
     978 1 84980 731 9 (paperback)

Typeset by Servis Filmsetting Ltd, Stockport, Cheshire
Printed and bound by MPG Books Group, UK

Contents

List of tables	vi
List of abbreviations	vii
Preface	ix
1 The genesis of a governing institution	1
2 The corporation as a political actor	21
3 Globalisation and the enhanced power of multinational corporations	42
4 Corporate power in the UK: the rise of the corporate elite	64
5 The politics of the New Corporate State	95
6 Partnership and policy in Britain's New Corporate State	117
7 Multinational corporations as partners in global governance	147
8 Corporations, culture and accountability	177
9 How persuasive is corporate social responsibility?	197
10 The explosion of interest in corporate governance	217
11 Conclusion: fairy-tales, facts, foci and futures	251
Bibliography	269
Index	303

Tables

1.1	National distribution of the world's largest corporations	5
1.2	Comparison of the economic size of countries and corporations	7
3.1	Transnationality index for countries, 2005	49
3.2	Largest stocks of outward FDI, by emergent countries	55
4.1	Party positions in a left–right scale	72
4.2	Corporations in politically vulnerable sectors, 2012	76
4.3	The UK Big 4 accountants	80
4.4	The elite city law firms	82
4.5	The largest UK management consultancies, 2007	83
4.6	Illustrative composition of the UK corporate elite	88
4.7	UK income before tax	89
4.8	Share in UK total income before tax and (after tax)	91
5.1	Public trust in the professions	98
6.1	Summary of the main UK privatisations	123
6.2	The Big 6 energy corporations: UK electricity market shares, 2010	130
6.3	Components of the public services industry	134
6.4	Approval for private provision of public services	144
7.1	WEF country competitiveness rankings: 2011–12 compared with 2001–02	162
8.1	Levels of trust in business and in government	195
10.1	Comparing national and corporate governance	220
10.2	Major reforms to German corporate governance	237

Abbreviations

AGM	Annual General Meeting
APPC	Association of Professional Political Consultants
BDI	Bundesverband der Deutschen Industrie (Federation of German Industry)
BERR	Department of Business Enterprise and Regulatory Reform (UK)
BIS	Department of Business Innovation and Skills (UK)
BITC	Business in the Community
BRICS	Brazil, Russia, India and China
CBI	Confederation of British Industry
CCP	Chinese Communist Party
CEO	Chief Executive Officer
CIPFA	Chartered Institute of Public Finance and Accounting
CME	Coordinated Market Economy
CSR	Corporate Social Responsibility
DBIS	Department of Business Innovation and Skills (UK)
EMNC	Emergent Country Multinational Corporations
FDI	Foreign Direct Investment
FDP	Free Democratic Party (Germany)
FSA	Financial Services Authority
GATT	General Agreement on Tariffs and Trade
GDP	Gross Domestic Product
GRI	Global Reporting Initiative
HMRC	Her Majesty's Revenue and Customs
ICC	International Chamber of Commerce
IEA	Institute of Economic Affairs
IFS	Institute of Fiscal Studies
IMF	International Monetary Fund
IPPR	Institute of Public Policy Research
ISO	International Organization for Standardization
LDP	Liberal Democratic Party (Japan)
LME	Liberal Market Economy
LSE	London Stock Exchange
MNC	Multinational Corporation

NAO	National Audit Office
NED	Non-Executive Director
NEDC	National Economic Development Council
NYSE	New York Stock Exchange
OECD	Organization for Economic Cooperation and Development
Ofcom	The Office of Communications
OFGEM	Office of Gas and Electricity Markets
OFWAT	Water Services Regulation Authority
ONS	Office of National Statistics
PAC	Public Accounts Committee
PASC	Public Administration Select Committee
PFI	Private Finance Initiative
PIC	Public Interest Companies
PPP	Public–Private Partnerships
PSI	Public Services Industry
PWC	PriceWaterhouseCoopers
SME	Small and Medium Sized Enterprises
SoS	Secretary of State
SPAD	Special Adviser (UK)
SPD	Social Democratic Party (Germany)
TCC	Transnational Capitalist Class
TNC	Transnational Corporation
TUC	Trades Union Congress
UNCTAD	United Nations Conference on Trade and Development
VoC	Varieties of Capitalism
WTO	World Trade Organization

Preface

In 1974, when I first became intrigued by the power of business corporations, and particularly by their ability to wrest concessions from national governments, it seemed perfectly possible to bring these concentrations of economic power under democratic control. Now I'm not so sure. It seems to me that many of the democratic gains fought for so heroically over the last 150 years have simultaneously created a set of nominally economic forces which have emptied many of those gains of real meaning. The truly worrying prospect is that those forces, call them corporate capitalism, managerial dominance or simply corporate power, have created new autocrats, immune from effective popular control. Business corporations are often creative and can be brilliant and enriching, but their economic and cultural achievements cloak their ability to dictate political choices. This is far from an original insight. It was expressed brilliantly by Charles Lindblom, and ironically by John Kenneth Galbraith, whose insights into the power of corporations in society have been a constant source of inspiration. Both Galbraith and Lindblom offered reform proposals to counter corporate power but that power has been, as argued in the following pages, vastly increased since the 1970s. The universal resort to market solutions, the emancipation of management, and the loss of faith in the active state, have conspired together to embed corporate power so deeply into our institutions that it appears invulnerable.

We used to be concerned about selecting a government we approved of and calling it to account. Now we should be concerned about our inability to exert influence over a government of corporations and to call them to account. And this matters. A national and a global society in which business corporations share in government has inherent dynamics which threaten economic collapse and environmental destruction, and also herald a destabilising new age of political activism including quasi-revolutionary struggle against corporate privileges. This slide towards the precipice is widely acknowledged but its causes are shrouded in confusion. To clarify those causes, in the shape of a clearer diagnosis of the nature of corporate power, is the motivation behind this book.

The origins of my deepening concern about the irresponsible business corporation began with my PhD on policy towards the British motor industry and developed through research on industrial policy, switching to competition policy as Thatcherite market fundamentalism discredited state intervention and unleashed market forces. My engagement with scholarly research on relations between government and corporations has been tempered by practical involvement with the dynamics of markets and dilemmas of corporate strategies through the enforcement of competition policy. As a Member of the Competition Commission from 2000 to 2008, and subsequently as a Member of the Competition Appeal Tribunal, I have had the opportunity to contrast rational economic (and political) theories with the often messy realities of corporate ambitions, regulatory uncertainty and managerial misconceptions. Insight into the power of management and its ideologies was provided, somewhat unpredictably, by four years as Deputy Vice Chancellor of Exeter University. Business management is not confined to the business corporation.

Universities still allow for the luxury of the critical exploration of political change. I am grateful to my colleagues in the Politics Department at Exeter for, to put it bluntly, leaving me alone, and to the undergraduates for not leaving me alone. For the past eight years I have taught a third-year seminar on business and politics, which has allowed me to explore aspects of business power intensively and speculatively. My students have similarly become explorers. They have been enthusiastic, questioning, sometimes brilliant, and sometimes startling in their analyses and their attitudes. This book is for them and for their generation who will have to face the challenges summarised in its conclusions. To that extent this is designed as a textbook, aimed at critical advanced undergraduates. I hope it will also reach a wider audience of those many people who are similarly concerned about, or implicated in, concentrations of corporate power and challenges to democracy. An audience in business schools and in business – partly academic, partly lay – will, I hope, find material here which helps to re-conceptualise the corporation. Accordingly, although this is a research-based study, I have tried to avoid engaging in arcane disciplinary debates just as I have tried to avoid too much jargon and too many references overburdening the text.

Since the ideas feeding into this book have matured over a disconcerting period of time I have accumulated many debts, intellectual and practical. I'm going to avoid a roll call of the many sources of generous inspiration but I must mention one or two colleagues and especially David Coen (UCL), Mark Thatcher (LSE) and Paul Jones (Warwick), with all of whom I have discussed these issues and who have read parts of the draft book. Among thoughtful and creative students it is perhaps invidious to pick out individuals, but of the recent cohorts, Chris Ford, Alison O'Connor, Sam Knight and Aleksandra Fernandes da Costa provided valuable insights as well as commentary on draft chapters. My thanks also go to Edward Elgar Publishers, in the shape of Alex Pettifer, who has been efficient, quietly supportive and above all patient. Finally, this book is dedicated to Philippa, for her heroically sustained encouragement, and to Laura, Susannah and Verity for their inspiration.

1. The genesis of a governing institution

APPRAISING THE BUSINESS CORPORATION

Sometimes hero, sometimes villain, from the emancipatory brilliance of Apple to the environmental incompetence of BP, the business corporation presents radically contrasting images. For the most part, however, it is simply part of the landscape, a law-abiding corporate citizen whose presence we take completely for granted, much like the weather. The weather only provokes comment when it is unusual, but it conditions the environment in which we live. In similar fashion the business corporation conditions our social and economic environment, it is a defining factor in our social biosphere but its sheer familiarity, its ubiquitous presence, leads us to assume that we understand its influence on our lives, our society and our politics. We do not. The business corporation is arguably the most influential and the least studied institution in contemporary political life.

This book focuses on the business corporation rather than on 'business' collectively, on the market, or on capitalism, although all three concepts enter the analysis as helpful theoretical frameworks. The term 'corporation' is used in preference to the 'company' or the 'firm' partly for consistency but also to exploit the mildly alien usage of this American term with its connotations of size and unfamiliarity. Four themes infuse the following chapters. They are first, the huge variety of business corporations, which requires better tools to interpret the corporation as a political actor and as an operational unit of political analysis. Second, is the idea of the business corporation as a 'governing institution' which simultaneously introduces an institutionalist approach and directs attention to the circumstances in which business corporations take on a governing role. Third, is the complex relationship between the large corporation and its management. A generalised assumption of managerial control runs through the following pages, extending into analysis of managerial elites, managerial rewards and the corrosive effects of managerialism as an ideology. Fourth, there is the vexing question of accountability. This covers a range of issues from the debate about corporate social responsibility to questions of corporate governance and relationships with the elected governments of nation states.

Underlying these themes is an intellectual puzzle and a disciplinary frustration. Until very recently there has been little systematic analysis of the impact of the business corporation on contemporary society. In particular political scientists have been myopic on the subject to the point that instead of mountains of scholarly achievement we have a few oases in an arid landscape. These oases, provided by scholars such as Gamble, Grant, Coen, Vogel, Moran and Fuchs, feature in the following pages but their insights underline the difficulties of coping with a multi-dimensional, multi-disciplinary understanding of the corporation as a governing institution. The argument is perhaps better presented as a matter of relative priority. The impact of business corporations, as analysed in this book, is not about participation in a political process, it is about dominating the political process and defining the structures of national and global politics. The ascendency of the business corporation has been consolidated since 1990 and has reached the point where contemporary politics can simply not be understood without a comprehensive account of business influence. It is this challenge that motivates this study.

The analytical difficulties of locating the business corporation in a political setting can be illustrated by a series of fascinating but ambiguous features of the corporation which inhibit clear conclusions. Consider four ambiguities. First, the corporation is an astonishing vehicle for creating wealth. The economic growth and prosperity of the 20th century was built on profitable corporate growth, but it often appears that corporate success demands individual exploitation, inequality, inappropriate technological choices and environmental destruction which threaten the very gains that it has achieved. Second, the corporation has a paradoxical relationship with the market. It operates in the market and professes loyalty to market principles but companies themselves are hierarchies and as they grow bigger they subdue and dominate markets, hence the origins of antitrust and the 'corporatization of the market' (Harrod, 2006: 45). Third, corporations operate as economic institutions and in disciplinary terms are analysed through the tools of industrial economics, yet their accumulated economic power inevitably translates into political power and business corporations not only influence politics, they are nurtured and privileged within capitalist societies. Their privileges have expanded in a post-communist world and are increasingly studied in the comparative setting of 'varieties of capitalism' in which the political coordination and distribution of values undertaken by corporations become a defining feature of national governmental systems. Finally, the ultimate ambiguity has been expressed by polemicists but has best been captured by science fiction; it is the progression from an historical position in which corporations were licensed by the state, to a 21st century position in which states are licensed by corporations. To be more specific, Gamble and Kelly (2000: 22, 23) explore the great reluctance of the British state to encourage the creation of joint stock companies in the 1840s by permitting limited liability. They conceptualise the eventual legal permissions as a 'license to operate' granted by the state to the joint stock company. Hence they emphasise the early understanding of the corporation as a creature of the state, but that creature has grown in size, status, reach and global power to the point at which governments, and potentially states themselves, survive on the basis of corporate approval. The corporation with a license to operate has become, in Mary Shelley's image, a Frankenstein's monster, threatening the state that gave it life.

These four areas of ambiguity point up the normative approach which transcends market economics and asserts not only that corporations deploy political power, but that they are privileged to the point where they can escape state control. The arguments advanced in this book are therefore critical. They accept the business corporation as an economic institution but also regard it as a 'governing institution' to be analysed through the joint lenses of institutionalism and traditional political economy. Hence it is almost taken for granted that large corporations possess political power which must be understood and analysed in order to identify how it can be held to account. But the arguments go further to assess the role of the business corporation as a social institution which shapes the lives of the majority of the citizens of the majority of countries. The corporation generates wealth which it holds hostage for individuals in the shape of jobs, shares and pensions. It determines technological trajectories embodied in production processes, products and services. It provides consumer products and is engaged in an ever-expanding extension of commercialisation and the creation of a global consumer society. In the process it defines identities and lifestyles through branding and control over the media. It therefore defines the very discourse by which societies define the good life and individuals pursue fulfilling lifestyles (Barber, 2001; Klein, 2002; Skidelsky and Skidelsky, 2012). The suggestion, in other words, is that we have in the West entered a world of corporate hegemony which is railed against by the anti-capitalists (Monbiot, 2000; Hertz, 2001; Bakan, 2004); by social democrats (Marquand, 2004; Crouch, 2004, 2011; Stiglitz, 2012); and by communitarians who re-emphasise the republican traditions of hostility to corporate dominance (Sandel, 1996, 2012; Etzioni, 2001); but which has proved ultimately seductive and has been packaged for global consumption.

THE NORM OF THE LARGE CORPORATION

In the 150 years since modern business corporations first came into existence they have grown in number, in scope and in size. It is hardly surprising that huge corporations have developed since the corporate form was a reaction to the need to create and to manage the massive accumulations of capital necessary to create efficient productive industries (Gamble and Kelly, 2000: 31; Micklethwait and Wooldridge, 2003: 54). The prototypes for the large corporations were the 19th-century railway companies and, in the USA, the consolidations following the creation of the Standard Oil Trust in 1882 produced industrial concentration and the development of oligopoly with the dominance of most markets by a small number of large corporations. Business historians such as Chandler have charted corporate organisation and growth in loving detail and have stressed the typical US model of oligopolistic competition (Chandler, 1990: 90). Classic studies such as Berle and Means (1932) stressed the growth of giant firms whilst Galbraith (1952: 58) took oligopoly as a defining feature of American capitalism. But although large corporations have become even larger in the closing decades of the 20th century, have expanded globally and have become the norm in the former Communist states, much of our understanding of managerial or corporate capitalism is unduly influenced by American experience and research. In many ways the US is special, not least in its response to corporate power through antitrust, dating back to the Sherman Act of 1890. One theme of later chapters is the influence of Americanisation – of ideas, corporate forms, antitrust and the American corporation itself.

Notwithstanding the American experience, the growth of industrial concentration, oligopoly and the large corporation has been a global phenomenon. The giant firm in Britain generated much sceptical interest in the 1970s (Holland, 1975; Prais, 1976) but in Continental Europe and Japan corporations developed in a less adversarial atmosphere and often in alliance with the state. The developed capitalist economies have had over 100 years to get used to working with and through business corporations. Since 1990 the corporate form has spread across the post-Communist societies and the emergent economies so that it has become the orthodox vehicle of wealth creation, most strikingly in China, as we see in Chapter 3.

From a political perspective we are less concerned with the legions of small firms, such as the 4.8 million active firms operating within the US economy in 1998 (Mueller, 2003: 2), although, as Vogel (1989: 12) notes, when they work together these millions of firms have the potential to be an important political force (see also Moran, 2009: ch. 5). Corporations with individual political interests and influence are typically large, either in absolute terms or in respect of a given market or sector. Firms with political power are likely also to have market power through oligopolistic advantages in their markets. Galbraith (1975: 54) argued that 'when firms become large: in fact a transformation of the very nature of economic society occurs'. The extraordinary scale of the biggest corporations is genuinely difficult to grasp but it confirms the visceral certainty, expressed eloquently by crusaders such as the US Supreme Court judge Louis Brandeis (Adelstein, 1989), that these corporations wield substantial political power. In George Monbiot's words, 'we hear plenty about the economies of scale, but there is a politics of scale too: the bigger business becomes, the more we, as consumers and citizens, shrink by comparison' (2000: 14).

Since the early 1990s the league table of corporate grandeur has appeared as the annual *Fortune Global 500*. Corporations are ranked by global revenue and the results for 2011 show Wal-Mart as the largest corporation in the world with revenues of $422 billion and employing an astonishing 2,100,000 people. The biggest companies are in the biggest global industries including oil, motor vehicles and financial services. Thus some of the totemic companies symbolising global consumerism are surprisingly low in the league table. MacDonald appears at 403; Boeing at 114; while NewsCorp is at 284. The league table is relatively stable year by year but in the 15 years between 1996 and 2011 some clear trends have emerged. There are fewer large Japanese companies, the US predominance is decaying with more large companies now headquartered in Europe, and there has been a remarkable globalisation of the large corporation with the rise of the BRICS, and especially China, as shown in Table 1.1 The dominance of 'the Triad' (the USA, Europe and Japan) is thus breaking down and there are increasing numbers of government owned global corporations.

Table 1.1 National distribution of the world's largest corporations

	1996	2007	2011
Europe (EU)	153	167	145
USA	153	153	133
Japan	141	64	68
China	2	29	61
Russia, Brazil, India	5	17	22
Others (in 2011, 12 countries)	46	70	71
Total Fortune 500	500	500	500

Source: Fortune Global 500, 2012, available at http://money.cnn.com.

Most large corporations are multinationals with subsidiaries in a number of countries. Again, the scale of multinational operation is spectacular. UNCTAD (2009: 9) note that 'an estimated 79,000 TNCs control some 790,000 foreign affiliates . . . the value added activity . . . of foreign affiliates worldwide accounted for 11 per cent of global GDP in 2007 . . . the number of employees reached 82 million'. Multinationals are likely to be more powerful than predominately national companies since they can exploit their flexibility to negotiate with nation-states. The UNCTAD league table of the top 100 multinationals ranks companies by the total value of foreign assets and placed General Electric in first place (with Wal-Mart relegated to tenth place). In the rankings of multinationals the Triad dominance is much more marked. There were no BRIC companies in the top-100 and the predominance of Europe is even more striking, over half of these multinationals are headquartered in Europe (UNCTAD, 2008: 220–22).

Since it is difficult to grasp the scale and importance of these economic units, one popular device has been to compare the revenues of large corporations with the GDP of nation-states. Serious analysts have pointed out that such comparisons are potentially misleading and overstate the power of multinationals (De Grauwe and Camerman, 2003) but as long as they are not used as some precise indicator of relative influence they do present a dramatic contrast between the resources available to corporations and those available to states. Thus, of the 100 largest economic units in the world, in 2007, 52 were countries and 48 were corporations. Table 1.2 shows approximately every fifth ranking to give some indication of the ordering of units (see also Chandler and Mazlish, 2005; Fuchs, 2007: 54). The table indicates that Wal-Mart was bigger than Denmark, and five corporations, including Toyota, were bigger than Portugal. Hitachi, at 100 on the list, was bigger than the remaining 80 countries on the World Bank schedule including such populous countries as Bangladesh (159 mn), Congo (62 mn), Ethiopia (79 mn) or Vietnam (85 mn). Harrod (2006: 24) actually suggests that we should compare corporate revenues with government budgets to get a more accurate idea of discretionary spend. That would, of course, paint corporations as even larger and more powerful units. The corporate pursuit of growth and sheer size is unsettling. It seems no longer to be driven by the imperatives of investment but by a search for market power, political influence and managerial ambition.

As explored in later chapters, there is a debate about whether giant corporations, operating as complex organisations, are being superseded by 'unbundled' network organisations. Indeed, the decline and bankruptcy of General Motors in 2009 was a powerful testament to the fragility of huge corporations. But, while some corporations decline, the post-1990 era has

Table 1.2 Comparison of the economic size of countries and corporations

		GDP or revenue $ billion, 2007
1	USA	13,811
5	UK	2,728
10	Brazil	1,314
15	Australia	821
20	Indonesia	432
25	Wal-Mart	379
30	Denmark	308
38	Toyota	230
40	Portugal	220
45	Conoco Philips	179
50	Czech Republic	168
55	Axa	163
60	Volkswagen	149
65	BNP/Paribas	141
70	Algeria	135
75	Egypt	128
80	BerkshireHathaway	118
86	Peru	109
90	Arcelor Mittal	105
95	Societe General	103
100	Hitachi	98

Note: ordered by ranking in top 100 economic units.

Sources: *Fortune Global 500, 2007,* available at http://money.cnn.com; World Bank, 2009.

seen a consolidation of corporations and the corporate form in the shape of an organisational hegemony in which the corporation has become the norm. This is evident in three respects. First, as the *Fortune Global 500* data conveys, the important emergent economies have chosen to operate nationally and globally through giant corporations, even if many of them are ultimately owned by government agencies. The giant corporation is no longer a Western creature, it may be the Chinese Sinopec, the Indian Reliance, or the Korean Samsung. Fukuyama (1992) celebrated the triumph of the market and the triumph of capitalism; that victory has also been manifest in the triumph of the corporation. Second, corporations have expanded into areas traditionally dominated by government provision through privatisation, partnerships and contracting out. The list of areas extends from commercial activities like transport, energy utilities and defence industries to huge service areas like health and pensions, and even to the basic functions of the state such as prisons, public safety and military training. Increasingly public services have become marketised services and government secures delivery by negotiation with, and regulation of, private providers. Direct provision through state bureaucracies and the mixed economy has become less common (see Chapter 6). This leads to a third victory of the corporate form, but one that is more normative: the assumed superiority of the corporate form has given rise to government departments, processes and decision-making being reformed around a corporate model (Crouch, 2004: 41; Wilks, 2007). Governments have become more 'businesslike' (James, 2001) and the prescriptions offered through the 'new public management' have brought a remodelling of the public sector in Anglo-Saxon countries and attempts to pursue such remodelling more widely, encouraged by agencies such as the IMF (Stiglitz, 2002; Woods, 2006). Public authorities have suffered a loss of self-respect in the face of constant assertion of the superiority of successful firms (see Crouch, 2004 and Chapter 6). The model of the large corporation becomes the organisational norm but the corporations themselves take on a life of their own, they become a legal entity, an independent 'person'.

THE JOINT STOCK COMPANY AND THE PURSUIT OF WEALTH

In the post-Second World War era of big government and big corporations, these two institutions have come to dominate the life of most people in Western societies – government through taxation, spending and ubiquitous regulation; corporations through employment, product development, entertainment and consumerism. In some ways the corporation has come to replace the role played in people's lives by the Church in earlier centuries. As Micklethwait and Wooldridge (2003: 2–3) observe approvingly,

> the most important organisation in the world is the company: the basis of the prosperity of the West and the best hope for the future of the world. Indeed, for most of us, the company's only real rival for our time and energy is the one that is taken for granted – the family.

Yet the government is made legitimate and accountable through elections and elaborate parliamentary processes, while the company is neither legitimate nor accountable, it has simply to obey the law and survive in the market. So what is the origin, purpose and justification for the business corporation? There is an economist's answer to that question which is simply that the business corporation is more efficient in organising economic activity than the market. But for mainstream economists this response smacks of economic heresy – nothing is more efficient than the market, and so the question of the firm was under-emphasised within economics and the early work of Ronald Coase (1937) was ignored until brought back into debate by the transaction costs approach of Oliver Williamson (1981; Mueller, 2003) which treated the firm as a response to market failure. Some economists outside of the main-stream, such as Lazonick, have emphasised the corporation as an alternative to the market, arguing that 'the historical experience of capitalist development demonstrates the growing importance of *organizational coordination* relative to *market coordination* in the value-creation process' (Lazonick, 1991: 59). This poses the paradox that the corporation succeeds in the global market precisely by substituting internal organisation and hierarchy for market relations. Later chapters come back to this paradox and to the often uneasy co-existence of the market and the corporation but, at this point, we should simply emphasise that the business corporation is a stunningly effective way of creating wealth. This simple reality provides a *de facto* legitimation of the corporation, it is, for this reason alone, 'in the public interest'.

We can go on to examine the basic building blocks of the corporation by presenting an account of the large Anglo-Saxon corporation as the most familiar model, although subsequent chapters point out that it has developed rather differently in non-Anglo-Saxon economies in Continental Europe, Japan and emergent economies. In an idealised form a large, publicly quoted business corporation such as Unilever or Exxon, registered in the UK or the USA, would display four characteristics: limited liability; legal personality; managerial control; and focus on shareholder value. Combined together these four characteristics provide substantial independence and provide the basis for the deployment of economic, social and political power. Each of these characteristics deserves examination.

The truly revolutionary and liberating basis for the corporation is the nowadays familiar and prosaic concept of 'limited liability'. Joint stock companies, which allowed the pooling of the resources of several individuals to finance major commercial enterprises, had existed prior to limited liability. But, if the venture went badly, creditors could pursue the individual owners whose personal liability could result in impoverishment and bankruptcy. Limited liability avoided that risk by limiting the owner's liability to the funding subscribed in shares. Although its practical benefits were apparent, early Victorian public and commercial opinion was sceptical if not outright hostile to the joint stock company in both the UK and the USA (Nace, 2003, ch. 5). One source of hostility had already been articulated by Adam Smith who thought that owner-managed firms were by far the most superior and famously observed that,

> The directors of such companies ... being the managers rather of other people's money than their own, it cannot well be expected that they should watch over it with the same anxious vigilance ... Negligence and profusion, therefore, must always prevail, more or less, in the management of the affairs of such a company' (Smith, 1776, Book IV, Ch. 1, part 3).

The debates over the merits of the corporation were prolonged (see Gamble and Kelly, 2000: 27–34) and included arguments about protecting the savings of working class investors, but the economic imperatives were pressing, especially the pressures to raise the huge amounts of capital required by the railway companies. The outcome was endorsement of the joint stock principle in 1844 followed by legislative approval of the limited liability right in the Joint Stock Companies Act of 1856. In the United States similar provisions were enacted piecemeal by the States who are responsible for company law and registration. Gamble and Kelly stress the autonomy of the companies incorporated under the UK legislation and the *laissez-faire* view that they should be left free to contract and to accumulate, 'although the huge privilege of limited liability had been granted, the exponents of laissez-faire were very unwilling that anything substantial should be conceded ... to ensure that companies acted in the public interest' (Gamble and Kelly, 2000: 34). Limited liability therefore constituted a formative moment in the development of the giant corporation. It provided a potential for a great expansion in corporate size with the capital of hundreds of thousands of investors combined together and with a sanctioned purpose of individual and collective wealth maximisation. The limited liability corporation emerged to enrich its shareholders, its managers and society at large.

The joint stock, limited liability corporation was constituted as a legal entity, able to enjoy individual legal rights – to own property, to enter into contracts, to sue and be sued. This included the right to own shares in other corporations which was again an important tool in building even larger and more complex corporate networks. Nowadays this seems very obvious but it deserves careful consideration because legal personality reinforces the separation between managers and shareholders. It represents the corporation as a property owner with the rights and duties that society expects from property owners, and it raises profound moral issues about whether a 'soulless' corporation has moral duties and can commit crimes as an 'individual' separable from its managers or owners.

As a separate legal entity the corporation is legally distinct from its owners. The shareholders own the company but the company owns its assets. As Bakan (2004: 16) puts it 'by the end of the nineteenth century, through a bizarre legal alchemy, courts had fully transformed the corporation into a "person", with its own identity, separate from the flesh and blood people who were its owners and managers'. As a legal person the corporation has economic rights but the principle has been extended to allow corporations social rights, political rights, and even rights traditionally regarded as 'human rights' such as free speech. The elaboration of these rights has been far more explicit in the USA than in the UK due to constitutional law and a more litigious culture (Ireland, 2000: 143). Thus, as far back as 1886, the Supreme Court appeared to decide that corporations should enjoy the safeguards of the Fourteenth Amendment rights of 'due process of law' and 'equal protection of the laws' which were originally designed to protect freed slaves (Nace, 2003; Bakan, 2004:16). That appearance was consolidated by later decisions including the 1978 decision, led by Chief Justice Lewis Powell, which created 'a constitutional right of "corporate speech"' (Monks, 2008: 50) and attached Fourteenth Amendment rights to corporate free speech with the effect of allowing political spending and corporate financing of politicians (Nace, 2003: 156). This was extended by the controversial *Citizens United* Supreme Court judgement of 2010 which effectively lifted all limits on corporate political spending (*Citizens United v Federal Election Commission*, 2010, see also http://reclaimdemocracy.org/personhood/). Hence, under the influential US model, the political rights of individual citizens came to be conferred on corporations, extending the concept of democracy to 'government of the people by the people ... and corporations'. It is curious to attach such rights to corporations who are not individuals with moral values. But perhaps legal personality can be seen in a less jaundiced light. Corporations are concerned with legal compliance, with identity, good brand image and reputation. Corporations tend to obey the rules and are 'amoral' until appropriate rules require them to behave as if they are moral (Wilks, 1997). In fact, on one interpretation of morality, as seen in the Japanese setting and Benedict's (1948) identification of the 'shame culture', a corporation concerned to avoid the adverse criticism that generates shame could be regarded as a moral creature, a point returned to in Chapter 10 and the discussion of corporate governance.

The third characteristic of the large Anglo-Saxon corporation is managerial control. The conventional view is that shareholding in large quoted corporations has become so dispersed that no one shareholder or coordinated group of shareholders has significant influence over the company. Recognising their ineffective ownership rights shareholders become passive and instrumental and, if discontented, will exit by selling their shares. The corporation is therefore controlled by professional managers who have little or no shareholding and ownership becomes divorced from control. Hence we have the development of 'managerial capitalism' and attention turns from the rights and goals of shareholders to the power and objectives of managers, either individually or as a cadre or elite of professional managers. This conventional wisdom is associated with one book and one man. The book is *The Modern Corporation and Private Property* published by Adolf Berle and Gardner Means in 1932. They argued first that the giant corporation had come to dominate American business; and second, that the family-owned firm had been replaced by the managerially controlled firm. Their analysis had substantial popular impact and is cited as a turning point although it was widely ignored by economists. Mueller (2003: 116) notes that 'a large fraction of the economics profession regarded Berle and Means as cranks' and only with the arrival of principal–agent theory did respectable academic economists begin fully to engage with issues of corporate governance. The man is Alfred Chandler, the doyen of US business historians who has diligently charted the rise of 'the system I have called managerial capitalism. Salaried managers not owners, came to make the decisions about current operating activities and long-term growth and investment' (Chandler, 1990: 9). Chandler argues that the managerially dominated corporation emerged first in the USA between the 1880s and the 1920s. Its emergence was initially linked to the multi-divisional (M-form) organisational form pioneered by Alfred Sloan at General Motors and it was steadily emulated across the Western world until, by the 1980s, the managerial model had become dominant.

While the divorce of ownership and control is a central concern in analysing the corporation, the story is far more complex than the conventional wisdom suggests. We come back to a detailed analysis of corporate governance in Chapter 10 but here we should take into account four qualifications to the model of managerial dominance. First, it has been suggested that Chandler's chronology is too US-centric and too deterministic. Managerial capitalism in France and Britain developed earlier than in the USA and, rather than a remorseless expansion of those ownership patterns, it waxed and waned through the 20th century. Hannah (2007: 426) presents ownership patterns as changeable, reflecting experimentation, major economic events and a gradual separation of ownership from control rather than the rupture of a 'divorce'. Second, it has recently become clear how much international variability exists in corporate models and how understanding has been distorted by a concentration on Anglo-American stock market systems. Gourevitch and Shinn (2005: 4) propose two contemporary models of ownership, 'an external diffuse shareholder model and an internal concentrated blockholder model' (see Chapter 10). The blockholder model embraces large controlling shareholdings held by financial institutions, family or ethnic networks or the state itself. They observe that 'most of the world operates through the blockholder model' (2005: 5) which provides an important corrective to suggestions of global managerial dominance.

The third qualification emerges from the changing composition of share ownership. The managerial model is most persuasive when shareholdings are widely dispersed, but savings and investment patterns have concentrated shareholdings in the hands of financial institutions, especially pension funds. Under these circumstances shareholders are inclined to be more interventionist, especially over major strategic decisions, and the whole issue of ownership becomes obscured. If employees invest a large proportion of their savings in pension funds, which in turn own the corporations for which they work, then the traditional adversarial class basis of capitalism is transformed and we enter a 'post capitalist society' (Drucker, 1993) in which the respective interests of owners and managers are less clear cut and possibly less opposed.

The final qualification concerns the role of 'management'. The very term management conceals the division and variability within the managerial function. Management is divided between the senior management, the board, and the chief executive; between functional specialisms such as finance and sales; between different locations or countries in a multinational; and between loyalty to the employing corporation, the industry, the profession, or the general interests of the managerial class. As discussed in Chapter 2, 'the corporation' is a miniature political system in which the concept of gaining control over the corporation can be misleading (Tivey, 1978: 41). Instead it might be more productive to consider 'policy making' within the corporation and to avoid reification (to avoid assuming that the corporation operates as a monolithic entity). There is a tension between managers, workers and owners over who controls the corporation and in whose interests it operates (see Chapter 10). Managers appear to be dominant in many countries and certainly in the UK. Thus the predominant Anglo-Saxon model, widely regarded as proper and productive, is the large, managerially controlled, publicly quoted corporation such as GlaxoSmithKline or HSBC. Such companies are powerful incumbents and in the political contestation over modes of corporate governance their senior managers are capable of very effective protection of their existing interests.

The fourth characteristic of the Anglo-Saxon corporation is the pursuit of 'shareholder value'. This has become a cliché of corporate reporting but it rests on a foundation of legal and economic theory that seeks to define the proper purpose of the corporation and which provides significant constraints on managerial autonomy through legal challenge and financial expectations (Lazonick and O'Sullivan, 2004). The model that has developed in the USA and the UK regards the corporation as a private association operating in the interests of its owners (the shareholders) and is referred to by Parkinson (1993: 74) as 'the legal model'. The corporation should be operated to the benefit of shareholders whose interests may diverge from the interests of managers who may seek an easy life or pursue status, luxury, salary or security against the interests of the shareholders in profit. Hence there has developed a legal requirement going under the innocent title of the 'fiduciary duty' of directors to act in the interests of shareholders (Parkinson, 1993: 75). This could be operationalised as a duty to maximise profits but shareholders are concerned to maximise the value of their ownership, and not only the income stream, so the concept evolved to suggest that 'directors should attempt to maximise the present value of the company' (Parkinson, 1993: 91). In the 1980s this concept underwent a further redefinition under the influence of 'efficient markets' theory which suggests that the stock market price of its shares will accurately reflect the real value of the corporation. This, in turn, will be enforced by the market for corporate control, an issue and set of assumptions that are highly problematic (Culpepper, 2011). Nonetheless, efficient market theory directed attention to the share price which came to provide a pragmatic, convenient and common-sense expression of shareholder interests. Thus fiduciary duty became equated with a duty to maximise the share price, expressed as a commitment to shareholder value, and easily realised by selling the shares.

The shareholder value concept has therefore developed a great weight and influence over corporate behaviour, especially for those companies quoted in London and New York. At the extreme it can be argued that it is actually illegal for the directors of a quoted UK company to pursue social or charitable activities that do not clearly enhance the share price. This provides a hostile legal environment for the pursuit of corporate social responsibility. In a less extreme interpretation it creates expectations among investors, intermediaries and the financial press that maximisation of shareholder value is the proper and legitimate goal of senior management and that this provides a yardstick against which to measure their performance. This position could unkindly be characterised as the legalisation and legitimation of shareholder greed and corporate exploitation.

This critique of the UK-style shareholder model is thrown into relief by international comparisons. In other developed countries, with different traditions of society and social justice, corporations tend to have a wider legal definition of purpose which pays attention to other stakeholders such as employees, suppliers and local communities. These 'stakeholder systems' are widely studied and are examined in more detail in Chapter 10. In stakeholder societies the market for corporate control does not operate and the corporation is visualised more nearly as a public institution with responsibilities to the society rather than as a private association aimed at individual enrichment. Of course these contrasts can be overdrawn but other countries, and especially Germany, provide clear alternative models which demonstrate that alternatives to shareholder value objectives are viable.

These four features of the contemporary Anglo-Saxon corporation – limited liability; legal personality; managerial control; and pursuit of shareholder value – developed over the 20th century and by the late 1990s had cohered into a dominant institutional model. None of these features are inevitable. The approach taken in this book is Polanyian (Polanyi, 1944) in that it sees corporations as creatures of the state, created by legislation, operating within a framework of economic laws and mandated by governments. The fact that the state has constituted the corporation and has, in effect, granted it a 'license to operate' logically provides that government could demand certain standards of behaviour in return for that license. These four features of the corporation have created a stunningly successful vehicle within which owners of capital, entrepreneurs, innovators and capable managers can pursue, increase, protect and extract wealth. It is the pursuit of wealth which animates the corporate form and critics argue that the state has been far too generous in its license to generate and distribute wealth. For Ireland (2000: 173) 'put simply and bluntly ... the (public) constitution and protection of (private) corporate property rights by the state is more accurately seen not as the neutral enforcement of "natural" individual rights over things but as the use of collective force of have over have-nots'. This argument takes us into questions of the distribution, as well as the creation, of wealth and will be taken up in later chapters. At this point we can simply suggest that corporate privileges and the license to operate have constantly to be reaffirmed and legitimised by corporations acting individually and collectively within the political system as political as well as economic actors.

THE ARGUMENT: INSTITUTIONAL FOUNDATIONS OF CORPORATE POWER

Since the industrial revolution, economic development has generated an increase in political freedoms. It is an extraordinary historical fact that all democracies have employed some form of capitalist system although, sadly, the reverse does not hold. Many capitalist systems still operate within oppressive and autocratic political regimes although there has always been an assumption that the development of capitalism will nurture political freedoms. Capitalism demands independence of mind and innovation, it creates economic power to counter political repression and it provides economic actors with resources, influence and self-confidence which allows them to demand political rights. This assumption of smouldering democratization seemed to find expression in the Arab spring of 2011 and it has raised the great question mark over Chinese economic development, how will it be deployed in political challenge to the oppressive post-communist regime?

Every democratizing nation state has devised some mode of engagement with economic actors in the form of a settlement which encourages them to generate wealth in return for a secure and stable position within the political system. The settlement will typically allow economic actors a position as part of a wider governing elite. Almost always the settlement has taken the form of some variant of 'liberal democracy' in which political freedoms of participation and free elections have co-existed with economic freedoms of markets and private property. The range of liberal democratic possibilities has been captured in the literature on comparative democracy (see Lijphart, 1999). The common feature of this compromise over the political organisation of the state is that democratic principles and processes have limited the power of economic interests but allowed the operation of a capitalist system (Dryzek, 1996). The ensuing equilibrium has secured economic growth but tolerated extensive inequality in return for the protection of minorities and provision of the basic necessities of civilised existence. In this setting the power of the business corporation was constrained and held accountable through elected governments. It is argued in subsequent chapters that this liberal democratic equilibrium has broken down so that the business corporation has become an even more powerful political actor over the decades since 1990. This applies especially in the UK where the case is made in Chapter 4 that large corporations have gone from being subjects of government to sources of governance, a role they also play in global governance. In the West the accretion of power has been gradual and less visible but in the former communist countries the rise of the corporate form and corporate power has been dramatic, a 'revolution without flags', while in the developing world the business corporation has come to dominate many areas of social as well as economic life. To argue that these transitions have positioned the business corporation as a 'governing institution' is to claim more than simply that it enjoys political power. A justification of this claim will be developed in the following chapters together with the logical conclusion that if corporations have (political) power they need also to assume a sense of (political) responsibility but first we need to say a bit more about what is meant by 'political power'.

The concern with the political power of business invites consideration of what is meant by 'power', how we recognise it, and when power is legitimate or is improperly exploited. Since 'power' is the central focus of political science there is a substantial literature that distinguishes direct, indirect and hegemonic power (see Lukes, 2005 for an influential presentation of the 'three faces' of power and Fuchs, 2007: ch. 3 for applying it). Authors discuss the possession of power in terms of abilities and effects, and evaluate power against justifications for its use such as justice, contract, and consent: and especially democratically based consent. There are some valuable discussions of power in relation to business corporations (Dahl, 1985; Grant, 1993, ch. 2; May (ed.), 2006; Bernhagen, 2007; Fuchs, 2007) which are deployed in later chapters. The approach taken in this study is pragmatic. It focuses on the ability of corporations and their leaders to participate in political decision-making in respect of public policies; this means examining the impact of corporations on the government activities that define public priorities and distribute values. In this focus on public policy business corporations are expected to pursue policies that are in the interests of the corporation as defined by its managers in the name of shareholders (see Chapter 6). When they are successful in securing favourable policies they can be said to be 'powerful'. When is such power proper or improper? The standard criterion in developed liberal democracies is the democratic criterion of whether power conforms to, or is held accountable by, the popular will. But the processes of democratic accountability are typically ambiguous, and the practice of democracy is frequently flawed, which makes it difficult to define clear criteria by which to judge the legitimacy of corporate power. In the global setting, of course, criteria for democratic accountability become even more tenuous.

Power over public policy includes direct pressure, indirect influence (agenda setting) and hegemonic power, the ability to secure desired outcomes by creating systems of norms, expectations and meanings. In this sense the concept of power running through the book is 'institutional' and borrows from the insights offered by sociological institutionalism which Vivien Schmidt has developed in the form of 'discursive institutionalism' (Schmidt, 2002; Schmidt and Radaelli, 2004; Schmidt, 2006). From this perspective the business corporation is conceived as 'an institution' which certainly has organisational manifestation and control over resources, but which also has normative and cognitive dimensions (North 1990; Scott, 1995). Institutions are locations of authority and by definition powerful. The approach to the institutionalisation of corporate power employed in the following chapters draws in particular on the work of Richard Scott (1995, 2008) and his institutional trinity of rules, norms and meanings. For a theory of institutional change this study follows the discursive institutionalism emphasis on the role of ideas in redefining institutional paradigms (see also Blyth, 2002; Hay, 2006; and Béland, 2010: 150). For Scott, an institutional order rests on three bases. First and most obvious is a regulatory system which embodies formal rules, regulations, soft law and also less tangible rules based on agreements and transparency such as codes of conduct. The rule system needs to be monitored and subject to effective sanctions. The second basis is normative which introduces an apparently simple set of ideas that are in fact highly complex and difficult to operationalize. Scott defines normative systems to include 'both values and norms. Values are conceptions of the preferred or the desirable ... norms specify how things should be done; they define legitimate means to pursue valued ends' (Scott, 1995: 37). Some norms are widely held and highly generalised such as reciprocity, egalitarianism or democracy itself. Others are more specifically applied to certain categories of actions in social settings and can be termed 'roles' so that a UN official or a CEO (chief executive officer) will be expected to behave in certain ways to fulfil that role. One of the earliest political gospels of the new institutionalism, March and Olsen's (1989) study, presented a primarily normative account of institutions which stressed social obligations. Thus,

> the terminology is one of duties and obligations rather than anticipatory, consequential decision making. Political actors associate specific actions with specific situations by rules of appropriateness. What is appropriate for a particular person in a particular situation is defined by political and social institutions and transmitted through socialization. (March and Olsen, 1989: 23)

This image of normative conformity and doing what seems appropriate has a great appeal but also brings a danger that verges on entropy, a dreadful circularity by which people do what they do because it seems right; and it seems right because they do it. A normative analysis has therefore to be applied with care and to include a theory of institutional change.

Scott's third pillar of institutional analysis is meanings, a 'cultural–cognitive' dimension. This is a more anthropological or psychological perspective which deals with how people and organisations make sense of social reality, how they 'frame' issues and by framing in certain ways follow, quite often involuntarily, customary patterns of behaviour. This is the difficult world of culture and identity, of symbolism and meaning. In this cognitive dimension people behave in a certain way in reaction to how they perceive reality; no other course of action occurs to them. But perceptions of reality are based on 'constitutive rules' (Scott, 1995: 41) through which actors are socially constructed, defined by interactions and given meaning by familiarity. There is arguably a 'politics of identity' (Scott, 1995: 45) 'in which actors create goals, identities and solidarities that provide meaning and generate ongoing social commitments'. A politics of identity has created a framing of the large business corporation as a cultural definer of social relations as explored further in Chapter 8.

In his summary of these three components of an institutional order Scott (2008: 429) observes that:

> each offers a different rationale for claiming legitimacy, whether by virtue of being legally sanctioned, morally authorized or culturally supported . . . Thus, it makes a difference whether one complies out of expedience (to avoid a punishment), because one feels morally obligated to do so, or because one cannot conceive any other way of acting.

This analytical approach is employed in subsequent chapters to provide a broader-based account of corporate power which relates it to institutional authority and therefore regards it as a property of all large corporations.

CONCLUSION: THE ORIGINS, EXERCISE AND CONTROL OF CORPORATE POWER

The following chapters fall into three broad sections. Chapters 2 and 3 continue to examine the origins of corporate power by looking in Chapter 2 at the available theories about the position of corporations within the political system. It goes on to characterise the corporation as a political actor and proposes a framework within which to assess its political engagement. Chapter 3 takes the discussion to the global level and examines the distinctive additional power enjoyed by the larger multinational corporations. Chapters 4, 5, 6 and 7 move from the origins of corporate power to analyse its exercise. This requires a shift from theory to practice and chapters 4, 5 and 6 undertake a detailed study of corporate power in the UK. A wider comparative study is beyond the scope of a single volume but the focus on the UK has some advantages. It examines a pioneering political economy and there is a case, explored in Chapter 7, for arguing that the experience of the UK has influenced wider patterns of global governance. Meanwhile Chapter 4 advances the case for an approach based on elitism and examines the formation of a corporate elite and the creation in the UK of a 'New Corporate State'. This new political settlement is examined in greater depth in Chapter 5 which puts the case that opposition to the corporate elite is modest and the elite itself has become both coherent and successful in securing a disproportionate share of financial rewards.

Chapter 6 explores the way in which an alliance of political and corporate elites has changed the face of UK political economy and extended markets through privatisation and a public services industry. It follows up the idea of partnership first advanced in Chapter 2 to outline the way in which public–private partnerships have become the characteristic mode of delivering public policy in the New Corporate State. The partnership theme is carried over into Chapter 7 which returns to issues of globalisation and the constitutive role of corporations within global governance. It identifies the components of an institutional role for corporations within global governance which will constrain national governments, will increase corporate power at the national level, and which displays a degree of similarity to the UK model.

The third section turns from the origins and exercise of corporate power to engage with issues of control and accountability. Chapter 8 presents an account of the way in which the corporation is embedded in society and outlines critiques of the corporation in popular culture. This leads into an analysis in Chapter 9 of the major corporate response which is to develop programmes of corporate social responsibility. The discussion identifies serious flaws with CSR but sees more merit in stakeholder approaches and in theories of corporate citizenship. This sets the scene for the discussion in Chapter 10 of corporate governance which is seen in its present form to be a wholly inadequate way of holding corporations to account. Examination of corporate governance models in Germany and Japan highlights the defects in the UK model and the chapter calls for a reinvention of a corporate governance based on a reconceptualization of the corporation itself. Chapter 11 provides a conclusion. It reviews the major arguments advanced in earlier chapters and seeks to revitalise a debate on corporate power by discounting several aspects of conventional approaches, presenting factual alternatives and focusing on corporate managerialism, corporate elites and the way in which the corporation has become embedded in the contemporary state. The chapter concludes with some speculative comments on directions for reform.

2. The corporation as a political actor

THE NATURE OF CORPORATE RATIONALITY

It is usual in everyday commentary to talk of 'the corporation' acting so that 'Apple' has launched a new iPhone, 'Daimler' has bribed foreign governments or 'Monsanto' is developing GM crops. We have seen from the qualities of the large corporation in Chapter 1 that this attribution of actions to corporations is a realistic expression of the corporation as a legal person and as an economic actor. The identification of the corporation as a purposeful actor presupposes, of course, that we are dealing with large corporations that enjoy market power. Smaller corporations operating in competitive markets are significantly constrained by market forces and have limited time, money and flexibility to devote to political engagement. Large oligopolistic corporations, on the other hand, have time, money, flexibility and, above all, discretionary room for manoeuvre. So how do they exercise that discretion? The treatment of the corporation as a 'person' provides a convenient approach. Theorists as far back as Hobbes have treated the state as an artificial person (Skinner, 1999) and students of international relations have built on that philosophical perspective. In a defence of the idea of states as persons Wendt notes that 'if state personhood is merely a useful fiction, then why does its attribution work so well in helping us make sense of world politics? Why, in short, is the concept so "useful"?' (Wendt, 2004: 290). He stresses the role of the state as an intentional or purposive actor and we could apply the same insights and concepts to corporations.

Treating the corporation as a person has the great virtue of emphasising the possibility of corporate choice with the implication that corporations can choose to be benevolent or cynical, generous or exploitative, to support elected politicians or to manipulate them. For Hobbes the artificial person of the state operated through the sovereign, to whom the people surrendered power (Skinner, 1999: 26); for the corporation the equivalent would be the executive directors generally or the CEO specifically. But while corporate personhood may be, as Wendt observes, a pragmatically useful shorthand there are some dangers in this approach including a resort to pop-psychology or to conflating the leader with the corporation. On the first danger there is a tendency in popular appraisals to treat the corporation as 'a personality' with human characteristics. Corporations are described as ruthless, caring or generous. Indeed, they may be described as schizophrenic or, in Bakan's searing critique, as psychopaths (Bakan, 2004: 56–9). This may seem absurd but corporations do have 'cultures' which express certain characteristics and they often seek to define and project their cultures through mission statements, advertising and branding. Good examples are the caring approach of Bodyshop, the environmental responsibility of Honda or the community loyalty of the Hershey Corporation and its governing foundation's benign governance of Hershey Pennsylvania (Monks and Minow, 2004: 114). To talk of 'corporate culture' rather than corporate personality may therefore be more defensible. The second danger is to identify the corporation with its leader, and especially the CEO (Haigh, 2004). This tends to be a more Anglo-Saxon syndrome and it can be tempting but misleading to take the views and personality of a strong CEO and treat them as the defining mind of the corporation. Thus Jack Welch at General Electric, (Lord) John Browne at BP, Terry Leahy at Tesco or Fred Goodwin at RBS have been dominant leaders, but leaders come and go whilst the corporation continues and, as in the cases of Browne and Goodwin, rapidly disown the CEO legacy.

It may be useful, and actually unavoidable, to treat the corporation as a 'person' but in understanding the evolution of corporate choice and the processes by which it arrives at choices it is more accurate to visualise the corporation as a political system in its own right (see March, 1962). From this perspective the corporate 'person' is shorthand for 'corporate policy' which emerges from the dynamics of the corporation as a complex organisation. After all, the corporation is an arena in which multiple interests compete for control. The interests of owners, managers and workers are clearly different in principle and can be expected to conflict in practice. In assessing politics within the corporation we can recognise that the corporation is an abstraction that does not have willpower, consciousness or the ability to make decisions. To treat it as if it could make conscious decisions would be to engage in reification (to attribute a material existence to an abstraction). The more accurate perspective might be to treat corporate decisions as emanating from the chief executive, the board or senior managers, and to recognise that they might be ambiguous and so contested within the organisation that they are fragile compromises. The nature of those compromises becomes clearer when we look at policy making within the corporation.

Large corporations are complex organisations and are more or less hierarchical, legally as well as organisationally. They have internal decision-making and policy-making processes that can be analysed through public-policy theories in the same way as we might analyse the policies of a government or government department. For example, in his comprehensive study of Unilever, Jones remarks that up to the early 1970s 'Unilever functioned as a kind of 'parliamentary democracy' in which individual components formulated goals and put forward cases' (Jones, 2005b: 20). Through its internal policy-making processes a corporation can be expected to develop a portfolio of policies concerning product development, market positioning, outsourcing, growth and so on. These policies will be developed, debated and decided by senior management and endorsed by the board in an elaborate process studied in business schools under the rubrics of corporate strategy and organisational behaviour. The subsequent implementation of policy is the applied work of business management and, as with the world of government, implementation will diverge from formal policy, it will be subject to managerial adaptation and competition and may produce unanticipated consequences. From this perspective the corporation emerges as a complex, ambiguous and sometimes contradictory actor that certainly cannot be regarded as predictable and which, far from being a fully rational market participant, will 'satisfice' in the fashion analysed by Herbert Simon (1957).

This chapter therefore accepts the popular simplification and treats the corporation as a 'person' but the behaviour of that person is a product of policy-making processes within the firm. That internal policy-making process is discussed further in Chapter 10 in relation to the idea that the corporation has a constitution which structures internal policy making. For now the important insight is to accept that corporations have discretion, exercise choice, but are not 'rational' in their policy making. Corporations can be inconsistent, contradictory, illogical or perverse in their decision making so that the 'legal person' of corporate law becomes a social and a political as well as an economic actor. In assessing its actions the policy approach involves the analysis of corporate behaviour in terms of powerful interests within and outside the corporation, in terms of corporate goals and cultures, and in terms of the implementation process and the competence of management. The policy approach challenges the assumptions of rational utility maximisation that underpin many economic models of corporate behaviour, just as it challenges assumptions about the deterministic influence of market forces.

THE POLITICAL ANALYSIS OF CORPORATE POWER

The political power of the business corporation will manifest itself in influence over governments and the policies they pursue. Extreme views of corporate power would extend to the idea that corporations influence entire political systems so that they control the state regardless of whichever government is in office; and in the international arena that corporations are more powerful than nation-states and can select governments as well as policies. Clearly gross generalisations about corporate political power are unhelpful. Power is relative and will be subject to many variables including the country, the time period, the political system, the policy area and the electoral cycle. In order to understand the deployment of corporate power and the extent of influence we can look to the analytical approaches and the range of conclusions offered by political science.

Politics is about the study of power, just as economics is the study of efficiency. Whereas economics studies how wealth is created, politics studies how it is distributed and it could therefore be expected that the literature of political science would have rather a lot to say about the business corporation as a 'governing institution' and as a vehicle for allocating values. In fact the relative neglect of the economics of the corporation has been matched by a relative neglect of its politics. There are some productive bodies of work but they could be likened to islands in a sea of ignorance. Here we can briefly summarise the main areas of research and their broad conclusions about corporate power. A valuable collection of research on government and business is also available in Coen et al. (2010) whilst Bernhagen (2007: ch. 2) provides a useful summary of the main theoretical approaches. At the risk of excessive generalisation we can identify five broad theoretical perspectives on business power in the shape of pluralism, partnership, structuralism, comparison and internationalisation.

The Pluralist Conceit

The mainstream approach to assessing the exercise of power in liberal democracies is to use the framework of pluralism. There is a substantial literature on pluralism but essentially it maintains that all interests and demands within society are articulated within the political system by individuals and by groups and are evaluated by democratically accountable government. The government will weigh demands, balance pressures, negotiate compromises and respond by adjusting public policy. In its idealised version, which assumes that all interests are equally articulated, and that a disinterested and neutral government apparatus evaluates the best interests of society, pluralism is a deeply complacent perspective. The power of business corporations can be analysed convincingly through the pluralist lens. Individually, or collectively through industry associations, corporations act as pressure groups and press their demands on the political system through all the mechanisms available to any pressure group including publicity, persuasion and direct support for politicians or parties. Pressure group theory would freely accept that business interests are likely to be unusually powerful. They are typically well organised, well resourced, and as 'producer interests' they are in a strong negotiating position. Nonetheless, they work within the rules, their arguments can be challenged by other interests such as consumers, unions or local communities, and, like any other interest, they are supplicants, deferring to the judgement of elected governments.

In this pluralist setting the characteristic political activity of corporations is lobbying, and a substantial literature has grown up to assess lobbying targets, content, strategies and success. The literature is full of insights and is discussed further in chapters 5 and 6. It examines the relative dynamics of lobbying through business associations or directly by a single corporation (Lang et al., 2008) and it accepts that some corporations and associations enjoy exceptional influence. Thus, while Richardson and Coen (2009: 347) continue to place corporate lobbying in a pluralist setting, Coen (2009: 160) identifies a syndrome of 'elite pluralism' in which some large firms gain favoured access to policy makers. The pluralist perspective therefore sees the political power of business and individual corporations as conjunctural, as dependent on circumstances and the strength of opposition. Business is not always powerful and corporations often do not get their own way. In part, as Grant (1993) has emphasised, this is because corporations are frequently poor at defining their own interests and are often reluctant to join with other businesses and competitors in business associations. They are, in Cawson et al.'s (1990) inspired quote from Marx, 'hostile brothers', and scholars such as Moran (2006) and Vogel (1989) have pointed to the political weakness of organised business. From this perspective business power is not exceptional and is certainly not constant. Vogel (1989: 8) has suggested that, in the United States, there is an inverse relationship between business influence and economic prosperity. When the economy is booming business loses power, when recession threatens business becomes more powerful. This insight appears less accurate in the UK's long boom from 1995 to 2008 but it does apply wonderfully to the power of banks during the 2007–08 financial crisis and beyond.

As a general theory of business power the pluralist perspective therefore regards the business corporation as subordinate to the political process and to elected government. Business corporations may be powerful citizens, but they are just citizens. They are not part of government, they do not 'own' officials or politicians and would not be regarded as 'governing institutions'. This conventional, mainstream view is the orthodox position embraced by most political commentators and the media. It is not only a descriptive perspective, it is normative. Corporations 'should' be subordinate, they have no special constitutional privileges and when they exert undue influence it can occasion principled criticism and moral indignation.

The Partnership Perspective

The idea of partnership captures a far less adversarial relationship between corporations and government in which shared power is evident and tolerated. The mutual toleration forms part of the traditions of political economy in later developing states like Germany or Japan and has been analysed in political science through the concept of corporatism or neo-corporatism. In its classic European form neo-corporatism refers to the voluntary sharing of economic governance between businesses, labour and government in the form of negotiated tripartite agreements over issues such as investment, taxation and wage bargaining. This relationship of mutual trust and accommodation can be taken down to the level of the industrial sector or even to the level of the individual large corporation so that Cawson et al. (1990: 7) argued that we could characterise close working relations as 'micro-corporatism'. The essential element has been a conceptualisation of the corporation as accepting certain public duties and national responsibilities which may override crude profit maximisation. Thus, in Germany, firms 'are social institutions, not just networks of private contracts or the property of their shareholders. Their internal order is a matter of public interest and is subject to extensive social regulation' (Streeck, 1997: 37). A similar set of expectations would apply in Japan and the traditionally neo-corporatist countries of Northern Europe.

While neo-corporatism began to be regarded with increased scepticism after the early 1990s, and has been challenged by the pressures of globalisation, the idea of partnership has increased in respectability. Under the influence of the new public management and marketisation we have seen the turn to 'governance' in which the state does less, and seeks to deliver public services through networks and partnership working. Corporations are the key partners whose role has been formalised in the UK through public/private partnerships and the PFI (private finance initiative). For corporations to enter into partnership with government a longer-term relationship is implied. In the partnership business model corporations are designed to supply services to government and good relations with government agencies become a core component of their business strategy. Thus a whole new category of 'support service companies' such as Capita, Carillion and Serco has grown up whose success depends on winning government contracts and working in partnership with the multiple levels of government (see Chapter 6). For sustainable success these companies must build up a relationship of trust and reliability with government, which in turn requires a degree of civic responsibility. In the international setting the partnership imperative has become a standard expectation in theories of, and research on, global governance, as explored further in Chapter 7 (see also Fuchs, 2007; Ougaard and Leander (eds), 2010).

The wide range of partnership models, and the varying national contexts in which they operate, are explored in later chapters. At this point we can contrast the more subordinated interpretation of corporate power intrinsic to the pluralist perspective with a more self-confident deployment of corporate power under partnership arrangements. A government partnership requires that, in some small way, the corporation takes on public obligations enforced either by cultural conventions and a sense of duty or, more mechanically, by contractual terms and economic incentives. To a greater or lesser degree corporations hence become 'governing institutions' which help to make policy and which interpret and adapt policy in the process of implementation.

Structural Perspectives

A range of influential theories maintain that the structure of the nation-state, and the constraints on government presented by liberal democracy and the market system, systematically bias politics in favour of business. From this perspective business power does not have to be deployed (as in pluralism), or sanctioned (as in partnership), it is simply built into political priorities. It may be invisible, it will be incorporated into expectations, and it is ubiquitous and unavoidable. In a particularly haunting passage Charles Lindblom (1977: 175) writes that:

> Any government official who understands the requirements of his position and the responsibilities that market-oriented systems throw on businessmen will therefore grant them a privileged position. He does not need to be bribed, duped or pressed to do so . . . he simply understands . . . that public affairs in market-oriented systems are in the hands of two groups of leaders, government and business.

Here we see the analytical tensions between agency and structure that is found across the social sciences. Is the possession of power a result of human agency? Or is it built into the cognitive and institutional structures of society?

Lindblom's diagnosis of business privilege emerges from dissatisfaction with the pluralist legacy. In contrast, much structuralist writing reflects Marxist antecedents. The Marxist analysis of the opposition between the capitalist and working classes interprets continued capitalist dominance as due to capitalist control over 'the state'. For Marxists the bourgeois (or liberal democratic) state operates in the interests of capital and structures politics and policy in the interests of capital accumulation. But the analysis operates at the level of capital and the generalised interests of capitalists; there is no traditional Marxist theory of the business corporation or corporate power, although there are many studies that seek to apply a Marxist framework (for instance, Soederberg, 2010). In contrast Lindblom offers an elegant and compelling theory of the structural power of the corporation in what has become known as the 'structural dependency thesis'. Lindblom argues that in a market system corporate executives control investment and economic activity, they 'decide a nation's industrial technology' (Lindblom, 1977: 171). Corporate executives cannot be controlled or directed, neither are market signals sufficient to ensure that they perform well, they must be induced by government. A rational government will engage in inducements in the awareness that, in a democracy, growth and the perception of economic prosperity is a necessity for staying in office. Since Lindblom wrote it has become steadily more evident that national elections are strongly influenced by perceptions of economic well being; that is what gains the support of voters. Politicians thus have a strong motivation to induce business corporations to perform well in order to set up the virtuous circle of growth, prosperity, low unemployment, rising incomes, buoyant tax revenue and a perception of well-being that will encourage voters to keep incumbent governments in power.

Lindblom expresses his argument in terms of 'the privileged position of business' arguing that 'business officials are privileged not only with respect to the care with which government satisfies business needs in general but also in privileged roles as participants in policy deliberations in government'. To talk of business 'privilege' poses a provocative formulation but the roots of privilege are clearly structural, hence 'mutual adjustment [between government and business] is often impersonal and distant. It operates through an unspoken deference of administrations, legislators and courts to the needs of business' (Lindblom, 1977: 178, 179). Lindblom's arguments were developed in a US setting but they provide an influential theoretical foundation for the study of business power. In the UK Colin Hay (1999: 140) explored the extent to which a 'modified' structural dependency thesis could explain the political economy of New Labour. The thesis is 'modified' by using the work of Przeworski and Wallerstein (1988) to argue that Labour accepted the dependency relationship and anticipated the need to court and placate business. He concludes by observing, 'That the British Labour Party won the 1997 general election is surely testament to the success of its internalisation of a form of modified structural dependency theory' (Hay, 1999: 172). This provides a plausible electoral rationale for the historic compromise of New Labour with Thatcherism and the business friendly policies of post-1997 Labour governments.

In later chapters the structural dependency thesis is examined in more depth. It appears to be limited in its application to Anglo-Saxon liberal democracies. The electoral rationale would not be so powerful in corporatist states experiencing coalition governments. Similarly it does not obviously apply to developing countries where business prosperity has less electoral impact or where there is no effective democratic electoral process. But structural dependency may have a greater reach. At one level all but the most authoritarian regimes have an interest in legitimating their role through economic prosperity. Further, the structural dependency thesis merges into a larger debate about neoliberalism and the need, in a globalised world economy, for states to compete for the approval of international business by creating a low-cost, business-friendly environment for investment. Cerny (2010) and Evans (2010) have analysed this tendency in their concept of the 'competition state', a set of propositions we can come back to in chapters 6 and 7.

The Comparative Perspective

The comparative method has been used to excellent effect to contextualise corporate power both in varying national settings and in terms of the industrial systems within which business corporations are embedded. The focus has been on 'comparative capitalism' which was a sadly underdeveloped area prior to the collapse of communism when it was addressed by only a few revealing studies (notably Shonfield, 1965) and research programmes (Wilks and Wright, 1987). The collapse of communism and the rise of alternative capitalist models, especially Japan, provoked a sustained research effort throughout the 1990s. Research on corporations and comparative capitalism is employed in later chapters. It provides an essential counterweight to the Anglo-Saxon bias in the literature on corporate power but generates few grand generalisations about corporate power in leading economies. As Whitley (1999: 25) notes, '"firms" are by no means the same sorts of economic actors in different economies' and he proposes a categorisation of five 'ideal types of firms' defined in terms of their governance and capabilities (ibid.: 75). He locates them within national business systems in an analysis that anticipates the most influential recent study of comparative capitalism, the analysis of *Varieties of Capitalism* in a chapter published in 2001 by Hall and Soskice. The varieties of capitalism approach is extremely useful and has spawned a research industry in comparative political economy (for instance, Hancké et al., 2007). The comparative framework developed by Hall and Soskice is a 'firm-centred political economy that regards companies as the central actors in the capitalist economy' and it is 'relational' in that it is based on the various relationships corporations develop with other economic actors such as unions, other firms and investors (Hall and Soskice, 2001: 6–7). This leads them to emphasise modes of economic coordination and to propose a major distinction between 'liberal market economies' (LMEs) and 'coordinated market economies' (CMEs). In LMEs corporations operate more individualistically and the dominant mode of coordination is markets in products, capital and labour. In CMEs corporations operate more collectively and coordinate through mechanisms of deliberation, negotiation and consensus building facilitated by linkages (such as cross shareholdings) with other economic actors and government bodies. This distinction maps easily (almost too easily) onto the contrasts between the Anglo-Saxon, English-speaking countries such as the USA, UK and Australia; and the continental European countries such as Germany and Sweden, as well as Japan. A persuasive element of their analysis is the proposition that either system can deliver efficiency and comparative advantage, but only if it reinforces its own distinctive modes of coordination and institutional complementarities. The framework is therefore sceptical about convergence between systems and predicts continuing national divergence.

The varieties of capitalism perspective underlines the common sense view that corporate power varies according to context but it also provides generalisations about the effectiveness and mode of expression of corporate power in given national settings. Thus a large corporation is likely to gain power in the UK through direct contact with government, in Germany by having an influential voice in a business association, in Japan through close ties with influential bureaucrats, and in the USA (and Japan) by substantial, targeted campaign contributions. These variations surface in later chapters to provide many insights from a research effort that is rapidly evolving. There are helpful overviews which point out that national diversity is still the norm even if the international reach of corporations, and the all too apparent globalisation of markets, could reasonably have been expected to erode the distinctions among capitalist systems (Jackson and Deeg, 2008: 680; Thelen, 2012). In relation to the specifics of corporate power and accountability recent research has also exploited the increasing salience given to corporate governance. Thus the work of Gourevitch and Shinn (2005), employed in Chapter 9, uses a political science approach unusual in studies of corporate governance to produce some very creative suggestions about the controlling influence of various coalitions of owners, managers and workers across a wide range of market economies. Their study serves to emphasise the many alternatives to Anglo-American managerial capitalism and we come back to this argument in Chapter 10. To round off this section, it bears emphasising that the comparative capitalisms approach affirms the importance of the nation state as a location for institutional continuity, as an arena for the deployment of corporate power, and with a potential for control by the state over the activities of large business corporations. This leads into the debate within international relations about the increasing power of international capital and the ability of large multinational corporations to escape effective control by the nation state.

The International Perspective

From a critical standpoint the terms 'multinational corporation' and 'corporate power' are often regarded as synonymous. A stream of studies from the late 1960s presented a jaundiced and often exaggerated view of the power enjoyed by multinationals, especially American multinationals, as they exploited their economic power, political connections and international mobility to out-manoeuvre national governments. The exploits of the Chrysler Corporation in 1975 as it extracted industrial subsidies from the Wilson Labour government were totemic of multinational power (Lindblom, 1977: 182; Wilks, 1988). Raymond Vernon's *Sovereignty at Bay* (1971) presented a judicious analysis which stressed 'the basic asymmetry between multinational enterprises and national governments' (ibid.: 271) but some of the more extreme fears of multinational dominance proved misleading. Writing 30 years later May (2006a: 16) notes that it would be a mistake to underestimate the latent strength of governments and nation-states so that 'states' ability to hold corporations (at least partly) accountable for their actions has allowed a more nuanced position to emerge' and part of that nuance is to steer away from a confrontational view of the nation-state and the multinational corporation.

The substantial literature within international relations concerning the corporate power of multinationals is deployed in Chapter 3. At this stage three points are worth noting. First, influential authors, and especially Susan Strange, have argued that multinational corporations should be placed at the centre of international political economy and need to be evaluated as global political units with powers comparable to nation-states. One rendering of this is the idea of 'triangular diplomacy' whereby nation-states bargain bilaterally with one another but also trilaterally with corporations (Stopford and Strange, 1991: 19). Second, one of the most important elements in evaluating international corporate power is to understand the relationship between home countries and international corporate activity. This may involve US support for US corporations operating overseas as, historically, with the infamous 'banana republics' of the 1900s dominated by the United Fruit Corporation (now Chiquita; Jones, 2005a: 51) but it might equally concern Russian or Chinese support for 'their' corporations operating in global markets. Third, Sklair rather reluctantly sounds a more optimistic note in his work on the 'transnational capitalist class'. He speculates on whether we should expect to find a dominant global class of corporate executives, bureaucrats, professionals and the media (Sklair, 2001: 17). This transnational corporate class may, however, have progressive features, specifically in the form of a long-term commitment to economic growth in developing countries and global environmental responsibility. Whether global corporate citizenship can be taken seriously is an issue we come back to in Chapter 9.

AN ELITE OF BUSINESS CORPORATIONS?

The perspectives reviewed above offer a repertoire of insights and concepts which can be used in a variety of settings to analyse corporate power. Those settings may involve different countries, time periods or policy issues and in some settings pluralist concepts may appear more important, in others structural determinants may appear decisive. One setting examined in chapters 4–6 is that of the UK since 1990. Here theories of structural dependence appear particularly revealing and a 'modified' structural dependency thesis appears to have had a substantial impact on the strategies adopted by New Labour. But corporations clearly also used their increasing structural authority to their own advantage and exploited pluralist avenues of lobbying. In parallel they also worked to popularise ideas of 'partnership' within a developing new economic orthodoxy that reduced the role of the state in delivering public policies and economic growth. Succeeding chapters will therefore come back to the ideas and frameworks outlined above.

It remains the case, however, that all these frameworks tend to treat corporations as relatively monolithic, in other words as 'persons' with predictable goals which they pursue through political means. As outlined in the opening section of this chapter, it appears necessary to qualify this perception of the corporation as a single actor with a recognition of the corporation as a complex political system. This leads to a staged analysis. First, we can consider the question of an elite of corporations; second, we can address the nature of the elite that directs those corporations. The first stage follows up the suggestion in Chapter 1 that not all corporations enjoy political influence. We are concerned with a small number of large, influential corporations which dominate their economic sectors and can be regarded as an 'elite' of corporations. The second stage is to ask who in practice controls those elite corporations? There are two possibilities. One is that the shareholders control the corporations, the second is that it is the management. This book stresses the influence of managers although, as we see in later chapters, the role of shareholders or, ostensibly working on their behalf, the role of the financial sector qualifies managerial control. The suggestion, therefore, is that certainly in the UK, and arguably in the majority of capitalist countries, a managerial elite exists and works in conjunction with political elites to create corporate strategies which favour their own and wider elite interests. This dual elite focus, an elite of corporations providing the foundation for a managerial elite, is elaborated in relation to the UK in chapters 4 and 5 but for the moment we consider the development of elite theories of corporate power in more detail.

The incontestable influence of a grouping of powerful corporations invites recourse to elite theory, which is based on the natural and regularly observed tendency to hierarchy in social organisation. There have been rigorous research efforts which have sought to demonstrate elite dominance in a variety of social settings, and an elitist element enters into influential approaches to studying public policy, such as policy network theory (Evans, 2006: 45). Elite theory seeks to do more than simply to point to the dominance of a minority of decision-makers or leaders in an organisation or society, it is also built on ideas of elite coherence, reproduction and conscious exertion of power and dominance. In a re-affirmation of the relevance of elite theory Scott (2008: 32) maintains that elites are defined by their holding and exercise of power so that 'elites are those groups that hold or exercise domination within a society or within a particular area of social life'. The concepts developed in elite theory can be employed to explore both the power of business in society, and the power of an elite within the corporate sector. The elitist approach assumes that those making up the elite become a 'governing elite' who dominate decision-making, bias policy making and play the major role in allocating values for society. They may not themselves directly control the major institutions of the state but they have dominating influence over public policy and render the democratic process ineffectual in establishing real control over government. As part of this exertion of hidden power the elite could be expected to construct a dominant narrative to legitimise their control over government and the state, which renders the conclusions of the elitist analysis similar to conclusions of Marxist analysis. Presented in this form elitism has a pejorative flavour since, by definition, it subverts the political equality embodied in pluralist interpretations of representative democracy. But elites could be regarded as benign as well as objectionable. They may pursue goals that are favourable to society at large and elite theory also merges with pluralist positions in the plausible concept of 'a plurality of elites' who compete for control of government and allow some popular accountability.

There is a well-established body of research on the existence and composition of a 'business elite' of individuals who derive their influence as owners of capital or as senior managers. The classic elitist critique of pluralism was undertaken by C. Wright Mills in his study of *The Power Elite* (Mills, 1956) which argued that three elites dominated the key institutional hierarchies in American society. The economic elite controlled large business corporations, the other two elites being the political elite and the military elite. The identification of a business elite has been followed through in research at the national and local levels, again mainly in the United States, and often by sociologists. Thus an impressive body of work has been undertaken by Useem whose book *The Inner Circle* (Useem, 1984) identified a cadre of business executives in the USA and the UK who took a broad, class-wide view of business representation so that 'the inner circle has . . . become the leading edge of business political activity, a special leadership cadre . . . (with) . . . a unique role on behalf of all business corporations' (Useem, 1984: 115). Useem defined a business elite which was exclusive, coherent, purposeful and which shared common goals. He argued that the elite influence exerted by the inner circle applied in the USA and also in the UK with the two countries converging to produce a new institutional capitalism in which 'the firm remains a primary unit of action, but the transcorporate network becomes a quasi-autonomous network in its own right' (ibid.: 195). Neo-corporatists might observe that the inner circle appears as the functional equivalent of the dense neo-corporate networks and representative associations that have grown up in continental Europe and Japan and indeed, one method used by Useem and others to chart the corporate elite was the existence of interlocking directorships whereby executives sit on the boards of several corporations. Such interlocks express the links, dependencies and cross-shareholdings that have always been a part of German or Japanese coordinated capitalism but the US/UK version is managerial and excludes workers and other stakeholders (see Chapter 10). Later work on business elites by Maclean et al. (2006, 2010) tends to endorse the idea of a managerial network, with business elites in both France and the UK cooperating to provide mutual understanding and coordination. Their empirically rich study is employed extensively in Chapter 4 but their conclusions are less critical than Useem and they are more cautious in advancing claims of corporate elite dominance.

Efforts to identify a business elite could also be employed to suggest that here we have a 'ruling class' that fits into a Marxist framework in the way that it represents capital and seeks to ensure that the state operates in the interests of capital. This approach informs the work of John Scott on interlocking directorships in the UK which he uses to develop a more explicitly Marxist analysis of a ruling class (Scott, 1984, 1997, 2008). The Marxist class framework leads Scott to argue that the corporate elite is still strongly associated with owners of capital and to argue that the managerial revolution is misleading. From this viewpoint corporate political and economic activity should continue to be seen as an expression of class struggle (Scott, 1997) which focuses the evaluation and critique of the business corporation on to traditional class concerns and expresses control of the corporation in terms of class exploitation. This viewpoint has been expressed very clearly by Soederberg (2010: 83) who sees the corporation 'as a capitalist institution based on the extraction of surplus value through exploitative activities'. The identification of a business elite with a capitalist ruling class is intriguing but it downplays the importance of managerial control and leads towards a more confrontational and constrained analysis of corporate power than the approach taken in this book.

Working also in a Marxist framework, but in a more eclectic fashion, Sklair extends the concept of a business elite to the global level with his analysis of the 'transnational capitalist class' (TCC). The TCC is defined as a dominant global class made up of four fractions (or elites) to include the executives of multinationals, globalising bureaucrats, globalising professionals, and consumerists (merchants and the media) (Sklair, 2001: 17). His framework is employed in Chapter 4 to analyse the UK corporate elite. He goes on to argue that the TCC 'is dominated by those who own and control the major corporations and through them, the global economy. The TNCs are the honey pot around which all those who are dependent on the capitalist global system circulate ... we need to identify those corporations' (ibid.: 41) and he chooses to focus on the *Fortune Global 500*. Sklair treats the global business elite as a 'class' which has class-consciousness, coherent ideologies and a vision which might have benign components inasmuch as the TCC wish to alleviate world poverty and to moderate environmental degradation. While he defines a need to oppose global capitalism he does not see that opposition strictly in terms of class conflict and in any case, and most interesting for this analysis, he slides from a class of people (corporate executives) to a class of corporations (the *Fortune Global 500*) which feeds into the approach of analysing corporate power through the corporations themselves rather than their managers or owners.

The proposition that there is an elite of corporations promises more explanatory purchase than the idea of a class elite. It is less transitory, less individualistic and less constrained by a commitment to neo-Marxist class analysis. We therefore focus on the power of corporations without forgetting the importance of corporate governance (see Chapter 10), which analyses the influence of those who own and control them. One of the earliest expressions of an elite of business corporations could be seen in the trusts of the late 19th-century United States. The big corporations and trusts that grew up after 1860 were seen as a threat to republican values and likened to a new feudalism. The popular concern was expressed in the Sherman Antitrust Act of 1890 and the raw economic and political power of trusts such as the Standard Oil Trust created in 1882 (and broken up in 1911) fuelled a long tradition of anti-big-business crusading. The challengers to the business elite included the lawyer Louis Brandeis, appointed to the Supreme Court in 1916, and a passionate early critic of big combinations which he saw as a threat to republican self-government and to democracy itself (Freyer, 1992: 66; Strum, 1993: 76). Current inheritors of the crusade are still highly vocal and include polemicists such as Klein, Bakan and, of course, Michael Moore (for instance his 2009 film, *Capitalism: A Love Story*). Nonetheless, government measures to constrain large corporations have had a limited or perverse effect. The antitrust regime actually encouraged corporate consolidation and the growth of large business corporations (Freyer, 2006). Thus, by the early 1950s, Galbraith (1952) diagnosed consistent oligopoly as one of the main characteristics of the American economy with most industries dominated by a small number of large corporations. His influential work on *The New Industrial State* (Galbraith, 1967) provided a provocative but stimulating analysis of the way in which large corporations exerted control over the US economy in their search for certainty and effective planning.

In the UK a similar recognition of corporate power prompted the postwar Labour government to nationalise 'the commanding heights of the economy' which at that time were identified with the heavy industries of coal, steel, rail and energy. On the Morrisonian principle of operation on a commercial basis the nationalised industries were organised as public corporations and only tangentially used as vehicles of public policy. By the 1960s more socialist orientated Labour thinkers were again considering how to identify and control the UK corporate elite. Influenced by French indicative planning, and by state alliances with leading French companies, there was again debate about how government could gain some control over large corporations. In opposition in the early 1970s Labour policy makers developed an industrial strategy which was influenced by the work of Stuart Holland who argued that the government should work in partnership with the 100 or so leading corporations, including multinationals. He proposed (again under the influence of French experience) that government should negotiate 'planning agreements' with leading companies (Holland, 1975; Wilks, 1988). In the event Labour's interventionist industrial strategy was abandoned in 1975 and only one planning agreement was signed, with Chrysler UK in 1977 (Wilks, 1981). But the Labour policy debates, and Holland's emphasis on the strategic importance of an elite of major corporations, signalled a realisation of the strategic economic importance of a corporate elite. After 1979 the UK elite of large corporations was expanded and strengthened by the privatisation policies of the Thatcher governments analysed in Chapter 6. The idea of an elite of business corporations is therefore relatively familiar. It is easy to define such an elite by size (turnover, employees or market capitalisation) because a variety of league tables are compiled by *Fortune*, the *Financial Times* and stock markets. Thus the trailblazing Harvard study of multinationals defined an elite population of the 187 multinationals in the *Fortune 500* list of US manufacturing corporations (Vernon, 1971). We could similarly define an elite of giant corporations at the national level (for the UK the *FT100*); at the regional level (the *FT European 500*; see also Whittington and Mayer, 2000); and at the global level (the *Fortune Global 500*), which provides the first stage of analysis, the identification of an elite of corporations. The second stage, identifying the elite of individuals who lead them is more complex and is undertaken in Chapter 4 in respect of the UK, but this is not the same as defining a business 'power elite' of influential individuals.

ASSESSING THE POLITICAL POWER OF ELITE CORPORATIONS

In order to go beyond a definition of the potential members of an elite of business corporations by size alone, it is helpful to identify in more detail the attributes of a politically powerful corporation. One of these attributes is a conscious intention to pursue political power and to embody that intention in corporate strategy. A framework to capture the attributes of politically powerful corporations can be derived eclectically from the theoretical perspectives outlined above. To achieve political influence we can suggest that a business corporation should have substantial resources; it should have the motivation to pursue political or policy goals; and it should have the opportunity to intervene or participate in the political process. These three elements of resources, motivations and opportunities could be assessed using a wide range of indicators. Here we take three indicators for each element to build a model of a politically powerful corporation.

Resources: does the corporation have the resources to be influential?

1. *size*: size in terms of investment, employees, turnover, trade and access to technology will make the corporation valuable to governments and communities and provide it with potential bargaining power. Its size relative to other economic actors will clearly be significant.
2. *market power*: a corporation which is a substantial oligopolist or near monopolist becomes significant in its ability to offer access to the relevant market and it will enjoy much more substantial discretion than corporations constrained by market forces.
3. *global reach*: the degree to which a corporation enjoys a multinational network provides it with independence and the ability to negotiate with national governments. Although support from a home government can be important Chapter 3 argues that the more multinational a corporation is the more influential it is likely to be.

The resource element is perhaps the most obvious component of potential political power. It is concerned with economic power and with the assumption that economic power can be converted into political power. The indicators are therefore dealing essentially with structural power. The structural argument suggests that corporations with substantial resources will receive favourable treatment automatically.

Motivation: many companies will have commercial motivations to seek political power because they are significantly exposed to government regulation, because their interests are deeply affected by public policy or because the public sector is a major customer.

4. *regulated products or markets*: government regulation is a key competitive factor in relation to a vast number of products including foodstuffs, cars and drugs. Other products are governed by product standards, which similarly provide a motivation to influence standards in favour of the corporation's products. For some corporations the entire market is regulated, as with regulated utilities, where a government agency becomes the single most important driver of market access (through licensing) and of commercial success (through price control).
5. *favourable public policy*: there is a wide spectrum of possibilities here stretching from the basic requirements of conducting business, such as legal certainty and currency convertibility; to specific policies such

as R&D subsidies or regional development; to a generalised interest in a favourable climate for investment. This merges into a preference for policies such as low corporate taxation and permissive labour relations explored in Chapter 6 and captured in the range of competitiveness indices explored in more depth in Chapter 7.
6. *government contracting*: for some corporations a contractual relationship with government is a major factor in their business models. This may involve the government as major purchaser, as with defence equipment or clinical drugs in the UK; or it may involve the corporation delivering public services under contract. As seen in Chapter 6, corporations are increasingly providing a whole range of services from mundane garbage collection to the PFI in the UK in which companies provide public infrastructure such as hospitals.

The motivational element reflects the reality of mutual dependence between government and industry. To that extent it exemplifies a partnership perspective on the political power of business in which there is negotiation and lobbying but also relationships of mutual trust and the creation of long standing networks. Many companies, small as well as large, have a motivation to influence government and for some of them, such as the utilities and contractors, government may be the single most important driver of commercial survival.

Opportunity: does the corporation have favourable access to the policy making process?

7. *lobbying capacity*: lobbying covers a range of activities from party campaign contributions to responding to government consultation exercises. The decisive factor is whether the corporation has identified a set of areas where it wishes to influence government and whether it has organised to exert influence. There are several avenues available including the creation of a 'government affairs' division, setting up lobbying offices in capital cities, lobbying through local politicians or in concert with stakeholders and local communities.
8. *associational involvement*: the standard routes of business political representation are through trade associations and 'umbrella' business associations such as *Keidanren* in Japan and the CBI in the UK. Some corporations will be in a position to influence the lobbying priorities of associations and through that route to influence government. Membership of business associations, contributions to funding and membership of key committees therefore provide routes to political influence.

9. *reputation and visibility*: corporations devote huge resources to marketing their products and they have the capacity also to market themselves as responsible members of society and to develop a reputation for integrity which would persuade government to support their priorities. This aspect of corporate social responsibility is examined in Chapter 9. A benign reputation also positions corporate executives to act as advisers to government and their executives will be invited to join committees to advise on reform.

The opportunity indicators have a pluralist flavour. They identify areas where corporations do not rely on structural power but organise deliberately to exert political influence based on the characteristics of the particular national or global process of public policy making. Opportunity may be enhanced by good fortune, by being in the right place at the right time, or being able to draw on charismatic directors or personal ties to the political elite, but none of these advantages can be realised unless the corporation formulates political priorities and builds then into its strategy.

CONCLUSION: NORMALISING CORPORATE POWER

There is no single theoretical perspective that provides an adequate understanding of the corporation as a political actor. Accordingly this book borrows eclectically from the perspectives reviewed in this chapter and from the research that informs them. It outlines a pragmatic theory of the three elements of resources, motivation and opportunity and it rehearses nine indicators within which the political power of individual business corporations can be assessed. In taking this approach it is recognised that business power is variable and conjunctural, it varies between countries, industrial sectors, policy arenas and the conjunctures of issues, forces and timing. This is not to argue that generalisations are impossible or that conclusions cannot be drawn. The following chapters operate on the basis that there are patterns in the operation of corporate power which allow us to evaluate its effects and, to some extent, to predict outcomes. Although this study is theoretically eclectic it does have a normative stance. It explores the power of the business corporations on the basis that its political power is substantial, is growing, is often excessive and needs to be constrained by the political process. This is hardly a novel position but this study seeks to contribute towards the debate about business power by offering a comprehensive treatment and by maintaining that business power is part of the political landscape.

Not only are large corporations political actors, their political power is exerted on an everyday basis as part of our political systems. The self-interested goals which corporations seek are discussed in greater depth in Chapter 6, but corporations also share political goals that are of the essence of good government such as stability, prosperity, economic freedom, good public services and a sustainable environment. Their role in contributing to these goals is ubiquitous but poorly recognised in prevailing images of government, and especially in pluralism. Hence this book regards pluralist theory as potentially misleading and places more emphasis on the structuralism and the partnership theories reviewed above. Structural dependency helps to explain why elected governments have become more business friendly and partnership theories help to define what form that cooperation takes. The collaboration between government and corporations leads to a mutual understanding between political and corporate leaders which, it was argued above, can be creatively and accurately analysed through the lens of elitism. Later chapters employ these ideas in exploring the nature of contemporary British politics but in most of this chapter, and in relation to the UK, the ideas are applied at the level of the nation-state. At this national level there remains a balance of power between political actors within society which is maintained by constitutions, by elected governments and by political bargains or settlements between elites. That balance has always been disturbed by the international operation of corporations and is in danger of being destroyed by globalisation. Chapter 3 assesses the qualitative increase in corporate power when large corporations become institutions of global governance.

3. Globalisation and the enhanced power of multinational corporations

WHEN CORPORATIONS TRANSCEND THE NATION-STATE

The unease felt widely across society about the growth and deployment of corporate power originates, as we saw in Chapter 1, in the implied challenge to democratic government. As democratic theory explores in depth, governments are regarded as legitimate thanks to elections and to the consent embodied in the exercise of popular will operating through the electoral process within a constitutionally agreed legal system. Corporate political power does not enjoy electoral legitimacy and although it may lay claim to alternative modes of legitimation, corporate power is commonly regarded as legitimate only if it is exercised in ways consistent with a democratic political process. Much of the discussion of the corporation as a political actor advanced in Chapter 2 therefore reflected the dynamics of relations between corporate actors and (legitimate) governments. The traditional pluralist view of corporate power visualised corporations making demands on governments but recent scholarship has emphasised a view of societies ordered not only by 'government' but by a range of actors in a process of 'governance' (Chhotray and Stoker, 2009). The governance perspective is more consistent with the partnership view of corporate power discussed in Chapter 2 and visualises multiple actors and sources of authority working together to define and enforce rule systems.

The governance literature visualises a regime of 'power sharing' which requires cooperation between diverse units of government, organisations within civil society and economic institutions. This sort of power sharing might operate through formal organisations or through less tangible networks, and partnership working is typically formalised through contracts which become a distinct mode of policy implementation. But, whilst government may share power, it is the ultimate sovereign authority and effectively the senior partner, able to change the terms of engagement and to disenfranchise other actors. This basic constitutional principle of ultimate sovereignty collapses when governance extends beyond the boundaries of the nation-state. When corporations go international their dependency on legitimate government begins to melt away. Corporations operating internationally transcend dependency on national governments, there is no source of international (electoral) legitimacy and corporations themselves become agents of governance with a degree of absolute autonomy. Moreover, their enhanced international authority comes full circle to reinforce their domestic power so that governments dealing with international corporations suffer reduced sovereignty.

The proposition that the large corporation should be visualised as a governing institution was advanced in Chapter 1. In the international arena, the idea that the corporation shares in governance has been debated and researched enough for it to become widely accepted (Hale and Held, 2011: 10). In a measured study of global business power Fuchs (2007) charts the areas where business is increasing its influence and centres her study on the contribution of business to 'global governance'. The corporation has become a constituent institution of global governance so that Fuchs observes that 'business has become a pivotal participant in global governance and an important source of global rules and regulation' (Fuchs, 2007: 164; see also Vogel, 2008; Ougaard, 2010: 20). It is attractive, therefore, to consider international corporate power as an element within global governance, although we need also to bear in mind the risk of attaching too much stability, permanence and even legitimacy to such a contested idea. Global governance has become a focus for study and sustained research but it remains an ill-defined location of authority. In the following discussion it is therefore necessary to reach conclusions as to whether multinationals engaged in global governance have taken on a degree of institutional autonomy which enables them to exercise power in a fashion divorced from the perceived interests of dominant states.

Independence from nation-states need not take on a confrontational character; it may be more about sharing the power of the nation-state than evading it. The confrontational attitudes of the 1970s and 1980s have been replaced by a far more positive and tolerant attitude since the early 1990s. Thus, at the turn of the century, one of the leading American scholars of international political economy could write that 'as an institution the MNC is beneficial to peoples everywhere' (Gilpin, 2000: 171). This viewpoint, reflective of the deepening neoliberal consensus, made it both instrumentally and ideologically respectable for governments to work with corporations in patterns of cooperation so we could characterise the role of multinationals in global governance as one of 'partnership' (see Chapter 2 and Stern and Seligman, 2004). Thus Dunning (1997: 15) identified a move from an adversarial relationship to 'a more cooperative relationship between *firms and governments*', a theme echoed with a more critical colouration by van Apeldoorn (2000: 159). The steady proliferation of 'transnational public–private partnerships' has become a distinct area of research in international relations. These public–private partnerships (PPPs) tend to operate over more technical niche areas relating to industrial sectors or public policies and for Schäferhoff et al. (2009: 452) 'PPPs are . . . an expression of the ongoing reconfiguration of authority in world politics, and reflect the fact that non-state actors, such as non-governments organisations (NGOs) . . . and transnational corporations (TNCs) . . ., are increasingly engaged in authoritative decision making'. Indeed, some authors go further to maintain that the public governance that traditionally took the form of international cooperation between nation-states has been replaced by private governance based on cooperation between global corporations (Pattberg, 2007; see also Ougaard, 2008; Büthe and Mattli, 2011).

If this partnership interpretation can be sustained, then something extraordinary has happened in relation to the powers of multinational business. There has been a qualitative shift from being the subject of government to becoming a seat of government. If corporations were individuals we might say that they had achieved emancipation and had gained office. This is close to the position advanced by Harrod (2006: 23) who identifies an historical discontinuity whereby 'the current corporation has assumed a size, power and nature that distinguishes it from its past manifestations'. Harrod argues for new theories of the corporation which would 'delink the current corporation from the language of past theories' (ibid.: 32). In the same vein Goldman and Palan echo this viewpoint of corporate emancipation by extending the idea of traditional, individual citizenship. They 'argue that MNCs transform themselves and, in so doing, change the nature of the "constitution" of the international political economy' (Goldman and Palan, 2006: 182). We come back to the idea of corporate citizenship in Chapter 9. It feeds into ideas of a redesigned global polity with a new constitutional settlement which also implies a global society, a theme explored by Cutler who analyses an 'emerging global business civilization as a dimension of the expanding "private" authority in global government'. For Cutler this heroic idea of a 'global business civilization' provides 'a unity of purpose and increasingly homogenous design for global private norms and practices' (Cutler, 2006: 201, 202). Hence this review of existing understandings of multinational corporate power has brought us from an adversarial understanding of multinationals and the state up to the 1980s to a position of partnership in the late 2000s in which state and corporations are jointly, with other actors, constructing a global society and generating rules, norms and frameworks which begin to look like the ingredients for a global constitution.

To claim that even a partial and implicit global constitution exists which empowers MNCs would amount to a comprehensive affirmation of a generalised power of multinationals. Put more formally, the proposition would be that 'there has been a constitutionalisation of the political power of the multinational corporate elite'. This is a strong version of the proposition that the MNC has become a 'governing institution' and is a controversial suggestion that has to be tested against, and defended by, a more rigorous application of theory and appeal to existing knowledge. This exercise is undertaken in the following sections using the theoretical perspectives reviewed in chapters 1 and 2. It draws on the concepts of institutionalism and explores how the emergence of the corporation as a governing institution has been projected into the international arena to produce a qualitative change which has transformed the influence of corporations operating on a multinational scale. The transformation is threefold. First, MNCs have become more powerful due to the global spread of markets as the universal method of organising the economy. Second, MNCs have become more diverse as the large emergent economies, especially the BRICS (Brazil, Russia, India and China), have adopted the corporate form. Third, and more controversially, MNCs have become more 'responsible' as they enter into governance and factor the long-term threats of economic hardship and environmental degradation into their longer-term strategies. This chapter therefore reviews our existing understanding of the economics and politics of multinational corporations before presenting the recent transformations. In the process it reviews the emergence of the new wave of MNCs from emergent economies. The chapter concludes with a summary of the arguments advanced in these first three chapters. Together these chapters present an account of the origins of contemporary corporate power.

ENHANCED CORPORATE POWER DERIVED FROM INTERNATIONAL OPERATIONS

Operation in several countries provides a corporation with potential political power for two straightforward reasons. First, it detaches the corporation from the exclusive jurisdiction of any one nation-state; second, there is no global government capable of taking an overall view of the corporation's activities. These features, combined with sheer size and nationalist sensibilities, have traditionally made 'the multinational corporation' (MNC) a source of interest and suspicion. The suspicion was fuelled by cultural differences and resistance to 'foreigners' controlling national industries, especially when the foreigners are taking unpopular decisions or can be portrayed as agents of neo-colonialism. Since the mid-1980s, however, suspicion has been converted into welcome, if not outright celebration. Governments have competed to attract multinational investment and the tide of economic globalisation has operated through multinational corporations to make them both ubiquitous and, on the whole, attractive routes to economic prosperity. This section outlines the economic and organisational landscape to delineate the salient features of multinational investment, also known as FDI (foreign direct investment) and its prominence within global markets.

The extensive literature on globalisation identifies the growth of a 'new global economy' which was recognised by 1990 and which has continued to deepen and to integrate economic activity. Jones (2005a: 20) talks of this as a 'second global economy' (the first stretching from 1880 to 1929) which has been created by a wide range of factors, some of which are technological, such as communications technologies and cheap transportation; but many of which are political involving conscious political decisions by nation states (Leys, 2001: 12) in areas like exchange rates and trade policy. For international investment Dunning (1997: 35) stresses 'the renaissance of market-orientated policies pursued by national and regional authorities' which has resulted in a mass global liberalisation of policies on FDI. This new golden age for MNCs has led them to be regarded as the leading agents of globalisation breaking down national barriers and remorselessly extending markets. As we see below, the role of multinationals is far more substantial than mere agency. They have substantially defined the very nature of globalisation, its modalities, goals, processes and benefits are constructed in a normative and cognitive framework that originates from corporations. Perhaps even more so than national politicians, multinational corporations produce ideas as well as marketable products (Amoore, 2006: 48).

Globalisation has brought an expansion of markets as well as a deepening of integration. The year 1989 and the end of the cold war was as important for corporate power as for world peace. The disintegration of the Soviet Union and the marketisation of previously centrally planned economies both legitimised MNCs and opened up huge new markets. Combined with the de facto embrace of capitalism by China, and the liberalisation of the huge economies of India and Brazil, the global economy became a truly global market accessible to MNCs. The magic of markets and the enticement of peaceful commerce operated as historians of political thought might have predicted, to integrate peoples and civilisations. Thus the French and American wars to control Vietnam, and to integrate it into a global capitalist economy emerge as futile as well as tragic, with a liberalised Vietnamese economy taking its place in a global market

20 years after the victory of the Vietcong. In a piquant piece of symbolism the 2007 ATKearney 'FDI Confidence Index', which ranks countries on their attractiveness to multinationals, placed Russia in sixth place and Vietnam in ninth place (more attractive than France or Canada). The American-model global corporation thus emerges as a far more effective defender of the 'free enterprise system' than the formidable American military in a pattern that is hardly coincidental. Critics would argue that the new right crusade to roll back socialism was succeeding on the international as well as the national stage (Leys, 2001: 12; Hanahoe, 2003; Klein, 2007). The few countries that still substantially reject multinational investment, such as Cuba, North Korea or Venezuela, are small and troubled.

The multinationals which operate in the global economy are bewilderingly diverse and the great majority, like smaller domestic corporations, will have very little individual influence. The usual working definition of a multinational is a corporation that has operations in at least two other countries in addition to its home state. Its operations will be the result of 'foreign direct investment' (FDI) which must be distinguished from portfolio investment – the arms-length ownership of shares and bonds. Defined in this way UNCTAD (2008: 9–10) identified 79,000 transnational corporations and up to 2007 it noted continued record growth in FDI which was growing three times faster than world trade. Increasingly MNCs are growing through cross-border mergers and acquisitions which is far easier in the Anglo-Saxon countries which encourage a 'market for corporate control' that is not tolerated in countries such as Germany and Japan.

The term 'transnational corporation' is often used synonymously with 'multinational' but, strictly speaking, a 'transnational' is a corporation with no pre-eminent links to a single nation-state in terms of ownership or management. The prevailing view is that genuine transnationals are very rare. Most corporations have a strong identification with a 'home' country reflected in the location of production, the make up of the board of directors, a nationally orientated corporate culture or an expectation of support from the home government. Prominent analysts of the corporation, notably Richard Whitley (2001, 2005) have repeatedly emphasised the embeddedness of firms and their competitive strategies in national business systems. He has speculated on the development of 'new cross national business systems' (Whitley, 1999: 131) but doubted that they were yet emerging. Similarly Jones (2005a: 40) notes that 'Rugman and D'Cruz (2000) could only find nine "global firms"' (see also Rugman, 2005; Wilks, 2013). While the continued influence of national origins does need to be emphasised it is striking how genuinely global many large corporations have become and, as examined below, this could be expected to yield an increasing level of autonomy. UNCTAD identifies the top 100 transnationals and applies a transnationality index based on the foreign percentage of assets, sales and employees. Of the top 100, 82 per cent have a transnationality index of over 50 per cent which indicates a high level of independence from home country operations. An increase in the proportion of such highly multinationalised corporations does raise the prospect of a globally 'denationalised' corporate sector. Some will object that the data for European multinationals are deceptive because we might regard the EU as the 'home' state. On the other hand the UNCTAD transnationality index only measures the internalised transactions within the hierarchy of the corporate organisation. As we see below, corporations are increasingly operating through networks and alliances which increase their influence.

The scale of economic activity undertaken by MNCs can be indicated in a variety of ways. One UNCTAD statistic is that 11 per cent of global GDP is accounted for by the foreign affiliates of MNCs (UNCTAD, 2008: 9). If we estimated that on average MNCs generated one third of their value added 'overseas' then the MNC GDP would amount to 33 per cent of global GDP. Perhaps more significant is the fact that multinationals account for one third of world trade, this is a statistic that has huge implications for economic theory and economic policy. A great proportion of this trade will be internal to the corporation and will be priced at internally defined prices (known as 'transfer prices') which are insulated from market forces. This means that traditional trade policy instruments such as devaluations or tariffs have only an indirect effect through their impact on corporate strategy. It also means that MNCs can manipulate their revenues and costs to declare profits in whichever country is most advantageous in terms of negotiations (with governments and workers) and tax bills. Multinationals therefore operate within an alternative global economy in which investment and production is internal to the corporation and is organised through hierarchies and corporate strategy rather than by market forces. This is a coordinated sector of the global economy in which the conscious hand of corporate strategy supplements or even replaces the invisible hand of market forces.

Some countries are much more exposed to multinational economic influence through operating as host or home country for MNCs, or in some cases as both. The largest hosts and home countries for multinationals are the market-orientated developed OECD countries and especially the UK, the USA, Germany, France and the Netherlands. Among these dominant players some countries are far more internationalised than others. UNCTAD also provides an index of country 'transnationality'. On this index Table 3.1 indicates the most internationalised economies.

Table 3.1   Transnationality index for countries, 2005

Belgium	66
Singapore	65
Chile	33
Netherlands	32
New Zealand	28
South Africa	25
UK	22
France	19
Switzerland	18
Egypt	17
Australia	16
Brazil	14
China	12
Germany	11
USA	7
India	4
Japan	2

Note: the index is based on four indicators of FDI flows, FDI stock, foreign affiliate value-added and employment by foreign affiliates.

Source: UNCTAD (2008: 12).

The high internationalisation of Belgium or Singapore is not surprising but the table also emphasises the high level of internationalisation of the Netherlands, the UK and France. Perhaps more surprising is that the large economies of Brazil, China and Germany are only modestly internationalised and the USA, despite its huge role as home and host to MNCs, has a far smaller exposure to international pressures than the UK. The UK has an exceptionally 'denationalised' industrial economy due partly to a very permissive (or neoliberal) stance by post-1979 governments which has allowed the market for corporate control to transfer a sequence of quintessentially 'British' companies to foreign control. Examples include P&O (now Dubai World), Pilkington (now Nippon Glass) and Cadbury (now part of the US Kraft Group).

This portrayal of a globalising economy being created and dominated by an elite of huge global corporations has been challenged by analysts who identify a fragmentation and 'deverticalisation' of large corporations. The 'new economy' thesis argues that the key features of globalisation, such as access to information, rapid communication and ease of transportation are changing the way in which corporations compete and organise themselves. Corporations have to be nimble, flexible, responsive, engage in rapid innovation and be prepared for continuous adaptation. Cairncross (2002: 152) anticipated that 'Companies will resemble constellations more than pyramids ... Corporate structure grows diffuse and fluid, more kaleidoscope in design'. It is argued that the traditional corporate hierarchy will become a competitive disadvantage and will be replaced by franchises, joint ventures, networks, alliances and outsourcing. In turn this will militate against vertical integration, it will increase competition and lead to deconcentration of the global economy with more but smaller and less powerful MNCs.

While the pressures for change are real enough the prognosis of decline of corporate control is far less persuasive. The new globalising technologies have the potential to increase control. Corporations are adopting alternative organisational forms and as well as relying on internal organisation and direct ownership and employment they are controlling economic activity through networks as well as hierarchies. As Perrow (2009: 218) concludes, 'huge firms may have more concentrated power than a simple market share statistic will reveal because of their de facto (as opposed to de jure) control over their suppliers or even customers'. This reaffirmation of the continued influence of giant corporations is shared by Dunning (1997: 78) and by Jones (2005a: 288) who observes that in the new global economy 'far more than before 1914, a small number of global giants held dominant positions in many industries'. Paradoxically, a shift to dominance through networks and alliances rather than through hierarchy may make MNCs more exploitative and less easy to hold to account. Increasingly corporations are outsourcing their operations (Amoore, 2006) with a supply chain of contactors and sub-contractors which begin to look like the model used for decades by the *keiretsu*, the large Japanese industrial groupings (Gerlach, 1992; Héritier et al., 2011). This strategy allows corporations to transfer risk but does not necessarily make the suppliers any less dependent. As seen in the supermarket supply chains, producers may become entirely dependent on their large customers who can use their monopsony power to impose terms and withdraw contracts whilst disclaiming direct responsibility. Perrow (2009: 241) sees 'the tight coupling of a product and service chain that is increasingly integrated around very large players'. In some cases brands provide the integrating focus and source of corporate power. This was the basis for Klein's brilliant polemic *No Logo* (2002) with her rather startling revelations such as, for instance, the fact that no-one employed by Nike makes shoes (Klein, 2002: 198; Roach, 2005: 30). Nonetheless, Nike, as the world's largest apparel and footwear retailer, controls the whole production chain. This and similar examples imply that the economic power deployed by MNCs should be analysed more widely as spheres of control rather than strictly defined by ownership.

PERSPECTIVES ON THE POWER OF MULTINATIONALS

There are a range of theories which seek to explain the existence of multinational corporations, their success, geographical distribution, political influence and contribution to economic development or exploitation. The economic theories are nowadays looking rather tired and do not provide an adequate framework. The various economic theories were brought together by John Dunning, a leading British economic student of MNCs, who developed his 'eclectic paradigm' which combined ownership, locational and internalisation approaches (Dunning, 1993). The 'OLI' eclectic paradigm combines some useful ideas but it does not provide a sufficiently robust theory to deal with the complex phenomenon of multinational investment despite attempts to adapt and update it (Dunning, 2007: ch. 3). In addition it has very little to say about the politics of MNCs which is a serious shortcoming since it is in the interplay of the economics and the politics of multinational investment that persuasive interpretations have to be found (Geppert and Dörrenbächer, 2011: 8). What, then, of the political theories of the MNC?

Theories of comparative politics have until recently had very little to say about the enhanced power of MNCs and their effect on national politics. There is an increased recognition that transnational political processes affect national politics but as yet few clear theories about how those effects operate (Jackson and Deeg, 2008: 702). We have to turn instead to international political economy (IPE) in which the MNC features in many guises as a vehicle of globalisation, a participant in global governance, and a member of global regulatory networks. Working within IPE, Fuchs (2007) has come closest to developing a persuasive theory of multinational corporate power in the context of the vacuum in global governance which corporations, even more than governments, have an interest in filling.

Perhaps the best place to start is with the paradoxical position of the corporation within the market economy. Corporations value market freedoms and reject the intervention of governments but they also crave certainty, stability, and the regulated, supportive environment which government provides. Corporations both detest and adore governments, which gives rise to the range of political compromises at the domestic level which were examined in Chapter 2. At the international level there is no government, and capital mobility allows corporations to free themselves from government intervention. Unlike trade or finance there are no binding international agreements or oversight agencies governing investment and no global antitrust regime. There is no global tax, no global unions, no global product regulation and no global environmental standards – and hence the paradox kicks in. Corporations cannot thrive in conditions of anarchy and there is clearly some level of global order in all these areas. In the absence of global government, multinational corporations co-operate to regulate the global economy. They co-operate with each other, with governments, NGOs and unions. In terms of the perspectives on corporate power reviewed in Chapter 2 this co-operation cannot be seen as pluralist since there is no neutral governmental authority to hold the ring; it is not structuralist because there is no government to control; it might best be termed 'partnership' in which corporations and nation-states co-operate to provide a degree of global governance. In this sense, and most clearly at the international level, corporations become 'governing institutions'.

This growth of corporate global regulation raises expectations of confrontational relations with the nation-state which has coloured many assessments of the power of MNCs. The development of global markets and of global corporations could be expected to threaten the integrity of the nation-state and to detract from its sovereignty. Clearly this is an important issue. In areas such as macro-economic policy, utilisation of technology, promotion of trade and consumer protection, national governments have less autonomy and less control over national policies and outcomes. But the tendency has been to reduce this attenuation of sovereignty to a crude confrontation between the nation-state which is said to be weakened in a 'borderless world', and multinationals which have escaped from the control of the nation-state. This opposition can be expressed as Strange (1996), *The Retreat of the State*, versus Weiss (1997), *The Myth of the Powerless State*.

Susan Strange was a particularly evangelical proponent of theories that stressed the influence of markets and firms in the international economy (Strange, 1994). Her analysis of the declining power of the state was controversial and could be caricatured as overly one-sided but she was one of the first to advance the hypothesis that 'the shift from state to market has actually made political players of the TNCs ... They themselves are political institutions, having political relations with civil society. These political relations are even more important than their political involvement with other firms or with specific governments' (Strange, 1996: 44). In charting the growing political role of MNCs Strange was therefore inviting a more sophisticated analysis of the reconfiguration of state authority and a consideration of the political power of MNCs independent from the state. It is hard to see that Strange's invitation was widely accepted. Writing more recently, scholars of IPE have regretted the continued baleful influence of the zero-sum sovereignty debate. Goldman and Palan (2006: 182) bemoan the preoccupation with two types of corporate entities, 'states' and 'nonstate actors'. 'Within such a dichotomised conception of the world', they write, 'IPE scholars have also tended to regard MNCs as constituting a direct challenge to state authority . . . the debates that focus on the interaction between states and MNCs are really a distraction from the real importance of these corporations'. One exception is Sklair, who accepted Strange's exhortation to concentrate on the corporation rather than the state and attempted 'to replace the state-centric paradigm . . . with a paradigm of transnational practices'. But he, like Strange, was too dismissive of the great variety of government–corporate relationships captured by comparativists in the 'varieties of capitalism' school of research (Sklair, 2001: 10, 72). It is necessary to retain a focus on the various modes by which corporations engage with national governments without an obsession with loss of state authority. The state's power has not been reduced, it has been redistributed.

Rather than concentrating on a loss of sovereignty by the state we should focus on how the state itself has changed, with new configurations of institutions and a redefinition of security and purpose in terms of economic competitiveness. The state has adapted to globalisation in which corporations have become both beneficiaries and agents of governance. We examine the emergence of the 'market state' in relation to the UK in Chapter 4 but it remains unclear as to how the increased power of multinationals in global governance is reproduced within national politics. At the global level Fuchs has presented a comprehensive account of the sources of business power which she reviews under the three categories of instrumental power, structural power and discursive power; these roughly map onto the three power sources of rules, norms and cognitive power discussed in Chapter 1. Her main focus is global governance and she concludes that 'business has become a pivotal participant in global governance and an important source of global rules and regulations' (Fuchs, 2007: 164). She points out that corporations can choose to act at the local, national or transnational level (ibid.: 94). As conscious political actors they work with and through states to shape regulatory regimes which in turn discipline governments (Murphy, 2004: 237).

The image of the corporation as a governing institution therefore appears as obvious at the global level where corporations are involved in processes of transnational governance in a myriad complex forms of 'governance beyond the state' (Hale and Held, 2011: 5). As corporations engage in processes of government, and incorporate political activism into their corporate strategies, it might be expected that they will accept a greater level of social responsibility and themselves become more mature in working with governments rather than seeking to undermine or confront them (Maclean and Crouch, 2011). But here we are dealing with a volatile and rapidly changing set of expectations. Are all global corporations becoming more responsible, are they working together, do their leaders form collective views as part of a transnational managerial elite? In particular, how will the increased power of business in global governance be affected by the emergence of a cadre of new giant corporations from the BRICs? Western governments may find it easy and even congenial to enter into partnerships with culturally familiar and socially responsible corporations from Europe or North America, but what about corporations from China or India? In the next section we consider how this disconcertingly new expression of a shift in global power relations is likely to find expression through the power of emergent country multinationals.

GLOBAL DIFFUSION OF THE MULTINATIONAL CORPORATE FORM

We saw in Chapter 1 that large corporations are no longer the preserve of the big Western developed economies. Corporations from emergent economies are not only growing in size, they have begun to internationalise and, since the turn of the century, this new breed of non-Western MNCs has become a formidable economic force which needs to be accommodated within theories of corporate power. Accordingly this section first sketches this major development of the growth of emergent country multinational corporations (EMNCs) before evaluating its significance for the global deployment of corporate power. In particular it is necessary to conclude whether EMNCs are likely to converge with traditional Western MNCs; whether their relationship with their home states is one of dependency or autonomy; and whether they are likely to intensify the development of a transcendent global business civilisation.

The EMNCs which have grown up since the mid-1990s have developed at a startling pace which would not have been anticipated by contemporary economic theory (Nölke and Taylor, 2010). They constitute an important new element in the intensified globalisation of the world economy inasmuch as they incorporate new industrial and service activities and integrate new geographical regions. Most spectacularly they integrate their 'home' countries which are no longer passive recipients of foreign direct investment but, as Table 3.2 shows, they themselves become investors in other countries and acquire an interest in global markets and in sustaining the global market system. These countries have to be aware that measures

Table 3.2 Largest stocks of outward FDI, by emergent countries

	$ billion, 2011
Hong Kong	1,046
China	336
Total China	1,382
British Virgin Islands	402
Russia	362
Singapore	339
Taiwan	213
Brazil	203
Korea	159
India	111
(for comparison)	
UK	1,731
Japan	963

Source: UNCTAD (2012, Annex table I.2).

taken to regulate MNCs within their own borders may make their own companies vulnerable to retaliatory measures in other countries. Their support for a regime of global market regulation therefore becomes more substantial and self-interested. During the 2000s the share of EMNCs in the global stock of FDI stabilised at about 15 per cent. Measured by the total of investment undertaken abroad, the largest home countries for EMNCs are shown in Table 3.2. The figures stress the importance of China and East Asia but also pick out the importance of the BRICS, with India as something of a latecomer. The comparison shows that China is already a larger home country than Japan and that it will exceed UK levels of outward FDI over the next decade. The UK is, of course, the second largest home of outward FDI after the USA. Comparing the top-100 global MNCs with the top-100 EMNCs indicated that the emergent country multinationals were growing very substantially to the point that by 2009 the total assets and employment of the top-100 EMNCs were equivalent to 31 per cent and 58 per cent respectively of the total assets and employment of the top-100 MNCs worldwide (UNCTAD, 2012: 25). Indeed, the 2008 UNCTAD listing of the top-100 MNCs contained seven corporations from emergent economies. The pattern of EMNC investment defies sensible generalisation and the statistics are notoriously unreliable. Investment has gone into services as well as manufacturing and extractive industries but EMNCs are also likely to be conglomerates. The main sources of investment are East Asia. The main motives include gaining access to markets, to technology and to cheaper labour. Beyond these sorts of generalisations there are no fixed patterns.

The 2006 UNCTAD World Investment Report made a particular study of FDI from emergent economies and rehearsed the eclectic sources of motivation and advantages that allowed these EMNCs to succeed. Two key attributes emerge from this and other studies. One is the importance of networks and family connections, the other is the importance of state ownership and support to the extent that some of this investment is a manifestation of 'state capitalism'. The family ownership is often enhanced by political connections and has given rise to extraordinary accumulations of wealth such as that enjoyed by Carlos Slim (the Mexican businessman who was the richest person in the world in 2011); the Korean chaebol families; or the Indian dynasties such as the Hinduja brothers, the Tata family or the remarkable Mittall family. Lakshmi Mittall has lived in Britain for three decades and has been, since 2005, the richest man in Britain, with a fortune of £13 bn based on his family ownership of the steel corporation ArcelorMittall (*Sunday Times Rich List*, 2012). The corporation is registered in the Netherlands and is perhaps an expression of entrepreneurial talent rather than political support. More formal state connections are commonplace, especially for Chinese corporations, and Goldstein (2007: 150) notes that 'there is no doubt that many EMNCs have closer ties with their governments than their OECD peers, often because they remain state-owned or state-controlled'. Many developing states have shifted to policies to encourage outward investment and many EMNCs owe their ability to build a global presence on state support through favourable regulation, direct economic assistance and diplomatic links. Indeed, this pattern replicates the early expansion of European and American corporations where 'investment followed the flag' and investment had a quasi-mercantalist character as an expression of national interests.

In relation to corporate power the three big questions about non-Western multinationals are first, whether they are emulating the Western corporate form of institution; second, to what extent they will become managerially controlled; and third, the degree to which they are becoming relatively autonomous from their home states and governments to become part of a global business economy (or civilisation).

On the first point, of apparent convergence with Western corporate forms, it was noted in Chapter 1 that the business corporation has become the standard mode of organising economic activity in market economies. The model has spread to emergent economies and has eclipsed various alternatives such as state-managed industries, cooperatives, individual traders, partnerships and so on. Moreover, the corporate form typically shares many of the characteristics of the limited liability joint stock corporation with larger corporations quoted on the rapidly developing stock markets of emergent economies (by 2012 the Hong Kong and Shanghai stock markets were the fifth and sixth largest in the world by market capitalisation, WFE, 2012). Within this general pattern of convergence there are a variety of alternative legal forms and governance structures which include such striking models as the huge Korean *chaebols* which are similar in organisation to the pre-war Japanese *zaibatsu*; the rambling Indian conglomerate groupings and the Russian industrial empires headed by the so-called oligarchs such as the Sibneft oil group (now part of Gazprom) which formed the basis of the fortune of Roman Abramovich. Perhaps the most interesting embrace of the corporate form is provided by China which began to encourage private enterprise after 1993. By 2000 the CCP officially moved to encourage development of privately owned businesses and 'gave the private sector the same status as the public sector' (Dickson, 2008, 39), a move followed by granting permission in 2001 for private entrepreneurs to become members of the Party (a measure so profoundly antagonistic to Maoist doctrine that it still seems bizarre) and by membership of the WTO in 2001. The corporatization of state-owned enterprises proceeded from the late 1990s by converting them into shareholder-owned corporations quoted on the new domestic Shanghai and Shenzhen stock exchanges. At the same time China began actively to promote inward investment thus accepting the presence and legal rights of foreign corporations (Hsueh, 2011: 42). Indeed, Story (2010: 348) notes that China began 'to make global corporations key allies for the regime in the global polity. China's adaptation is a magnificent achievement'.

This striking convergence on the corporate form is one of the most important examples of 'isomorphism' in the global economy. Isomorphism is the term used by organisational sociologists to explain convergence towards a particular organisational form. A standard explanation would be in terms of economic efficiency, so that the corporate form is adopted simply because it generates greater added value, but theories of isomorphism go beyond the efficiency perspective to try to explain convergence in non-economic settings. In one of the most influential treatments DiMaggio and Powell (1991) identify coercive, mimetic and normative sources of isomorphism and this analytical approach is helpful in identifying the mix of factors that have led emergent countries towards endorsing the model of the corporation. The Chinese example is both fascinating and important so we can use it as an example of a more general syndrome.

From a coercive perspective the corporate model provided an entry ticket to participation in the global market by making Chinese economic organisations respectable in foreign markets and by gaining the endorsement and legitimacy provided by membership of the WTO in 2001. This was not coercion by blunt threats or ultimatums; the Chinese leadership has been spectacularly resistant to overseas pressure. Instead it was soft coercion through the acceptance of the rules, standards and expectation that characterise corporate trading practices so that Chinese corporations could be understood and trusted as trading partners. The Chinese leadership has proceeded gradually in its market reforms which has made 'mimetic isomorphism' another significant factor. Mimetic pressures take the form of copying or contagion, of borrowing models that appear effective and offer convenient solutions. The American corporate model has, as we have seen, been disseminated successfully across the globe. As the dominant economic unit in the most successful global economy it was similarly attractive to a Chinese leadership who became determined to beat the Americans at their own game (see Story, 2010: 348). These coercive and mimetic influences are relatively straightforward but the Chinese leadership arguably had a far more powerful, pragmatic and self-interested motive for building up Chinese corporations under the influence of a normative isomorphism. The corporate form provided a means to create and to access markets but it preserved the key normative considerations of stability and control (see *The Economist*, 2012a: 5). State-owned industries could be corporatized and privatised thus protecting vested interests whilst opening up new possibilities for enrichment of elites in the CCP. At the same time the Party could retain control by becoming a major shareholder, by taking seats on the boards of corporations, and in many cases by appointing senior Party members as chief executives. We have thus seen an extraordinary interpenetration of political and economic elites. Dickson (2008: 238) observes that 'the CCP's strategy of integrating itself with the private sector, both by encouraging party members to go into business and co-opting entrepreneurs into the party, continues to provide dividends'. Forecasts for the future development of the Chinese economy and polity tend to emphasise the apparent tensions arising from massive economic change confronting autocratic political continuity. But the Party has played the wealth card. Multinational corporations are now welcome in China and Chinese corporations have become the dominant domestic economic organisations and have established power in global markets. Thus, barely 30 years after the death of Mao Zedong in 1976, political power is no longer exerted through class struggle, but through the operations and strategies of business corporations whose boardrooms are the new battleground for control over corporate decision making between the Party, business managers and shareholders (see McGregor, 2010, ch. 2). Indeed a revolutionary change, but not quite the one that Marxist–Leninist–Maoist theory anticipated.

In China, therefore, there has been substantial convergence on the Western corporate model, and the same is true of the bulk of emergent economies. The second key question posed above was whether these EMNCs will remain subject to family or state control, or whether they will become managerially controlled with a separation of ownership and control. As noted in Chapter 1, 'blockholding', where a family or the state owns a large proportion of the shares in a corporation, is more typical outside the Anglo-Saxon countries and characteristic of Chinese SMEs (Redding and Witt, 2007: 222). Even with the family influence, however, large and internationalised corporations will tend to be controlled by professional managers and the specific corporate governance arrangements of the home country will structure the balance of power between managers, workers and owners. For emergent economies there is a familiar transitional phase between control by the family and the first generation entrepreneurs and the transition either to professional managers or to a second and third generation of the family. There is an observable syndrome of large corporations being ruined by conflicts within the family or by incompetent second-generation owners. The syndrome has been at work in some of the Korean *chaebol* and in Indian family conglomerates (Damodaran, 2008). The state also appears a less effective manager than professional managers working within a familiar corporate framework and we see EMNCs turning to professional management cadres. As Jones (2010) comments, 'the leaders of many of the largest firms in developing countries, such as Mexico's Cemex, were typically educated at leading American business schools'. Again China provides an important example of growing managerial influence.

Chinese corporations have managerial structures and corporate governance arrangements based largely on the regulations and practices of the West (Chen et al., 2010: 110). Thus, in a short space of time they have reproduced some of the least attractive features of the Western corporate model including over-powerful chief executives, poor protection for minority shareholders and excessive executive compensation. The state capitalist economic reforms in China have conceded a substantial measure of independence to corporate managers, thus 'the managerial discretion in Chinese listed firms originates from the increasing autonomy delegated by the government to firms during the market-orientated reforms' (Chen et al., 2010: 110). This has allowed CEOs to indulge their hubris in ways familiar to Western patterns (Haigh, 2004) to engage in ambitious and risky ventures (Li and Tang, 2010) and has permitted them to benchmark executive pay against foreign firms so that one by-product of foreign multinational investment in China has been for Chinese companies to emulate high executive pay (Chen et al., 2010; 112). The growth of management independence has also seen the development of autonomous business associations (organised within civil society rather than by the state) (Dickson, 2008: 116) but this has been accompanied by a remarkable blending together of party and corporate elites. Thus a third of China's 100 richest people were members of the National People's Congress in 2004 (Dickson, 2008: 171) and Dickson has charted the deliberate way in which the CCP has co-opted entrepreneurs into the Party. He paints a picture of the Party brilliantly embracing entrepreneurs so that 'the integration of political and economic elites in China may serve to sustain the existing authoritarian political system rather than pose a direct challenge to it' (ibid.: 238) but this does not rule out the possibility of a corporate elite steadily gaining additional influence within the Party to produce a 'crony communism' in which policy is tilted towards corporate interests and the state is operated in favour of the 'red capitalists' and the corporations they control, rather than of society at large. Gourevitch and Shinn (2005: 192) rather provocatively term this 'a unique form of insider kleptocracy, a sort of managerism with Chinese characteristics'. It seems therefore that in China a managerial cadre has emerged which has a substantial degree of discretion. Minority shareholders have little protection and the CCP has engaged with entrepreneurs rather than workers, with norms of global competitiveness and with global market penetration. This remains a partnership between the corporations and the state. Thus Chinese corporations, like those from India, are charged with pursuing strategic objectives and particularly access to vital inputs such as raw materials. UNCTAD has observed that 'in the case of Chinese TNCs, the quest for raw materials is complemented by parallel and sustained Chinese diplomatic efforts' (UNCTAD, 2006: xxvii; see also McGregor, 2010: 58 and Nölke and Taylor, 2010: 169). The proposition is therefore that China's model of state capitalism has conceded a substantial element of control to corporate managers (*The Economist*, 2012a: 11) and that their discretion could be expected to be enhanced in those cases of Chinese MNCs operating outside the framework of domestic constraints. Although the emphasis here has been on China it seems to be a more general phenomenon in which many EMNCs have developed substantial managerial autonomy.

Our third big question was whether EMNCs are becoming part of a self-regulating global governance and whether they are joining what can be described as a global business civilisation. EMNCs have become full participants in global business representative bodies such as the ICC (International Chamber of Commerce) and UNCTAD (2006: xxxii) notes that 'more than half of the participating companies in the United Nations Global Compact are based in developing countries'. Similarly they are involved in global standard setting through private sector bodies and especially the ISO (International Organization for Standards), and with their governments they are involved in the international dispute resolution processes in the WTO, thus engaging with international trade law. A more interesting question is whether their senior managers are becoming integrated into an international corporate elite through entry into the international executive labour market. This could happen through recruitment from business schools or through executives moving freely between Western and non-Western MNCs. While there are some hints that emergent country executives are becoming integrated into a global business elite, in the main they retain their home country identification although that does not prevent them from engaging fully in policy formulation for global business. The Davos meetings, for instance, encompass Indian and Chinese corporations and their chief executives. One of the beguiling and civilised aspects of multinational business is, of course, precisely its devotion to commerce and the absence of xenophobia and nationalistic hostility that drives nations to pointless wars (Hirschman, 1986: 107)

CONCLUSION

This chapter reflects a paradox in the study of corporate power. On the one hand multinational corporations enjoy substantial additional sources of power and in popular debate are credited with extensive and often sinister influence. On the other hand our understanding of the politics of multinationals is underdeveloped. The surge of interest in the 1970s, symbolised by Vernon's (1971) *Sovereignty at Bay* and extending to Stopford and Strange's (1991) *Rival States: Rival Firms*, faded out in the 1990s and has only recently been revived. Chapter 7 explores the continuing disjuncture between the study of corporate power at the national level and its study at the international level. The unrealised potential is underlined by the few studies which have made the link between domestic politics and the influence of multinational corporations (see particularly, Leys, 2001). The disjuncture is doubly unfortunate as we see the corporatisation of the large emergent economies and the explosion onto the world stage of new and barely understood multinationals corporations from emergent countries.

More broadly, these first three chapters have presented an account of the origins of corporate power and it is necessary to bring the threads together in a brief summary to set the scene for the next four chapters which move on from the origins of corporate power to explore how it has been exercised in practice. The political power of the business corporation, what we can term 'corporate power', originates with the state. The state has 'licensed' the corporation and granted it extensive legal rights including legal personality and limited liability. Over the 20th century corporations grew in size, in authority, in political influence and in international reach to dominate the developed economies of the OECD. These concentrated economies are home to the huge corporations who feature in the Fortune league tables. They are autocracies; hierarchical and without the representative features which attach legitimacy to liberal democracies. Instead their legitimacy is grounded in property rights, in familiarity as an economic institution, and in economic success. Corporations generate economic growth and historically unprecedented levels of wealth which have driven the Western, capitalist, economic miracles of the second half of the 20th century. In the process they have become politically as well as economically powerful. This study has adopted a pragmatic definition of 'power' which regards power as the ability by corporations to influence public policy. This becomes quintessentially political when it translates into the distribution of resources and the business corporation is not only the source of cherished economic and social resources, but has come to influence the political process by which resources are distributed and re-distributed. As such it was identified in Chapter 1 as a governing institution which has transcended mere political influence to become a vehicle of government with a partnership status in making and implementing public policy.

To see the corporation as a governing institution is to identify a qualitative shift in the nature and origins of its power. As seen in Chapter 2, this approach rejects the assumptions of pluralism and sees the large corporation as a privileged institution integrated into government itself through elite interaction. The qualitative shift came during the 1990s in the UK and in many liberal democracies. It reflected an ideologically driven reduction in the status and responsibilities of the state, a triumph of the market system, and an acceptance of business elites as important partners for political elites. Chapter 2 outlined a framework within which the influence of large corporations as political actors could be assessed, but of course we are interested in collective business power as well as the influence of individual corporations. That collective power is expressed in the governing institution discourse, corporations are treated with respect and possess authority by virtue of their status, as much as by their political activism. Collective power is also, however, expressed through more instrumental (and sociological) routes through the empowerment and integration of business elites. Those elites are dependent on their ability to control an elite of large corporations and may in some countries be owners, and in other countries may be managers. In an Anglo-American setting this book puts the emphasis on managers as dominating the business elite. The origins of business power hence merge into the origins of managerial power.

The national origins of business power stand in complex relationship to global politics. The corporation as an institution has become the standard unit of economic activity across all the world's larger economies and multinational corporations have become indispensable components of global governance. Large global corporations enjoy additional sources of political power, most obviously through their command of economic resources, which allows them to bargain with national governments from a position of strength and a position of equality. They have an existence independent from any one state and can exploit their viability and mobility. As a matter of course they will also operate as political as well as economic actors employing the resources, motivations and opportunities analysed in Chapter 2. This makes them formidable political actors in host countries, able to influence domestic politics, to build alliances and mobilise domestic supporters, especially in smaller, poorer states with underdeveloped political institutions. This direct political engagement, bolstered by the structural power of a contribution to economic growth, is also increasingly enhanced by 'constitutional' weight. The post-1990 international acceptance of global markets and capitalist economies has attached greatly enhanced legitimacy to corporations who operate with greater self-confidence and can mobilise what Fuchs calls 'discursive power', the 'power of ideas' (Fuchs, 2007: 139) in the shape of favourable discourses emphasising the benefits of markets, the corporate sources of competitiveness and the virtually universal elite endorsement of liberalisation. In this globalised setting the power of the corporation as a governing institution becomes unambiguous, and its manifestation in an international managerial elite has created a powerful cadre with a collective influence unprecedented in world history.

This concentration of power in corporations as governing institutions at national and at international levels demands a reconsideration of the corporate form. There is a crying need to reinvent the corporation to ensure that it can contribute to civilised ends. The corporation has created huge wealth and nurtured extraordinary technical progress; it could equally destroy that wealth through misuse of the power it has acquired over material goods, whole communities and ecosystems. The potential for reinvention is explored in the closing chapters but before that, how corporate power is exercised is the subject of the next four chapters. Chapters 4, 5 and 6 take up the concepts outlined above focusing mainly on developments in the UK. As we saw above, the UK is one of the most transnational of the world's larger economies and therefore exceptionally subject to influence by multinational as well as domestic corporations. Chapter 7 comes back to the international issues picked up in this chapter to explore the exercise of power by MNCs based on, and generalised from, the UK experience.

4. Corporate power in the UK: the rise of the corporate elite

DEMOCRATIC SETTLEMENTS AND CORPORATE POWER

The three earlier chapters dealt broadly with the origins of corporate power in a relatively abstract fashion. The next four chapters turn the emphasis towards the exercise of corporate power and focus in Chapters 4, 5 and 6 mainly on the UK. They examine the factors that have consolidated corporate power since the 1980s and how that power has been exercised through the influence of a corporate elite. The discussion moves on to examine the ways in which corporate power moulds public policy and produces distinctive distributional outcomes. The focus on the UK tries not to be too parochial and draws on comparative material where space allows. It also has a broader relevance in defining a model of corporate capitalism which serves as an example and perhaps a warning to other states. The UK has been a capitalist market pioneer and offers a prototype of an emerging form of corporate state in which partnerships between government and corporations, and between corporate and political elites, dictate political choices. In fact the influence travels beyond other national market economies to affect governance at the international level. It has been a cliché of recent international relations that the global economy has been governed (in as far as it is governed at all) on the basis of principles and organisation that are constituted along US lines, the so-called 'Washington consensus'. The study of how corporate power has moulded governance in the UK also offers insights into how the Anglo-American model influences governance at the global level where corporations are similarly partners in governance. This perspective is developed further in Chapter 7 where the forces that militated towards corporate dominance in the UK setting are explored in the international setting. The corporations, the rules, the agendas and the market cultures that are so influential in the UK have a parallel existence in the global economy and the reciprocal influence between domestic and global politics needs to be brought into clearer focus, Chapter 7 seeks therefore to analyse the exercise of corporate power within global governance.

Initially we can locate the UK in a comparative context. Studies of comparative capitalism and comparative lobbying identify marked differences in the extent and operation of corporate power varying systematically between countries and over time (Hall and Soskice, 2001; Grote et al., 2008; Coen and Richardson, 2009). Each country and political system has devised some compromise between the exercise of political and of economic power. This chapter examines this 'settlement' in the UK, what it implies for the political process and how it is changing to accommodate and embed a more dominant political role for business and for large corporations. Democratic and constitutional settlements have been constructed within the boundaries of a nation-state as a result of negotiation and confrontation between the major centres of power. The focus of negotiation and the substance of the settlement concerns the control of the state with its apparatus of administration, security and law making. The question of 'who controls' the state is a perennial focus of political science, but even in highly developed liberal democracies control by 'the people' is an impossible ideal and the people select elite representatives through some majoritarian or consensual process (Lijphart, 1999: 2). Accordingly, the approach taken here is to apply an elitist framework to examine the shifting power and compromises negotiated between a plurality of elites.

Elitism was introduced in Chapter 2 and provides a classic approach to understanding the distribution of power in society (Dryzek and Dunleavy, 2009: ch.3; Savage and Williams, 2008). Traditional elitism argued not only that inequality was inevitable in any society, but also that the elite of leaders possessed some sort of exceptional qualities of moral superiority. The assumption of natural superiority is no longer credible but elitism continues to provide a persuasive interpretation of many features of industrialised modern societies. Contemporary democratic societies are extensively organized, subject to bureaucratic or managerial control and are mass societies in which individuals are represented by leaders. Elites exist in every walk of life, social and economic equality is unusual and, like the classic elitists, we can observe a ubiquitous social arrangement of followers and leaders in which the leaders increasingly provide subjects for popular admiration. The saving grace of elite domination of society, and the antidote to an unduly cynical or fatalistic application of elite theories, is that elites compete. The idea of a plurality of elites giving rise to a circulation of elites provides the reassurance of a degree of accountability and popular influence. Economic elites may be powerful but they are constrained by constitutional settlements enforced by the state, and competitor elites remain influential.

THE CIRCULATION OF ELITES IN THE UK

From the 1940s up until the mid-1980s British ruling elites continued to be traditional, familiar, often fiercely criticised but idiosyncratically British (or more correctly, English). They were dissected in a variety of studies such as the wry and mildly sympathetic 'anatomies' of Britain first produced in 1962 by Anthony Sampson (1962, 1992). The traditional elites in the early 1970s, as captured in a snapshot by Giddens (1974), were those of the still powerful class system and included the monarch and the aristocracy with their power embedded in landowning and the financial institutions of the City. The traditional elite reached out to the Church of England and the military, reproducing itself through the public school system. Part of the traditional elite was what might be called the 'constitutional elite' in the shape of the civil service and the judiciary. Together these institutional elites could be termed 'the Establishment' (see Hennessy, 1989, ch.13; Annan, 1990: ch. 25; Du Gay, 2008) and their governing arm operated through the Conservative Party as a major component of the political elite in the Commons and the Lords.

The business elite of service, and especially manufacturing, corporations was semi-detached from the Establishment. There were links and sympathies but also marginalisation and incomprehension, expressed in a contempt for the vulgarities of business and markets which was diagnosed as a root cause of the British disease and condemned in a range of critiques of Britain's anti-manufacturing culture (Wiener, 1981; Pollard, 1984; Barnett, 1986; Wilks, 1988). Against the Establishment and business elites were arrayed the union elites representing organised labour, and to some extent a cultural and arts-based elite critical of traditional privileges and values. The Labour Party, as the second major component of the political elite, articulated alternatives but was committed to the essential foundations of the Post-war Settlement crafted during the Second World War and consolidated under the Attlee government of 1945–51.

The Post-war Settlement originated in wartime negotiation conducted against a background of nationalism and idealism. Its seminal gospel was, for Middlemas (1986: 341), the 1944 Employment White Paper which enshrined agreement to high and stable employment. The Settlement rested on compromises embodied in the mixed economy and the welfare state. The Establishment accepted nationalised industries and extensive state intervention in, and management of, the economy. The unions and labour accepted a private-enterprise, market-based economy in return for rising living standards, full employment and the welfare state. Within this Settlement the power of business and corporate elites was constrained within predominately national economies by interventionist governments inspired by Keynesian self-confidence, by a widespread suspicion of the free market, by the unions, and by self-doubt. Management was regarded with suspicion and 'entrepreneur' was a curious French word with vulgar connotations of sharp dealing and opportunism. Corporate political engagement took the form of lobbying and, from the early 1960s, there were attempts at partnership through tripartism as symbolised by the NEDC (National Economic Development Council). Business interests tended to be poorly articulated and were often ignored. Relations reached a low point with the 1974–79 Labour government when 'the CBI Leadership would lock with the government in relations of anger, sullen acquiescence or recoil, or at best joint crisis management' (Boswell and Peters, 1997: 122). It was these relations that persuaded Grant and Marsh (1977) that the CBI was a relatively weak political actor although, in contrast, Moran argued that the leaders of giant corporations were well integrated into policy elites so that 'their chief executives just had everyday access to the policy-making elite in a private political world' (Moran, 2009: 64). We come back to these contrasting interpretations of business influence in Chapter 5 when examining the further development of effective single-corporation lobbying from the late 1980s. Writing in 1991 Middlemas observed the steady deterioration of the Post-war Settlement. He did not attempt to define a new settlement but, 20 years later, we can be more definitive about the shape of a new settlement by examining the forces that undermined the Post-war Settlement, by outlining the decline and rise of elites, and by characterising the shape of the new post-Thatcher settlement.

The forces that undermined the Post-war Settlement have driven the changed configuration of governing elites in British society. Four sets of forces deserve emphasis. First, is the raw fact of Britain's relative economic decline for virtually the whole of the post-war period. Michael Porter's important comparative study placed Britain firmly at the bottom of the annual growth tables of advanced economies for the 1950–87 period. In his discussion of 'the slide of Britain' he remarks that 'as a result of the economy's slow rate of upgrading, the British standard of living has been losing ground relative to other advanced nations for many decades' (Porter, 1990: 572 and 279). The deep-seated, gut-wrenching despair which decline evoked sometimes erupted in anger, but also generated a dismal resignation and atmosphere of pessimism which gave way to crisis over the course of the 1974–79 Labour government. Those who experienced the hyper-inflation (over 20 per cent in 1976), perpetual strikes, IMF Bailout in 1976 and the miserable Winter of Discontent in 1978–79 were willing to tolerate radical change. Middlemas captures the mood of the times, 'individuals who lived through it recall a dangerous, disorientating time when what counted most was to survive. To recapture the feeling of being without landmarks, somewhere between panic and exaltation, requires an effort of imagination comparable to understanding the consequences of an immense natural disaster' (Middlemas, 1991: 3). The crises of the 1970s became the midwives of Thatcherism, partly by discrediting the elites in government, the civil service, industry and of course the unions, which became the antagonists of early Thatcherism.

Linked to economic decline is the second force in the shape of the fundamental redefinition of the conditions for economic success away from Keynesianism and towards market forces and neoliberalism. The free market orthodoxy that was constructed during the 1980s was originally debated in terms of Thatcherism. Following its acceptance by New Labour it might better be termed 'the British business model' or even a 'market society' (both terms employed by Faucher-King and Le Galès, 2010: 17, 141). The Thatcherite project rested on liberalised market solutions, and in order to impose them some elites had to be marginalised, some confronted and some empowered. The Thatcher governments employed the power of the state to remove constraints on the operation of the market including reducing the size and influence of the state itself in a paradox captured by Gamble's (1994) study of *The Free Economy and the Strong State*. Similar processes were underway in the United States with market principles gaining ascendancy and, of course, a cross-fertilisation of ideas and policies between the two leading free market economies. In an influential assertion of the power of ideas, Blyth analysed the way in which a new neoliberal institutional order was created in the USA. He argued that the battles over ideas were fought deliberately and ruthlessly by business elites and their associates with the result that 'organized business groups and their political allies displaced states as the principal actors responding to economic dislocation' due in part to the way in which 'business ... used ideas as weapons to promote institutional change. The ideas of monetarists, new classical macroeconomists, and public choice theorists were used to attack and delegitimate existing institutions' (Blyth, 2002: 258). In Britain, a similar battle also resulted in the eventual dominance of market principles, although in this case it perhaps owed more to Conservative and libertarian thinkers, to think tanks and to monetarist economists. The Labour Party embraced market principles, the imperatives of globalisation and the primacy of competitiveness in the 'modernization' of the Party which rested on a 'Third Way political economy' (Hay, 2002: 206) which consolidated the British version of American market supremacy. Business and financial leaders found these ideas highly congenial and the corporate elite both benefited from and absorbed the new market orthodoxy.

The third force driving a reconfiguration of elites is globalisation. The arenas within which traditional elites had created and sustained their dominance were transformed by globalisation which created new elites. As we saw with the expansion of multinationals in Chapter 3, markets have been globalised and industrial success is less likely to be achievable within the confines of the UK market. From the first Thatcher government Britain enthusiastically embraced globalisation with the elimination of exchange controls in 1979, deregulation of banking, and the 'big bang' deregulation of the stock exchange in 1986. Residual commitment to protecting British ownership of British corporations evaporated so that corporations which might once have been regarded as national champions were subject to foreign takeovers in a trend that stretched from Rowntree (Nestlé since 1988) to Land Rover (BMW in 1994 then Ford, now Tata), Pilkington (Nippon Glass since 2008) and to the widely regretted takeover of Cadbury by the US Kraft Corporation in 2010. Hence global markets reached quickly and deeply into the British economy with global corporations able to use their international flexibility and corporate authority to redefine their relationships with national governments. These trends are seen above all in the absolute incorporation of the UK into global financial markets. The globalisation of finance has been at once the cause and the symbol of the financial crisis and has redefined the institutional foundations of elite power.

The fourth factor influencing elite transformation is a growing tolerance of economic inequality which originates with the Thatcherite transformation of economic doctrine and the accompanying shift in social values and standards of morality. The Thatcherite emphasis on individual achievement, entrepreneurship, market values and pursuit of self-interest were all part of the reaffirmation of Britain as a market society. By its very nature a free market society is an acquisitive society and the acquisition of wealth became admirable and enviable rather than vulgar and selfish. Surveys indicate that governmental acceptance of inequality chimed with public attitudes. The proportion of people believing that it is 'the government's responsibility to reduce income differences' fell from 75 per cent in 1985 to 67 per cent in 2006 with the fall in the number of people saying government 'definitely should act' falling more dramatically from 48 per cent to 27 per cent (Park et al., 2010: 45), thus demonstrating a declining support for government measures to aid redistribution. This mattered for economic elites whose wealth could be admired and could earn respect and celebrity status by inclusion, for instance, in the *Sunday Times Rich List* which began publishing in 1988. Curiously, there was a major exception to this pattern. Extraordinary rewards have been tolerated for corporate and financial elites, for the professions, and even for a new wealthy section of the public sector in people like local authority chief executives and the senior management of the BBC. But the media and the public draw the line at the political elite. Ministers forgo pay rises, thousands of public sector employees earn more than the derisory £148,000 that the Prime Minister is paid and, when MPs supplement their modest salaries (of £66,000 in 2011) with inflated expenses, the nation is outraged while, in bizarre contrast, corporate directors pocket annual remuneration in the millions. To participate in the world of the wealthy, politicians either need private wealth (as enjoyed by the 18 millionaires in the 2010 Cameron/Clegg Cabinet, *Sunday Times*, 23 May 2011) or they need to cultivate the private sector for lucrative post-politics employment. We come back to inequality at the end of this chapter whilst noting that it is increasingly seen as the responsibility of the individual, not of society, and the tolerance of inequality implies a society more at ease with the influence of elites.

THE NEW CORPORATE STATE

The factors outlined above transformed the balance of elite power in the UK. The old 'Establishment' elites declined, to be replaced or overshadowed by an empowered corporate and financial elite. The evidence of this transition was apparent from the late 1980s but it was only with the 1997 general election, and the ascendency of Blair, Brown and New Labour, that the balance became sufficiently stable to be regarded as a new settlement. The embedding of a culture of business dominance is at the heart of the new settlement which is conceptualised here as a 'New Corporate State' in a deliberate echo of Galbraith's (1967) *New Industrial State* and in order to emphasise (as did he) the central role of the large corporation and to distance the discussion from a preoccupation with neoliberalism.

The agreement on a new settlement, and the consensus which the political elite crafted around markets and competitiveness, owed much to the genius of Tony Blair. It created for him a virtuous circle in which his unprecedented achievement of three Labour election victories embedded the settlement as a basis for the exercise of public power. Under the joint Blair and Brown leadership New Labour made an astonishing ideological shift which was, of course, symbolised by the re-writing of its constitution. The highpoint was the April 1995 special conference of the Labour Party which voted by 65 per cent to abandon the Clause IV commitment to 'the common ownership of the means of production, distribution and exchange' in favour of a social market acceptance of private ownership. It was, says Seldon (2004: 228), 'as important to him as his victory in the leadership in July 1994'. On this foundation Blair and Brown moved to strengthen bridges with industry and finance in what became known as the 'prawn cocktail offensive' as they and their City linkman, the wealthy and influential MP Geoffrey Robinson, dined their way around City boardrooms (Peston, 2005: 103). They won over many leading business figures including Sir Colin Marshall and Adair (now Lord) Turner as President and Director-General of the CBI (Bower, 2007: 178–9). This campaign culminated in a special election manifesto in 1997 aimed at the business community and designed to confirm a 'positive engagement' with employers. In Taylor's interpretation, the functions of the state under the Blair/Brown vision 'were to liberate private companies from excessive regulation and help to create the kind of competitive framework that would help them to flourish in a global economy' (Taylor, 2007: 217). Like many commentators, Taylor also remarks on 'the Prime Minister's unsettling adoration of corporate wealth' (2007: 224) but the real driver was straightforward electoral calculation. In Hay's interpretation of events Blair and Brown understood and accepted the structural dependency thesis outlined in Chapter 2. They agreed that electoral success depended on a successful and cooperative corporate sector that should therefore be supported and incentivised by government. As Hay observes, 'what is so remarkable about such a thesis is the extent to which it seems to capture New Labour's strategic assessment' (Hay, 1999: 149). This interpretation of the New Labour strategy was confirmed over the next ten years during which the Labour government deepened and broadened their relationship with the corporate elite. Only during the decaying Brown government did the relationship begin to sour. In mordant phrases, which captured his own partnership with business, Blair commented on the swansong of New Labour. It lost the 2010 election, says Blair, 'because it stopped being New Labour' and, he adds, in a revelatory passage,

> tellingly, we lost business. This was crucial. When the Tories brought out thirty or so chief executives who were against the National Insurance rise, I knew the game was up ... If thirty chief executives, employing thousands of people in companies worth billions of pounds, say it's Labour that will put the economy at risk, who does the voter believe? Answer; the chief executive. Once you lose them, you lose more than a few votes. You lose your economic credibility. (Blair, 2010: 679, 680–81)

Like Thatcher, Tony Blair was a leader of extraordinary ability and influence. Like Thatcher he dominated the political scene but the new settlement rests on a broader and by now well-entrenched consensus. Both the Conservatives and Labour made an ideological shift to a new centre ground. The British Social Attitudes Survey observed that,

Table 4.1   Party positions in a left–right scale

	1983	1992	1997	2001	2005
Labour	−39	−30	8	6	−3
Conservatives	29	28	26	15	15
distance	68	58	18	9	18

Note: left −ve; right +ve.

Source: Padgett and John (2010: 42).

> the British party system has been characterised by a pronounced convergence ... In 1983 there was a 68-point gap between Labour and the Conservatives. By 2001 it had shrunk to just nine points reflecting the repositioning of both parties in relation to the role of government, welfare and the market economy. (Padgett and John, 2010: 41)

This remarkable ideological convergence is one of the largest in Europe and is based on a 'left–right' scale derived from party manifestos. Table 4.1 shows Labour moving much more substantially than the Conservatives.

Ideological convergence provided the party-political foundation of the new settlement but, as in 1945, it is the Labour Party that has defined the new politics. In Moran's (2009: 134–5) summary,

> New Labour has been determined to present itself as a business-friendly party. In short, for over a quarter of a century now, determined efforts have been made by governing elites in Britain to reinforce business domination. We are seeing an attempted creation of a Gramscian-hegemony – the attempt to establish a culture where business domination seems part of the natural order of things.

The stability of the New Corporate State was threatened by the financial crisis of 2008, with the possibility of the resurgence of state intervention and a discrediting of free market economics, but in a remarkable demonstration of the power of the corporate and financial elite, and a dismal failure of political imagination, the settlement appears to have survived those setbacks (Crouch, 2011; Engelen et al., 2011: 13; Kay, 2011). Indeed, the 2010 general election which brought Cameron and Clegg to power had, if anything, further consolidated the post-Thatcher governing consensus.

Although the consensus is regularly characterised as 'neoliberal' this is a misleading label. The reality is of oligopolistic markets organised by corporations, not the emancipated markets of neoliberal legend. As explored in Chapter 1, the political economies which large corporations create may be justified by the rhetoric of markets, but they are not the pure, spontaneous markets of Hayekian myth. They are hierarchically governed, regulated and biased. Like Braithwaite (2008: 4) this study regards neoliberalism as a 'fairy tale' and, like Crouch (2011: 54), it emphasises the contradiction between neoliberal rhetoric and managed markets which are dominated by large corporations. We may appear to live in a marketised world but it is a world of regulatory capitalism in which markets are created and manipulated by partnerships of governments and corporations. The New Corporate State in the UK is probably the most advanced example of corporatisation among the larger developed economies, as such it provides an inspiration, or a warning. How, then, was it brought into existence?

The explanation offered here is of a rise to dominance of a financial and corporate elite operating in partnership with an electorally successful political elite. This elite thesis is easy enough to assert but it tends to be employed as a sweeping generalisation and to be informative it needs to be analysed systematically. We can therefore seek to substantiate a claim of dominance by a financial and corporate elite by examining four questions in a UK context:

1. what is the nature and composition of the corporate elite?
2. what is its relationship to the political elite?
3. what is its mode of operation in pursuit of its interests?
4. how much is it constrained by countervailing elites?

The rest of this chapter addresses the first question, the other three questions are addressed in Chapter 5.

THE COMPOSITION OF THE CORPORATE ELITE

Corporate elites are regularly referred to in the press and popular debate and are a staple in the analysis of elite power. The concept of the corporate elite was reviewed in Chapter 2. Identifying a contemporary British corporate elite presents a challenge which must be met if we are to have any chance of understanding the exercise of corporate power, the goals which it pursues and the options for calling it to account. One place to start is with Sklair's analysis of corporate elites discussed further in Chapter 7 where he defines the main components of the 'transnational capitalist class'. Although he is undertaking analysis at a global level his categories can be applied at the national level. His four components are executives; politicians and bureaucrats; professionals; and merchants and the media (Sklair, 2001: 17). This approach takes the corporation as the centre of gravity of the elite and it is valuable in supplementing an examination of corporate executives by taking account of supportive organisations which service and benefit from corporate wealth generation. The chapter goes on to examine each of these elite components.

Corporate Executives

Corporate directors and senior executives are at the core of the corporate elite. Just as the political elite is defined by the posts they hold within the state, so the corporate elite is primarily defined by their posts in the corporate world. Thus, although the corporate elite in the UK has a personalised dimension and does exploit social and family ties, it is better thought of as an elite of corporations and therefore defined as the individuals who hold the directive leadership roles within those corporations (see Chapter 2). But which corporations? In his study of *The Inner Circle* Useem looked at about 2000 directors of the largest 196 manufacturing and financial corporations. In defining the corporate elite he looked for (and found) 'a leadership cadre ... whose powers extend far beyond the individual firm, whose responsibilities are those of managing no less than the broadest political affairs of the entire big-business community' (Useem, 1984: 17). These people share a 'classwide' vision which extends beyond the particular preferences of individual corporations and, for Useem, they can be identified through multiple corporate connections; by advisory service to government; involvement with non-profit organisations; with political parties; with the media; and with business associations. These are the 'statesmen' of the business world. Of course Useem was writing in the early days of the Thatcherite transformation but his analysis can be updated with the work of Maclean, Harvey and Press in their study of *Business Elites and Corporate Governance in France and the UK* (Maclean et al., 2006, 2010).

The corporations which form the platform of elite activity cannot be defined with complete precision but include the following four elements:

1. The largest corporations quoted on the LSE. In fact equity investment is highly concentrated and the FTSE 100 corporations account for a remarkable 85 per cent per cent of total equity (ONS, 2010: 2). The very largest of these, for instance the top 33 with a market value in 2010 of over £10 bn, are automatic members of the elite.
2. Most of the FTSE 100 corporations also dominate the industrial sectors within which they operate. The FTSE allocates corporations to one of 50 industrial sectors, the largest of which is oil and gas, and the smallest leisure goods. It is striking how most of these sectors are

dominated by two or three corporations. Following the analysis of political activism in Chapter 2 we can identify some sectors where dominant corporations may not be huge but will prioritise political activity, and where CEOs and senior managers are likely to be active in the corporate elite. Table 4.2 gives examples of politically vulnerable sectors where we could expect intense political activism.

3. Many members of the corporate elite will be associated with corporations which are not quoted on the LSE but are still dominant players in the British economy. Such corporations may be privately owned by families and private equity groups but are more likely to be subsidiaries of global corporations quoted on overseas stock exchanges. Obvious examples would include ASDA (part of Wal-Mart) or Nissan. For key sectors such as energy and water only a few companies are quoted in London and the big players are members of multinational groups. In energy, for instance, there is no London quotation for RWE, EON, EdF or Iberdrola (see Ch. 6). The UK corporate elite includes the CEOs of the UK subsidiaries of such corporations but they will have less independence, and an ambiguous role in balancing UK engagement with the strategies of their multinational parents.

4. In a special category are the corporate financial elite. The financial sector has a peculiarly central role in organising and representing the corporate elite. Leading financiers in banks, investment banks, insurance and fund managers have exceptional influence in three respects. First, they provide the essential life support system of capitalist economies. Banks have to be protected, they are special and cannot be allowed to collapse, as we saw only too graphically in the financial crisis. Second, banks and finance establish the criteria by which capital is allocated to corporations and sectors. They influence the direction of economic and technological development and have great influence over the other members of the corporate elite. This may be through markets, as in the UK, or more directly through shareholdings and appointments as in Germany, but whatever the instrumentalities, finance has oversight over the system. Third, the financial sector imposes discipline. It is the carrier and reproducer of operating norms whether related to shareholder value, governance or debt levels. Finance requires conformity and defines acceptable economic behaviour by corporations, by corporate leaders and also, of course, in relation to the economic policies and sovereign debt of government itself. The financial elite is at the core of the broader corporate elite, indeed, for some observers it has come to dominate the whole economy, with levels of reward that put even FTSE chief executives in the shade (Peston, 2008: 341). The analysis presented here does not

Table 4.2 Corporations in politically vulnerable sectors, 2012

Sector	Largest corporation	FTSE rank	CEO
Oil	BP	1	Peter Voser
Banks	HSBC	2	Stuart Gulliver
Pharmaceuticals	GlaxoSmithKline	5	Sir Andrew Witty
Gas/Water	National Grid	23	Steve Holliday
Aerospace	Rolls Royce	29	John Rishton
Electricity	Scottish & Southern	31	Ian Marchant
Media	BSkyB	33	Jeremy Darroch
Support services	Experion	38	Don Robert
Health	Smith & Nephew	57	Olivier Buhuon
Financial services	Schroders	66	Michael Dobson

Source: FT UK 500, sector analysis, ranking on market capitalisation, March 2012, available at http://media.ft.com/cms/a6e7a5e8-ca80-11e1-89f8-00144feabdc0.pdf, (accessed 5 August 2012).

accept the pre-eminence of the financial element of the corporate elite but it does accept that elements of that elite have come to threaten the legitimacy of the New Corporate State. In a US context Johnson and Kwak (2010: 89, 118) talk of a financial oligarchy which developed into a 'Wall Street–Treasury Complex' and which conspired in the regulatory laxity which led to the financial crash. Elements of that financial elite, in areas like hedge funds and the speculative activities of investment banks, have accepted a level of financial irresponsibility that threatens even the licensed self-enrichment of the corporate elite. These financial engineers and speculators are arguably outside the elite consensus and their development of markets to their logical extremes could be regarded as a classic Marxist 'contradiction of capitalism' which undermines the very system that sustains it.

In summary, the classic British corporate elite has become less attached to the traditional locations of British social prestige and has, in fact, been significantly 'denationalised'. In the early 1970s Whitley (1974) could map the elites of 'City and industry' by reference to gentleman's clubs, public schools and interlocking directorships. Nowadays the elite is less cohesive so that business schools, consulting networks and sporting interests may provide equally important links. However, whilst the elite may be less socially cohesive it is both stronger and more united in its ideological beliefs and self-confidence. The corporate elite has gone from advising, exhorting and sometimes confronting government to being in government.

It has a presence through partnership, through positions on public sector boards and even through appointment as ministers. Maclean et al. (2006) have sought to define the core corporate elite with some precision. Taking 1998 as their sample year they use a composite definition to identify the 100 most powerful corporations in the UK (and rank them by degree of power). They go on to analyse the composition of their directors and build a data base of the 1050 individual directors and a ranking of the 100 most powerful individuals. Their fascinating ranking was headed by Mark Moody-Stuart, then Chairman and Joint CEO of Shell, and extended to Christopher Tugendhat, then Executive Chairman of Abbey National, at 100. There was only one woman on this list (at 87, Lydia Dunn, Vice Chairman of HSBC). The Maclean et al. ranking presents a profile of the CEOs, chairmen and directors at the core of the British corporate elite. These are among the most powerful men in Britain and globally. Their policy preferences are individually influential and, when expressed collectively, verge on the irresistible.

Supporting Bureaucrats

The corporate elite portrayed above is far from isolated. It is nested within a supportive environment of corporations, organisations and social networks whose *raison d'être* is to service the core corporations and their boards. Sklair's second component of the 'transnational capitalist class' is made up of 'globalising politicians and bureaucrats'. The UK equivalent is discussed in Chapter 5, here we can briefly comment on the bureaucratic expression of the New Corporate State. Under the Post-war Settlement the British civil service provided stable government, measured consensual policy making, expertise, dedication and a quasi-constitutional limitation on the more divisive preferences of politicians. The undermining of that traditional Whitehall model under Mrs Thatcher, and its gradual disintegration under New Labour created a civil service that became partially absorbed into the corporate elite through four routes.

First, ministers pressed for a more open civil service in which the approximately 4,000 posts in the senior civil service would be opened up to competition. The result has been that over 20 per cent of senior posts are occupied by people recruited from outside the service, mainly from the private sector. At the very top of the service is the 'Top 200' group of civil service leaders. The PASC (2010: 6) notes that 'since 2005, more than half of all new entrants to the Top 200 have come from outside the civil service' (overwhelmingly from the private sector). The leadership of the British civil service is now predominantly composed of private sector appointees. They can be expected to deploy corporate management strategies, to be aware of business interests, and to base their leadership on corporate management norms. Second, the civil service has resorted on a grand scale to the employment of management consultants for advice, project management and policy implementation. The NAO 'estimate that in 2009–10 total spending on consultants across central government, including arms-length bodies, was £1.5 billion' (NAO, 2010b: 11). This is a huge amount and the sheer weight of consultant's influence becomes more fully apparent when the spending is expressed as a percentage of staff costs. Thus, in 2009–10 five departments spent the equivalent of over 40 per cent of their staff costs on consultants and the Department for Transport spent a jaw-dropping amount equivalent to 70 per cent of its staff costs. The Chair of the Public Accounts Committee, Margaret Hodge, described these numbers as 'shocking', adding that 'so for every £10 spent even in the Home Office on staffing, £4 is spent on consultants. It's crazy' (PAC, 2010: oral evidence, 17 November 2010). Crazy or not, this level of input from consultants gives them substantial influence over the development and implementation of public policy. Their wider influence is discussed below.

Thirdly, senior civil servants often pursue rewarding careers after retirement at 60. This has always raised concerns about their relationships with the corporations with whom they deal (Dowding, 1995: 126). Senior officials are independent people with high levels of integrity, but they have many routine contacts with large corporations with whom they deal on terms of mutual respect, understanding and often a degree of accommodation. There is a danger that accommodation might go too far when future corporate employment is in prospect. Thus, not only does the corporate elite enter Whitehall, so also does the civil service elite enter the boardroom. This 'revolving door' is a classic route for business influence and is far further developed in Japan and France, as well as in the United States, but it has always generated suspicion, which prompted Harold Wilson to create an Advisory Committee on Business Appointments whose annual reports make fascinating reading. The 2009–10 report reveals that 33 retiring diplomats, top members of the armed forces and senior civil servants accepted 42 corporate appointments. Often they were linked to their civil service careers so that Mark Britnell, Director General of Commissioning at the Department of Health, became a partner and head of healthcare at KPMG; Sir John Scarlett, the high profile Chief of the Secret Intelligence Service, took no fewer than five appointments including a partnership with PWC (Acoba, 2010).

A fourth source of corporate influence comes through the management boards that have been created to manage all accounting units of central government and even departments themselves. The management boards are modelled on private sector corporate governance and they inject private sector experience, expectations and techniques, including management accounting. More particularly they also include non-executive directors (NEDs) who are invariably from private sector corporations. This further reinforces a deceptive and counter-productive private sector model (Wilks, 2007, 2008) but the board device has been reinforced under the Coalition government. David Cameron invited Lord Browne (former CEO of BP) to recruit up to 60 top flight private sector directors to become NEDs in Whitehall. Thus, for example, Andrew Witty (CEO of GlaxoSmithKline) was appointed as the lead NED at BIS (Department of Business Innovation and Skills) and Sam Laidlaw (CEO of Centrica) as lead NED at the Department for Transport (Sherman, 2010). The extent of business influence was further emphasised by the extraordinary introduction of a 'buddy' system by Cameron in September 2011 whereby CEOs of major corporations were given direct access to named ministers who were expected to trouble shoot on their behalf. The senior Conservative, David Davis, used this as 'proof that the government pays too much attention to big business' (Davis, 2012: 24). The picture, then, is of a civil service colonised by business ideas, models and people so that its independence is moderated and its leaders are either constrained or replaced. The effect has been to shift the institution of the civil service towards supporting, and to some extent joining, the corporate elite.

Professionals and 'Reputational Intermediaries'

Sklair's third component of the transnational capitalist class is 'globalizing professionals'. Adapting this category to the UK context introduces the supporting chorus of dependent technical firms whose main clients are the big corporations and who are themselves often giant firms. The main professional services are provided by accountants, law firms, management consultants and business schools. These organisations enhance and protect the reputations of big corporations and their leaders. Accordingly Gourevitch and Shinn (2005: 114) call them 'reputational intermediaries'. They provide services to the corporate elite but they have a wider role in explaining and justifying the new corporate state in an ideological debate about how the corporate system enhances public benefits and the public interest.

Reputational intermediaries are more or less committed to protecting standards and maintaining the stability of the system but they are also, of course, beneficiaries. They may define their roles as protecting shareholder interests or wider stakeholder interests although in practice they tend to be most sympathetic to the interests of senior managers. At the senior levels, these intermediary organisations are headed by people who are themselves

Table 4.3   The UK Big 4 accountants

	Partners	Fee income £m	Profit p. partner 2010 £'000	No. of audits FTSE100	FTSE350
PWC	885	2,248	770	40	108
Deloitte	758	1,969	744	23	79
KPMG	569	1,626	684	20	87
Ernst & Young	515	1,383	633	16	63
next largest:					
Grant Thornton	235	378	237	0	6

Sources: Singh (2011); Select Committee on Economic Affairs (2011: 162).

members of the corporate elite and who share in lavish rewards. The reputational intermediaries tend to be impressive, authoritative bodies deploying considerable professional and intellectual resources to defend the prevailing system and to drive profitable innovation. They are the cheerleaders of the New Corporate State who often define the terms of the debate in areas like national competitiveness, public sector productivity, public–private partnerships, the future of occupational pensions and, of course, business-friendly regulation. Whether as City accountants, lawyers or management consultants, or as deans of business schools, this element of the corporate elite deploys discursive power, it uses the power of ideas to build trust, to advance rationales and to legitimise the New Corporate State.

The big accounting firms are central actors in the UK and the global corporate system. Following the collapse of Arthur Andersen, resulting from its incrimination in the Enron scandal, the UK, and indeed the global, market has come to be dominated by the 'Big 4' firms. They are massive: PWC employs 162,000 people in 154 countries and in the UK its income comes fairly equally from audit fees, management consultancy and tax planning (2012 figures from www.pwc.com). Their UK operations are summarised in Table 4.3 and their dominance is illustrated by their oligopoly over the audit of large corporations. They audit 99 of the FTSE 100 and 337 of the FTSE 350 and the rewards of partnership are substantial, an average of £770,000 for a partner in PWC.

The Big 4 recruit from the cream of university graduates. They supply many of those who will go on to be chief financial officers of the biggest corporations and they are at the centre of the network of professional accountants. The senior partners of the Big 4 are influential members of the corporate elite. Through the audit process they are the definitive protectors of corporate reputations and, as outlined in Chapter 10, they are the custodians of the British model of self-regulatory corporate governance. Their influence is such that they have avoided a separation of their audit and consultancy arms, despite widespread unease at conflicts of interest. They fended off investigation by the competition authorities until October 2011 when, after pressure from the House of Lords Select Committee on Economic Affairs (Select Committee, 2011), the OFT referred the accounting market to the Competition Commission for a two year investigation. Whether the Big 4 will retain their oligopolistic dominance was in 2012 still an open question. As global enterprises they employ the same strategies as global corporations when arguing against more stringent national regulation. Thus John Connolly, then Head of Deloitte, told a sceptical House of Lords Committee that break-up of the firm was not feasible, 'we have big global networks . . . 80 per cent of the business of the FTSE100 companies anyway is outside of the UK. So I don't see the feasibility' (of break-up) (Select Committee on Economic Affairs, 2011: 219). Here, as in the corporate sector itself, we see a concentration of benefits and influence into a very small elite with global connections.

Turning to the lawyers, again the pattern is of concentration but, rather than the Big 4, we have 'the Magic Circle'. The big London law firms provide a striking example of the recent emergence of a legal elite closely integrated into the demands and priorities of a global corporate elite. By now the big law firms have become a feature of the City landscape. They are outlined in Table 4.4 which ranks them by the number of FTSE 100 clients they service. It was not always so. Freshfields had three partners in 1890, only 10 by 1960 and still only 46 by 1986. The huge expansion came after the 1986 'big bang' liberalisation of the London financial markets with a huge increase in demand for legal services and financially driven legal innovation. The bigger firms embarked on a process of organisational innovation and growth. They moved away from a pattern of conservative, risk averse lawyers towards services to facilitate financial marketization and globalisation and they reaped the rewards. The PWC law firms survey showed profit per equity partner of the 'Top 10' law firms peaking at £1.1 mn in 2008 (PWC, 2010). City law practice has become a very lucrative activity with remuneration packages comparable to corporate CEOs.

The firms were still partnerships in 2012 although the Legal Services Act would allow them to incorporate. If they did so the six biggest would be truly huge enterprises large enough to enter the FTSE 100 (Binham, 2012). In a pattern analogous to the Big 4 accountants the group of the four largest of the five magic circle law firms has come to dominate the global market for legal services. They are consistently in the top 10 of international law firms, measured by revenue, all the others are American. But the US

Table 4.4 The elite city law firms

		FTSE 100 clients	Partners, 2011 total	Partners, 2011 profit p.p.	Lawyers employed	% outside UK
Slaughter & May	MC	29	123	2.6	*	*
Freshfields	MC	23	418	2.0	2,034	69
Linklaters	MC	22	440	1.8	2,134	63
Herbert Smith		21	133	1.4	1,060	41
Allen & Overy	MC	18	398	1.7	2,112	64
Addleshaw Goddard		8	*	*	594	0
Ashurst		7	150	1.1	788	48
Clifford Chance	MC	7	455	1.6	2,466	70

Notes: MC = 'magic circle' firms; * = not ranked in top 100; profit p.p. = 2011 profit per equity partner in $mn.

Sources: FTSE 100 clients, Hemscott rankings, reported in *The Lawyer* 6 June 2011; other data from *The American Lawyer*: 'The Global 100, 2011', available at http://www.americanlawyer.com/PubArticleTAL.jsp?id=1202514395108 (accessed 7 September 2012).

firms are large due to domestic activity, the UK big four have developed a 'global law firm' model (Morgan and Quack, 2005: 19) enabling them to service the multinationals operating in London on an equivalently global basis. Their character as innovative, business-orientated firms, operating in a flexible common law system, and with a legacy of international networks, has enabled the magic circle firms to acquire their own elite status.

The magic circle firms recruit and promote disproportionately from the public schools and Oxbridge. They have become more centralised with senior management and a senior partner who is effectively the CEO. Summarising recent evolution, Galanter and Roberts (2008: 17, 168) conclude that 'firms came to look and behave much more like international businesses'. Crucially, these firms act as enterprising and innovative facilitators for international business operating creatively to facilitate mergers and acquisitions, novel corporate forms, joint ventures, creative contracting and so on. Rather than reinforcing a legal philosophy that controls and limits corporate activity (which German law firms tend to do) they have lubricated corporate strategy and profit seeking. Morgan and Quack (2005: 7) identify 'a positive orientation to business, mostly around acting as intermediaries that facilitate new forms of activity (rather than acting as a constraint on that activity)'. In other words, the magic circle firms and their senior partners have become part of the elite that organises and benefits from the New Corporate State.

Table 4.5 The largest UK management consultancies, 2007

	Fee income, £mn
Accenture	979
IBM Business Consulting	753
Deloitte	469
Steria	467
PriceWaterhouseCoopers	402
Capgemini	337

Source: 'Insider report', *Accountancy Age*, 9 October 2008: 17.

A third set of reputational intermediaries whose senior managers form part of the corporate elite is the management consultants. We encountered them earlier in the chapter in relation to government services and they have also experienced two decades of striking growth. Some firms like McKinsey can trace their roots back to the 1930s (O'Shea and Madigan, 1999: 19) and, although the industry is US inspired and dominated, it has expanded rapidly in the UK. The *Accountancy Age* survey (Abbott, 2008: 17) of the consultancy industry showed 2007 fee income at £7 bn which would place the industry as a whole, on the basis of turnover, safely in the FTSE 100, about the same size as Reckitt Benckiser. But of course it is made up of a whole range of firms headed by 17 firms with income over £100 mn. The top six UK firms are listed in Table 4.5, although the UK operations are typically dwarfed by the US presence. Accenture, for instance, employs 10,500 in the UK but in 2012 had 249,000 employees globally. The rewards for directors and senior consultants are substantial but the firms are secretive about remuneration packages. Accenture, for instance, operates a fiendishly complicated salary, bonus and stock option package which in 2011 delivered to its then Executive Chairman, William D. Green, a package of $16.1 mn (Forbes, 2012). It seems safe to assume that senior consultants in the UK will enjoy compensation packages at least as generous as others of the corporate elite.

The main consultancy clients are financial services, central government and the communications industry. Consultancy in a 'knowledge industry' in which the big firms live on their reputations which they zealously nurture by recruiting, allegedly, the brightest graduates from universities and business schools, by engaging in thought leadership, and through research links with business school academics. The big consultancies have developed distinctive cultures and are prized for their status, their role in channelling best practice, and their networks. The McKinsey old boy network is legendary. A nice network example was provided by Ian Watmore who in November 2010 joined forces with the Head of the Civil Service, Sir Gus O'Donnell, in explaining to the PAC why government spent so much on consultancy (PAC, 2010). At this point Watmore was Chief Operating Officer of the Efficiency and Reform Group of the Cabinet Office, one of the key groups responsible for managing spending cuts. Watmore was in a good position to assess the utility of consultants. From 2000 to 2004 he was Managing Director of Accenture UK and he entered Whitehall with the status and the networks which his career at the peak of the consulting profession provided. Consulting networks evidently penetrate the public sector at the highest level.

The management consultancies are famously demanding of their staff. Without the independent professional standards and integrity that, at least residually, influences accountants and lawyers, their people are wholly committed to corporate interests, to serving their clients, and to maximising income. This is a world of corporate aggrandisement served through extremely bright people who share a managerial mind-set concerned with financial efficiency, marketization and strategic opportunity. It is tempting to characterise the big consultancies as the priesthood of the corporate elite. As O'Shea and Madigan (1999: 255) observe, 'comparison of McKinsey to the religious order [of Jesuits] has come up so many times that it has almost reached the status of cliché. McKinsey's own insiders describe themselves as combinations of Jesuits and US Marines.'

Thus the management consultancy industry has been extremely important in expanding profitable corporate opportunities, from mergers and outsourcing to supply chain management and IT projects. In the process it has been a crucial disseminator of US managerial orthodoxy into government as well as into UK industry. Most important for our purposes has been its role in nurturing, and at the senior levels joining, the UK corporate elite.

These three sets of reputational intermediaries are, of course, located within a broader set of providers of corporate services, from head-hunters to bond-rating agencies. But they are the biggest and most powerful. We can conclude the discussion of this component of the corporate elite with four observations. First, their expansion is strongly linked to the financial sector and to the post-Thatcher celebration of corporate ascendancy in deregulated markets. Second, despite the core ethics of these professions (true accounts and legal compliance) there is very little expression of countervailing power. The intermediaries operate to facilitate corporate expansion and profitability. Third, all three intermediaries operate across the public and private sectors and contribute to a business-friendly approach in public policy and regulation. Finally, the big law, accounting and consulting firms have become amongst the most respected and authoritative bodies within the contemporary economy and political system. They are prestigious, recruit the brightest graduates into the corporate elite, and are the lead battalions in the ideological warfare over models of the capitalist economy. Perhaps their most important role is in generating legitimating ideas and constructing persuasive discourses that support the New Corporate State.

Merchants and the Media

Sklair's fourth component of the transnational capitalist class is 'merchants and the media'. Here he is concerned with those forces and interests which define and preserve 'the culture-ideology of consumerism'. In the UK we can agree that 'the media' comprises a distinctive and essential element of the corporate elite. The media, defined broadly to include print, broadcasting, advertising, public relations, creative industries and internet providers, has a special significance for the corporate elite. One of the major functions of the media is to engage with, respond to, and often to manipulate public attitudes and standards. Its very product is ideas; ideas about lifestyle, about behaviour, about health, politics, and the market and capitalist system itself. Today the volume and availability of media outlets has made the media the prime originator of attitudes. For Hutton (2010: 315) 'it has become the dominant element in the public realm and the prism through which politics is seen'. The political influence of the media has changed the very nature of politics with the rise of spin and the permanent campaign (see Wring, 2006; and Kuhn, 2007). The relationship between political parties, their leaders and the media has become a sort of political family life often defining the tempo and even the content of ministerial activity, as the memoirs of such accomplished media managers as Campbell (Campbell and Scott, 2007) and Mandelson (2010) attest. Politicians seek endlessly to impress and influence the media whilst the political influence of those who control media empires underlines the importance of keeping the media onside. Thus, in 2012 Cameron's Business Advisory Group included Sir Martin Sorrell of WPP and Eric Schmidt, the CEO of Google. In a similar vein the constant massaging of representatives of Rupert Murdoch's News Corporation was exposed during the 2011 phone tapping scandal which prompted the resignation of Andy Coulson, the former editor of Murdoch's *News of the World*, as David Cameron's Director of Communications in January 2011 (Wintour and Davies, 2011). Two of the greatest architects of media power, Silvio Berlusconi and Rupert Murdoch, illustrate the peculiar influence of the media in politics but the same argument applies to the corporate elite. If corporations can equally impress and influence the media they not only secure support for their strategies, their products and their brands, they also create a sympathetic political environment.

Although a free, critical media is regarded as a vital safeguard in a liberal democracy the media has itself become an industry dominated by large corporations. To cite Hutton (2010: 316) again, 'the media is big business ... All the trends observable in any business sector facing such convulsive change have happened here: consolidation and concentration'. The big media corporations are thus subject to the familiar corporate incentives and financial market pressures. They must be sensitive to City comment and sentiment, and their profits are driven by advertising revenues and the marketing strategies of the big advertisers. The big three British corporations, BSkyB, WPP and Pearson, share many of the incentives to become effective political actors outlined in Chapter 2. They wield great political influence but they are also vulnerable to policy and regulatory change. Even the seemingly invulnerable Murdoch empire could be disciplined, as we saw with the 2011 phone hacking scandal, the closure of the *News of the World*, the painful collapse of the takeover of BSkyB by Newscorp, the criticisms of Newscorp's family dominated corporate governance and the subsequent inquiry by Lord Justice Leveson during 2012. The media sector may have a lingering commitment to critical and investigative reporting but at its senior levels it has come to share the priorities and agenda of the New Corporate State and the media has become thoroughly commercialised. In the UK the BBC provides a hugely important corrective but even here commercial pressures and the lobbying of private corporations to constrain the BBC have limited its critical independence (see Leys, 2001: ch. 5).

The media component of the corporate elite can be a less reliable, more uncomfortable partner than the accountants or lawyers. Sometimes the media will see financial opportunities in biting the very hand that feeds it, as with the Hollywood films such as *Avatar* or *Wall Street* which criticise the corporate system. Similarly, the media may be intensely critical of corporate greed, banker's bonuses, the hidden costs of PFI, or corporate complicity in bribery or environmental damage (see also McClusky and Swinner, 2010). But, notwithstanding these elements of unpredictability or hostility, those who control the media act as members and supporters of the corporate elite. That world would therefore include the leading editors and commentators of the financial press, the senior executives and directors of the main media groups (such as Pearson, ITV, News International, WPP and the *Daily Mail*) and, of course, the proprietors of those groups which still experience family influence.

THE CORPORATE ELITE, POWER AND INEQUALITY

This chapter has presented a profile of the corporate elite in the UK adapting Sklair's methodology but applying it to a national rather than a global business elite (see Scott, 2008: 38). The bedrock of the corporate elite is the largest corporations and professional firms, and it is composed of the individuals who have effective control over them. The elite is powerful through its control over institutional resources which include systematic influence over political decision-making as a core element of the New Corporate State. This presumption of elite power needs to be teased out more fully, however, to avoid the danger of a circular argument. It is argued that powerful people form an elite, but if the elite is defined as a body of powerful people, the term 'elite' merely becomes a synonym for 'powerful'. To operate as an explanatory concept we should establish that the elite have collective goals, operate with cohesion and share in the fruits of power.

The elite exercises power through control of elite corporations which are themselves power-seeking. The motives for seeking to gain and retain power are multiple and would include status, security and the ability to dominate others, so that many discussions of power regard the power-seeking imperative as obvious and self-evident, akin to satisfying basic needs like food or shelter. In considering elite goals we can consider how power is employed, how it affects policy outcomes, how it affects people's life chances and levels of inequality, in short, who gains from the exercise of corporate power? This directs attention to indicators of economic advantage which benefit corporations generally and the elite specifically. These might include:

- Share of corporate profits in national income
- Absolute value of corporations and distribution of ownership
- Level of corporation tax as a proportion of government revenue
- Level of management remuneration
- Distribution of income between richest and poorest
- Distribution of wealth and of extreme wealth

All these indicators are, to a greater or lesser degree, also indicators of inequality. Indeed, as we saw in Chapter 2, inequality can be regarded as a defining feature of power, since power is deployed to secure privileges and to gain a disproportionate share of desirable values. The group in society which has succeeded in gaining a disproportionate share of the benefits which corporate power yields is, of course, the corporate elite.

Table 4.6   Illustrative composition of the UK corporate elite

FTSE 100 and some FTSE 350 directors	1,200
Senior non-director executives	500
Financial operators, hedge funds, private equity etc	500
Intermediaries	800
Sundry others, economic regulators, media	600
Executives of non-quoted multinationals	1,000
Total	4,600

The corporate elite is small. Maclean et al. (2006) studied 1,050 FTSE board directors but a wider definition, drawing on Sklair's categories, would encompass perhaps 5,000 people, equivalent to about 0.01 per cent of the adult population. An illustrative composition could be presented as shown in Table 4.6.

Not all elites are materialistic or rich. Religious, civil service and even military elites may not be particularly wealthy but here we are analysing an economic elite for whom wealth is both materially and symbolically valued. It can therefore be argued that the ability to acquire, accumulate and retain substantial wealth can be used as an indicator of the identity of the corporate elite, and changes in the level of economic inequality are an indicator of the waxing and waning of their power.

Any student of elitism or advocate of markets would expect a degree of inequality as a normal part of social life. Equality is not a natural state of affairs and inequality may have beneficial aspects as a factor promoting competition, the pursuit of profit and advantage, and therefore wealth, which can be redistributed as society determines. But gross inequality arising from exploitation, denial of rights and lack of moral scruple is perceived as unfair, even intolerable, and may lead to violent protest. Virtually all societies therefore place limits on inequality and one of the puzzles, and flaws, of vulgar Marxism has been the willingness by capitalist classes and the capitalist state to prevent exploitation developing to such an intolerable extent that it provokes revolution, a prospect ominously re-emerging in the wake of the financial crisis as the politics of inequality feed an outrage provoked by the politics of austerity (Stiglitz, 2012). Thus the traditional genius of liberal democracy has been to constrain markets and capitalists, to tax, and to redistribute through the welfare state so that the excesses of capitalism are restrained, the benefits of wealth generation are distributed, and popular support is sustained for a capitalist system. Business corporations have compromised with democratic processes because they too need certainty and stability; the managerial elite accept the necessity for the system to sustain its legitimacy. Moreover, many aspects of government redistribution and the welfare state provide an infrastructure which is essential for corporate success. Thus the promotion of scientific research, training, energy supply, transport, health and safety or the socialisation of health care and retirement costs are among the many necessities that corporations value and benefit from. Accordingly, the presence of inequalities in society can be taken as a measure of corporate privilege, but limits on inequality may similarly be accepted by corporations in recognition of the need to sustain a favourable environment for profitable activity. While accepting that there is what could be termed a spectrum of tolerable inequality we can sketch out the pattern of inequality in the UK.

As far as incomes are concerned, income before tax is highly unequal, as the following figures demonstrate:

Table 4.7 UK income before tax

	5 percentile point	95 percentile point	multiple
1997–98	5,220	39,000	7.47
2007–08	6,870	61,500	8.95
2009–10	7,970	63,200	7.91

Source: *Survey of Personal Incomes*, Inland Revenue, table 3.1, available at http://www.hmrc.gov.uk/stats/income_distribution/3-1table-feb2012.pdf (accessed 30 August 2012).

It shows that the ninety-fifth highest income percentile group had an income eight to nine times that of the fifth highest. In 1999, 36.3 per cent of the total of national income went to the top 10 per cent of taxpayers (Hills, 2004: 27), and over the following ten years this disproportion increased, as reflected in the Gini coefficient which is a standard measure of income inequality. The higher the number, the greater the degree of income inequality (with 1.0 indicating 'perfect' inequality). Thus the IFS measured 'the Gini coefficient in 2007–08 at 0.36, its highest level since our comparable time series began in 1961' (IFS, 2010: 30). The UK therefore continues to have one of the most unequal income distributions in the OECD (Hills, 2004: 29).

Of course taxation moderates the level of inequality, but it is striking how modest are the taxes on capital and profits. Capital taxes accounted for only 2.2 per cent of the total tax take in 2008–09 (and the take from capital gains tax was scheduled to fall dramatically) whilst corporation tax raised a mere 8.6 per cent of total tax, way behind the 30.3 per cent raised by income tax (HM Treasury, *Budget 2010*, June, Annex C, Table C11).

The whole question of tax avoidance, the advantages enjoyed by non-domiciled taxpayers and the avoidance of corporate taxes through tax havens means, of course, that the official figures understate the levels of corporate profits and the incomes of very highly paid individuals. Indeed, for Beetham (2011: 9) the tax avoidance industry undermines democracy as well as fiscal justice. The hesitation to create or enforce redistributive taxes means that wealth in the UK remains highly concentrated. The statistics have been elusive but the ONS has undertaken a massive survey of household wealth which registered total wealth (including pension wealth) in the UK in 2008 at £9 trillion (£9 million million). It found that the top 10 per cent of households possessed 44 per cent of that wealth against 9 per cent possessed by the bottom 50 per cent of households (ONS, 2009: 9). Pause for a moment to reconsider these numbers. '10/44: 50/9' speaks of a society so grotesquely unequal that it magnifies the pathologies of injustice identified, for instance, by Barry (2005, ch. 13). What is more, these numbers almost certainly underestimate the share of total wealth possessed by the very richest segment of the population and are slightly lower than earlier estimates. Thus Hills (2004: 31) noted that in 2001 the top 10 per cent enjoyed 56 per cent of marketable wealth; the top 5 per cent enjoyed 43 per cent and the top 1 per cent controlled 23 per cent. This is an extraordinary concentration of wealth and the concentration is much higher than the concentration of incomes, with a Gini coefficient of wealth distribution which rose from an already stratospheric 66 per cent in 1976 to 70 per cent in 2001. In other words, wealth in the UK is very disproportionately distributed and that distribution (like the distribution of income) is becoming more unequal.

At the very top end of the scale of income and wealth lie what Haseler (2000) calls 'the super rich', those individuals like Bill Gates or Warren Buffet whose wealth genuinely defies imagination. Haseler identifies such people as the visible component of a new 'class' of extraordinarily rich individuals who are insulated from unpleasant aspects of society, no longer have any national loyalties and are defined by their control over capital. They are often visible as celebrities by virtue of their wealth and are enumerated in league tables such as the *Sunday Times Rich List* which estimated the richest 1,000 families in the UK as worth £414 bn in 2012, which approaches 5 per cent of total national wealth. Philip Beresford, who compiles the List, noted that 'the first decade of new labour was in fact a golden age for the rich in Britain' (Beresford, 2010: 4).

Since the late 19th century the receipt of income and accumulation of wealth has been closely associated with control over capital, which meant ownership of corporate capital, whether finance assets or industrial assets. The increased power and prosperity of corporations in the post 1980s New

Table 4.8 Share in UK total income before tax and (after tax)

	Top 10%	Top 1%	Top 0.1%	Top 0.01%
1937	38.4	17.0	6.6	2.8
	(35.6)	(12.6)	(3.6)	
1979	28.4	5.9	1.3	0.3
	(26.2)	(4.7)	(0.9)	
2000	38.4	12.7	4.6	n/a
	(34.3)	(10.0)	(3.5)	
2008	44.0	16.2	6.8	n/a

Sources: Atkinson (2007: 93, table 4.1); 2008 figures derived from High Pay Commission growth figures (HPC, 2011a: 23).

Corporate State has supplemented ownership enrichment with managerial enrichment. Individuals have extracted income and wealth through share ownership but also increasingly through managerial remuneration, and this dimension of inequality deserves emphasis. The corporate elite in the UK is a managerial elite. It will include the major shareholders who have a managerial or strategic engagement with their corporations, and of course managers often have significant shareholdings. But broadly speaking, UK corporations are controlled by their managers, often, but not always through the boardroom. This managerial corporate elite is therefore rich, but in income rather than absolute wealth. Studies of the share of top incomes in national income show a pattern of increasing returns at the very top of the distribution which displays an uncanny correspondence to the Thatcherite empowerment of business and the rise of the New Corporate State. Research by Atkinson shows a gross inequality of incomes in the UK prior to the Second World War, growing equality up to 1979, followed by an increase in inequality until, in 2011, the income distribution had returned to the 1930s pattern of gross inequality. The pattern is shown in Table 4.8. Including trends since 2000, it shows that the share of the top 10 per cent is now larger than in 1937 and the share of the top 0.1 per cent is back to 1937 levels. In fact, with the favourable tax regime, the after-tax share of the top 0.1 per cent is higher than 1937 and, of course, that overlooks the opportunities for tax planning and tax avoidance. The Inland Revenue estimates the 'tax gap' through avoidance and evasion to be at least £40 bn, about the same as the tax yield from corporation tax (Jagger, 2010). Atkinson (2007: 110) also shows a major shift away from investment income so that about 70 per cent of the income of the top 1 per cent is derived from employment, confirming that these people are managers, not rentiers. The corporate elite is located within the top 0.1 per cent which comprises about 47,000 individual taxpayers with a gross income estimated at £533,000 and above (High Pay Commission, 2011a: 24). Within that group it is estimated that 35 per cent are company directors. Whether directors or not, 30 per cent work in financial intermediation, 38 per cent in real estate and other business activity, and the residual 32 per cent will generate high income from a range of non-corporate activities including sport, entertainment, inheritance, overseas income and so on.

The pay levels of US executives and board members has always been extraordinarily high and it seems that this pattern has been reproduced in the UK, across Europe and into the emergent economies (Cheffins, 2003). There are periodic expressions of outrage at the sheer scale of executive rewards, which forge remorselessly upwards. The forceful analysis by Ertürk et al. (2005) observed that CEOs had, by 2002, established a going rate for the job of CEO of a large corporation as over £1 million. By the end of the decade this had become small beer. Toynbee and Walker (2008: 43) note that, by 2007, pay for FTSE 100 chief executives had advanced to an average of £3.2 mn. Bart Becht, the CEO of Reckitt Benckiser became the highest paid CEO of 2009 with a package of £93 mn (Stiff, 2010). Press comment began to compare CEO remuneration with that of the average employee and the High Pay Commission produced a startling analysis which showed CEO remuneration rising from a multiple of 69 times average earnings in 1999 to 161 times average earnings in 2007, by which time the average remuneration package of a FTSE executive director was about £3.8 mn (High Pay Commission, 2011b: 28). To add to this picture of executive self-enrichment, and reflecting the peculiar power of the financial elite, the FSA reported that, in 2009, 2,800 employees of banks received more that £1 mn and that Barclays had paid out three times as much in bonuses as it had paid in dividends, a revealing indication of managerial power (cited in High Pay Commission, 2011b: 8).

The rationales for such huge pay increases are based on agency theory and the supposed identification of board interests with those of shareholders. But the Ertürk et al. (2005) study is emphatic that there has been no great increase in job sophistication or risk, an argument confirmed in the well researched reports of the High Pay Commission (HPC, 2011a, b). Rather, Ertürk et al suggest that executives have entered into an elite conspiracy which has resulted in 'value skimming', the extraction of huge rewards in a blatant exploitation of managerial power. They suggested that value skimming is a 'victimless crime' in that the amount extracted would make little difference to the rewards available to workers or to shareholders (see also Froud and Williams, 2007). More recently that diagnosis appears misleading. In the finance sector ministers have exhorted banks to reduce their bonus levels to bolster reserves. Remuneration has reached the point where it is materially weakening financial institutions and depriving other stakeholders. In such corporations managers have captured the rewards of the capitalist owners. Kaletsky (2010: 300, 301) wryly observes that banks 'have been managed as workers cooperatives' giving rise to 'looting' by employees, but the issue of remuneration is not, of course, simply about unfair rewards, it provides a highly skewed incentive structure to the decision makers in large corporations. It can be expected to distort corporate strategies in ways that seek to maximise short-term profits and share prices. In the financial sector we have seen the damage this licensing of greed has done in contributing to the 2008 crash.

CONCLUSION

Few people would disagree with the proposition that there exists in the UK a privileged group of leaders of the largest business and financial corporations. Many observers have shared this conclusion, including Mount (2012) who presents his critique of the economic and political oligarchs through a more anecdotal route. This chapter has gone further, to argue that this privileged group constitutes an identifiable elite, that has become politically influential through entering into a partnership with the political elite, to share control over the institutions of the state. The politico-corporate partnership became solidified into a new Settlement by the end of the 20th century in the shape of the New Corporate State which has become relatively stable, embedded in the institutional order through legal provisions, a normative consensus and cultural adaptation. The effect is to bias public policy processes and political priorities towards policies that favour the interests of large corporations and the elite which leads them. It is further argued that we can partially identify the corporate elite not only by their holding leading positions within the corporate world, but also by their success in harvesting the material benefits of corporate wealth creation through massive executive remuneration and accumulating personal wealth.

It is not argued that the corporate elite entirely controls the New Corporate State. Britain remains a liberal democracy with many factors and forces constraining the corporate elite within government and, indeed, constraining the influence of the state itself. Rather, it is argued that corporations have become governing institutions which share power with the traditional institutions of government. This new reality has generated increasing concern about threats to democracy, thus Democratic Audit (2012: 15) expressed grave concern that 'corporate power is growing, partly as a result of wider patterns of globalisation and deregulation, and threatens to undermine some of the most basic principles of democratic decision-making'. This argument about a new, entrenched, corporate elite raises questions about the stability of the New Corporate State and the likelihood of this Settlement being sustained. Chapter 5 addresses these questions by examining the position and influence of competing elites in politics, the civil service and civil society. There is also, of course, the question of whether this analysis is peculiar to Britain. This chapter has concentrated in the UK but the corporate state diagnosis would apply relatively well also to the USA. Indeed, this shift in Britain's political economy looks very much like Americanisation and is paralleled by an equivalent Americanisation of electoral politics. More widely, several of the drivers that have enabled the rise of the UK corporate elite apply on an international scale, especially globalisation and the competitiveness agenda. The increased power of giant corporations and the emergence of a privileged corporate elite is an international phenomenon that can be found equally in countries as diverse as France, Israel, India, and of course China. In this the UK is an exemplar of a global shift in the location and exercise of political power, an argument elaborated in Chapter 7.

5. The politics of the New Corporate State

This chapter extends the discussion initiated in Chapter 4 about the integration of the corporate elite into the New Corporate State. It follows up the three questions posed there first by analysing the relationship between the corporate elite and political elites in the parties and the civil service. It goes on to examine how business corporations organise themselves individually and collectively to pursue elite interests. As part of this review it assesses the stability of the New Corporate State by dissecting the influence of competitor elites. The conclusion comes back to one of the dominant themes of this book, the privileging of corporate interests and the shrinking of democratic choice in the UK's New Corporate State.

THE POLITICAL ELITE AND THE TRANSFORMED PARTY SYSTEM

Political parties are the lifeblood of the British political system. They mobilise voters, choose candidates, select leaders and animate governments. Whoever controls the Party with a majority in the House of Commons controls the British state. From 1979, and more emphatically from her second election victory in 1983, that person was Margaret Thatcher. As Prime Minister Margaret Thatcher initiated a transformation in the British political economy which involved a reconfiguration in the dominant ideologies, institutional complexes and governing elites. As noted in Chapter 4, the scale of the transformation was little short of revolutionary and was justified by the collapse of the British economy and the bankruptcy of the British Establishment in the dying days of the Callaghan government. In the paradox captured by Gamble (1994: 36), Margaret Thatcher used the strong centralised power of the British state to withdraw the state from many hallowed aspects of economic life and to create an internationalised free market. Margaret Thatcher was the midwife of the New Corporate State but whether she planned or envisaged the shape of the new settlement is very doubtful. As Gamble (1994: 6) affirms, the Conservatives under Thatcher did not have a grand plan.

They endorsed new economic policies, they had a visceral distaste for many of the institutions of the Post-war Settlement, and particularly for organised labour, and they were informed by a new right ideology that emphasised individualism, entrepreneurialism, self-help and a minimalist state. Thatcher set in train a series of transformations in areas like industrial relations, privatisation, deregulation, internationalisation, fiscal retrenchment and market solutions whose dynamics drove the policies of her successors, Major, Blair, Brown and now Cameron and Clegg, all of whom endorsed much of her legacy. To that extent Margaret Thatcher was something of a sorcerer's apprentice, releasing forces she neither controlled nor understood. If those forces are to be subject to effective control the only political bodies up to the task are those that released them, a strong party mobilising the authority of the British state, which brings us to the diminution in authority of British political parties.

The political parties continue to perform their historic functions of selecting and legitimating political leaders, but they do so from an increasingly fragile and tentative base. The two main parties are no longer the substantial, vibrant, social and political organisations of the mid-20th century. They have become vehicles for personalised leadership and no longer exhibit the independence, intellectual innovation or breadth of representation that characterised the mass parties in their heyday of the 1950s (Conservative Party membership peaked at 2.8 million in 1952, Ball, 1994: 291). In elaborating this argument of a more ephemeral party-political elite we can touch on membership, finance, organisation, trust and, above all, the celebrity party leadership.

Membership of political parties has been on a downward trend since the 1960s. By 2010 total membership of the three main parties (excluding union-affiliated members) was down to under 500,000. For Labour, in 2010 only 128,000 voted in the leadership election in which Ed Miliband succeeded Gordon Brown. With a turnout of 72 per cent, that gives a membership of about 178,000. The Conservatives had exactly equivalent numbers with 178,000 members eligible to vote, whilst the Liberal Democrats had 65,000 members (Heffernan, 2011: 170–71). British political parties have been transformed from mass parties to 'electoral-professional' parties, a modern variant of the elite cadre parties of the early 19th century (see Childs, 2006). A mass party could rely on the subscriptions of its members to finance organisation and elections. Although Labour can still benefit from subscriptions channelled through the unions both parties have come increasingly to rely on donations and have stumbled from one financial crisis to the next. Unlike the United States, company and electoral laws mean that donations from corporations are minor and transparent; instead the main sources of donations are wealthy individuals. Direct funding of candidates, parties and political causes gives US corporations immense and indefensible influence (see Moran, 2009: 119). In this respect British electoral politics is much cleaner than the USA but it still involves influence being secured by wealthy donors who tend to have made their money in finance or service industries and are typically themselves members of the corporate elite (see Grant, 2005: 71–88; Beetham, 2011: 12–13).

Shrinking party membership has also contributed to major shifts in party organisation towards centralisation, more direct control of candidate selection and of policy making. Since 1992 the Labour Party Parliamentary leadership has escaped the direct control of the Party Conference and of the NEC (National Executive Committee) (Heffernan, 2007: 154–5), whilst the Conservative Parliamentary Party leadership has always had extensive independence. This is important for party and for governmental policy making. It means that fewer policies emerge from party debates with their distinctive ideological contexts and further, that the party leadership has greater autonomy and is freer to negotiate policy programmes with other societal elites. This lack of deep roots may have contributed to a haemorrhage of 'trust'. In his study of *Why We Hate Politics* Hay (2007) charts the depressing disenchantment of most democratic electorates with the conventional electoral process and with professionalised politicians. A decline in deference might be regarded as welcome; a decline in respect for electoral politics and for professional politicians is far less positive, yet the trends are dismally clear. Since 1983 Ipsos/MORI has been surveying trends in trust for the main professional occupations in society. An extract from their polls appears at Table 5.1. The polls show a remarkable revival of faith in civil servants, a moderation in scepticism about trade union officials and increased trust in business leaders. In contrast, government ministers are one of the least trusted groups in society. Moran (2006: 459–60) uses the low relative trust for business leaders as an indicator of delegitimisation of business, but that scepticism does not seem to be growing and it is outweighed by a consistent distrust of ministers and a growing and quite shocking distrust of politicians generally who were, by 2011, the most distrusted professional group in society.

The distrusted politicians form a professionalised political elite who control the political parties but appear qualitatively different from the traditional party leadership. Prior to the 1980s political leaders tended to be 'men with a ready-made reputation . . . or . . . with exceptional experience outside government' (Guttsman, 1963: 369). From the 1980s the new party leaders were increasingly people who had made politics itself their career. The characteristic career path was via student politics, then

Table 5.1 Public trust in the professions

Question: 'do you generally trust them to tell the truth or not?'					
	1983	1997	2003	2011	Change '83–'11
Doctors (highest)	+68	+76	+85	+80	+12
Judges	+59	+53	+53	+55	−4
Ordinary people	+30	+28	+21	+30	0
Civil servants	−38	−14	+5	+13	+51
Trade union officials	−53	−29	−20	−12	+41
Business leaders	−40	−31	−32	−26	+14
Journalists	−54	−61	−57	−51	+3
Government ministers	−58	−68	−53	−57	+1
Politicians generally	−57	−63	−57	−66	−9

Source: http://www.ipsos-mori.com/researchpublications.aspx (accessed 15 July 2011).

employment as a special adviser (SPAD) or politics-related job (such as journalism) followed by candidate selection and promotion by virtue of ability and connections. This generation of leaders is less ideologically committed and with little experience of the world outside politics and the public sphere. They are intelligent, personable, exceptional networkers with great analytical abilities, and they display a social conscience and commitment to the public good. But they are also narrow careerists and, for critics such as Oborne, they constitute a 'Political Class' which now dominates British public life and is responsible for a style and content of politics that is populist, centralised, suppresses opposition and is committed to 'modernisation' (Oborne, 2008).

Oborne's attack on a 'political class' that is more interested in securing office than in changing policy is bitter and remorseless but it has a persuasive core. It chimes with more measured studies of Blair's leadership and changes in party organisation (see, for instance, Heffernan, 2007) and it squares with the careers of many ministers. For Oborne, New Labour's 1997 election victory brought the first Political Class government and, among the leading ministers, were the student politicians such as Jack Straw and Harriet Harman, the early activists such as Gordon Brown and David Blunkett, and of course the SPADs such as Ed Balls, Yvette Cooper and the Milibands. The exceptions included veterans such as John Prescott and, in the Coalition Cabinet, Vince Cable and Kenneth Clarke. But the majority of the Cabinet squared with Oborne's diagnosis of political professionals including David Cameron, Nick Clegg, David Osborne and William Hague. In fact by 2011 the leaders of the three main parties were all young men who had served one term or less in the Commons. The 'career politician' had arrived (see Cowley, 2011: 106).

While political sociology identifies a new type of politician the important factor is the pattern of alliances constructed by the political elite and their impact on the circulation of elites. In this regard Oborne presents a stark account of two trends found in many more scholarly studies. He argues first, that the Political Class continued the demolition of the traditional British Establishment and secondly, that in rejecting the institutions of the Establishment, it has embraced the world of business and entrepreneurship which the Establishment had found socially and culturally distasteful (see, for instance, Wiener, 1981: 10). Thus, 'the Political Class . . . prefers to work through the commercial or service sector . . . the Political Class highly esteems successful business men, rewards them, awards them patronage and looks to be rewarded with sinecures, consultancies and directorships on leaving office' (Oborne, 2007: 51).

The proliferation of post-political careers with business has been characteristic of Labour Cabinets so that Ruth Kelly (SoS Transport) became a senior manager with HSBC and Jacqui Smith became a consultant with KPMG. There are many other examples (see Acoba, 2010). In his emphasis on a business-friendly stance Oborne is also recognising the continuity from Thatcher to Blair, Brown and now Cameron and Clegg. In the words of another journalist, Blair and Brown appeared as *Thatcher's Sons* (Jenkins, 2007) and there is truth in the observation that Thatcher's greatest legacy was the transformation of the Labour Party. The Thatcherite assault on the pillars of the Establishment was consolidated under New Labour with a continued attack on public institutions alleged to be elitist. The new political elite presented itself as 'anti-elitist' leading Du Gay (2008: 81) to reflect on the Orwellian paradox of 'an elite of anti-elitists'. In place of alliances with the Establishment the political elite negotiated the Settlement of the New Corporate State which rested on a partnership between the corporate elite analysed in Chapter 4 and the party-political elite which dominates the cadre political parties.

Although the party-political leadership has established almost complete control over their respective parties, and operates with a high level of internal discipline and policy independence, this professionalised, political elite is weaker than the political leadership prior to the 1970s. It suffers from a decline in legitimacy arising from smaller parties, low electoral turnout, and the startling decline in trust outlined above. Moreover, permanent campaigning and the panicky, reactive attempts to manage a 24-hour news media contribute to an insecurity, which has been a curious dimension of Blair, Brown, Cameron and Clegg in power. This leads to the conclusion that the partnership between the political and corporate elites in early 21st century Britain is far more a partnership of equals. The New Corporate State has become embedded in the political landscape and it is difficult to see the possibility for a contemporary government to confront the corporate elite with the determination and success with which Margaret Thatcher confronted the unions and the traditional Establishment. In contrast, the confrontation with traditional elites continues and in dissecting the relative decline of the institutions of the old Establishment we can begin with the civil service.

THE 'MODERNISATION' OF THE CIVIL SERVICE

The increasing business influence over the British civil service was reviewed in Chapter 4. This trend is part of a wider subordination of the administrative elite which is one of the most important features of the circulation of elites and the transition to a New Corporate State. For over 100 years, ever since the Northcote-Trevelyan Report of 1854 was implemented (see Hennessy, 1989: 48), the British civil service has performed the role defined in Gladstone's vision of a selfless, gentlemanly public service as a key component of Britain's unwritten constitution. The senior civil service, the old 'administrative class', was a core component of the Establishment. Its constitutional role, seldom articulated and invisibly woven into the fabric of public life, was to operate the machinery of the state in accordance with norms and values held by the enlightened, educated classes. This involved curbing the excesses of elected politicians, persuading them to negotiate, to compromise and to build consensus. Deferential but determined, anonymous but unavoidable, the senior civil service was Gladstone's safety net to guard against the unknown consequences of extending the franchise. It was a deliberate device to counter the power of Parliament with the influence of a permanent, capable, enlightened and legitimate bureaucracy (Gowan, 1987). The civil service values in Gladstone's day were those of the great public schools, values of Christian service and gentlemanly obligations. Those values evolved in step with society and took on the standard virtues of an elite bureaucracy to emphasise impartiality, incorruptibility, loyalty and public service. At every stage, however, the civil service retained its power and authority; it remained an elite attracting, at the senior level, talented and often dedicated recruits from the cream of Oxbridge graduates.

The administrative elite played a key role in defining and maintaining the Post-war Settlement. The civil service enjoyed the classic bureaucratic advantages of permanence, expertise, networks and time, in addition to which it had a virtual monopoly of policy advice. Politicians decided between options defined by officials and government was operated as a partnership between politicians and officials in which officials often had the upper hand. In 1989 Peter Hennessy produced his study of Whitehall which was, in retrospect, an 'end of empire' examination of an administrative elite under siege. He charted the staying power of the Northcote-Trevelyan model and outlined the apparently timeless influence of The Establishment (Hennessy, 1989: 542–3). But he also sketched the gathering storms of criticism in the shape of the Thatcherite hostility to the civil service and the commitment to reform, including the managerial reforms initiated by Sir Derek (later Lord) Rayner, Mrs Thatcher's efficiency adviser, whose career as Managing Director of Marks and Spencer aroused (seriously misplaced) derision in Whitehall. Hennessy discusses, with some regret, the apparent inability of the civil service to realise the importance of 'management' and to realise that Whitehall departments are 'big business' (Hennessy, 1989: 732). Indeed, the civil service was dismissive of management and contemptuous of many of the businessmen they encountered, prone to write them off as having 'third-class minds'. Campbell and Wilson observed that 'many civil servants had chosen the service as a career almost to *avoid* management' (1995: 42) and the 'anti-industrial culture' of which the civil service was a leading bastion was increasingly identified as a root cause of Britain's relative industrial decline (see Wiener, 1981; Pollard, 1984). The administrative elite was living on borrowed time.

Even as he wrote, the institution which Hennessy sympathetically portrays was crumbling. In 1995 Campbell and Wilson published *The End of Whitehall: Death of a Paradigm?*; by 2005 Foster was identifying the 'end of Northcote-Trevelyan' and bemoaning 'the decline of the position of the civil service . . . (which) . . . has led to a precipitate decline in ministers' efficiency, certainly in their ability to get things done with thoroughness and practicality' (Foster, 2005: 207, 284–5). We have not, of course, seen the end of Whitehall as a permanent bureaucracy. It remains important, powerful and headed by an administrative elite, but it is a much-diminished elite. The civil service was undermined by the new right project with its emphasis on the small state, on market solutions and private sector managerialism. Campbell and Wilson also stress the influence of career politicians (the 'political class') and 'the ascendance of the politicians over the bureaucrats' (1995: 306). They point to the paradox that ministers have suppressed their own advisers and, 'since there is unlikely to be a satisfactory alternative source of advice' the result is 'policy failures now occurring almost weekly' (309), a problem we return to in Chapter 6 when assessing the problems generated by the New Corporate State.

The issue of policy advice sits at the heart of the loss of influence of the administrative elite. 'By 2003 the Cabinet Secretary had excluded policy making from the list of aptitudes civil servants needed' (Foster, 2005: 220). Instead the civil service was exposed to the rigours of 'the new public management' and the associated ideas of 'delivery' and 'modernisation' which justified the application of business models to Whitehall. In 2005 the then Head of the Civil Service, Sir Andrew Turnbull, stressed this alignment with big business arguing that civil servants 'looked at the models of CEOs of big businesses . . . and convinced ourselves that they were not for us. We have overturned that orthodoxy. We've swept away the belief that we are not leaders of public services' (Turnbull, cited in Wilks, 2007: 452).

The imperatives of modernisation became the narrative, expressed through the vocabulary and the machinery of 'delivery'. The civil service was no longer about making policy but instead about delivering results. An influential 'Delivery Unit' was created in Tony Blair's second term from 2001. In his memoirs of the effort devoted to delivering the Prime Minister's priorities Michael Barber, the head of the Unit, emphasised the Prime Minister's commitment to the delivery agenda and outlined the steps taken to cajole Whitehall departments into embracing the strategies and targets so central to the modernisation project. It is not hard to imagine how the traditional senior civil service must have loathed this public sector managerialism with its management jargon and league tables. The evangelical Barber notes, with atypical understatement, that 'not everyone in the public service likes league tables, but I love them. I have spent much of the last decade advocating them' (M. Barber, 2007: 96). The civil service was under comprehensive performance control and subject to the discipline of targets and league tables. The apogee came with Sir Gus O'Donnell's 'capability reviews' during 2006–07 when every department in Whitehall was ranked according to its capability to lead and to deliver (Wilks, 2007, 2008). The administrative elite had been thoroughly tamed and subordinated, to the extent that an apologist textbook could be entitled *Britain's Modernised Civil Service* (Burnham and Pyper, 2008).

The downgrading of policy advice and the shift to delivery signified an administrative elite brought under the control of politicians. Their reduced status took material form in the steady deterioration in civil service salaries in terms both of absolute decline and in relation to the remuneration of competitor elites. In a poignant review John Rimington, a former Permanent Secretary, charts the decline in remuneration and concludes that 'the British Civil Service is now recruited, organized and paid not as a professional instrument of government but as a tool of governments – of politicians' (Rimington, 2008: 1124). As part of that subordination the civil service adapted its values and norms to become more business-like and managerial. Partly this is a generational change. The new entrants to the civil service fast stream in 1980, when Margaret Thatcher began her critique, have only succeeded in a modernised civil service by accepting, however sincerely, the management credo and by adapting to a reduced role consistent with a reduced level of self-confidence (see Hay, 2007: 57). Foster agrees that 'what most threatened to undermine official's professional confidence was that the denigration to which they were subjected seeped into their souls' (2005: 215). Their function within government became infused with a priority to develop policies that met business requirements and were often developed in partnership with business. They became part of New Labour's 'enabling state' and undertook their responsibilities as one element within 'governance' rather than as 'the government'. This pattern was sustained under David Cameron and the Coalition government with continued criticism of the civil service. The 2011 *Open Public Services* White Paper opined that 'too many of our public services are still run according to the maxim "the man in Whitehall really does know best"' (Minister for Government Policy, 2011: 7) and it promised decentralisation and increased resort to alternative providers in a policy seen as further privatisation to deliver spending reductions (Sherman, 2011).

The enabling state, the transformed role of the civil service, and the positive support of business pursued by Blair and his advisers in Number 10 was part of a self-conscious historical mission as a response to economic globalisation. The aim was to create the sort of 'market state' advocated by the US historian Philip Bobbitt and Barber cites, with approval, Bobbitt's influential proposition that 'we are witnessing the emergence of "the market state", which depends on the international capital markets and ... on the modern multinational business network to create stability in the world economy' (M. Barber, 2007: 331). This deliberate programme of civil service reform in the shape of the new public management is not unique to the UK, it has been pursued in virtually all English-speaking countries. The New Labour endorsement of Britain as a 'market society' (Faucher-King and Le Galès, 2010: 141) is not therefore just about shifts in public policy it is, as Bobbitt's ambitious study argues, an epochal shift in the nature of the nation-state (Bobbitt, 2002). But to express this shift in terms of 'the market' as the animating dynamic of the state is misleading. Certainly market principles and market rhetoric have been employed, as in Europe, to highly persuasive effect (see Jabko, 2006), but this is a corporate state, not a market state. Policies and regulations are skewed towards the priorities of the corporate elite whose whole rationale and success is based on structuring markets in favour of their strategies and products. Markets are managed by a combination of politicians and corporate leaders, with the aid of the civil service. And the same syndrome has developed within government itself, with the civil service being managed by the Treasury.

The most significant agent in the modernisation of the civil service was, of course, the Treasury. Always powerful, under Brown it became the alternative centre of government with predominance in respect of domestic and economic policy. Gordon Brown famously ran the Treasury on the basis of his individual authority delegated through special advisers, junior ministers and a small number of trusted civil servants. The managerial apparatus he established was formidable and involved PSAs (Public Service Agreements) with each department, spending plans, performance targets and spending reviews. This was combined with measures to build management infrastructure through reforms of public accounting, clarification of leadership responsibilities and the creation of management boards for all accounting units. In many ways Brown was behaving like a private sector CEO and the organisation he created resembled the dominant organisational form of the large global corporation. He created in Whitehall an 'M-form' organisation so that central government began to resemble a giant corporation in which delivery of public services and regulation of public activities was designed, assessed and funded from the centre.

The M-form corporation is organised into a multi-divisional structure in which divisions are responsible for discrete activities, usually products but possibly also geographical areas or service functions (see Whittington and Mayer, 2000). Strategy is determined at the centre, resources are allocated and divisional managers are held responsible for performance, measured by budgets, targets and profits. The CEO and the central staff will delegate and allow discretion but can impose formidable and precise control from the centre. CEOs and boards of directors are driven by financial performance and by the post-1980s preoccupation with shareholder value. New Labour ministers were driven by performance in the opinion polls (and the media) and by a developing managerial concept of 'public value' (M. Barber, 2007: 326; Williams and Shearer, 2011). This transformation of a great institution, enjoying administrative discretion, employing due process and animated by ideals of public service; into a managerially dominated, quasi-corporation is one of the most remarkable developments of 21st-century British politics.

The transformation of the British civil service is of fundamental importance in the rise of the New Corporate State. The modernised civil service supports the corporate state in a number of important respects. First, it has accepted and internalised pro-corporation ideologies, including the importance of aiding corporations based in the UK to compete in world markets. Second, it has accepted a degree of capture, not so much by SPADS (which the service is still resisting) but by business appointees, advisers and management consultants. Third, it increasingly develops and accepts business-friendly policies, either spontaneously or in deference to the preferences of politicians, or the pressures of business lobbying. Fourth, it has surrendered control of major elements of government. As emphasised in Chapter 6, state responsibilities have been contracted out or simply transferred to the private sector and have been made subject to regulation by independent but deliberately market-friendly regulatory agencies. Finally, and rather shockingly, the semi-constitutional role of the original Gladstonian design has been virtually extinguished. Civil servants are less able 'to speak truth to power' and fail to speak out against misconceived policy initiatives (Du Gay, 2008: 97). Examples are legion, from the major fiascos such as rail privatisation and ID cards, to the more trivial such as the failed attempts to sell the Forestry Commission estate or failures to ensure parental child support. The key point for the argument developed in this chapter is that, when the political and the corporate elites come together to develop policies in favour of the corporate state, the sceptical, reasoned, challenging voice of the administrative elite is barely heard.

ORGANISING THE CORPORATE ELITE

The study of how business organises itself to pursue its interests in the political system is a specialised area which was relatively under-developed up to the 1980s (Grant, 1993) but has become a vibrant area of political economy since the mid-1990s. Within that field of study is a focus on lobbying and corporate political strategies at national and increasingly at the European level. At the risk of over-generalisation the tendency, the 'default option', is to regard business as a participant in a more or less pluralist system. Business has a powerful voice, and can mobilise huge resources, but other groups in society are also highly influential. While politicians and the state apparatus are receptive to business pressures they must also balance, negotiate, listen to other interests and business does not always get its own way. This perspective therefore defaults to the study of business as a pressure group, or multitude of pressure groups, engaged in a variety of ways with 'lobbying' governmental bodies either individually or collectively. The argument developed later in this section maintains that this perspective has become increasingly misleading but, before developing this argument, it is necessary briefly to rehearse the existing understanding of business representation in the UK to provide a profile of business organisations under the Post-war Settlement. The engagement between government and industry in Britain over the post-war period involved variants of 'tripartism' in which representative of labour (in the form of the TUC), and representatives of business, met government ministers and officials to debate the key issues of economic and industrial policy. The main voice of business was the CBI which was regarded in the 1960s as a powerful lobby group, in fact as one of the most powerful voices in the political system. But research by Grant and Marsh argued that the CBI's influence was actually rather modest and it placed this peak body of business representation as one more voice in a pluralist system, hence, 'the CBI has little consistent direct influence over the policies pursued by government' (Grant and Marsh, 1977: 213). They pointed out that it only represented manufacturing, it was divided by the differing interests of member corporations and industrial sectors, and it had very few means by which to discipline its members. While it was sometimes effective, on the whole 'government acts independently of business interests' and therefore the CBI 'seems to fit happily with a pluralist analysis' (Grant and Marsh 1977: 214; see also Grant, 1993: 116).

This theme of the collective weakness of business representation in Britain has been sustained by other studies including work by Moran. Indeed, he stresses 'the persistence of pluralism' (Moran, 2009: 150) and, despite his views on the growing power of business cited earlier in Chapter 4, he has argued that corporate power is increasingly constrained by a series of countervailing forces. Constraints include a decline in popular trust, a decline in business unity, an increase in cultural critiques and, above all, a shift from self-regulation to a more challenging 'adversarial regulation' that is typical of the USA and is being replicated in the UK, often under the influence of the EU (Moran, 2006, 2009: 170). This viewpoint emerged from Moran's portrayal of business power prior to the 1970s as based on an almost effortless access by business leaders to the political elites. The directors of giant British firms 'became incorporated into the policy-making elite' (Moran, 2008: 74; 2009: 64) and therefore, argues Moran, they enjoyed huge influence under the Post-war Settlement which has, if anything, been reduced in the post-Thatcher period. The discussion below takes issue with a diagnosis of sustained pluralism, with its implication that business and corporations should still be regarded essentially as pressure groups engaged in lobbying. Before coming on to that discussion it is useful to pick out two further features of research on British business representation. First, the contrast between manufacturing and finance; second, the shift from collective representation of business interests to lobbying by individual corporations.

As explored further in Chapter 7, banking and finance have always had a special role in capitalist systems. In the UK that role has been exceptionally important and has skewed Britain's economic history. In his study of the part played by finance and the City, Ingham charted the evolution of British capitalism away from industrial capitalism and towards finance, commerce and the global services provided by the City of London. He argued that it is the City that is politically influential, so that it formed part of the traditional Establishment and dominated business inputs into economic and industrial policy making. The problem for the CBI was that it did not include the City, and Grant and Marsh (1977: 70–71) observed that 'although the City is prepared to assist the CBI in its work, it does not regard the CBI as an additional channel of access to government . . . (the CBI) . . . does not really counterbalance the links developed over centuries between the City and government'. From the late 1970s City firms and banks began to join the CBI (Grant, 1993: 72) but it was something of a reverse takeover with the voice of manufacturing being further diluted. Manufacturing was a poor relation and economic policy was operated to benefit commerce and finance with relatively little concern for its impact on the prosperity of the manufacturing sector. As part of this syndrome the nexus of the Bank, the City, and the Treasury played the key role and Ingham points out that 'the City's access to the means of political domination is based upon the close and longstanding relationship with the Bank of England and the Treasury' (Ingham, 1984: 230). This elite intimacy, carried over into the New Corporate State, underpinned the regulatory permissiveness that contributed to the financial crisis and is being perpetuated with the increased regulatory role being entrusted to the Bank under the Coalition government.

Although Ingham was writing during the early years of Thatcherism, and before the 'big bang', the historical pattern that he analysed continues in a rather remarkable process of path dependence to form a cornerstone of the New Corporate State. By 2007 Turner (2009: 16, 18) noted 'a remarkable growth in the relative size of wholesale financial services within the overall economy' with UK debt as a percentage of GDP growing from about 100 per cent in 1990 to 180 per cent in 1997 but ballooning to 460 per cent by 2007 with the bulk of the growth accounted for by financial debt (bank borrowing using increased leverage). Hutton updated Ingham's diagnosis of a sympathetic regulatory regime in the Treasury, the Bank and the FSA which devoted itself to ensuring the growth and profitability of finance. He noted the overwhelming political support for banks and the City coming from Blair and Brown, as symbolised in Brown's annual Mansion House speech heaping praise on 'the leadership skills and entrepreneurship' of the City (Hutton, 2010: 146, citing Brown's 2007 Mansion House speech). In this context he argued that the financial plutocrats had taken over the state (2010: 176) and itemised the revolving door between the City and the regulators, along with the intensive and successful efforts made by the City to define the regulatory debate itself and to design the very instruments of regulation (see Chapter 10). This parallels the almost complete capture of the Washington regulatory structure by investment bankers, as recounted by Johnson and Kwak (2010). In both the US and the UK the size and hubris of the financial sector combined with deferential regulation to allow the 2008 financial crisis.

It seems, therefore, that the generalisations about the limited power enjoyed by business representative bodies in the UK are less valid from the early 1990s and, in any case, do not apply to the financial and commercial sectors of the City. Another way of looking at this relative influence is to argue that within the financial/business elite the financial interests are dominant. This is a conclusion strongly supported by the analysis of the top 100 corporations in Britain and the assessment of their relative power undertaken by Maclean et al. They identify 19 financial services corporations in the top 100 and judge that they exercise 23.5 per cent of corporate power. To put that in context, the equivalent figures for France are a mere two corporations and 4.9 per cent of power (Maclean et al., 2006: 13). Despite the continuing influence of the financial elite the composition of that elite has, of course, changed fundamentally. The big bang deregulation of City practices and financial markets resulted in the disintegration of the old British City firms and their trust-based, 'gentlemanly' ways of doing business (see Moran, 2003: 161). The handshake was replaced with the written contract and foreign investment banks, brokers and fund managers poured into London, often via takeovers of venerable British institutions. The legitimating discourse, constructed by the internationalised City elite, still emphasised the importance of the City in generating wealth, employment, foreign earnings and competitive advantage. This justified demands for lighter regulation, internationalisation of markets, tolerance of high profits and grotesquely high earnings, together with a permissive tax regime that would continue to attract the world's wealthy to London.

A second feature of research on business representation concerns the shift during the early 1990s away from reliance on collective representation of corporations and towards corporate lobbying by individual firms. This trend has been thoroughly examined in a series of studies by Coen (2009) and has been driven by the increased size and resources of large corporations, by the more international scale of their operations which means that a national focus is less relevant, and by the perceived need to protect corporate brands (rather than sectoral preferences). Coen stresses in particular the shift from lobbying at the national level to lobbying in Brussels which is, for some sectors and activities, now the major source of new regulations. He points out that the European institutions are deliberately open to lobbyists since, with limited resources, they need to tap into the information and technical expertise which lobbyists can supply (Coen, 2009: 148). The pattern has therefore been for business lobbying to become more focussed and professionalised, with rapid growth in the 'lobbying industry'. Specialised lobbyists in consultancies or law firms operate in London and Brussels. An inquiry by the Public Administration Select Committee reviewed the professional bodies such as the APCC (Association of Professional Political Consultants) which aim to represent the several thousand UK lobbyists (PASC, 2009) and in Brussels it is estimated that there may be as many as 20,000 business lobbyists (Moran, 2009: 41).

There are still, of course, a bewildering array of specialist trade, technical or issue-based bodies who lobby collectively on behalf of industry. For instance, dipping into a chapter on chemical industry lobbying finds mention of bodies ranging from the Fertilisers Manufacturing Association to the British Aerosol Manufacturers Association (Grote, 2008: 73–5; see also Moran, 2008: 70). But the most influential actors are the large corporations, so that Coen (2009: 160) talks of 'the current "elite pluralism" as a system where access is restricted to a few policy makers' and Tenbücken points to the ability of multinationals to use multiple routes of influence including 'an immense influence on the political institutions at the national level' and, at the EU level, an ability 'to gain acceptance even in areas that have traditionally been reserved for collective interest representation' (Tenbücken, 2008: 206, 208). Stepping back from the detail of business associations and lobbying tactics, and turning from a pluralist perspective to a governing institution perspective, in many areas corporations have evidently become partners in policy making. This is a logical extension of the theme of corporate political activism outlined in Chapter 2 where it was pointed out that some corporations are so involved in the delivery of public services, or so dependent on public regulation, that a defining element of their strategy is to 'enter government'. The resultant partnership creates a mode of governance with policy making and implementation undertaken jointly by one or a few corporations together with the specialised sections of government ministries or agencies (see Chapter 6).

Finally, the balance struck between collective representation of business interests and engagement at the level of the individual corporation is important for social cohesion. Collective representation of business interests will tend to articulate collective interests which benefit the whole of the business community, and will do so in a setting that also considers national interests and 'the public interest'. At its best, collective representation can contribute to a debate within civil society on key issues around growth, conditions of employment, distribution of benefits, and social and environmental impacts of economic activity. Collective institutions can give a voice to alternative philosophies of industrial and capitalist development expressed by business leaders. These voices are by no means always materialistic and self-interested. In their study of business ideologies Boswell and Peters review self-critical, altruistic, reform-minded and public-spirited business leaders such as the 'reconstructionists' who advanced early notions of stakeholder capitalism in the 1970s (Boswell and Peters, 1997, ch. 6). The CBI continued to engage in thoughtful, introspective debate, as represented in its post-crash discussion paper on *The Shape of Business: The Next 10 Years* (2009), which reviewed the decline in public trust in business, argues for better ethical credentials, and rather impressively anticipates that 'business recognises that demonstrating their accountability will be part of the new 'license to operate' (CBI, 2009: 5). This sort of expression of business responsibilities and obligations is, of course, characteristic of neo-corporatist business systems such as those of Germany and Japan explored in Chapter 9, where corporations are expected to display responsible behaviour and where collective bodies may discipline them if they do not. In contrast, engagement with government by one corporation will prioritise the interests of that corporation and its wider, probably global, goals. There will be less peer pressure to pursue industry-wide interests, and certainly less expectation that it will consider wider social or national interests. Its executives, negotiators, or paid lobbyists could be expected to pursue a far more instrumental agenda focussed on market growth, profitability and shareholder value. In the New Corporate State privileged access is the reality but the corporations are less likely to consider national interests and more likely to pursue their individual or selfish interests.

This account of the organisation of the corporate elite presents a picture of relative disorganisation, the sort of picture which has contributed to a pluralist diagnosis. Instead, this section concludes with an argument that the corporate elite is in fact far more united, purposeful and organised than the superficial picture implies. It is too easy, of course, simply to assert malign and omnipresent corporate manipulation as presented, for instance, in the entertaining edifice built in George Monbiot's (2000) *Captive State: The Corporate Takeover of Britain*. Conspiracy theories require substantiation. It is tempting to look for an organisational manifestation of elite power, a corporate equivalent of the Cabinet room which is the aspiration and definition of the political elite. There are symbolic expressions of the leading edge of the corporate elite such as the Prime Minister's Business Advisory Group, the Council of the CBI or, if we accept the argument of the leading role of the financiers, the Board of the British Bankers Association. Outside the UK similar attempts have been made to stress, for instance, the mobilising role of the ERT, the European Round Table of Industrialists (van Apeldoorn, 2000) or, for the USA, Hanahoe's (2003: 91) blood curdling account of a cohesive corporate elite coordinated by families and particularly by the Rockefeller network. We need something more solidly grounded than these critical accounts, based on a recognition that, in the UK at least, there is no single coordinating general staff willing or able to mobilise the various battalions of the corporate elite.

Traditional accounts of elite coherence tended to emphasise the family, educational and social linkages and loyalties. In their study of French and British business elites, Maclean et al. reviewed the traditional sources of coherence in interlocking directorships, educational background, membership of clubs, social and family networks and, strikingly, common sporting interests. They conclude, however, that 'while the ties that bind the French business elite tend to be institutional and strong, those that unite the business elite in Britain are in part social in nature and relatively weak' (Maclean et al., 2006: 240). They argued that weak ties can nonetheless be very effective but something more is required to establish the coherence of the corporate elite and its dominance of the New Corporate State. The argument here builds on earlier chapters and stresses three levels of coherence moving from systemic ideology, to economic policy and then to raw self-interest.

At the level of systemic ideology is the dominant neoliberal orthodoxy. We have examined the emergence of neoliberalism in earlier chapters but in this context it takes on importance as a mobilising and legitimating discourse for business leaders. Neoliberalism is not just about the small state, the free market and pro-business policies. It also embodies a vision of private sector competence based on Darwinian selection and an appreciation of the realities of economic relations. In their examination of business ideologies Boswell and Peters identify a 'hegemonic ideal type' which they term 'liberationism'. This is a set of ideas espoused by business leaders based on 'the core notion ... of business leadership in society by virtue of its incomparable contribution to both wealth-creation and liberty' so that, 'the concept is of the full potential of business energies released and stimulated for the public good ... with ... a maximum of resources in private, not public, hands' (Boswell and Peters, 1997: 17). This business ideology, on the margins throughout the 1960s and 1970s, came into its own during the Thatcher governments. Boswell and Peters plot the rise and entrenchment of liberationism, although in their conclusion they speculate that its future was 'cloudy' (ibid.: 193). That was before the New Labour consolidation of the Thatcherite project, which inspired business self-confidence and even a sense of mission. Liberationism emerged from the clouds to enter the sunlit uplands of a dominant systemic ideology, widely shared, valuably legitimising, and providing a public and private ideological coherence for the New Corporate State.

The second level of coherence relates to economic policy and is embedded in an elite consensus about the proper role of the state in relation to the economy and regulation of corporations. The consensus centres on the role of 'competitiveness' and the need for governments to provide a supportive environment to allow British-based corporations to compete successfully in global markets. The competitiveness agenda empowers multinationals, as outlined in Chapter 7, and generates a programme of policy demands which are evident in the New Labour 'British business model' and form the basis for Cerny's (2010) critical model of the British competition state (see also Horsfall, 2010). Competitiveness policies are derived from the 'liberationist' corporate ideology. They profess to exploit the genius of markets by encouraging entrepreneurship, stimulating innovation, attracting talent and rewarding success. This is a familiar, even a hegemonic, discourse but it also has the tremendous benefit for the corporate elite of articulating in a persuasive fashion a set of understandings and prescriptions which can be shared by business leaders. They have become normalised as a way of conceiving economic policy that is obvious, common sense and is reinforced by consultancies, corporate leaders and the whole apparatus of financial appraisal.

The liberationist and competitiveness discourses provide cohesion for the corporate elite and are, of course, presented in terms of the common interests of society. They are a recipe for economic success which benefits all strata of society and, until the onset of financial tribulations in 2007, they underpinned the UK 'economic miracle'. These ostensibly public-spirited sources of pride and cohesion conceal a third level of elite solidarity based on raw self-interest. The corporate elite is engaged in an astonishing project of self-enrichment which is extraordinary in its scale and defiance. The increase in inequality, the rise of the super-rich, and the escalation in executive remuneration was outlined in Chapter 4. The members of the corporate elite have visceral motives of self-interest to perpetuate that self-enrichment through devices such as remuneration committees, recruitment consultants, and votes in Board meetings, all as part of defending the allegedly global market for top managerial talent. Thus ideological and social ties are cemented by financial self-interest which delivers an extraordinary privileged life style, benefits for families and friends, and that classic motive for all elites, the creation of a dynasty through the provision of exceptional education and wealth for children. A distinctive life style for the corporate elite with a wealth management industry, luxury as a commodity, gated communities and access to life-prolonging health care carries a risk of losing touch with public opinion. A small example was provided by Tony Hayward, the CEO of BP at the height of the Deepwater Horizon Gulf oil spillage, when a bemused press and incandescent public saw him spending a relaxing day at the Isle of Wight on his £470,000 yacht attending the plutocratic 'J.P.Morgan Asset Management Round the Island Race' (*New York Times*, 19 June 2010). Hayward's subsequent departure gave substance to Sklair's (2001: 26) observation that 'members of the corporate elite have commonly and with good reason felt insecure', but Hayward bounced back and, even after the financial crash, the UK corporate elite continued to appear arrogant and even complacent. Remarking on this appearance of defiance, manifested in stratospheric executive remuneration, Richard Lambert, outgoing Director-General of the CBI, warned in a thoughtful speech that, 'if leaders of big companies seem to be occupying a different galaxy from the rest of the community, they risk being treated as aliens' (Lambert, 2010: 4). Reports from the High Pay Commission (2011a, b) indicated that his warnings had little visible effect.

CONCLUSION: CORPORATE BIAS AND THE SHRINKING OF DEMOCRATIC CHOICE

The overarching theme of chapters 4 and 5, has been the suppression of the UK 1944 Post-war Settlement and its replacement with a new settlement in the shape of the New Corporate State. To claim a transformation in the nature of the British state is hardly novel, virtually stating the obvious. The more challenging questions are to define the nature of the new state and to identify the forces that will sustain it. Several different labels have been attached to the new British state but it is instructive to return to the work of the US historian, Philip Bobbitt, to locate the transformed state as something more than a transformation in political economy and as something larger than a purely British phenomenon. In his magisterial account Bobbitt sees a transition from the nation-state, which dominated the 20th century, to a 'market state'. For Bobbitt the market state is the product of universal historical forces including technology, the nature of warfare and the effectiveness of law, as well as shifts in political economy and globalised markets. The certainties of the nation-state have given way so that 'within the most prominent market-states, the groundwork was laid by Margaret Thatcher and Ronald Reagan, who did so much to discredit the welfare rationale of the welfare state. The rationale that underpins the legitimacy of the market-state, by contrast, is that it maximises opportunity' (Bobbitt, 2001: 339). His stance on the merits of the market-state range from the fatalistic to the frankly celebratory. In an account very close to the structural dependency theory examined in Chapter 2, he concludes that 'the market-state promises a "virtuous" circle to those states that copy its form and obey its strictures' (2001: 668) and observes that 'it seems not unlikely that virtually all major states will accept for themselves the fundamental assumptions that Margaret Thatcher and Tony Blair urged for Britain' (2001: 667).

The significance of Bobbitt's argument is not only in his political economy, which is less impressive than his accounts of warfare and diplomacy, but in his endorsement of an epochal transformation towards a new sort of state defined by its relationship to markets. His whole emphasis on the legitimisation of the new state through offering opportunities to individuals is an elaboration of Thatcherite market ideology but he sees a continued role for the state in market economies. The state may be mercantilist, managerial or, as in the case of the UK and the USA, entrepreneurial. Oddly he also sees regulation as declining in importance (2001: 671), perhaps because he fails to emphasise the importance of the corporation which, individually and collectively, has moved to constitute and structure markets through its influence over economic regulation.

The New Corporate State can therefore be seen as the product of historic forces and as a prototype of the newly emergent model of the market state. It is based on an alliance between political, corporate and financial elites and it attaches central priority to economic growth achieved through international competitiveness based on steadily increasing productivity. Although the primary discourse stresses the effectiveness of markets, the imperative is the attraction of dominant market players who are the large corporations. In practice this means regulations that are sympathetic to corporate interests. Thus the rise of the New Corporate State is also expressed in the move towards a 'regulatory state'. This might sound ominous, since corporations allegedly have an aversion to regulation, but it all depends on what sort of regulation. As Stigler (1971) pointed out, large corporations often love regulation. It provides certainty, excludes competitors, facilitates planning and underpins investment. Or at least it does when the corporations have a hand in designing, implementing or even undertaking regulation themselves. As discussed in Chapter 2, this is not a world of free market neoliberalism, it is a world of regulatory capitalism composed of markets which in Polanyian fashion are constituted by rules and laws. The key point is that those rules and laws are created through a partnership of political and corporate elites.

It has been argued in chapters 4 and 5 that the corporate elite has at its core the directors of large financial, service and manufacturing corporations. This elite is embedded in a wider corporate elite which includes supportive and reputational elements located in government, in corporate services, and in the media. The corporate elite displays coherence and self-discipline which is based only partially on classic elite characteristics of social background, family and education. Coherence is provided more directly by a shared commitment to a market rhetoric, a competitiveness agenda, and to a self-interested access to corporate income. It is an elite based an a managerial cadre that has established exceptional autonomy with only limited countervailing influence from workers or owners, although it is highly responsive to financial markets. The alliance with the political elite is of paramount importance. The corporate elite enjoys power, status and wealth; the political elite enjoys power, status and re-election. Both have high stakes in a system that generates income, wealth and the material benefits of economic growth.

There are, of course, challenges to the dominance of the corporate elite and the New Corporate State. It is in any case a model with elements of instability, including the unhealthy level of crude self-interest that prompted James Galbraith to attack the US equivalent as a *Predator State* (Galbraith, 2009: 131). The sources of instability are important in helping to understand the dynamics of the New Corporate State and the prospects for its survival or adaptation. First, the corporate elite is to some extent fragmented with internal tensions. As explored above, corporations do compete for resources and markets, whilst the critical voices of the old elite can still be heard. The UK corporate elite has to a large extent been 'denationalised'. It is no longer committed to the British national interest or even to continued location in Britain. Comparison with corporate elites in other countries emphasises this fragility and the eroding social base. For instance, Maclean et al.'s (2006) analysis of France paints a picture of very strong social and educational ties embedded deeply in the institutions of the state and with an organic integration of the economic and the political. In Britain, in contrast, important elements of the elite are either themselves non-British or are working for overseas corporations. Second, policy making dominated by an alliance of career politicians and senior executives is prone to be dysfunctional. Marginalisation of the traditional elites, and especially worker representatives and the civil service, removes expertise, judgement and dissenting voices, with the risk of increased policy failure. The list is depressingly long, from rail privatisation and failed computerisation of the NHS, to uncontrolled immigration and insecure energy supply, and most recently the financial crisis itself, which Engelen et al. (2011: 9) analyse as an 'elite debacle'. This dysfunctional dimension of elite policy domination is explored in later chapters but the New Corporate State has managed to survive such policy failures. It has even managed to survive the greatest policy failure of all, the financial crisis of 2007–08.

We should, in any case, emphasise that the argument about the dominance of the politico-corporate elite is relative. The New Corporate State attaches priority to corporate interests but, despite arguments to the contrary (Crouch, 2004), it remains a liberal democracy which accommodates a range of interests. The corporate elite enjoys disproportionate power but it does not enjoy a monopoly of power. The argument is more about the shrinking of democratic choice or, more correctly, the shrinking of political choice. This is seen in a variety of settings but here let us enumerate five. First, the New Corporate State does less, in the sense that it spends less on direct delivery of public services. Second, the private sector does more, either as direct deliverer, often regulated by the state, or under contract from state agencies. Third, the state continues to engage in regulation and there has been continued regulatory growth, but the regulation is increasingly 'depoliticised' and operates independently, responsive to market rules rather than political choice. Fourth, the state service itself has been marginalised and the civil service has been in part colonised by the corporate elite. Fifth, where policy choices are made, and initiatives undertaken, the range of policy choices is limited by parameters of competitiveness and corporate needs. The cumulative effect of these constraints is to reduce the range of options available for political debate, to limit the room for manoeuvre by government, and to shrink the public space of collective debate whilst expanding the private, market-orientated space within which individuals, to use Bobbitt's phrase, can pursue 'opportunities'. This, of course, reduces the role of individuals as citizens, with responsibilities, public obligations and the opportunity to deliberate on the shape of society. Instead the individual is a consumer within an increasingly commodified society. The practical effects of such developments are explored in Chapter 6 which examines the New Corporate State in action and explores the influence of the corporate elite.

6. Partnership and policy in Britain's New Corporate State

Chapters 4 and 5 explored the creation of the New Corporate State in Britain and the shape of a new political economy jointly dominated by corporate and political elites. This chapter examines how those developments were boosted by privatisation and demonstrates the exercise of corporate power through the example of the public services industry. This chapter therefore argues that the New Corporate State has created new opportunities for the expansion of the corporate sector, involving new configurations of economic regulation and public policy, and new distributional patterns which favour the interests of the corporate elite. In the process the New Corporate State has matured and become embedded in a stable institutional configuration to an extent that makes alternative economic models difficult to visualise, both ideologically and practically. The economic relationship that has become institutionalised is that of 'partnership' as outlined in Chapter 2. This is a partnership in the delivery of public services, in the development of policy options, and in the very process of governance. Partnership is a term imbued with benign associations and in the economic sphere it might well be regarded with approval, as many positive assessments of German neo-corporatism affirm (Schmitter, 2010: 249). But equally, partnership may have negative effects if it is exclusionary and energised by private gain rather than public interest. This chapter therefore seeks to identify the impact of the New Corporate State on individuals and communities. It begins with a review of the sorts of policy options likely to be pursued by corporations as they exploit the resources, incentives and opportunities identified in Chapter 2 as the drivers of their political activism.

WHAT DO CORPORATIONS WANT FROM GOVERNMENT?

As Chapter 5 outlined, there is an influential line of argument that says that corporations do not know what they want. While it is true that corporations are often unclear or incoherent about the most desirable policy environment in which they operate, they can safely be expected to have some very clear preferences which can be anticipated by politicians and civil servants and which are articulated strongly by business leaders. It is also true that businesses often have contradictory interests and one of the most interesting questions about business representation is which groups, sectors or collection of corporations impose their preferences on business generally and then on government. Nonetheless it is feasible to define a series of preferences and interests which corporations could be expected to pursue and which, if successfully achieved, would stand as evidence of the exercise of power.

The obvious place to visit for a corporate wish list is the business representative bodies such as the CBI which are there precisely to articulate business interests. But their publications tend to be coy, evasive or cloaked in a facade of collective benefits. An alternative approach is to extrapolate from business ideology and hypothetical self-interests to define a set of preferences that we could expect corporations to pursue. Chapter 5 outlined the 'liberationist' business ideology in the UK that emerged during the Thatcher years seeking to liberate business from control and regulation by the state (Boswell and Peters, 1997: 163). It insisted that business should be set free from constraints posed by unions, governments and society. The liberationist position was joined by the 'shareholder value' discourse to define a set of general freedoms which business wished to pursue, together with more specific corporate strategies defined by their ability to add shareholder value, so that, by the early 2000s, we could construct a fairly coherent set of expected corporate preferences. Those preferences can be discussed under the four categories of generalised interests common to all corporations; contradictory interests which benefit some corporations more than others; distributive interests which are more concerned with governance and the position of owners and managers; and finally fractional interests which considers how different fractions of capital can be expected to present their interests and, indeed, which interests are dominant.

The collective interests of business would include governmental policies that could be expected to benefit the vast majority of corporations and associations. These would go beyond the normal legal protections and the framework of markets such as contractual protection and trading standards which can be taken for granted. They would form part of the competitiveness agenda and Horsfall (2010) has made a trailblazing effort to identify these policies as part of research on the competition state. Such policies include the following:

- low rates of business taxation, especially low corporation tax;
- low and reducing levels of welfare state spending;

Partnership and policy in Britain's New Corporate State

- flexible labour laws with limitation on the rights of labour and industrial action, but unrestricted immigration;
- reduction in employment costs in areas such as minimum wage, employment subsidies and protection for temporary workers;
- the expansion of markets and creation of new markets through privatisation and contracting out;
- de-regulation through minimising regulatory costs seen as burdens on business, and light touch regulation;
- socialising business costs such as training, health and safety, environmental mitigation and so on.

The category of 'contradictory' interests of corporations deals with those areas where policies favour the market position of certain corporations but hinder others. In these settings some corporations will seek advantageous policies and others will resist those same policies which they will find disadvantageous. For instance:

- stricter sectoral regulation leading to regulatory capture which may exclude competitors through requirements such as licensing or professional qualifications;
- regulations on business conduct which favour SMEs such as preferential lending rates or prompt payment codes which disadvantage large corporations;
- policies that assist exporters at the cost of importers, or vice versa, such as guarantee schemes, encouragement of inward investment, tariff barriers or exchange rate policy;
- regulations on business services which push up costs such as universal service requirements for utilities, or low tariffs for those in fuel poverty;
- policies to encourage research such as patent protection which protects research intensives at the cost of generic substitutes.

The distributive interests pursued by corporations concern the benefits that corporate management is able to distribute to managers, owners and other stakeholders. This encompasses questions of corporate governance and social and environmental responsibility. Here policies would include:

- strong autonomy for the board and limited rights of employee participation and consultation;
- arms-length relations with major shareholders and banks;
- a transparent market for corporate control with self-regulation of takeovers;

- low levels of taxation on higher incomes and favourable rules concerning domicile and allowances;
- permissive rules relating to remuneration including stock options and bonuses;
- permissive rules on the payment and taxation of dividends, share buybacks, loans and securities;
- favourable rules on free capital movements, double taxation provisions, setting of transfer prices and repatriation of profits.

This brief sketch of some of the key corporate policy preferences illustrates the difficulty of business coming to a consensus on desirable policy content. A series of fault lines emerge between different sectors of industry which Marxists term 'fractions' of capital. The most important divisions are between large and small corporations; between importers and exporters; between the retail sector and the productive sector; between multinational and national corporations; and between services and manufacturing. One further opposition, which is especially important in the UK, is the distinction between the interests of finance and those of manufacturing. Traditionally finance has wanted a strong currency, high interest rates, easy takeover rules and a highly liquid market in shares and securities. Manufacturing has wanted a cheaper currency, low interest rates, protection from takeover and patient long term investors. For the entirety of the post-war period the interests of the City and finance have prevailed (see Chapter 5). Criticism of financial or City dominance was submerged during the long boom but concerns were raised about the 'financialisation' of British and global capitalism. The financial crisis demonstrated how justified those concerns were but the New Corporate State has survived the aftermath of the financial crisis and the influence of the corporate and financial elite outlined in chapters 4 and 5 has been sustained. In part due to the embedded power which is explored in this chapter.

A shorthand description of the range of policy preferences outlined above would be that a neoliberal framework has come to the fore (Leys, 2001; Gamble, 2009b; Cerny, 2010). The profile of policy preferences advanced above certainly shares a neoliberal bias, but in many accounts of neoliberalism policies consistent with a neoliberal agenda seem to emerge almost spontaneously as governments anticipate business preferences. This deterministic tendency of critical and Marxist analysis underplays the complexity of the exercise of corporate power and the various agencies through which it is exerted. In fact the dominance of the market discourse, which has become the zeitgeist of the 21st century, has become so pervasive that it is easy to forget how hard fought were the ascendency of market principles. In the USA and in the UK the revolutionary shift to a free market economic paradigm involved a struggle of ideas mediated by business leaders, economists and political parties in an intense process of ideological conflict. As studies by Boswell and Peters (1997), Blyth (2002) and Marangos (2008) affirm, new paradigms have to be fought for but once achieved they change the balance of advantage and begin to yield vast benefits for the victors. In reality the paradigms of the market and of neoliberalism have become dominant but are grossly misleading. They offer extraordinarily powerful arguments and generate eloquent and impassioned defences but they conceal a very different reality, which is one of markets organised by a small number of large and dominant corporations. Markets are organised within the hierarchies of firms, through agreements between corporations, and through government policies and regulations which constitute markets but which also reflect corporate preferences. Recently Crouch has come to term such markets as expressions of a 'Chicago economy' (Crouch, 2011: 122) in a reference to the toleration of large corporations in American antitrust, but in reality oligopolistic domination of markets is of much longer standing (especially in the United States: Galbraith, 1952), what has perhaps changed is a governmental and even public tolerance of such market concentration.

The parallel processes of the expansion of markets and the extension of arenas of corporate control within those markets are explored in this chapter in relation to the UK, and in Chapter 7 are extrapolated into aspects of global governance. These transformations share the common denominator of a transition from public services defined and administered by government organisations, to the meeting of public needs through activities undertaken by private or third sector organisations. There has been an extension of the areas of economic and social life subject to corporate influence or corporate strategies, and associated with that extension is the reduced repertoire of democratic policy choices. The chapter concentrates on two crucial areas of the extension of corporate power; areas in which it could be said that there has been corporate colonisation of the public sphere – privatisation and the creation of a new public services industry.

PRIVATISATION

In the early 1980s privatisation was still regarded as a new, ugly and unwelcome word describing a policy of doubtful validity. Now it is, of course, a major component of economic policy in all market economies and an essential part of the toolkit of international organisations and fiscal retrenchment. The earlier post-war norm was the 'mixed economy' in which public and private corporations co-existed (Young with Lowe, 1974). It was felt important for the state to retain control of 'the commanding heights of the economy' and new public enterprise was regarded as a possible wave of the future with innovations such as Labour's 1976 National Enterprise Board (Wilks, 1988: 48–9). In 1979 public corporations employed 8 per cent of the workforce and accounted for 10.5 per cent of GDP (Cook, 1998: 220), by 2007 there was nothing (except Royal Mail and the BBC) left to sell. The way in which the first Thatcher government stumbled on privatisation is a familiar story (McLean, 2004: 60; Parker, 2009) but it became a defining feature of the Thatcher reign from 1983 onwards and gained wide acceptance. A common assumption is that privatisation was driven by economic logic and by the efficiency gains and increments to growth that were claimed for privatised industries. Those on the left saw privatisation in a far less flattering light: as a political campaign to change the political landscape and to embed markets as the dominant feature of the British political economy. In retrospect they were right.

The privatisation project stands as a stunningly successful campaign to create a hegemonic market regime. It is an economic transformation comparable with the institutionalised neoliberalism which Blyth (2002) dissected in the United States. In fact economic efficiency was not increased by privatisation, either in Britain (Parker, 2012: 524–6) or across Europe (Parker, 1998). Instead privatisation is best understood as a political project, a point reflected in the official history (Parker, 2012: 505), which charts the evolution of the sales summarised in Table 6.1.

Looking down the list of industries the scale of change is breathtaking. It is hard to imagine this scale of economic transformation being achieved in countries with a less powerful and centralised executive although the scale of opposition was relatively modest, except for some controversial privatisations such as water in 1989. The economic and industrial transition is obvious enough, the political effects are far less clear cut and less widely debated but can be summarised in six elements which were pursued under Conservative governments up to 1997 and consolidated under Labour.

The first element targeted the political power base of the traditional Labour Party. The failure of Labour's industrial policy, which helped the Conservatives to win the 1979 election, also implicated the public sector trades unions which had been prominent in the 'winter of discontent' strikes in 1978–79. The unpopularity of the public sector unions reduced the credibility of opposition to privatisation and, after a hesitant start, the privatisation of the bastions of the public sector workforce in gas, electricity and then those ultimate strongholds of coal and the railways

Table 6.1   Summary of the main UK privatisations

British Aerospace	1981
Cable and Wireless	1981
Britoil	1982
British Petroleum	1983
Associated British Ports	1983
Jaguar	1984
British Telecom	1984
British Shipbuilders	1985
British Gas	1986
Rolls Royce	1987
British Airports Authority	1987
British Airways	1987
British Steel	1988
Rover Group	1988
Water	1989
Electricity Distribution	1990
Electricity Generation	1991
Coal Industry	1994
Railways	1995–97
British (Nuclear) Energy	1996

Source: Parker (2012: 4, 504).

undermined one of the most powerful political forces of 1970s Britain. The transfer of the workforce to private sector corporations exposed them to market pressures and to an assertive management empowered by the trade union reforms under the Conservatives. The industrial power of the unions was undermined, their ability to contribute membership and funding to the Labour Party was reduced, and the self-interested and tribalised Labour electoral support was diminished. This was a political campaign little short of brilliant.

The second element was the mirror image of the assault on Labour support. Privatisation was also used to create and to reward Conservative supporters. Privatisation revealed a more acquisitive instinct across a wider spectrum of the British population than many had expected. The Yuppie generation and the increasingly strident celebration of individualism and greed found expression in the enthusiasm for purchasing privatisation shares. The proportion of the population owning shares increased from about 7 per cent in 1979 to 22 per cent in 1997 (Parker, 2012: 520). These new enthusiasts for 'popular capitalism' were amply rewarded by premiums on the new share issues which, for example, Feigenbaum et al.

(1998: 77) put at 92 per cent for British Telecom and 70 per cent for British Airways. These were immediate profits from the first day of trading but most of these early share issues, and especially water and electricity, continued to experience rising share prices thus creating a new sector of small capitalists who later realised their gains (and the proportion of private shareholders declined). A transition from Labour to Conservative support could also have been expected from the non-industrial privatisation of council housing owned by local government but offered for sale to tenants at deep discounts through the 'right to buy'. Since 1980 2.5 million homes have been sold, reducing council house tenants from 33 per cent of households in 1980 to 11 per cent in 2011. The value of houses sold, at £86 billion, exceeded the total of all privatisations (HSBC, 2011). This huge increase in home ownership enlarged the population of pro-Conservative property owners (see McLean, 2004: 60) while the expanded markets created further profitable opportunities for private landlords, house builders and housing finance. Ultimately, of course, it also contributed to the property credit bubble.

The third element lay in the fiscal gain from privatisation. This has become a global driver of privatisation. For any government experiencing fiscal pressure, sale of state assets has attractions, and for the Conservative governments those attractions were fully exploited. The proceeds over the period 1979–97 were £69 billion (Parker, 2012: 505) yielding an average annual bonus of 1.7 per cent of public expenditure and providing Conservative Chancellors with a substantial fiscal advantage equivalent to about 2 pence off the rate of income tax. Privatisation proceeds thus allowed government to sustain public spending whilst cutting taxes to create electoral advantage. This short-term advantage was clearly transient and the Conservatives were criticised for fiscal opportunism. In particular it seemed that some industries such as British Telecom, Gas and British Airways were sold as monopolies precisely to increase their attractions to potential purchasers. Moreover, the privatisations proceeded rapidly and before effective regulatory provisions were in place, meaning that regulation of price, profit and competition had to be undertaken as part of an exercise in belatedly addressing the monopolistic advantages of the privatised corporations.

These three elements combined to undermine Labour support, to bolster Conservative support, and helped to create a favourable electoral climate which sustained the Conservatives in power from 1979 to 1997. They appear in retrospect to constitute a stunningly successful political exercise and McLean cites Brittan to the effect 'that people always overestimated Mrs Thatcher's grasp of economics while underestimating her grasp of politics' (McLean, 2004: 63). The political dimensions have been downplayed in popular discourse, in Hood's (1994: 49) phrase they are 'the unmentionable politics of privatisation'. Those short-term benefits had been exhausted by 1997. Most obviously the money had been spent but the unwinding of traditional Labour politics in favour of 'New Labour' meant that the Labour Party had accepted the validity of privatisation. The political centre of gravity had moved to the right and Labour was now an equally enthusiastic exponent of markets. It was no longer the threat to house owners, share owners and employers that it had appeared in the early 1990s, a transition which underlines the three longer-term elements of the privatisation rationale.

The fourth element of the privatisation project concerns the transfer of property rights. Industrial assets once owned by the state were now firmly in the hands of private corporations and their shareholders. Short of crisis re-nationalisation (such as the rescue of the banks in 2008) those assets could not in practice be transferred back to the state. Expropriation would destroy credibility in global financial markets and to purchase the shares would be prohibitively expensive. The transfer of property rights was in practice irreversible. These new corporations were also operating in markets that had been created, policed and regulated by government. A whole industry of market regulation had been created through competition policy at the UK and European levels and by the utility regulatory agencies such as OfCom, OFWAT and Ofgem. These markets, and the corporations within them, were therefore operating in a stable, legitimate and familiar economic environment that had comprehensively replaced public control with market dynamics and market values. Hood (1994: 55) observed that public enterprise had not been discredited in principle or in practice and hazarded the thought that it might re-emerge. By 2010 it remained a threatened species, certainly in the UK and, as we see below, in the global economy.

The embedding of markets and the creation of a new orthodoxy around private sector delivery comprises the fifth element of privatisation. Left-wing critics such as Colin Leys have produced eloquent polemics opposing 'the commercialisation of everyday life' but sharing the conclusion that the markets had become embedded so that 'there was little resistance to all these changes. Within two decades the omnipresence of business and business culture had become as commonplace and apparently inevitable as the rain' (2001: 53, 54). He examined the detailed impact of market forces on traditionally non-market areas (in this case public service broadcasting and health care) and he analysed 'the penetration of non-market spheres by market forces and their conversion into fields of capital accumulation' (Leys, 2001: 87). Thus the cultural crusade of the Conservatives led by Sir Keith Joseph, Margaret Thatcher, the IEA and like-minded think tanks achieved a level of success that few would have anticipated in the early 1980s. The 'enterprise culture' which became their holy grail was achieved, and with it a decisive enhancement of corporate power. Feigenbaum et al. (1998: 42) see this project as a strategy of 'systemic privatization' which 'is intended to reshape the entire society by fundamentally altering economic and political institutions and by transforming economic and political interests'. Privatisation thus constitutes a major episode of institutional change involving a normative acceptance of the proper role of government as a regulator of services delivered by market organisations. The institutional change includes a cultural or cognitive shift which places individuals as consumers of public services, rather than as citizens with entitlements.

The sixth and final element of privatisation lies in the creation of a new set of economic interests. Hood (1994: 56) remarked on the rise of a 'privatization complex' of corporations and policy entrepreneurs seeking to defend and expand the gains from privatisation. The idea that privatisation creates new interests (and in Eastern Europe new classes) is of fundamental importance. Feigenbaum et al. (1998: 56) similarly stress the emergence of new interest groups which seek to influence political institutions. This is actually too modest a statement of the change in interests and the creation of an important governmental element exercised by corporations. The networks which govern vital services important to the public, such as water, energy, transport and housing, now revolve around private corporations which themselves are highly influential within corporate politics and within society more widely.

The influence of formerly privatised companies can be gauged from their size. In 2009, 132 of the corporations on the *Financial Times* list of the world's 500 most valuable corporations had been privatised. They had a combined market capitalisation of $4.7 trillion and accounted for 30 per cent of the total market capitalisation of the top 500. Excluding the 181 US corporations from the FT500 gives a privatisation share of the non-US market capitalisation at a remarkable 50.2 per cent (*Privatization Barometer*, 2009: 16). In other words, over half of the world's most valuable non-US corporations were former state-owned corporations that had been privatised. These figures emphasise the irreversibility of privatisation, the extraordinary expansion of markets, and the scale of the vested interests in protecting and extending the privatisation process. *Privatization Barometer* also undertakes an analysis of the largest corporations in 32 of the world's most important economies judged by market capitalisation. In 20 of those economies the largest corporation is privatised and: 'privatized companies are the first, second, and third most valuable firms in Austria, The Czech Republic, France, Greece, Hungary, Poland, Portugal and Hong Kong – and, unsurprisingly, all the most valuable companies in

China and Russia are privatized firms' (*Privatization Barometer*, 2009: 16). For the UK, 11 of the corporations in the 2009 *FT Global 500* are wholly or partly former UK state-owned corporations. The UK initiative in creating huge private sector corporations in politically sensitive areas clearly became a global phenomenon creating a momentum towards further privatisation and enhancing corporate political influence. These privatised firms are inescapably powerful political actors by virtue of their absolute size, their motivations, and their position in the corporate elite.

The presentation of privatisation as essentially a political project invites analysis of the changed political relationships in a privatised market economy. Again the discussion concentrates on the UK but we should note that the UK experience has an altered ideological significance in other European countries. The UK was certainly a trailblazer, and has acted as a model for privatisations in other countries, but the UK emphasis on the ideological virtues of privatisation, and the pursuit of 'systemic' transformation, was far less typical of other European countries. Indeed, Clifton et al. (2006: 739) conclude that 'the UK was not a privatisation leader but an anomaly'. They point out that, although virtually all European governments embarked on privatisation programmes after 1993, their motives were opportunist, financial and driven by European imperatives of market integration instead of neoliberal principles. Indeed, Germany and Sweden in particular were very reluctant privatisers with Sweden following a public enterprise policy of 'active owner'. Later research suggests that the neoliberal policy pressure came through the European Commission which informally pressed for privatisation since 'a primary way to advance its own institutional powers was to implement the economic programme enshrined in the Single European Act, which is to a considerable extent based on neo-liberal ideas' (Schneider and Häge, 2008: 16). This is a familiar theme of the European Commission as a facilitator of neoliberal policies thus opening the door to pan-European corporate power. The pressure on Eurozone member states to meet the Euro convergence criteria and reduce budget deficits provided another pressure towards privatisation which became irresistible for high deficit Eurozone countries after 2008. Nonetheless, across Europe privatisation took place mainly in the sectors of manufacturing, finance, telecommunications and transportation. The UK privatisation of basic utilities was followed only partially in energy and avoided in water. Nonetheless the share of public enterprise in GDP fell from 10.9 per cent in the EU 14 in 1990 to 8.5 per cent in 2000 with the UK at the lowest at 1.9 per cent, and Sweden at the highest at 13.7 per cent (Clifton et al., 2006: 743).

Privatisation in the UK created new political forces in a number of ways which include the following:

- a reduction in the influence of public sector workers and their trade unions and an increase in the authority of directors and senior managers;
- an increase in management rewards seen in boardroom remuneration and salaries of senior managers;
- an increase in income and capital gains to shareholders with the corollary of increased costs to consumers (depending on the extent and distribution of operating efficiencies);
- the creation of large companies in a consolidated industry (an oligopoly) with the likelihood of greater benefit for multinationals as opposed to SMEs;
- a greater corporate role in shared governance of key industrial sectors including defence, transport, energy and basic utilities.

These changes are all fairly obvious and the justification for tolerating them would be the standard market arguments of greater efficiency, enhanced productivity, economic growth and a general increase in national wealth; this would not be seen as a zero-sum gain. Unfortunately the increments to efficiency are contested and the welfare implications of wealth distribution are as likely to be negative as they are to be positive.

The efficiency debate in the UK petered out in the early 2000s as it became clear that privatisation was a fact of economic life. Parker notes that economic research was sceptical about efficiency gains and he observes that 'it seems fair to conclude that the strident claims of ministers during the 1980s and 1990s about the benefits of privatisation were exaggerated' (Parker, 2012: 526). Privatisation thus emerges as a reconfiguration of political forces as much as an improvement in economic organisation. Similar conclusions can be reached about performance and efficiency in other privatisation locations including the former communist regimes, continental Europe and developing countries (e.g. Megginson and Sutter, 2006). The literature is immense but it could fairly be argued that there is no consensus that privatisation unambiguously contributed to efficiency or improved economic welfare. Indeed, the ideological assumption that privatisation is positive, which has been part of the core assumptions of the IMF and the World Bank, has been extensively criticised as part of the general critique of the Washington Consensus. Moreover, the key question is the distributional effect. If privatisation enhances efficiency (and here there are dynamic effects of change as well as better business models) the overwhelming concern is with how those benefits are distributed. Feigenbaum et al. (1998: 76) captured the disillusion of the late 1990s with the observation that 'the privatized utility monopolies were apparently far more concerned to increase profits, dividends and share price than they were to reduce prices to the consumer'. They might have added the popular outrage at the inflated salaries and bonuses that newly privatised directors managed to pay themselves, symbolised by the British Gas AGM in 1994 when the CEO, Cedric Brown, was pilloried as 'Cedric the Pig' for taking a salary increase of 75 per cent to £450,000, a horrifying sum at that time, small beer 20 years later (Apostolides and Boden, 2005).

The monopoly profits and managerial self-enrichment appeared to affect popular attitudes to privatisation in the UK which became negative at the turn of the century (see Table 6.4). The popular mood seemed to be characterised by a resigned scepticism which was stoked by a series of corporate debacles including the steady monopolisation of the bus industry, with a series of actions against the predatory practices of Stagecoach; the desperate failures in the rail industry and the eventual de facto re-nationalisation of Network Rail; the woeful competitive performance of BA; the pathetic collapse and asset stripping of MG Rover before its bankruptcy in 2005; and the decline of steel making under the control of the Indian Tata Steel Europe. These episodes of corporate failure were not what the evangelical prophets of privatisation had promised a grateful nation, and that is before we consider energy.

The energy sector provides a revealing case study of the implications of privatisation for corporate power and public policy. Energy is a policy area of crucial importance for economic growth, economic (and political) stability, for medium-term security, for quality of life and, increasingly, quality of the environment. As such it is a major concern for the public and governments. From the early 1990s, after privatisation, energy policy in the UK became centred on the corporate strategies of the big energy corporations in a pattern of shared governance. The 'Big 6', as they became after 2002, are outlined in Table 6.2 which shows their dominance of the retail supply market (which is still based on historic regional monopolies) and emphasises that 56 per cent of the market is supplied by four European multinationals. The key issues, which were previously decided by ministers and civil servants, now became contingent on the strategic decisions of the corporations, their boards and multinational parents. Thus important questions included the development of hydro-electric power in Scotland, the advisability of building huge gas storage facilities, differential tariffs to reduce fuel poverty, carbon reduction through carbon capture in coal generation, or the security issues of sourcing gas from Russia. These and a medley of equally urgent questions could only be decided in consultation and negotiation with the energy corporations, in Helm's words, 'decisions were transferred from Whitehall to boardrooms and the regulatory offices. Apart from dealing with crises and handling privatizations, there was little for civil servants to do' (Helm, 2004: 424–5). This was not necessarily

Table 6.2 The Big 6 energy corporations: UK electricity market shares, 2010

Corporation	Generation	Retail supply
EDF Energy (French)	18.9	13.3
RWE npower (German)	9.9	13.5
Centrica (ex British Gas)	9.9	21.8
E ON UK (German)	9.1	17.7
SSE (Scottish and Southern)	9.0	19.0
Scottish Power (Iberdrola, Spanish)	8.2	11.3
Total	65.0	96.6

Source: Bloomberg New Energy Finance (2012: 4).

an unproductive governance system. Governance in conjunction with responsible corporations might yield better results than governance by inadequate public bodies. Market signals might yield admirable outcomes such as investment in gas storage, and liaison with corporations in a transparent and accountable fashion could yield some caring policy outcomes.

The energy regime therefore illustrates many of the dilemmas of the operation of corporate power within liberal democracy. The essential interests of the corporations are with profitability, which generates benefits for management and shareholders. There is therefore an imperative to exploit the market and, where possible, to collude with other companies to drive up prices, extract surplus and conceal actions from the regulator. Indeed, regulatory theories would expect that corporations would seek to build a co-operative relationship with the regulatory agency and seek a good working relationship leading to sympathetic regulation and hopefully into some semblance of 'capture'. The corporations would also be working towards toleration of behaviour in other aspects where their interests were in principle opposed to those of the public interest. At the most basic level energy corporations make their money by selling energy. There is fundamental incongruity about expecting them to encourage energy saving and lowering consumer spend, yet that is exactly what consumer and environmental groups would press for. In terms of corporate strategy there is also potential for strategies to clash with British national interests. The European corporations have invested abroad in part to protect their domestic markets (Thatcher, 2007: 215–16). Their strategic presence in the UK is part of a pan-European struggle for market share by national champions supported discreetly (or in the French case overtly) by their national governments. Their inclination to extract surplus is clear, and their commitment to the UK consumer must be qualified.

Within this kaleidoscope of hugely important issues, with immense long-term implications, the abdication of the UK government and the market theories of Ofgem have an air of naivety verging on delusion. The major political issues that emerged from 2006 onwards required policy initiatives that were outside the ability of the regime of regulatory governance to deal with. There was, for instance, the question of fuel price in an environment of rapidly increasing input prices driven by spikes in the cost of oil; then the question of energy security and dependence on the supply of gas from Russia; then the question of how to define and encourage the best way of building up electricity generation from renewable sources; and the new emphasis on climate change, emphasised by the Stern Review of 2006, and the acute political imperative for change. The political salience was symbolised by the creation in 2008 of the new Department of Energy and Climate Change (DECC) headed by Ed Miliband. The new Minister found it difficult to define and articulate climate change policy and almost impossible to push through major new measures (such as a carbon tax) partly due to vested interests in government, but partly because of the power of the energy corporations who had to be courted and persuaded. Dependence was further illustrated by energy policy decisions to build new nuclear generation capacity. The Coalition government had to negotiate with two private sector consortia and during 2012 implementation was confronted by the withdrawal of the two German corporations, RWE and E.ON, driven by the German government's decision to exit from nuclear generation, and energy policy became centred on the need to persuade EDF to proceed by providing long-term price guarantees. The merits of the policies are less important than how this case study illustrates the way in which governmental processes, political choices and the public interest are conditioned by corporate strategies.

In summing up this discussion of privatisation and the energy industry example it is worth emphasising the politicisation of corporate behaviour and yet its apparent invulnerability from popular discontent. Privatisation by definition intensifies the involvement of corporations with issues of public concern and political sensitivity. Nationalised industries were created in areas of national importance so that industries which have been privatised in areas like defence, transportation, energy, electricity, mail, banking and water are of deep concern to the public and to national security. At the risk of melodrama they are of 'life or death' importance, sometimes literally so. For instance, fuel poverty kills vulnerable people and it is a reflection of political salience (and a challenge to corporate social responsibility) that the state provides winter fuel payments for the elderly rather than requiring the energy corporations to safeguard those with the most extreme vulnerability. Equally, the availability of clean water is a basic necessity of life and the government intervened in the 1998 Water Act to prohibit the increasing tendency for water corporations to disconnect supplies for those unwilling or unable to pay. These are therefore areas that cannot be separated from political dispute, they cannot (or should not) be 'depoliticised' and corporations operating in those fields should be willing to accept a degree of public-regarding obligations as a supplement to their pursuit of efficiency and profit.

In reality we encounter the unapologetic commercialisation of privatised corporations which has contributed to the more general unpopularity of private provision touched on below (see Table 6.4). But, despite the evidence of popular disillusion, the effectiveness of opposition appears limited. Judged in terms of outcomes, the privatised sector enjoys substantial benefits that speak of a very effective deployment of power by a corporate elite fully integrated into the dynamics of the New Corporate State. Regulation is conducted according to market principles with defined legal boundaries and is a limited threat to well-resourced corporations. The corporate elite has been expanded to include the managers, directors, shareholders and professional intermediaries who share in the wealth generated by privatised corporations. The large privatised corporations participate in the governance of the policy sectors in which they are the dominant economic forces. There have always been critics of the market and of capitalism; indeed complaints about the exercise of power are one of its defining features. The privatised sector continues to reward its corporate controllers who ensure that, to use that ancient phrase, 'the dogs bark but the caravan passes by'.

PARTNERSHIP AND THE NEW PUBLIC SERVICES INDUSTRY

The emphasis on the market, entrepreneurship and competition which lies at the heart of the Thatcherite turn to neoliberalism did not, of course, stop with privatisation. It brought comprehensive attempts to reform the whole public sector in a wave of change through 'the new public management'. As discussed in Chapter 5, the new public management gained credibility from the generalised questioning of the large provider state and gained inspiration from the organisational and management practices of the private sector. It often seemed that anything originating in the private sector was illuminated by a halo of progressive efficiency, and any traditional public sector activity was tarnished with the image of sclerotic bureaucracy. The emphasis on efficiency, as measured by management accounts, by operating budgets and by financial outcomes opened up fertile ground for the operation of private sector corporations who could promise and demonstrate efficiency gains. The unease felt by defenders of the public sector lay in the subordination of other criteria by which public services had conventionally been operated and especially professional standards and administrative values of egalitarianism, accountability and societal stability. It bears repetition that there is a persistent divergence of key public and private values with the public sector stressing lawfulness and impartiality against the private sector's profitability and efficiency (see van der Wal et al., 2008: 473).

Running through the whole debate about the role of the private sector in delivering public services is therefore a fundamental clash of values which on the one hand stress a pragmatic concern with delivery, symbolised by the Blairite phrase that 'what matters is what works'; and on the other hand argue that public services comprise collective entitlements which should be delivered with respect as part of the reciprocal obligations of citizenship between the individual and the government. The pragmatic response is illustrated by the Julius Review of the public services industry which concluded that although government bears the responsibility for delivering high quality public services, 'the question of who delivers them – whether it be the public, private or third sector – is essentially a practical one' (BERR, 2008: 70). Critics of delivery by private corporations would reject this appeal to common sense and instead would argue that services will deteriorate through managerial cynicism and a prime goal of profitability, leading to the corrosion of the intangible trust between the citizen and her government. Plant, for instance, is 'worried about the idea of abandoning the idea of service' and he notes that 'the idea of contract cannot replace the idea of common purpose which was central to the idea of the public service ethic' (Plant, 2003: 576–7). Since the compelling arguments in favour of private delivery tend to be precisely those pragmatic appeals to financial efficiency, it is especially poignant when reservations are expressed by accountants who challenge not only the financial advantages but also the very principles of private delivery. Thus, in a critical treatment of PFI, Shaoul (2005: 466) writes that 'PFI has the potential to destabilise the wider healthcare system' while Asenova and Beck (2010: 12) allege that 'PFI procurement in the UK and elsewhere, carries the possibility of establishing a new legacy of anti-democratic public sector governance'. As with privatisation, therefore, private delivery of public services alters the terms of the political debate as well as the balance of political forces. The following section explores the way in which corporations have come to create and operate within markets as partners in the area of non-privatised public services.

The creation of a public services industry is a major change in the provision of public services and in what used to be called 'public administration'.

It is a revolution comparable in importance to privatisation but is far less visible and far more complicated. The corporations that make up the public services industry are working with governmental bodies in public–private partnerships (PPPs) which include relationships of contracting, collaboration and complex networks. We are seeing a consolidation of 'partnership' between the public and the private sector in which the very terms public and private begin to lose their significance. The Julius review (BERR, 2008: 49) outlined seven types of partnership ranging from 'alliancing' to PFI. Bovaird (2006: 99) proposed a typology of types of partnership and speculated that we need new ways of visualising service delivery in which services are 'co-produced' with the involvement of citizens so that the production of services takes place within 'self-organising systems' that are distinguishable from either hierarchies or markets. This process of co-production through partnership began in the late 1980s with the extension of compulsory competitive tendering in the Local Government Act 1988 as a way of encouraging contracting out of services; and with the creation of the PFI and the change in procurement rules which originated from 1992 (Flinders, 2005: 220). The 1994 Conservative White Paper on competitiveness pressed for a new partnership with business declaring that 'this partnership requires detailed understanding and appreciation of business needs across all sectors of the economy' (DTI, 1994: 18). The Labour government accepted and built upon those developments after 1997 and became an enthusiastic proponent of partnerships as an expression of the collaborative approach embodied in the ideology of the 'Third Way'.

The public services industry represents the most advanced form of the partnership that is at the heart of the New Corporate State. The industrial side of this collaboration grew from a turnover of £42 bn in 1995–96 to £79 bn in 2007–08 at which point it accounted for about 33 per cent of the total cost of delivery of public services (BERR, 2008: 13). The service sectors involved are presented in Table 6.3 with examples of the corporations involved. Some corporations, such as Serco and Capita, are present in a

Table 6.3 Components of the public services industry

Managed Services – (Serco, Group 4 Securicor (G4S))
Information and Communication Technologies – (Capita, BAE Systems)
Business Process Outsourcing – (EDS, IBM)
Facilities Management – (Sodexho, Rentokil)
Construction services – (Balfour Beatty, Carillion)
Professional services and consulting – (Accenture, KPMG)

Source: BERR (2008: 22–3).

number of sectors, some are multinationals such as Skanska (Sweden) or Sodexho (France), and there are a range of associated corporations such as banks, infrastructure funds and private equity funds. In addition there are a range of third sector providers who account for perhaps 15 or 20 per cent of the market (UNISON, 2008: 21).

The study by Gosling analyses the corporations across 23 supply categories such as defence and long-term care (UNISON, 2008). This illustrates the huge variety of activities undertaken through the partnership route. So, for instance, the transfer of residential care for the elderly to the private sector is by now a familiar phenomenon but more than half of children's residential care places are now also provided by the private sector and even fostering is now a partnership activity. The National Fostering Agency, a large supplier of fostering services, is owned by the private equity firm Sovereign Capital (UNISON, 2008: 14).

PPP is a globalised phenomenon with the US by far the largest market, due partly to the private provision of health care, but PPP has become big business in a range of countries (Greve, 2010: 593). In Europe PPP and PFI has grown substantially but the UK public services industry is the most advanced and it is mainly in the anglophone countries that PPP has become an accepted tool of policy delivery. By the end of 2008 UK PPP contracts were worth about €61bn with contracts in the whole of the rest of Europe at only half that level (at €37bn, see IFSL, 2009: 3). Spain, France and Italy have substantial PPP sectors with Germany less enthusiastic. Most European investment is going into infrastructure and especially transport, rather than public services. The government has explored ways of assisting the UK PPP corporations to expand abroad and the CBI sees this as an area of UK comparative advantage (see CBI, 2007; BERR, 2008: 60) with great opportunities for market growth.

In her review of the UK industry DeAnne Julius noted that 'we have found a large and diverse collection of big and small, private and third sector enterprises which together produce nearly 6 per cent of GDP and whose 1.2 mn staff are proud to be engaged in delivering high quality services to the public and best value for money to the taxpayer' (BERR, 2008: Foreword). The industry lobbies hard for expansion of the market both in extending the services to be delivered by corporations and in extending the corporate share of the public finance committed to those services. The arguments employed include a critique of traditional bureaucratic delivery and profuse examples of where partnership has worked well. A powerful case has been made by the CBI which focuses on the decline in productivity in the public sector and compares it unfavourably with productivity increases in the market sector. The compelling argument is that 'this growing waste of resources has to be tackled urgently' (CBI, 2010a: 11) specifically by turning to private sector corporations and perhaps using them in new ways. Delivery through PPP has become a mainstream tool of government but it is still fragmented and corporations tend to be commissioned or contracted to deliver a service defined and monitored by public bodies. The CBI has pressed for a move to 'output-based commissioning' in which the corporation is paid by desirable outcomes (like people finding jobs or lowering the rate of re-offending) rather than being paid for inputs (such as training or counselling). The corollary is that the corporation should be given far greater discretion to design policy programmes and to implement them; this could be a creative process but it puts limits on political control and the very process of implementing policy can change the nature of the policy itself. There is a favourable environment for such radical ideas as committing whole policy or service areas to private delivery. The House of Lords report on PFI (Select Committee, 2010: 32) noted that 'there is scope to transfer more demand or output-related risk' (to the private sector); while the Julius Review observed that government could 'involve potential bidders at a higher level thereby commissioning an overall service, rather than combinations of individual inputs and services. This allows potential bidders greater flexibility in how to combine, procure and manage inputs to deliver services' (BERR, 2008: 73). This proposal visualises not only private delivery of services but entrusting corporations with the very process of defining policy options and choosing modes of implementation. So, for instance, instead of contracting out aspects of the prison service such as transporting prisoners, prison building, maintenance or training of offenders, why not commission the entire regime of punishment and remediation?

Serious evaluation of transfer of entire areas of public policy to the private sector is, of course, one aspect of the shift to governance and the rise of the regulatory state. Government does not have to deliver services 'in house' to secure desirable policy outcomes (Minister for Government Policy, 2011). It can exercise control though contracts, through regulation, and through negotiation in policy networks, including empowering local communities. This has happened in huge areas but the shift from public to private delivery is not neutral. It introduces different values, different organisations, different incentives and a different repertoire of choices. A nice example is provided by the unglamorous world of waste management. Municipal waste management was owned and provided by local government up to the late 1980s. Subsequently deregulation, contracting-out and privatisation have converted it into a significant market that is now dominated by consolidated waste management companies, many of them multinationals such as Onyx (French), SITA (French), Cleanaway (Australian) and Biffa (UK) (Davies, 2007). They are tending to pursue a model of integrated waste management which is attractive to government commissioners but it excludes smaller companies, is unsympathetic to recycling and leads to environmentally contentious solutions such as large scale incineration (Davies, 2007: 54). Moreover, as UNISON (2008: 35) has pointed out, the public services market has high transaction costs and there are pressures to negotiate large contracts which favour larger corporations. The tendency, as in waste management, has been to see the market consolidating into a few large suppliers. This allows the corporations to gain and exploit market power and to reduce the range of options on offer. In other words, turning to the public services industry has drawbacks in terms of a reduced capacity to develop policy options, to pursue alternative strategies, to control the corporations concerned and to ensure that the policy is not transformed in the process of implementation. These sorts of concerns prompted Flinders to ask whether PPP is a 'Faustian bargain' in which 'concerns regarding increased fragmentation, complexity and opaque accountability channels suggest that PPPs may involve substantial political and democratic costs' (Flinders, 2005: 234). His perceptive study of PPPs emphasises the curious commitment of the Labour governments to this approach which seemed ideologically doctrinaire in the absence of any clear, measureable evidence of efficiency benefits, and in the presence of vigorous opposition from the public sector unions. He attributes Labour's enthusiasm for PPPs to frustration with the slow pace of reform in the public services and to the Third Way strand of New Labour ideology but, in an otherwise perceptive article, he virtually ignores the lobbying influence of the corporations. The ability to expand PPP relied on a cadre of aggressive, ambitious corporations intent on building market share and on deploying political influence to do so. A key driver has been the political strategies of the larger public sector corporations.

There are good reasons for government bodies to enter into partnership with private providers and the industry has worked hard to make its case and to influence decision-makers. The campaigns waged by the corporations have been relatively open and included systematic efforts to win the support of Labour leaders. Such efforts have generated predictable criticism (see Osler, 2002: 127) including frequent attacks from the satirical magazine *Private Eye* and allegations of impropriety, such as the personal loan to the Labour Party of £1 mn made by the CEO of Capita, Ron Aldridge, who resigned in March 2006 partly to divert criticism. The political lobbying has exploited the elite linkages outlined in chapters 4 and 5 including a sophisticated programme of research and policy advocacy. For instance, the industry developed a close involvement with the IPPR which was very influential in the early years of the New Labour government and which promoted PPP through its reports and its

1999–2001 Commission on Public Private Partnerships. The CBI's Public Services Strategy Board has been an energetic source of lobbying. The Board describes its lobbying work as 'a campaign' and itemises a series of meetings and conferences to make their case and to engage closely with the 'public service practitioners' who are actually engaged in commissioning. It has pressed for 'a partnership approach' to develop creative and strategic commissioning so that 'conversations with ministers and shadow ministers showed a broad recognition of the value of pooling budgets and strategic commissioning in making services more effective and efficient' (CBI, 2010b: 11). The discourse is invariably about the noble and altruistic goal of delivering better services and lower costs; an innocent reader could overlook the underlying reality of profits, executive salaries and dividends.

Another effective mode of political engagement is to reach into government to influence policy postures. Labour welcomed the input of business advisers and the Business Secretary, John Hutton, commissioned a Public Services Industry Review chaired by DeAnne Julius which reported in July 2008. The conclusions of the Review were measured but amounted to an endorsement of private sector delivery and an argument that government should encourage its growth, at home and overseas. Hutton welcomed 'recommendations as to what more the government can do, as a policy maker, regulator and procurer to ensure that its full potential can be realised for the benefit of the public' (BERR, 2008: Forward). The Report was couched in the language of competition, arguing that 'government departments and local authorities should seek to introduce competitive challenge into areas of service delivery where it has not yet been tried and consider how best to incentivise further innovation in sectors where it already exists' (BERR, 2008: 70). The Review reinforced the standing and credibility of the public services industry and pointed up some intriguing aspects. It said almost nothing about corporate governance, about alternative corporate models such as PICs (public interest companies), or about social responsibility in the major corporations and therefore failed to address questions of trust and public confidence. Privatisation involves complete transfer of a service and is in practical terms irreversible. Partnership requires continuous engagement between corporations and government officials and is reversible. Government remains the source of funding and can choose to end some services or to bring others back 'in house'. Accordingly the Review observed that 'more than any other major industry the future of PSI is in the hands of government; conversely, the PSI can do more to directly affect the achievement of core government objectives than any other industry' (BERR, 2008: 75). This is a nice statement of the implications of partnership and shared governance and it underlines the imperative for the corporations to build reputation and trust, including persuasive demonstrations of corporate social responsibility, as a prerequisite for their commercial survival. In itself the Review also illustrated elite interpenetration and the integration of the industry into government policy formulation. It was undertaken by 30 members, including 13 officials or policy advisers, and 12 senior managers or business representatives. There were two union representatives but they were only added after protests from the TUC (UNISON, 2008: 34). The Review panel could hardly be described as disinterested, as symbolised in the person of the Chairman, DeAnne Julius. She had a distinguished career as a policy adviser but it is remarkable that up to December 2007, when she was appointed to head the Review, she was the senior non-executive director of Serco, one of the largest and most influential of the public service corporations.

The exercise of political influence by the public service corporations also takes the form of the classic ploy of recruitment of influentials. At the extreme this is a mode of elite circulation fairly typical of the 'revolving door' in the United States or France, or of the post-retirement careers of senior officials as seen in the *amakudari* system in Japan. The UNISON Report provides a remarkable account of recruitment of former ministers and officials. They itemise 13 Labour ministers and 11 senior civil servants or policy advisers who have taken on directorships or advisory posts with public service corporations. They include Alan Milburn (director of health care products firm Covidien); Patricia Hewitt (adviser to Cinven private hospitals group); and Hilary Armstrong (chair of waste company SITA's advisory committee). The officials include two former heads of the Civil Service (Lords Turnbull and Wilson) and the former industrialist and temporary civil servant, Sir Peter Gershon, the author of the influential Gershon efficiency review (Treasury, 2004) who became non-executive chairman of the outsourcing firm Vertex (see UNISON, 2008: 27–32). This cross-fertilisation of business people entering government, and the political and administrative elite joining corporations, was noted in Chapter 5. In many ways it is unexceptional and may be beneficial but it undoubtedly involves a degree of influence which can be criticised as part of a more general critique of elite dominance. Aside from this more general point, the pattern of appointments illustrates a new public services industry consolidating its position as an informed and respected partner in governance. Indeed, the industry is now the eighth largest sector (by market capitalisation) in the FT UK top 500 and has the largest number of corporations (*Financial Times*, 2012). Like the privatised utilities sector it has emerged as a new location of corporate power which has built up a constituency for continued expansion. In the UK there is still two thirds of government spending potentially available to boost profitable activity and an interesting new debate has opened up in the context of cutbacks in public spending. On the one hand, spending restraint is a threat to public sector contractors. On the other hand, it is also an opportunity as the spending crisis precipitates major cuts in direct government employment. A *Financial Times* headline captures the possibilities, 'outsourcing set to boom as contracts surge' (16 June 2012).

A nice parable was provided by the corporate engagement with the 2012 London Olympics. Allegedly the most commercialised in history, they were organised by a private company (LOCOG) whose CEO, Paul Deighton, was a millionaire former COO of Goldman Sachs Europe, and was paid £700,000 in 2011 (LOCOG, 2011). This corporate cross-fertilisation went further as Deighton was extraordinarily given a peerage and brought into government as Commercial Secretary to the Treasury by Cameron in September (Gibson, 2012). Were the Games organised primarily to meet the priorities of the public, or those of the 44 corporate sponsors such as Coca Cola, McDonalds and Samsung who contributed £700 million?

With the creation of this new market sector within the economy, balances of political interests and economic benefits have inevitably shifted; there will be gainers and losers. The hope is that the citizens as consumers and beneficiaries of public services will gain in quality and availability while the taxpayer will gain through greater efficiency. This has been the focus of most evaluations of PPP and the results remain ambiguous. But this is only one aspect of a redistribution of benefits. Since a new market has been created, market dynamics come into play and motives of profitability and personal gain enter the picture. In the efficiency-generating magic of competitive markets the profit motive is typically seen as a healthy incentive. Partnerships therefore accept the need for profit or 'return on capital' in commissioning and collaborating with the private sector. This does, however, introduce a new element into the delivery of core public services based on a radically different set of legitimate motivations for one of the partners. A public service ethos is complemented by a profit-seeking ethos; the two may be compatible but they may also conflict. A CBI report on globalisation of PPPs is rather upset to note that 'PPPs are still met with scepticism and a belief that the public interest is being sacrificed in favour of shareholder needs' (CBI, 2007: 8). Is this scepticism justified?

On profitability many of the public services corporations appear to have made very good profits from public sector work although overall figures are hard to come by. Some sub-sectors, such as consulting, have clearly yielded very substantial income streams and have generated criticism from observers and the press (Craig, 2006). Some corporations have grown very quickly from a very low base. Capita is a particularly impressive example of an enterprise that started life in 1984 as a modest consulting arm of CIPFA (Chartered Institute of Public Finance and Accountancy). After a management buyout it was listed in 1991 to become by 2012 the fourth largest corporation in the support services sector with revenues of £2.9 billion and 40,000 employees. Profits have enabled corporations to reward their shareholders, banks and senior management, and to that extent surplus has been extracted from the public sector. It would be argued, of course, that gains from efficiency mean that surplus has also been re-invested in the public sector. Since secure profits allow stability, innovation and longer-term planning, an important aspect of the governance partnership is whether government bodies should assume a responsibility similar to that of the utility regulators to ensure that corporations behaving reasonably should be assured of a reasonable return on capital. In other words, should negotiation over contracts be relatively generous in the interests of keeping the provider corporations profitable and therefore available to continue to supply services? There is clearly something of that attitude at work, with public bodies hesitant about enforcing good performance. The NAO has noted the soft treatment of corporations, commenting that 'we normally find very few penalties applied to payments to contractors. One reason for few penalties is that public clients do not always enforce the contract. . . . Sometimes public clients fear that applying penalties will harm their relationship with the contractors and cause further performance degradation' (NAO, 2010a: 108). Of course, corporations will experience similar pressures to maintain good relations and we could expect 'relational contracting' to develop in which a close working relationship is formed based on trust and mutual accommodation instead of strict adherence to contractual terms. Mutual accommodation over the level of profits was seen in the early actions of the Coalition in July 2010 when the Cabinet Office Minister, Frances Maude, began negotiations with the CEOs of 19 of the biggest public services contractors in order to renegotiate contracts as part of the public spending reductions overseen by the 'Efficiency and Reform Board' (Cabinet Office, 2010).

The profitability of the public services sector is not restricted to the operational corporations themselves. Benefits are shared across the corporate elite in law, accounting, consulting, and in finance through banks and private equity. The role of finance has been emphasised by some of the sternest critics of PPP and of its PFI dimension. For Asenova and Beck the huge attraction of government contracting for corporations is that it provides a secure, reliable and low-risk return on investment. Accordingly 'finance capital is itself the driver for the creation of PFI' and they argue that politicians have been complicit in creating returns for banks. Hence, 'it is part and parcel of the PFI agenda to create new profit opportunities for finance capital, irrespective of the negative effects which the creation of these new profit opportunities will have on other stakeholders including consumers of public services and public sector employees' (Asenova and Beck, 2010: 4, 3; see also Shaoul, 2005: 465). We do not have to accept the full weight of this critique to accept that substantial returns are being secured by the financial sector. On the now notorious Norfolk and Norwich Hospital Trust PFI it has been asserted that the average rate of interest over 37 years is 10 per cent (Edwards, 2010: 144) and it is clear that the financial sector has often outmanoeuvred the public sector commissioners. A notable example is refinancing of PFI contracts. Crudely the contract is awarded on the basis of an interest rate which reflects the risk of not securing the contract. Once the contract is awarded it represents a very low-risk income stream which can be refinanced at a much lower rate of interest. The public sector bodies did not anticipate this windfall gain which generated huge additional surpluses from some of the early Labour PFI contracts. Thus, again with the Norfolk and Norwich Hospital Trust, the contractors, which included Serco, operating through the Octagon Healthcare special purpose vehicle (UNISON, 2008: 42), generated a £116 mn refinancing gain. The NHS Trust managed to claw back only 29 per cent of this gain (NAO, 2010a: 109).

One final element of the gains and losses arising from PPP is the vexed question of risk. The transfer of risk has always been one of the key arguments in favour of PPP and particularly of the PFI component. If PPP contractors enter into supply contracts they accept the risk of not delivering against performance targets and are therefore strongly motivated to perform well and to avoid the risk of non-compliance. This shifting of risk from the public to the private sector is cited as one of the main benefits of employing the public services industry. The major flaw in this argument is the illusion that government can escape the ultimate responsibility for public service delivery, especially when those services are essential, visible or life threatening. As the NAO dryly remarked, 'ultimate responsibility for delivery always remains with the public sector' (NAO, 2010a: 88). The full horror of what can go wrong was seen in the failure of the Metronet contracts to upgrade sections of the London Underground. When two of the companies failed, Transport for London had to honour their loan guarantees with a net loss to the taxpayer of up to £410 mn (NAO, 2010a: 88) and further expense in setting up new arrangements to protect this totemic and indispensible piece of infrastructure. The Lords Select Committee report observed that 'the failure of the London Underground Metronet PFP gave private finance projects in general a bad name. Yet this project was exceptional' (Select Committee, 2010: 23). Perhaps not wholly exceptional. When the huge private security corporation G4S failed to deliver enough security staff to control the London Olympics the government was obliged to step in with army personnel in what the CEO, Nick Buckles, conceded to the Home Affairs Select Committee was 'a humiliating shambles' (Hyde, 2012). Other projects, such as the partnership between Siemens Business Systems and National Savings and Investments have produced good results and hugely improved the administration of the National Savings (see NAO, 2010a: 89). Perhaps the experience of the hapless Mr Buckles provides a remedy for corporate risk evasion. If senior corporate executives appeared routinely before Parliamentary Committees, like ministers or civil servants, new conventions of corporate political accountability could be developed.

The rapid development of this new public services industry is the corporate face of a startling transformation in the administration of public services and in the growth of shared 'governance'. Delivery of public services by corporations presents challenges for public sector officials who have to commission services; for the corporations who have to operate to deliver services to contract while maintaining profitability; and for politicians and the system of political accountability since new organisations are outside the standard expectations of control and accountability. If corporations are to work as contractors for government bodies they are operating in a peculiar market which is marked by competition over bidding for contracts, but by cooperation and partnership in the operation of services. The profit-making ethos must be supplemented with a public service ethos and a relationship of trust and meaningful partnership is necessary on both sides. Big corporations like Siemens and Serco are in the business for the long run; reputations and brands become part of their capital and need to be protected. Hence we might expect the public services industry to develop modes of operation and of organisation that were less purely profit driven than corporations operating in conventional markets. Alternative non-profit modes of delivery include charities and the variety of third sector corporations who are important but operate on a small scale, with around 15 per cent of the market. Another possibility would be to encourage the formation of public interest companies (PICs) although these are formed by, and dependent on, government (e.g. Prabhakar, 2004; Flinders, 2005: 219). Despite the partnership protestations, therefore, the public service industry is predominately made up of corporations with conventional UK or multinational corporate governance arrangements who are mandated to pursue profit and shareholder value. There are no exceptional social obligations built into their corporate governance principles, and it is not surprising if the public sector partners retain a latent concern that goals of profitability, financial gain and shareholder benefit skew their service delivery commitments.

Concerns about the merits of private sector delivery are shared by the wider public. Polling by MORI has shown a strong vein of scepticism

Table 6.4   Approval for private provision of public services

Question: To what extent do you agree or disagree with the following statement? 'In principle, public services should be run by government or local authorities, rather than by private companies'.

	agree	disagree	strongly agree	strongly disagree
2000	66	17	27	3
June 2001	78	9	45	3
June 2008	79	14	50	5

Source: Ipsos-MORI, Trend Poll, available at www.ipsos-mori.com/research (accessed 16 July 2010).

about private sector delivery which has intensified over the 2000s, as indicated in Table 6.4.

The polls hence show a strongly felt objection to private delivery which had risen from a quarter to half of the population by 2008. This takes us back to the discussion of trust in business in Chapter 5 and underlines the mismatch between a governmental enthusiasm for private sector delivery and a resigned scepticism felt by many citizens (or consumers).

CONCLUSIONS

This chapter has sought to illustrate how the political power of business has been deployed in the UK to create new markets and in the process to extend the role of corporations as governing institutions. The extension of markets has been a generalised trend for 30 years but this chapter has emphasised its extent through privatisation and through partnership with the public services industry. Extension of markets is in fact a code for transfer of influence to large corporations and transfer of policy initiative from government to negotiated governance involving cooperation with corporations in models of partnership. Government has been explicit in advocacy of partnership which has become the characteristic policy-making model in an increasing number of important policy areas of key importance to the public and political debate. Energy policy and social care were mentioned above, but partnership working applies to a range of areas such as transport, personal security, housing and communications. State provision remains central in health and education but here too market alternatives are serious contenders. The sharing of governance with corporations means that corporate priorities are more likely to be built into policy options and the process becomes self-replicating in a pattern of path dependency as corporations use their governing authority to sustain market relations.

The extension of markets into what was formerly the sphere of public sector delivery through privatisation and PPPs is usually considered from the point of view of government and its ability to secure cheaper and more effective delivery of services, but it is assumed that government remains in the driving seat. In contrast, the discussion above has emphasised the institutional authority of the corporate sector which has metamorphosed from making demands on government bodies to actually making policy in areas such as energy policy and social policy. Here we see the practical impact of corporations becoming governing institutions. Their role in governance has been consolidated as the competence of state administration of services has been both questioned and partially dismantled. The role of government and the state has been reduced as public services have been 'commodified' and government has retreated to become a commissioner and a regulator of services provided by private sector corporations. Government by regulation is a very different creature than government by hierarchy. It replaces command and control with rule making, negotiation and persuasion. This might be benign but it is certainly different and requires new political understandings to secure public benefits.

We have seen therefore not only the increase in corporate power in the UK analysed in Chapter 5, but also the deployment of that power greatly to expand the corporate sector and therefore to expand the incomes and wealth under the control of corporations. That wealth has benefited those who control corporations – mainly their directors and senior managers but also shareholders, the professional corporate intermediaries and especially the financial sector. The expansion of the corporate sector has been accomplished in symbiosis with the huge accumulation of financial wealth analysed in Chapter 5. We have therefore also seen a maturing of the corporate elite which has increased its size, its wealth, its status and its influence over the other key institutions of the state. As argued in Chapter 4, this political redistribution is reflective of a new and relatively stable political settlement in the shape of the New Corporate State and it represents a distinctive new model of political economy.

We can round off these three chapters which have concentrated on Britain by considering the wider international influence of the British model. The first point to make is that this is a model of political economy that is a radical departure from the traditional 'English' model of a liberal capitalism marked by *laissez faire* and an arms-length relationship between the large corporation and the state. It is based on partnership rather than adversarial relations, on institutional integration and elite collaboration, and it is new. Forged in the foundries of Thatcherism it is a bold experiment in unleashing corporate capitalism. It was inspired by American experience but has substantial differences from the American model (Moran, 2009: 169–71), it may have more in common with New Zealand in its conscious attempts to create an opportunity society (Lunt, 2010: 32). Neither, of course, is it 'European' yet since Britain is inescapably part of Europe this creates tensions as Britain seeks to project its model onto a European canvas. Gamble (2003: 145) has explored these tensions and reflects that this new model of capitalism 'proclaimed its superiority over other models, and was set out as the template for all the world's economies to copy, including those in Europe'. This poses intriguing questions. The UK, or rather England, has historically been renowned as a model for others; is it still? Many of the drivers that created the New Corporate State in the UK are common to other OECD countries; are they following a similar route? Indeed, is the British model influential in global governance? Chapter 7 addresses these questions within a wider discussion of the political power of the corporation at the global level.

7. Multinational corporations as partners in global governance

INTRODUCTION: FROM NATIONAL TO GLOBAL CORPORATE POWER

Chapters 4, 5 and 6 explored the exercise of corporate power in the UK. This chapter continues the exploration but examines corporate power in the global arena and emphasises the complex interdependence of the national and international exercise of corporate influence. The earlier chapters sought to demonstrate that corporations have operated as governing institutions in the UK and that they have consolidated that institutional power through the elite construction of a 'New Corporate State'. Chapter 4 identified globalisation as one factor driving elite reconfigurations so that international operation within global markets emerges as a decisive enhancement of corporate power, arguably the factor that differentiates corporate power post-1990 from earlier incarnations. At the global level the exercise of corporate power is taken for granted as an obvious and constant element in governance (Fuchs, 2007; Ougaard, 2010), but how does global business power impact on the national setting, and vice versa? As we saw in Chapter 3, multinational corporations have distinctive sources of power, but every multinational political actor is simultaneously a multiple national political actor. Are we simply therefore seeing a reduction in the authority of the nation-state every time it deals with a single multinational, or corporations collectively, or is something more complex going on? It might be that the new relationship of partnership between corporations and government at the national level is also operating at the international level. Similarly we might be seeing the major features of the British New Corporate State also emerging as features of global governance.

Uncertainties about the interaction of national and global corporate power are not confronted in the literature on global governance or comparative politics. Very few authors examine the impact of multinationals on the operation of domestic politics and policy making in developed countries. A rare exception is Colin Leys (2001), who draws pessimistic conclusions about the vulnerability of British politics to global market forces. It is important to extend Leys' project for three reasons. First, the continued influence of global corporate power on domestic politics could pre-empt options for domestic policy reform. Second, it makes it more productive to generalise from the British experience if we can conclude that other states are subject to those same global pressures that bear on the British state. Third, there is the possibility that the British New Corporate State has projected or uploaded its partnership model of dealing with corporations onto the global level. Rather than using insights about global corporate power to explain developments in Britain, perhaps the British model can be used to explain developments at the global level?

It has become an orthodoxy in the study of global political economy that the neoliberal order was inspired and created by the Reagan and Thatcher governments to produce what Bobbitt identified as a new form of state, the 'market state' (see Chapter 5). As has constantly been reaffirmed, the neoliberal tag is misleading and it might be better to term this a 'post-liberal' order featuring competition between states for the benefits available from multinationals in globalised, oligopolistic markets. Hence the alternative term of 'competition state' employed by Cerny (1997, 2010). The origins of global post-liberalism are invariably ascribed to the USA with its influence over international organisations, its championing of market solutions, its assertion of corporate rights, and its articulation of the Washington Consensus (Germain, 2010: 57). And indeed, as the global hegemon at the turn of the century, the US influence was immense. But the post-liberal market model arguably owes as much to the UK pioneers as to those of the USA. As Leys notes, 'Thatcher was not reacting to pressure from forces operating in an already existing global economy but played a leading part in constructing a global economy' (Leys, 2001: 34; see also Gamble, 2009b: 105). The Anglo-Saxon model had to be manufactured before it could be exported. Multiple institutional forces led other countries to pursue the policies embodied in the Anglo-Saxon model as explored in a substantial comparative politics literature (for instance Horsfall, 2010 and Chapter 10) and those forces also evolved as constituent elements in regimes of global governance. The UK's New Corporate State became an inspiration for the evolution of a post-liberal political economy at the global level. The influence came through changes in rules (for instance, liberalisation of capital markets); by changes in norms (for instance, deregulation and privatisation); and by changes in cultures (managerialism penetrating the public sector). The UK was the success story of post-liberalism and the virtues of markets – recall its remarkable economic miracle with 15 years of continuous economic growth, second only to Canada in the G7, from 1997 to 2007.

If we can see elements of the UK model also operating within global governance, then conclusions about the extent of corporate power in the UK can be applied also to global governance and simultaneously we can recognise how the UK is integrated into global power relations. So, what are the similarities? First, the large corporation is a governing institution at both the national (UK) and global levels, an argument first advanced in chapters 1 and 3. Second, if there is an elite of large corporations at the national level, that is also evident at the international level. Most global industrial sectors are dominated by a small number of multinational corporations who similarly provide a power base for a financial and managerial elite. Third, they share a managerial outlook partially articulated by UK-based reputational intermediaries in the form of the global law, accounting and consultancy firms. Fourth, the UK argument about growing inequality as evidence of, and as a consequence of, corporate power also operates at the international level where we have seen striking increases in global income and wealth inequality at the top end of the income distribution (see Wade, 2007; Stiglitz, 2012). Fifth, distinctive institutional features of the UK or Anglo-Saxon model have been reproduced at the international level. We could point to flexible labour markets, to the global spread of competition policy, or to privatisation. A central institutional example, explored in greater depth in Chapter 10, is UK-style corporate governance.

In the UK these features of the Anglo-Saxon model were created in a distinctive political setting in which the power of the state was employed, paradoxically, to reduce the direct intervention of the apparatus of the state in the economy, welfare and the delivery of public services. In the international sphere the political framework of authority is far weaker or non-existent. Corporations and influential states have had to work almost in a vacuum to create modes of global governance and the UK has stood as an example of how the economy could be structured in the interests of global capital. The UK-style 'partnership' between government and business, outlined in chapters 2 and 6, was taken to the global level by UK-based corporations acting as vigorous 'norm entrepreneurs'. As Flohr et al (2010: 244–5) argue,

> UK business is used to a cooperative approach to policy-making with government as an individual partner – which above all stands in contrast to the US style of business–government relations. Therefore, British corporations are more likely to adopt the same expectations and style when interacting on the international level.

The foundations of a governance shaped by partnerships between states and corporations at the global level are explored in more depth in this chapter. It advances an institutional analysis of multinational corporate power and looks at the basis of that power through a consideration of institutional rules, norms and cultures. Most space is devoted to the most obvious source of power in the shape of favourable rules but the analysis of norms and cultures is equally important, and more novel, in discussion of MNCs. Running throughout the chapter is the theme of partnership, with governments and other global players working with corporations in a variety of modes including regulatory networks. Going beyond partnership the chapter also speculates about the way in which corporate power has become sufficiently independent of nation-states, and so embedded in global regimes that it has taken on almost a constitutional character. It considers the possibility that the institutional power of the multinational corporate form, and the collective weight of multinationals, has created a 'new global settlement' that has come to accept the role of multinationals as a cornerstone of the global political economy. Even more speculatively it then raises the question, which is examined in later chapters, of whether the corporate elite should accept a level of governmental responsibility and adopt a more overt leadership role in dealing with issues of global poverty and environmental degradation.

GLOBAL RULES FAVOURING MNCS

By the year 2000 'The West', under the leadership of the United States and the UK, had constructed a global market which provided an open, predictable and supportive framework within which multinationals could invest, coordinate operations and pursue profits and shareholder value. The global market can only partly be described as a 'free market'. It is skewed to the interests of global corporations, it is oligopolistic, competition is often constrained and the market regulations are aimed at controlling national governments as much as at regulating MNCs. This section outlines the regulatory regime that sustains the global market; the following two sections consider the issue of whether the global system of rules has attained a level of stability and autonomy, and the means by which these rules are enforced in practice.

The global market has been constructed on two simple legal principles that have the same profound, longstanding and largely unquestioned influence as limited liability. They are 'national treatment' and the 'most favoured nation' principles. These principles have been enshrined in the World Trade Organization (WTO) but they are applied in a variety of settings. The 'national treatment' principle prevents foreign goods, services or intellectual property being treated less favourably than the domestic equivalent. This prevents domestic products being assisted by subsidy, tax or favourable regulation in preference to foreign products. In effect it means that support and concessions secured by domestic corporations have to be extended also to foreign corporations. In fact the principle is asymmetric because, as Goldman and Palan (2006: 191) point out, it does not prevent more favourable treatment being given to foreign corporations. Multinationals may therefore secure more generous subsidies and tax breaks without breaching the national treatment principle. The 'most favoured nation' principle requires that a state must grant to all other nations the same terms that it offers to its most favoured nation (Picciotto, 2011: 301). This again requires equality of treatment for multinational corporations regardless of their national country of origin. If these two principles can be applied across all major economies, and if they can be policed effectively, then they provide the global market, the legal certainty, the predictability, and the restraint of competition that allows corporations to operate in a benign global legal environment.

These principles have become part of the DNA of the key international agencies and networks which regulate the global economy – the IMF, WTO, World Bank, the BIS, the G7/8 (or now G20) and the OECD. The WTO, created in 1995 as the more institutionalised successor to the GATT, is a central actor and lightning rod. It supervises multilateral agreements between the 155 members (China joined in 2001, Russia eventually joined in 2012) covering trade in goods, services, intellectual property and some investment issues. The WTO operates in a quasi-judicial fashion as a court overseeing a dispute resolution mechanism and appealing for legitimacy to procedural fairness and the involvement of developing countries. Like all international organisations the WTO is formally an association of nation-states but scholars such as Sell (2000: 174) have argued that the driving force behind the agreements have been 'US private sector actors' (see also Picciotto, 2011: 321). The conventional interpretation of international regulatory organisations is that they were reinvented during the 1980s, mainly by the USA, in the service of global neoliberalism. 'The World Bank and the IMF's loans and the GATT/WTO trade agreements played an especially important and visible role in the formulation of neoliberal prescriptions, to their legitimation and in their enforcement worldwide' (Chorev and Babb, 2009: 461). This is, of course, the Washington Consensus thesis ably described and criticised by Joseph Stiglitz (2002: 16). But the Washington Consensus was about liberalisation, privatisation, small government and freeing up markets. It does not appear directly to address the interests of corporations and one of the most intensive studies of these organisations, Ngaire Woods' *The Globalizers* (2006), barely mentions corporations.

Expressed in terms of institutional rules, the international organisations constructing the Washington Consensus support corporations through embedding the principles of national treatment and most favoured nation. More specifically the WTO and the IMF have opened up new markets by negotiating reductions in tariffs and in protectionist measures. To give two examples: (1) the IMF encouraged Mexico down the path of liberalisation after its debt crisis of 1982 (Woods, 2006: chapter 4) thus bolstering the influence of the new business elite orientated towards cooperation with foreign corporations (Gates, 2009: 65); similarly, (2) the IMF and the World Bank helped to persuade the Indian government to pursue a pro-market policy of liberalisation from 1991 onwards (Sengupta, 2009), again allowing MNCs to gain entry into the huge Indian market. New markets have also been encouraged through the consistent endorsement of reduced government, liberalisation of markets and privatisation which has created new industrial sectors in areas like telecoms where multinationals can expand or form joint ventures with privatised domestic corporations. Throughout these processes, although only nations can initiate dispute settlements within the WTO machinery, there is ample opportunity for states to further the interests of 'their' corporations. The record of WTO disputes shows the most disputes being initiated by the US and the EU who use the WTO machinery to provide a detailed, case-specific, but precedent-creating means of policing the national treatment and most favoured nation principles.

There has thus grown up an international legal framework and administrative apparatus which works to create free markets in respect of trade in goods, in services – where FDI has grown hugely in recent years – and also in intellectual property. It has been argued that this framework, and particularly the WTO, has created a global economic constitution. In formal legal terms this is almost certainly not the case (Cass, 2005), but the idea of a 'constitutionalisation' of rules does have analytical purchase when considered as the embedding of a dominant regime (Gill, 2002), a point we come back to in the conclusion. It is striking, however, that there is no constitutional apparatus for regulating investment or enforcing competition policy. The USA has, since 1947, consistently resisted a treaty on investment despite attempts to negotiate an agreement through the OECD. Again, this appears to have been driven by the interests of US corporations who do not want to be subject to international obligations in relation to trade, employment, local content and so on. There is therefore no codified international law regulating relations between MNCs and host countries. Governments can only control those elements of multinationals that operate within their domestic jurisdiction and have limited ability to respond to the substantial market power a multinational might possess through its 'ownership' advantages of access to finance, technology, brands or simply global market share. One conventional way to respond at a global level would be through reinforcing competition enforced by a global antitrust regime and by a competition agency such as DG Comp (Directorate General for Competition) which operates at the regional level in the EU. But, as with investment, the USA has opposed the creation of a global competition regime (Wilks, 2010: 742) and there are fragmented, partial and often weak domestic competition authorities equipped only with bilateral treaties to address on an international level the standard abuses of competition, including restrictive practices, anti-competitive mergers, abuse of dominance and international cartels. Thus, it can be argued, the US and other OECD countries have favoured multinationals by international rules which benefit corporations, whilst inhibiting international rules which control them.

The Stability and Autonomy of the Global Regime

The system of global rules favouring multinationals was consolidated in the 1990s as part of a post-liberal economic order, which prompts two questions. First, has global market regulation come under fatal challenge resulting from a wave of criticism and doubt stretching from the 1999 protests against the WTO in Seattle to the 2008–09 financial crisis? Second, is this global market still governed by US hegemony or has it become autonomous, regulated by a mix of bodies including the multinational elite as well as key nation-states?

On the first question, these rule systems appear vulnerable to the wave of criticism of international organisations and of global capitalism itself. The WTO has been suffering from a legitimacy crisis since the late 1990s (Esty, 2002), as symbolised by the chaotic breakdown of the Ministerial Meeting in Seattle in November 1999. The legitimacy crisis transmuted into a substantive crisis during the 2000s with repeated failures to deliver on the Doha Round, and the questioning of the neoliberal basis on which the WTO operates reinforced by the 2008–09 financial crisis. The symbolism of Seattle was matched ten years later by Gordon Brown's declaration at the end of the G20 London Summit on 2 April 2009 that 'the old Washington consensus is over' (Painter, 2009). The prolonged WTO crisis has been extensively analysed with critiques of unwieldy decision making, coalition game playing by its member countries and a determination by developing countries to protect their own interests (Capling and Higgott, 2009). What is less effectively considered in the trade-policy literature is the impact on the operations and influence of the organisations that actually dominate world trade, the corporations themselves.

It is the actual, the alleged and the potential exploitative practices of the MNCs that have fuelled the anti-WTO, anti-globalisation and anti-capitalist activists – what Schweickart (2011: 5) calls 'the counter project'. The scale of protest is wide with a sophisticated resort to digital technology and a profusion of critical websites, but it is often not very deep (Hatcher, 2003). Nonetheless, it spawned a passionate, highly visible and polemical critique which includes writers such as Hanahoe (2003) and Hertz (2001) but was most effectively captured in Klein's *No Logo* (2002). Klein concentrated on 'the all-star multinationals that have been the focus of this book [and] are the celebrity face of global capitalism'. She stressed the exploitation of brands and focused her criticism on the abusive behaviour of (mainly US) retail corporations. Her study is a litany of criticism of corporations from Nike and Wal-Mart to Mattel, Microsoft and, of course, McDonalds. But while many of the issues raised are important and emotive, and direct action intensified after the financial crisis, including the highly visible Occupy movement, the targets of the activists are ill-defined and the corporate response is impressive.

Corporations have responded to the protests of the activists by developing elaborate corporate social responsibility policies as examined in Chapter 10. Meanwhile, home governments have reacted to WTO weakness by turning to bilateral agreements. Over 400 such agreements had been notified to the WTO by the end of 2007 and Dieter notes that the big multinational home countries have been in the lead. These agreements are more favourable to MNCs than the WTO multilateral compromises, thus 'the United States now seems to offer PTAs (Preferential Trading Agreements) to those countries that are willing to accept the (market opening) US template . . . which puts particular emphasis on intellectual property rights and market opening in financial services' (Dieter, 2009: 395).

Here again the home country support of their multinationals continues to be important. While, therefore, criticism of bodies regulating the global market has become more acute, and popular trust in business and MNCs has deteriorated, the rule system that facilitates growth and profitable operations by MNCs appears to be intact.

The second question raised at the beginning of this section was whether the institutions governing the global market were still dependent on US intervention and hegemony, or whether the regulatory regime had acquired a degree of autonomy. Disentangling the power of multinationals from the power of the United States is no easy task. Until very recently MNCs have been predominantly associated with the USA which in 1980 accounted for over 40 per cent of the stock of FDI (Jones, 2005a: 33). Moreover, the very model of multinational corporate form and organisation was associated with the US invention of the corporate system of industrial production (Djelic, 1998: 23) whilst, by the end of the century, the USA was the world's most powerful nation, militarily as well as economically. The implications of its global dominance have been profound. Its ability to dominate international organisations and to set the rules for international economic governance could hardly be doubted. Indeed, the very phrase 'Washington Consensus' stresses a US design and the whole post-Reagan neoliberal global economic orthodoxy created a world order which empowered the world's largest MNCs (Hanahoe, 2003: 13). What is less often emphasised is the supportive role of Thatcher and the UK in promoting, inspiring and legitimating that order both globally and through European market creation.

It is interesting, in this light, to return to one of the classic fault lines in the study of international business power. Is the influence of multinationals simply an extension of the power of their home states (as state-centric comparativists would have it), or have global corporations, global markets and an international society taken on an autonomous and relatively stable existence? This book falls into the latter camp. As a governing institution the multinational corporation has become part of a global economic governance that is not fully autonomous from powerful nation-states, but it does share power with them. Two indicators of relative autonomy can be identified in the form of codes of conduct and partnerships resulting in shared regulation.

Codes of conduct for MNCs date back to the first code issued by Shell in 1976. Such codes would be more convincing if they were designed, negotiated and policed by international organisations such as the ILO and the OECD who have developed their own codes. The OECD Guidelines for Multinational Corporations originated in 1976 but are regarded as weak, with no enforcement mechanism, while the UN attempt to create guidelines through its Centre on Transnational Corporations was opposed by large corporations and fell by the wayside when the Centre was abolished in 1993. Instead, and often in reaction to activist campaigns, corporations have developed their own codes of conduct on an individual or sector-wide basis. Such codes proliferated in the mid-1990s and it is easy to be cynical about their vague, glossy and hyperbolic statements of good intent without any compliance mechanism. But even Klein (2002: 432) accepts that some codes 'are nonetheless more substantial than a simple statement of good intentions' and Ougaard (2006: 247) sees both codes and CSR initiatives as having the potential to improve global governance.

By the mid-2000s codes of conduct had become more serious, sophisticated and in some cases effective enough to be regarded as 'soft law'. In a thorough analysis Fuchs (2007: 119–33) plots five generations of code development which are stages in the evolution of self-regulation by individual corporations or groups of corporations building up to standards of international best practice. She sees this as contributing to the structural power of MNCs and observes that 'if standards with sufficiently stringent regulations for environmental and social conduct were to become the de facto norm for business practice ... international governmental regulation would indeed become unnecessary' (Fuchs, 2007: 133). In pursuit of this vision NGOs and advocacy bodies monitor conformity to codes and provide an informal international avenue of public accountability (Lloyd, 2008). The prospects for the implementation of stringent standards are mixed. There are, for instance, a bewildering profusion of codes covering issues from labour standards to corruption and environmental responsibility. There are some global standards in the form of global codes such as ISO 14000 (on environmental management) or SA8000 (on global social accountability) and there is the UN Global Compact launched by Kofi Annan, the UN Secretary General in 1999. All these codes are voluntaristic: the main sanctions and enforcement mechanisms come from transparency, monitoring by NGOs and campaigns in the media and on the web which can be surprisingly effective, especially for consumer-facing corporations reliant on brands and reputation.

The argument that these mechanisms of global market regulation have taken on a life of their own is substantiated by the growth of a global civil society. There has been a population explosion of NGOs and of highly visible initiatives such as the Fair Trade movement which has moved from instinctive critique of corporations towards engagement, partnership and cooperative monitoring or certification of corporate behaviour. This move to 'multi-stakeholder initiatives' (Haufler, 2006: 96) clearly causes concerns about co-optation (Jordan and Stevenson, 2003: 43) and there has, for instance, been criticism of the WWF programmatic engagement with a variety of prominent multinationals (Huisman, 2012), but it has also given rise to celebration. Thus Yaziji and Doh (2009: 182) conclude 'that corporations and NGOs will interact with increasing frequency, intensity and, potentially with greater creativity and innovativeness'. They see a joint interest in co-regulation in processes that may involve national governments but which are relatively independent from them. Indeed, Vogel (2010: 474) has identified a growth in 'civil regulation' in which the global civil society, centred on NGOs, has developed 'new non-state political mechanisms for governing global firms and markets'.

Judgements on the effectiveness and desirability of global self-regulation by corporations monitored by a global civil society will vary with the issue, the policy area, the corporation and, of course, the viewpoint of the observer. Corporations have an interest in keeping at arms' length from interventionist government regulators but they have no interest in anarchy. Galbraith might have overstated the drive towards stable corporate planning but he was right to emphasise the corporate desire for stability and predictability. Moreover, self-regulation is also a rational corporate strategy which helps the participants to shape market rules in ways that limit competition or inconvenience competitors (Haufler, 2006: 219; Yaziji and Doh, 2009: 181). In standard setting self-regulation is particularly well developed (Büthe and Mattli, 2011). The important point, from the perspective of our analysis, is that corporate self-regulation, in a global setting, establishes a degree of autonomy from home governments and particularly from the United States.

The growth in global regulatory autonomy by corporations can be examined more rigorously through a categorisation of modes of global regulation. Haufler (2006: 93) distinguished traditional regulation (top-down, enforced by national governments); self-regulation (by corporations and trade associations); co-regulation (by governments and corporations in partnership); and stakeholder regulation (by multiple stakeholders including NGOs and unions). She identifies a shift away from traditional regulation and towards co- and stakeholder regulation. The key development underlying this transition is the growth in 'partnership'. Despite the residual authority of the nation-state it can be argued that MNCs can govern sectors of the global economy alone, but, in addition, they demonstrably operate as partners in governance together with national governments, international agencies and not-for-profit organisations. A surge in research on transnational public–private partnerships has identified 'a hybrid type of governance, in which nonstate actors co-govern along with state actors for the provision of collective goods, and adopt governance functions that have formerly been the sole authority of sovereign nation-states' (Schäferhoff et al., 2009: 451–2; see also Hale and Held, 2011). The rules that PPPs develop provide a governance structure in relation to policy issues or to whole economic systems.

The discussion so far of the regime of global governance has stressed the way in which rules facilitate the operation and growth of MNCs. We have reviewed the role of national (home) governments and the influence of international organisations, both of which are founded on a system of sovereign nation-states. The post-liberal regime that developed from the late 1980s was structured most obviously by the USA but also drew on the UK model. The regime has maintained its essential operation despite a wave of 'anti-capitalist' protests and it has developed a substantial degree of autonomy and escaped the effective control of leading nation states. The argument therefore affirms the role of corporations not only in benefiting from the rules which constitute global governance, but actually making and enforcing those rules. But this argument is only credible if we can demonstrate how this governing role of multinationals is sustained and enforced.

Enforcing Global Rules

There are three primary mechanisms by which the global corporate rules are enforced. The familiar mechanism is by home country intervention either bilaterally or through international organisations. We could call this the 'OECD monitoring mechanism'. The second and third mechanisms are the financial markets and the competitiveness imperative; they are non-governmental and deserve more extensive examination.

The 2008–09 financial crisis revealed the extraordinary growth, diversification, obfuscation and irresponsibility of global financial markets. The irresponsibility is a product of market failure and of government failure. As Adair Turner's lucid analysis picked out, the crisis resulted from market failure – the financial markets were not self-correcting; and it resulted from a failure of regulation – in Turner's (2009: 36) phrase 'global finance without global government'. The impact of the crisis and the failures of imagination over reform are shaping the evolution of contemporary capitalism and have generated a substantial literature (for instance, Gamble, 2009; Germain, 2010; Kaletsky, 2010). The scale of the crisis serves to emphasise the reach and power of financial markets which have operated to sustain a global economy and to provide an implicit system of rules to constrain both corporations and governments. Defined broadly of course, the financial markets are no longer simply banks and stock markets. There has been a series of financial revolutions (Zhu and Morss, 2005; Johnson and Kwak, 2010) which have created new institutions and new markets in areas like structured investment vehicles, hedge funds and securitised credit; and more powerful global financial intermediaries in global consulting, accounting and law firms. Some of their activities are incestuous and parasitic but many of them are crucial for the financial health and prosperity of most corporations and countries. In effect global financial markets operate as an infrastructure providing a utility product of financial resources. It is essential for a corporation or a country to be connected to the network, but connection requires conformity to the rules, procedures and operating protocols which govern the network.

The rules and protocols of the financial markets essentially involve the imposition of a neoliberal policy programme so that:

> global financial markets are conceived as central to inducing a convergence of political and social agendas among governments of varied ideological

persuasions to 'market friendly' policies: a general commitment to price stability; low public deficits and indeed expenditure, especially on social goods; low direct taxation; privatization and labour market deregulation. (Held et al., 1999: 232)

The financial markets are concerned with key economic indicators such as currency rates, debt levels, inflation and growth, and have a considerable influence on macro-economic policy. They also impact on micro-economic policy and are sensitive to levels of corporate taxation, regulation, investment climate and labour relations – in short all those aspects which Cerny (2010) has captured in his idea of the 'competition state' which seeks to compete for mobile capital and foreign investment (Hay, 2004). The neoliberal disciplines imposed by the financial markets on governments are revealed in statistical trends such as the generalised reduction in rates of corporate taxation since the early 1980s (Swank, 2006: 849) but the agencies of that discipline are often subtle, invisible, and may simply take the form of advice within a neoliberal normative framework. Sometimes agency is revealed by scholarly research which picks out how liberalising pressures are mediated by individual corporations, groupings or even individuals. Thus Murphy (2004: 105) examines the growth of offshore finance and tax havens which accounted for over half of all international finance by the 1990s. He documents the creation of unregulated offshore markets which were positively encouraged by senior UK and US bankers and regulators but 'shaped by leading firms' (Murphy, 2004: 108) in the interests of open and liberalised markets (see also Palan, 2010). Another example is provided by pressures from international finance to formalise corporate governance in order to protect shareholders and to create a market in corporate control, as discussed in Chapter 10.

At times, of course, the pressure from financial markets becomes less subtle and approaches coercion. The classic example is the attempt between 1981 and 1983 by President Mitterrand's government to adopt a policy of 'socialism in one country'. Under the weight of adverse criticism and capital movements in financial and currency markets the neo-Keynesian and social welfare policies were sacrificed in favour of financial austerity and an abandonment of traditional French dirigisme. Schmidt (2002: 190) recounts the decisive French shift towards market capitalism. She observes that foreign direct investment proceeded to grow exponentially and Hancké (2001: 308) notes that in the 15 years 1980–93 'this crisis irreversibly shifted the balance of power from the state to the management of large firms'. This French example of the power of the financial markets to dictate national economic policy has been seen much more recently in the aftermath of the 2008 financial crisis and the ensuing European recession.

The likely breakup of the Eurozone was still undecided as this book went to press but Europe was in the grip of the politics of austerity and the relationship between the financial markets and the most indebted Eurozone countries provided a graphic and barely believable demonstration of the unconscious power of the markets. The successive bailouts of Greece, Ireland, Portugal and Spain were accompanied by market judgements symbolised in credit rating downgrades. The interest rates paid by countries on their bond auctions became a hot topic of public debate and the policy implications were grim. Cuts in spending and increases in taxation brought economic misery and political unrest, with historical resonances to the 1930s that were truly sinister. The imposition of neoliberal policy packages, historically applied by the IMF to developing countries in debt, was coming home to roost. Neither political nor corporate elites favoured these outcomes but they appeared powerless. Trust in European political institutions collapsed and during 2011 unelected technocratic governments were imposed on Italy and Greece to enforce austerity. Through processes of innovation, opportunism and resistance to regulation it seemed that financial markets had created complex interdependencies that political elites could not control. In their account of the remorseless convulsions that constituted the interminable Eurozone crisis the Manchester research group observed that 'politics *can't* control finance, *doesn't understand it*, and *doesn't know what to do* in order to control it ... the consequence is that powerful sectional interests define agendas in ways which limit scrutiny and control' (Ertürk et al., 2012: 46, emphasis in original). The accuracy of this apocalyptic vision remained unclear in 2012 but what was evident was precisely the by now immense and irresponsible power of financial markets to over-ride governments.

The discipline exerted by the financial markets on developed states tends to be macro-economic and concerned with public spending, debt and portfolio investment (Mosley, 2003: 305). A parallel discipline operates at a micro-economic level in respect of individual corporations and their investment strategies through the agency of the competitiveness discourse and the operation of political risk analysis. The competitiveness tables, which rank countries by reference to the openness of their markets and the permissiveness of their regulations tend to be regarded as a league table of neoliberalism. It is certainly the case that neoliberal theory emphasises the wealth-creating properties of open markets and competition on the one hand, and a small state and minimal regulation on the other. But although large companies prefer open markets they are ambiguous about competition, and whilst they approve of the low taxes imposed by minimalist governments, they welcome favourable regulation. Competitiveness league tables are not therefore a purely neoliberal badge of honour, they measure 'business friendly' national environments even if they are promoted through a normative discourse of neoliberalism.

Rankings of countries by reference to their level of competitiveness are a familiar feature of the media, and not just the financial media (see, for instance, WEF, 2011 and IMD, 2010). The league tables are taken seriously and the WEF (Davos) tables provide a revealing example of this method of policing business-friendly national policy stances. The World Economic Forum publishes an annual Global Competitiveness Index. It defines competitiveness 'as the set of institutions, policies and factors that determine the level of productivity of a country' (WEF, 2009: 4) but this is rather disingenuous. High productivity is seen to enhance 'the rates of return obtained by investments in an economy' so that the real focus is on profitable investment or, put another way, a supportive environment for business. The elaborate Index is built on 12 pillars of competitiveness, some of which are laudable such as good infrastructure and good healthcare and primary education. Others are more controversial and reveal a neoliberal pedigree such as a flexible labour market 'to allow for wage fluctuations without much social disruption' (ibid.: 6); sophisticated financial markets, and 'government attitudes to markets and freedom' (ibid.: 4). The indicators are combined together to produce a weighted index.

The 2011–12 Index covered 133 countries. Switzerland was rated as the most competitive economy in the world with the United States falling back to 5th. Table 7.1 gives the rankings of a sample of large economies. Some, such as China and Sweden scored surprisingly well, others, such as Italy, South Africa and Brazil did rather badly. The UK improved its position but France was probably further down the league table than free marketeers would like. The North European countries were increasingly well regarded and comprised five of the top ten (Sweden, Finland, Germany, Netherlands and Denmark). The detailed analysis is interesting. The UK was 7th on labour market efficiency whilst France was 68th (and Italy highly inflexible at 123rd). The UK was only 85th on macro-economic stability (thanks to bank rescues) while France was 4th on infrastructure. On institutions Singapore was ranked first with Hong Kong at 9th and Saudi Arabia at 12th, which is extraordinary given their dubious democratic credentials. The emphasis here is on economic efficiency and not political participation.

Like all league tables the Competitiveness Index has a certain intrinsic fascination and poses interesting questions; why was Vietnam so low (at 65th) yet such a popular destination for FDI? Why was Japan so high (at 9th) given the impermeability of its domestic market? But the Index only has effective significance if it is assumed that countries wish to attract FDI and will adapt their competitiveness profiles to do so. MNCs have the

Table 7.1 *WEF country competitiveness rankings: 2011–12 compared with 2001–02*

	2011–12	2001–02
Switzerland	1	15
Singapore	2	4
Sweden	3	9
USA	5	2
Germany	6	17
Denmark	8	14
Japan	9	21
UK	10	12
France	18	20
Korea	24	23
China	26	39
Italy	43	26
South Africa	50	34
Brazil	53	44
India	56	57
Vietnam	65	60
Russia	66	63

Note: selected countries.

Sources: WEF (2002, 2011).

potential to bring massive economic benefits, not just capital and global market access, but research, technology, training and so on. On the whole most countries have good reason to attract FDI and they try hard to do so. How then do MNCs calculate their risks, make their choices and protect their investments?

In this regard multinationals are concerned with specific investments in selected locations. They will undertake standard financial and economic appraisals but they also need to consider physical risk (will assets be expropriated or damaged?); operational risk (will there be strikes or import bans?); regulatory risks (intensified process or environmental regulation or increased taxes); and political risk (will a new government be hostile to their business?). This is the world of political risk assessment and when considering investments in any county lower than (say) 40 on the Competitiveness Index these political risks are likely to weigh almost as heavily as the technical economic business plan. A high level of risk will deter investment and this in itself acts to police the informal rules of business-friendly national environments. Risk is assessed by specialised political risk consultancies who are engaged in the fascinating process of 'applied international relations'. They deal with risks ranging from war and terrorism to governmental change and regulatory incompetence. The issues are explored in a study by Bremmer and Keat (2009) who run a leading political risk consultancy. Their book is packed with examples of what can go wrong, from the regulatory discrimination against Lone Star Funds in Korea, to the hostility to privatised business shown by the Law and Justice Party which governed Poland in 2006–07 (ibid.: 143, 146). Apart from the corrective they provide in picking out examples of business weakness the political risk industry serves in three ways to reinforce policing of national governments. First, it increases transparency and influences the intangible 'investment climate' for a country, region or industry. Second, it feeds information into the financial infrastructure so that hostile behaviour by a government will be punished by a fall in investment or an increase in its cost. Thirdly it sensitizes large corporations to political risk which many of them assess through a process of 'enterprise risk management' which steers them away from investments in potentially hostile environments (ibid.: 195).

This section has discussed the way in which global rules have been created in ways that provide a supportive environment for multinational investment and provide corporations with a role in global rule-making. Those rules are enforced in a highly variable but surprisingly effective fashion and present the visible and sometimes the unacceptable face of multinational dominance. But rules are not enough. Institutional authority rests on a far wider and less visible foundation which takes us from direct to indirect power, from explicit coercion to systemic influence. In the next section we accordingly turn to the normative foundation of institutional authority.

GLOBAL NORMS FAVOURING MULTINATIONALS

The second foundation of institutional authority is a framework of norms which incorporate a set of ideas about how global society and economy should be ordered. These ideas are partly prescriptive, partly evaluative, and they convey a sense of obligation. Here we are concerned with norms that help to legitimate corporate power, which provide what Fuchs (2007: 139) calls 'discursive power', and which imbue the multinational corporation with authority to participate as a partner institution in global governance. The analysis of a normative global framework could embrace a huge set of possibilities. Here we concentrate on five normative narratives. Two of them are relatively uncontested, namely the desirability of a market economy and the existence of a global economy; two are policy orientated in the form of national economic growth and national competitiveness; and one is the contested norm of neoliberal policy prescriptions.

The grand contextual norm is the desirability of 'the market' as a means for organising economic activity. Since the fall of the Berlin Wall in 1989, the end of the Cold War, and the Chinese acceptance of a social market economy from 1992 (Dickson, 2008: 38), the dominance of the market principle has become a fact of economic and social life, nationally and globally. The normative consensus facilitated the diffusion of free-market orientated economic reforms which became a defining feature of the late 20th century (Simmons et al., 2006: 781). The market norm is associated with a second norm that is rather more controversial: the belief that all economies are now operating within a global market. The whole globalisation debate is, of course, still in progress, but if any aspect of globalisation is generally accepted it is the unavoidable influence of economic globalisation through the global trading system and financial markets (Held and McGrew, 2002: 120). These two norms provide a barely questioned framework within which government leaders and economic policy operate. Their task is to exploit the market, to guide market forces in directions favourable to their political goals but to do so in a setting that recognises the constraints and opportunities offered by a global market.

It is possible to conclude from this normative position of globalised markets that states are obliged to construct policy not only in a market context but according to a neoliberal model. Thus, in his analysis of the western ideology, with neoliberalism at its core, Gamble argues that 'neoliberalism is more than just an ideological cloak for the interests of the powerful. Its ascendency also accurately reflects... The way in which the modern world is ordered' (Gamble, 2009a: 4–5). But, as we see below, neoliberalism constrains many policy options and is itself only one variant of organising capitalist markets. Outside the Anglo-Saxon states it is more contested as a norm than the market or economic globalisation and even in Anglo-Saxon states its influence on policy is mixed. Indeed, Braithwaite (2008: 4) calls it 'a fairy tale'. It is not, however, clear that the role of the corporation as a governing institution is necessarily dependent on a neoliberal policy paradigm. Like many Christians, multinationals proclaim the gospel but do not live by it. In fact a minimalist state, comprehensive deregulation and aggressive competition policy would make life very uncomfortable for many large corporations. A decline in the influence of neoliberalism would not therefore necessarily undermine corporate power as long as no alternative to a free global market emerges. At present there is no persuasive global alternative to the market on offer. There is an increased interest in greater social justice; in systematic environmental engagement and in principles of cosmopolitan social democracy; but large global corporations can adapt to and even incorporate many of these ideas, as we will see with sustainability. The present normative framework appears still to offer a congenial environment for the deployment of corporate power.

Economic growth is the holy grail of economic policy and the preeminent meta-policy goal of the majority of governments. There is a political dividend to be gained from the resources generated by economic growth, but it is also self-evidently the single most important way to improve human well-being and to lift populations out of poverty, misery and poor health. This is a norm which is widely shared and, until recently, only questioned by a fringe of communitarians, anti-capitalists and deep greens. Since the turn of the century, however, the environmental movement and the economics of happiness have begun to make the questioning of economic growth more respectable (see NEF, 2009; Coyle, 2011: 268; Skidelsky and Skidelsky, 2012: ch. 5) but growth continues to dominate the policy agenda of virtually all countries, posing the question of how best to achieve growth? Since the late 1980s the answer has, of course, been to use the market. But markets are now global, meaning that countries have to participate in global markets and compete with other countries. Hence we see the emergence of the competitiveness discourse and the norm of the constant need to improve national competitiveness. As we saw above, competitiveness can be analysed in great detail and presented in various forms in influential league tables. As the varieties of capitalism literature demonstrates, there are alternative routes to competitive success in world markets. Neoliberalism is certainly one possibility, which emerged as the single most persuasive policy posture in the long boom from 1994 to 2007. Other possibilities include co-ordinated market capitalism on the German or Japanese models, state-sponsored capitalism as seen in South Korea or Singapore, or outright state capitalism as in China. Whichever model of competitiveness is chosen, the key agent of competitive advantage is the corporation. The relative importance of corporations and governments in driving competitiveness is hotly debated but the predominant view remains that of Michael Porter and the Harvard School. In his influential study of *The Competitive Advantage of Nations* (Porter, 1990) he argued that it is not nations that compete, but corporations located in those nations. The task of governments is therefore to work in partnership with corporations, to provide a supportive environment and to persuade them to locate their value-adding activities in your country.

If government engagement with corporations is informed by a neoliberal framework then governments reconfigure their policies into what Cerny has called a 'competition state'. This concept captures the same set of ideas that Bobbitt expressed as the 'market state' (see Chapter 5) but it is more critical and more detailed in its examination of a model of economic policy in which the welfare state is subordinated to a new set of priorities which emphasise a smaller, more efficient state apparatus and a state which is open and responsive to market forces (Hay, 2004). It involves 'a shift in the focal point of party and governmental politics away from the general maximisation of welfare ... to the promotion of enterprise, innovation and profitability in both private and public sectors' (Cerny, 2000: 302). The competition state is seen in its most advanced form in the Anglo-American economies. It incorporates a normative position which lauds a free enterprise system and provides a favourable environment for corporations (Cerny, 2010; Horsfall, 2010). But whether neoliberal or not, in practice virtually all states will favour corporations and may do so directly rather than through market signals. In the recent past state sponsorship of favoured corporations was widespread, overt and took the form of 'national champions' (Hayward, 1995). The traditional national champions of the USA, Europe and Japan were aided by protection, outright subsidy, biased regulation and protection from takeovers. Since the early 1990s European competition policy has prohibited blatant state support but exactly this pattern has been employed in Korea and the BRICS. The national champion relationship has been modified by globalisation. Corporations are no longer dependent clients of their home states and the new global partnerships between states and corporations are more likely to be manifest in collaborations in transnational networks and sharing in regulation and economic governance. The norms of economic growth and the imperative of competitiveness thus underpin a procedural norm of partnership which, as noted above, is reproduced at the international level on the basis of corporate socialisation gained in national level business partnerships, especially those operating in the UK and Germany (Flohr, et al., 2010: 240).

The suggestion, then, is that these norms briefly outlined above form part of a normative system which supports an institutional order. It provides corporations with the second face of power, the discursive power of ideas to set the agenda, provide a conceptual framework, and to impose a sense of obligation on policy makers to conform to those accepted ideas. In a more overtly political setting this normative system could be labelled an 'ideology' and, of course, critics of neoliberalism would use exactly that terminology. The power of ideas and the mobilising potential of ideology has not been lost on the intelligentsia of the business world. The corporations themselves pay increasing attention to presenting their activities as both consistent with market norms and as operationalising those norms sympathetically through corporate citizenship and corporate social responsibility, as explored in Chapter 9 (see also Ougaard, 2006; Crane et al., 2008b: ch. 7; and Levy and Kaplan, 2008). In particular the response to environmental challenges has provoked a turbulent battle of ideas. The normative imperialism of business corporations is apparent in the love affair between corporations and the concept of 'sustainability'. The embrace of sustainability is an important facet of the whole CSR offensive analysed in Chapter 9. Sklair points to the way in which business corporations have hijacked the sustainability discourse. Corporate leaders borrowed the idea of sustainability from the 1987 Brundtland Report and repackaged it in the form of 'sustainable development' and 'sustainable growth'. 'From this powerful conceptual base big business successfully recruited much of the environmental movement in the 1990s to the cause of 'sustainable' global consumerist capitalism' (Sklair, 2001: 206). He presents a series of case studies of the environmental impact and policies of large corporations but comes back to the adjectival power of the sustainability norm. Sustainability has been reinforced and redefined by corporations, by some powerful industry groupings such as the influential WBCSD (World Business Council for Sustainable Development), and has been supported by government and the media. Most large corporations, intermediaries such as consultancies and lawyers, lobby groups and even accountants not only issue environmental sustainability reports (see, for instance, Mikler, 2009: ch. 6), they have entire sustainability divisions. Many of them do good work and make gains but all within a system which continues to pursue growth and consumer satisfaction. Thus the corporation, with its new-found devotion to sustainability, has metamorphosed away from the threat of 'conservation' and towards a solution of 'sustainability'. This provides a nice case study of the power of ideas adeptly employed to enhance corporate interests.

In summary, the six norms discussed in this section: the market economy, the global market, economic growth, competitiveness, neoliberalism and sustainability, constitute a mutually supportive set of ideas which embody orthodox wisdom and are widely accepted by economic policy makers. They define and rationalise a 'global capitalist market' which, in Kuhn's invaluable concept, becomes an economic paradigm. Further, they empower large multinational corporations and imbue them with a value and a legitimacy that positions them as governing institutions. The grand historical question is whether this global market paradigm has become self-sustaining and has given rise to the 'global business civilisation' which Cutler (2006: 201) has identified. In these circumstances the power of the MNCs would become autonomous and they would be less dependent on the power and support of specific nation-states, such as that exerted by the United States. One possible way in which the global market paradigm might have become self-sustaining, and corporations become autonomous, is through a 'constititionalisation' of the paradigm. This involves a removal of global economic governance out of the public sphere of nation-state control and into a private sphere of economic principles and market rules, but rules that are underpinned by a normative understanding. We come back to this idea of a global economic constitution in the conclusion to this chapter.

GLOBAL CULTURES FAVOURING MULTINATIONALS

The third element in the trinity of foundations for institutional authority is 'cognitive', denoting the way in which individuals and groups make sense of social reality. The cognitive explanation of why an institution is regarded as legitimate can also be termed 'cultural', or in March and Olsen's (1989) terms, a 'logic of appropriateness'. As noted in Chapter 1, whilst rules are obeyed due to coercion, and norms are complied with due to the power of roles, 'the cognitive framework stresses the importance of social identities; our concepts of who we are and what ways of action make sense to us in a given situation' (Scott, 1995: 44). In other words, we accept institutional authority because we cannot conceive of any other way of acting.

Globalisation involves a transition from traditional to modern society summarised in the concept of 'modernity' in which society becomes rationalised, more impersonal, calculative and individualised. The market and market relations are a central feature of modernity, and the business corporation is a core cultural form. In market economies market relations are accepted as natural, automatic, the standard means by which individuals conduct their material lives. Although, in theory, business corporations are not essential for the operation of markets, since the late 19th century the business corporation has become accepted as the visible face of the market system, as the irreplaceable organisation constituting the free enterprise system. Thus the business corporation becomes a defining foundation of modern society, less fundamental than the family but more definitive in the 21st century than organised religion or local communities. As a core component of modern culture the corporation performs a range of unquestioned functions. In addition to creating wealth and providing employment it defines a way of life by meeting the needs of individuals and families. Needs are met through a process of consumption in the market and fulfilled through the achievement of consumer satisfaction. If contemporary Western civilisation is characterised by a materialistic, market-driven consumer society, then its character is owed to the business corporation whose legitimacy is constantly and inevitably reinforced by the acceptance and celebration of a consumerist civilisation.

This presentation of the business corporation as an organic element in the life force of contemporary consumer society is important in understanding domestic political power and arguably even more important in understanding the international political power of multinational corporations. As the market extends its global reach, so the corporate form accompanies it. Societies acquire the 'package'; with the market comes the corporation but clothed in the same benevolent, wealth-creating, need-meeting, consumer-satisfying advantages that are associated with the market. This is doubly important because, while the market transforms social relations through arms-length pricing transactions, the corporation transforms commercial and employment relations through hierarchy. Employees are paid to accept the authority of the corporation but payment is only one side of a relationship that is culturally sanctioned. The corporate organisation of the market system also incorporates market disciplines and acceptance of 'the right to manage' which is justified by the manager's ability to exploit the market. Management earns deference as the priesthood of the market system. It becomes a specialised, professionalised caste and remarkable faith is vested in corporate leaders as the high priests of the market gods. Managers may be humane or inspirational but within the large corporation management too often deteriorates into 'managerialism', a US-inspired approach to management which is deeply calculative, morally cynical and embodied in a caste of business-school-educated corporate leaders (Locke and Spender, 2011). The corporate form hence shifts cultural expectations towards management and managerialism which creates new forces and criteria for collective decisions within society; a set of issues explored in greater depth in Chapter 8.

As with the efforts by corporations to pursue favourable rules and to define favourable norms, so also a pro-business cultural framework is pursued assiduously by corporations. This is not shy, reticent, secretive pursuit of political lobbying or popular mobilisation. This is core business pursued aggressively by the massed battalions of marketing, public relations, the fashion industry, the media, branding and consumer research. As in so many aspects of corporate analysis, Galbraith expressed the essence of the issue in his dismissal of the assumption of consumer sovereignty and his reformulation of a 'revised sequence' in which 'the producing firm reaches forward to control its markets and on beyond to manage the market behaviour and shape the social attitudes of those, ostensibly, that it serves' (Galbraith, 1967: 217). If, as is regularly maintained, people's social identities are defined by what they consume, then in manipulating consumer demand business corporations are creating social identities. This is not only a profoundly systemic source of power; it is a huge responsibility as we see the creation of consumer societies in Eastern Europe, India and China. Modern consumer capitalism is inescapably attractive and frighteningly dangerous. 'This global ramping up of global economic activity', writes Jackson (2009: 13), 'has no historical precedent' and has already embarked on an avalanche of destruction of finite resources and irreplaceable ecologies.

It is intriguing to examine consumer society through the eyes of its critics who have been numerous, erudite and only tangentially effective. These include classic treatments such as the aloof irony of Thorstein Veblen whose 1899 *Theory of the Leisure Class* protested at the excesses of 'ostentatious consumption' and who later feared the capture of American society by a 'pecuniary culture' (see Fraser, 2005: 296); or the existential angst of Herbert Marcuse whose 1964 study of *One-Dimensional Man* protested against febrile needs manipulated by vested interests to create an almost totalitarian consumer conformism. Contemporary critics remain highly visible, if somewhat strident. The globalising consumer culture is caricatured as 'McWorld' to emphasise American cultural influence. Thus Klein (2002) attacks the production of brands by powerful multinationals and adeptly uses that route to condemn their exploitative practices. Barber (2001) casts the culture in grand strategic terms as a dialectic between the global consumerism of McWorld and the localist resistance which he terms 'Jihad'. These and a profusion of like critiques are aimed as much at the culture and politics of MNCs as at their economic effects (Ritzer, 1996). For Barber, in his recent head-on confrontation with consumerism, 'Capitalism per se is not the issue. The question is not whether there is an alternative to markets but whether markets can be used to meet the needs capitalism is designed to serve, whether capitalists can adapt to the sovereignty of democratic authority that alone will allow it to survive' (B. Barber, 2007: 4). At present, he argues, US-style consumer capitalism has degenerated. It has 'infantilized' consumers by manufacturing false needs to create demand and sustain profitability. He advances a rhetorically powerful polemic but one that is not wholly pessimistic. Barber wants to reassert democratic control and pursue 'civic consumerism' (ibid.: 293) but he recognises that globalisation presents many obstacles and that the transnational capitalist class, the 'children of Davos', 'share a commitment to privatization and branding as well as to the ethos of infantilization that allow them to cooperate across international frontiers' (ibid.: 336). Barber's attack on consumerism attacks a culture as well as the corporations that are complicit in creating it. Sklair is far more focussed. For him major corporations determinedly pursue a 'culture-ideology of consumerism' which is part of their struggle for global hegemony so that 'the consumerist visions of global corporations . . . play a central role for the hegemonic agenda of the transnational capitalist class' (Sklair, 2001: 255, 288; see also Sklair, 2002, ch. 7; 2009). Both Barber and Sklair are intrigued by the potential for a more progressive global corporate citizenship, a point we come back to in Chapter 9.

Such critiques of a global consumer society are eloquent but the anti-consumer critique is a quiet voice when heard against the massed choirs of consumerism; the cognitive acceptance of multinationals and global consumer society appears remorseless. What is the evidence for this? The cultural source of institutional authority is relatively easy to express in the abstract but harder to establish in practice. Evidence could be sought in the creation of national and global markets; in the spread of Western patterns of popular consumption; in the reproduction of the corporate form in emergent economies; in the creation of a global media that celebrates Western lifestyles; and in the global consolidation of the status of corporate management reinforced by an apparatus of training (or indoctrination) in global business schools, the seminaries of the corporate priesthood. More specifically, we can focus attention on three types of evidence captured in the three clumsy words of commodification, marketisation and privatisation.

The concept of commodification is usually associated with a Marxist approach and refers to the process of turning social relations and human needs into 'commodities' which can be bought, sold, priced and operated to generate a surplus (a profit). Child care provides an example, with child minders and nurseries absorbing the wages of parents, and especially women, who enter the labour market. This is the territory of McWorld where domestic preparation of food is turned into the fast food industry and cooking is replaced by convenience foods. Sexual relations become a sex industry marked not only by the age-old existence of prostitution but by systematic exploitation of sex workers and commercialisation through pornography. There is plenty of room for censure and moral outrage in these extensions of market relations but the boundaries of the market are constantly being extended in the most ingenious and shocking fashion as illustrated by efforts to commodify genetic material through patenting and licensing. Marketisation is a more contemporary phrase employed by proponents of market solutions as much as by opponents, and it describes similar processes. Marketisation tends, however, to refer to the altered organisation of economic activity rather than rendering social relations economic. A prime example lies in sport and the conversion of the voluntary associations of football clubs into substantial companies with global brands, stock market listings and controversial takeovers – the

Manchester United phenomenon, registered in the Cayman islands, owned in Delaware by a secretive American family from Florida and floated on the NYSE (Marlow, 2012). The third term, privatisation, is a leitmotif of neoliberal capitalism and the very essence of the global transformation that followed the Reagan/Thatcher capitalist triumphs. Privatisation applies commodification and marketisation to the state and, as we saw in Chapter 6, the UK was the pioneer providing a model and a source of inspiration for international extensions of private markets.

This discussion of the cultural pillar of support for the corporation as a governing institution has presented a familiar picture of a seductive consumerist market culture which is becoming globalised and works to extend and 'naturalise' the power of large corporations. The attractions of the consumer society are thus projected forcibly, but its successful colonisation of a wide range of countries and cultures continues to puzzle and depress a swathe of left-wing intellectual opinion. Perhaps Polanyi identified one core reason for this success. Like early liberal society, the consumerist market culture unlocks the basic human motive of 'gain'. Nineteenth-century civilisation, he opines, was based on gain (for Smith, self-interest; for Wall Street, greed), thus 'the mechanism which the motive of gain set in motion was comparable in its effectiveness only to the most violent outburst of religious fervour in history. Within a generation the whole human world was subject to its undiluted influence' (Polanyi, 1944: 30). This captures something of the extraordinary transformation of societies from South Africa to Poland, from Mexico to China, and sets the scene for a review of the cultural critique of the corporation which follows in Chapter 8.

The conclusion that MNCs devote resources to extending a consumer society is banal. What is more interesting is to evaluate the way in which they identify themselves as the producers, guardians and interpreters of the wealth and consumer satisfaction upon which consumer society rests. For Amoore 'firms cease to be adequately conceived as producers of things . . . and must be recognised also as a producer of ideas, cultures and identities that extend across spatial boundaries' (Amoore, 2006: 48). One of those cultures is a management culture which imparts status, knowledge and authority to corporate management and is symbolised by the deference, respect (and fees) accorded to global management consultancies like McKinseys. Not only, therefore, is the multinational corporation itself legitimised by the global market and global consumer society, the management of the corporation takes on a legitimate role in defining and directing economic activity. The managerial elite operates in a cultural setting which defers to corporations in the United States, Europe and Japan, and which regards it as natural that corporations and managers should take on a leadership role. Their activity is seldom questioned, their corporations are, on the whole, trusted. If this deference can be globalised it provides a potent source of corporate power sustaining the large multinational corporation as a global governing institution.

CONCLUSION: A GLOBAL CONSTITUTION FOR CORPORATE PARTNERSHIP

This concluding section speculates first on whether the status of the large multinational corporation has become sufficiently embedded to be regarded as quasi-constitutional. It then goes on to bring together the discussion of 'partnership' as an expression of corporate power as discussed in chapters 4, 5 and 6 as well as at the international level. Finally we take stock of the deep concerns raised in these discussions about the restriction of democratic choice and the imperative to increase corporate accountability.

Initially this chapter has examined the way in which the large multinational corporation has become a governing institution within international regimes of global governance. The institutional sources of authority have been explored through the analytical framework of rules, norms and cultures outlined in Chapter 1. It is straightforward to conceptualise the MNC as an institution but the claim that it is a 'governing' institution requires elaboration. At the international level corporations take on an enhanced political role. By engaging in political discourse they constitute themselves as political actors (Schmidt, 2006) and, as political institutions, corporations undertake the classic functions of government. Their role in regulation is increasingly acknowledged (Büthe and Mattli, 2011); they spend (on labour, goods, research and so on); they redistribute (from consumers to producers, from labour to shareholders); and they impose economic and political order. In partnership with government they may also coerce (especially labour and subcontractors) and tax (through differential taxation and subsidies). Indeed, in some developing countries they are obliged to take on public responsibilities so that Valente and Crane (2010: 54) observe that 'company executives in developing countries have increasingly seen their firms called upon to play a role more akin to government than business'. In all these ways they allocate values, their activities are definitively political, and they participate in governance as partners, and sometimes without the involvement of state agencies, in the exercise of private governance.

The 'governing institution' claim therefore introduces preconceptions of corporate privilege into any discussion of global corporate power. In the hands of critical theorists such as Claire Cutler, corporations as institutions are seen to have reconfigured governance such that 'the transnational corporation has not so much replaced or eclipsed the state, but rather has contributed to processes of re-regulation and in so doing de-centred the state as subject, recasting the authority of both business and government in governance' (Cutler, 2010: 79). She emphasises the deployment of institutional authority through law and endorses a Gramscian analysis of the embedding of corporate authority in a 'constitution'.

In the introduction to this chapter a link was made between the exercise of corporate power at the national level and the way in which it has expanded and become legitimised at the global level. If corporations have become independent partners in global governance then we have seen a qualitative transformation in international political economy; a new settlement which could be likened to the transformation in the domestic political economy of the United States and the UK in the 1980s. The new settlements transformed those economies from an embedded liberal order of state intervention which defended labour, to a neoliberal order which protected business interests. As reviewed in Chapter 4, that domestic transformation was analysed by Mark Blyth who identified ways in which 'business also used ideas as weapons to promote institutional change' (Blyth, 2002: 258). The ideas he stressed included supply-side political economy and monetarism; the ideas stressed in this chapter include market-led growth and competitiveness but it is argued that the success of corporations in establishing themselves as institutions of global governance is comparable to, and in part emergent from, the domestic transformations to neoliberalism so effectively analysed by Blyth for the USA and by Gamble for the UK. The neoliberal (or post-liberal) global order thus owes much to the UK model. The global rules, norms and culture outlined above share their inspirations with the forces that created the New Corporate State in Britain, and their common ancestry is clear to students of British political economy. As in the UK, we are seeing not the power of markets but the power of corporation to structure markets and the power of a global corporate elite to capture rewards. As also with the UK, the financial components of the corporate elite have become particularly dominant and the post-2008 decade has become preoccupied with the issue of how to hold global finance to account.

The discussion in chapters 4, 5 and 6 emphasised the emerging partnership between government and the corporation. At the global level, in the absence of a global government, a far more equal partnership has developed between corporations and governments. Indeed, in some areas corporations have become the senior partners and the main agents of governance. The global rules and regulatory regimes that emerge from these partnerships have become the quasi-legal framework by which the global economy is regulated. But are these regulatory regimes? Or can we go further to regard them as constitutional settlements? If we take that further step then we can suggest that the New Corporate State in the UK has been replicated by an elite partnership at the global level. We can also suggest that nation-states, such as the UK, are operating within an international constitutional framework that restricts their options, supplements domestic regulation, and consolidates the New Corporate State with international disciplines that would make radical reform problematic.

Finally, the third section of this conclusion comes on to the concerns that are generated by corporate power and participation in governance. These trends towards governments sharing, or even abdicating from, certain areas of governance have generated substantial concern and a large literature devoted to woefully inadequate accountability and a global 'democratic deficit' (Held and Koenig-Archibugi, 2005; Bexell et al., 2010: 81). There is undoubtedly some degree of corporate accountability. Corporations are accountable to markets, competitors and consumers, to their shareholders and to legal process enforced by corporate law. They have to observe a degree of transparency and to answer to the media, activists and NGOs which monitor their activities. But, as we have seen in earlier chapters, these are all weak modes of accountability and have little democratic legitimacy. Global governance by corporations suffers from ambiguous, confused, contradictory or simply inadequate modes of accountability and its democratic legitimacy is almost non-existent. This presents a profound source of instability and a huge threat as global corporate capitalism ploughs remorselessly forward towards its own environmental destruction.

This chapter therefore concludes on a more speculative note by stressing the challenge a blatant lack of economic, social and environmental accountability presents to the new global corporate settlement. Much has been made of the individual and collective moves made by large corporations to embrace corporate social responsibility. With global corporate citizenship comes global governmental responsibility and it should be possible for a global corporate elite to concede that they deploy power and to accept a level of governmental responsibility. This is the implied contract in the 'license to operate' noted in Chapter 1 as the concession granted to the corporation by the national state and now by global society. The acceptance of responsibility is not only some abstract moral obligation, it is also an imperative of medium to long term self interest. As Sklair (2001) has pointed out, large corporations expect still to be operating in 10, 20 or 50 years' time in markets that remain profitable and in a (physical) environment in which they can do business. This conveys a self-interest in economic development and environmental sustainability. Big corporations and their investors have to think far further ahead than their next profit and loss account. A logical, enlightened response to these responsibilities would therefore be for corporations to go beyond CSR and promote CGR – 'Corporate Governmental Responsibility'. We explore that ambitious agenda in chapters 8, 9 and 10 which move the debate on corporate power from its origins and its exercise to a discussion of how it can be controlled.

8. Corporations, culture and accountability

INTRODUCTION

Up to this point the book has looked at the origins of corporate power and at its exercise, in the UK and globally. The case has been made that corporate political power is substantial and has undergone a transformation since the late 1980s. The result has been the development of a new institutional basis for the state and the consolidation of power by a corporate elite allied with a political elite. In itself power is acceptable if it can be made legitimate, which is another way of saying that it is tolerable if it can be made accountable. These next three chapters therefore examine the accountability of the corporation and the degree to which processes of accountability render its power legitimate. Accountability is one of the magic ingredients of successful societies with an instant ethical appeal, but it involves a complex set of ideas and processes with an ambiguous relationship to democracy. In respect of corporations there are important modes of accountability but also some indefensible shortcomings.

We can pick out four areas of accountability which are of particular importance for corporations. The first is economic accountability to the market. The ultimate defensive response of corporate leaders is that their corporations behave as they do simply in response to market signals and that the market provides inescapable discipline that secures economic welfare. Competition, they would say, is intensifying (see Reich, 2009: 10). There is clearly substance in this mode of accountability but it breaks down when corporations have market power through oligopoly or even monopoly. To prevent abuse of market power governments regulate corporations through competition policy, which has become ubiquitous since the early 1990s (Wilks, 2010), and through specialised regulatory agencies policing industrial sectors such as energy or telecommunications. Although these are important economic sources of accountability they are not examined in depth in the following chapters (but see Braithwaite and Drahos, 2000). The second is financial and legal accountability. Corporations are answerable to the providers of capital, who exert control through the financial markets (as discussed in Chapter 7), and to a special category of capital providers in the form of shareholders who have in company law control over the corporation. This involves accountability through corporate governance which is examined in Chapter 10. A third mode of accountability is internal to employees, whose well being is dependent on corporate success and who could be expected to be knowledgeable about the corporation and its activities. Employees will often be represented by unions who impose a potentially effective source of accountability. But that internal accountability is constrained by corporate hierarchy, internal corporate democracy is unusual and the power of management is substantial. We come back to the growth in managerial authority and power at the end of this chapter. Fourthly, there is external political accountability. This takes us into the territory of the relations between corporations and government and between corporations and society. It is a rapidly growing field embracing ideas of corporate social responsibility and corporate citizenship and is the subject of Chapter 9.

As corporate power has increased, so corporate accountability has attracted more attention. Within the political system left-leaning political parties have traditionally articulated concern about corporate power in unrestrained markets and have advocated ideological alternatives in the form of social democracy and socialism. On a practical level agencies of government are designed to ensure that corporations pursue publicly defined goals in areas stretching from the environment to health and safety. Political accountability is demanded by many of the critical academics cited in this book and by polemicists such as Hutton, Monbiot, Klein and Bakan. But we have encountered their work in earlier chapters; instead we turn in this chapter to cultural sources of concern and to the critiques advanced in film and fiction which might be expected to have an impact on popular perceptions of the corporation and on popular demands for greater accountability. In effect we are addressing the question 'who cares?' How deep are concerns about excessive corporate power? How strong are the demands for government to do something? How outraged should we be if governments fail to respond?

POPULAR IMAGES OF THE CORPORATION

A theme running through this book is that the business corporation is far more than simply an economic organisation. In a cultural setting the corporation can be considered as an abstraction, an image or constructed reality, which exists as a part of the mental framework of individuals within society. As one of the leading institutions within modern society the image of the business corporation provides a component in what March and Olsen (1989: 39–40) call 'the institutionalisation of meaning', helping individuals to make sense of the world they inhabit. These corporate images embrace a set of ideas about corporations as organic bodies, about their purposes, their resources and their benevolence. Such ideas recall Keynes's proposition that 'economic interests are not based on "given" interests, but instead on intuitive beliefs' (Blyth, 2002: 42). Ideas can be combined into conventions, which provide stability for institutions and coordinate expectations. Here we are concerned with conventional views about the corporation, so that ideas about its operations drive the interests of actors in co-operating with, or opposing, the corporate state.

Thus the image of 'the corporation' provides a reservoir of possibilities – of ways in which individuals seek satisfaction, define desirable lifestyles and even create identities. These are large corporations which control significant resources through substantial organisation and enjoy an air of authority. They convey a cluster of images which, analogous to images of the family, can be idealised to encompass a range of possibilities from the good supportive corporation (the happy family) to the destructive exploitative corporation (the dysfunctional family), the important point being that corporations are visualised as idealised institutions which are an important element in constituting society and representing the corporate state. Moreover, corporations as moulders of values and lifestyles have supplanted earlier sources of institutionalised meaning based on institutions such as the army in militarised societies; the aristocracy and the monarchy in class-based societies; or religion and the church in virtually every Western developed society. This central position of the corporation as a constitutive institution in modern society was prophesied by those pioneers of corporate studies, Berle and Means, who speculated that 'the future may see the economic organization now typified by the corporation, not only on an equal plane with the state, but possibly even superseding it as the dominant form of social organization' (Berle and Means, 1932: 357; cited in Parker, 2002: 55). Speculation on the future of the corporation has become a vibrant topic for literature and film, and in many of these representations the corporation has indeed supplanted the state. In the real world of the early 21st century the corporation has not yet displaced the state, but in many areas of contemporary life the corporation is a larger presence in most people's lives than is 'government'.

The corporation as an institution is therefore imagined as part of the way in which individuals understand society. The ideas which contribute to people's construction of meaning are derived from multiple sources ranging from TV news to corporate marketing. One approach to interpreting how the corporation is understood across the mass of the population is therefore to turn to popular entertainment and cultural representations.

But people also understand the corporation through personal experience in the lifeworld and we can briefly consider those changing sources of meaning before examining the important relationship between cultural influence and corporate power. Within modern society the large corporation has a presence in people's lives through their activities as employees, consumers, borrowers, social beings and practitioners of management.

Employment is important not only for economic well being but as a source of psychological well being, with feelings of self-worth, achievement, status, community and as a source of happiness (Coyle, 2011: 43). For many people employment is more important than friends or even family, and provides a source of identity. The days of 'company man' may be fading (see Sampson, 1995), and employment may ultimately be a financial relationship, but the nature of work, the expectations, disciplines and rhythms are defined by the corporate workplace, even for those people who work outside the corporate sector. The importance of employment can be simply underlined by the stigma of unemployment and, as a provider of employment, the corporation features as a source of reassurance, trust, familiarity and, as we discuss below, of authority.

If employment is central for those in work, so consumption is important for virtually every member of the population. With the exception of the tiny elements of society who are ascetics or self-sufficient, we all meet needs from survival to spiritual fulfilment through processes of consumption. As consumers our needs are fulfilled within markets that are impossible to escape (Kozinets, 2002), whose dominant providers are corporations and whose whole rationale is to define and meet consumer demands, to the point that consumption becomes an art form. Western society is consumer society and its materialistic, often superficial nature has been subject to extended critiques which tend to emphasise corporate influence through marketing, manipulation of demand and product innovation. From a negative perspective this is the consumer society defined as 'Macdonaldization' (Ritzer, 1996) with the mass-produced and mass-consumed homogenous products offering only transient satisfaction (see Frank, 2001; B. Barber, 2007). Even from a less critical perspective, which celebrates the affluence of Western society, the central role of the corporation in meeting consumer demand would also accept its importance in moulding taste, defining lifestyles, branding people as well as products and defining demands to be met by markets and by governments.

Changing lifestyles in late modern society also increase the exposure of the individual to a world of markets organised and dominated by large corporations. As borrowers, individuals and households have taken on debt to an extraordinary extent, as revealed by the 2007–08 financial crisis. The stigma against debt has faded; many individuals have bank debt, credit card debt and mortgages. Their relationship to the large financial corporations that provide and police that debt becomes one of the most important in the lives of indebted households. It becomes more important to be a good credit risk than a good citizen (although in advanced market societies to be an active consumer with manageable debt is to be a good citizen) and people's financial profiles are constructed, exploited and even traded by the financial industry. Meanwhile, as social beings, individuals increasingly find their social intercourse mediated by corporations. In the digital world individuals seek information through Google, consume through Amazon, are entertained via their Apple iPads, and enter relationships through Facebook. Communication is no longer undertaken round the family dining table or by means of Her Majesty's Post Office, but by the ubiquitous mobile phone supplied by Vodaphone, Telefonica (O2), Everything Everywhere (Orange) or Hutchinson (3). The digital world not only influences, it literally creates identities through media such as Facebook. Again, a world defined by highly profitable giant corporations creates the social reality in which much of the population, and the majority of the younger population, experience lifeworlds which they regard as normal.

The proposition that individuals in western societies are absorbed into a corporate world reaches out beyond employment, consumption and debt to encompass thought processes. The ordering of information, defining of priorities, and criteria for decisions which are the bases of human cognition have increasingly become framed by ideas of 'management' absorbed from the corporation. Thus Parker argues that

> people believe that management is a precondition for organised society, for social progress and economic growth. If we have a difficulty with our jobs, our lives, our government or our world, then the answer is often supposed to be better management. (Parker, 2002: 2)

In his eloquent critique of management he observes that 'my broader target is "managerialism", the generalised ideology of management' (ibid.:10). Locke and Spender (2011) see managerialism as characterised by quantification and financial calculation, practiced by a caste of managers originating in American business schools who impose a universalised but impoverishing system for organizing human activity. We are enjoined to 'manage' almost every aspect of existence; we manage our time, our relationships, our money, our careers, our children and our anger. Indeed, the idea of 'anger management' nicely encapsulates the managerial reassurance that even personalities and emotions can be analysed, controlled and their performance assessed. Thus cultural theorists, such as Hancock and Tyler, argue 'that management discourse has come to "colonize" the life world' so that management thinking enters 'into all life spheres, and lifestyle magazines particularly deploy that to urge that lives are things to be managed' (in Rhodes and Westwood, 2008: 19).

The appeal of managerial modes of thought parallels the rise of the corporation as an institution. The calculation and optimisation of goals intrinsic to managerial approaches provides criteria for decisions which are very different from the criteria operated by other institutions. It differs from criteria of discipline and hierarchy in militarised societies, from faith and doctrine in religious societies, or from loyalty and deference in familial societies. This is important in normalising the behaviour of corporations, in bolstering the power of the corporate elite, and in reducing the ability to imagine alternative ways of organising society. Thus Grey (1999: 577) explores the idea of 'management' not only as a specialised occupation, but as a universal activity and 'as somehow an essential attribute of human life'. But he warns that the extension of ideas of management into society through expectations of 'self-management' carries a danger of managerial colonisation which 'installs this coordination and control in an ever-wider set of activities . . . By drawing the many rather than the few into management, managerial power – if not the power of managers – is extended rather than diminished' (ibid.: 578). To an increasing extent 'we are all managers now'. For many this is literally the case. In the UK the occupational census showed an extraordinary growth in the number of managers from 3.0 million in 1981 to 4.7 million in 2001, around 18 per cent of the workforce (see Wilson and Thomson, 2006: 18). This growth is reflected in management education in schools, universities and beyond. Of the 67 subjects researched in British universities, as assessed in the 2008 Research Assessment Exercise, the biggest by far, with about 3,500 academics, was 'Business and Management Studies'. The mental framework of managerialism has become ubiquitous.

Whether practiced in work or in private life, the influence of managerialism is important in the evaluation of corporate power. The imperative to be a good manager and to improve management skills and outcomes translates into respect and admiration for senior managers in corporations. It is they who provide the role models and who inspire the best selling 'airport' management gospels which 'typically represent the senior manager as heroic, central and critical to the success of the organisation' (Rhodes and Westwood, 2008: 18). This reinforces the legitimacy and authority of those in the corporate elite who as directors, management consultants or, above all, as CEOs act as the supreme exponents of management skills. Hence the engagement of the individual with the corporation at so many different levels has become infused with an admiration of the managerial dexterity with which successful corporations are run, and with an acceptance of the authority exercised by corporate managers and, indeed, of their leadership within society. In this way managerialism as an ideology provides a foundation for the power of management in its most advanced form in large corporations. Hence corporate ascendancy and managerial ascendency are closely associated and mutually supportive, with the reciprocal that criticism of management, or of corporate power, is simultaneously an attack on both.

This cultural positioning of the corporation as a central constituent of modern society and individual lifestyles makes it powerful. This is not the direct power of corporate lobbying, or the indirect power of corporate agenda setting; rather it is the third face of power – the power of normality. This ability of ruling elites to create systems of symbols, expectations and frameworks of meaning which legitimise their privileges has been addressed in Gramsci's elusive theories of 'hegemony' in which 'dominant classes do not simply rule but lead society through moral and intellectual guidance' (Hassard and Holliday, 1998: 2–3). As reviewed in earlier chapters, Fuchs discusses this source of power as an expression of 'the power of ideas' and terms it 'discursive power' (Fuchs, 2007: 140; see also Hay, 2006 and Schmidt, 2011). The discursive power of business is of fundamental importance. It amplifies the lobbying and agenda-setting power but, since it is embedded in prevailing ideas and societal norms, 'it is difficult to recognise and assess the discursive power of actors and to hold those actors responsible' (Fuchs, 2007: 147). The cultures of the market and competitiveness that underpinned the growth of this discursive power were discussed in Chapter 7 and are relatively recent. We have seen how they have been a constituent element of the New Corporate State discussed in Chapter 4, and the project to build discursive power was quite deliberately undertaken. But what can be built can also be demolished. Fuchs observes that 'while discursive power can thus be a particularly strong source of influence, it simultaneously is the most fragile dimension of an actor's power' (Fuchs, 2007: 148) and she examines challenges to the legitimacy of business as a political actor. Those challenges include corporate scandals and, of course, the 2008 financial crisis of capitalism. A particular danger for business would be a decline in the normative supports explored in Chapter 7; the norms of economic growth, competitiveness and neoliberalism. Normative support is embodied in popular perceptions and we can explore the threats to discursive power revealed in critical accounts of business, the corporation and management in popular film and literature.

THE CRITIQUE OF THE CORPORATION IN POPULAR CULTURE

There has been a steadily increasing recognition that political processes and institutions take on meaning through cultural representation. Politics operates through confrontations of interests, but also through confrontations of ideas. Explicit systems of political ideas can be expressed as ideologies but there is an implicit process of creating, disseminating and justifying ideas about institutions operating through the media by which populations make sense of what is going on around them – through television, papers, books, films and electronic media. Earlier chapters have emphasised the importance of ideas, and this chapter picks up the way in which ideas are incorporated into 'discourses'. We can gain insight into those discourses by examining how institutions are portrayed in fiction and film looking, for instance, at British political institutions and processes (see Fielding, 2011); or at management and business organisations (Lilley and McKinley, 2009). Indeed, such cultural representations may affect how political institutions operate as well as how they are perceived. It was suspected that the Number 10 staff in the Blair era thought of themselves as 'acting out a British version of *The West Wing*' (Randall, 2011: 274).

From the point of view of critique, fiction and film have a vastly greater potential to reach and mobilise large audiences than the output of scholars. Academic books and scholarly articles reach audiences of a few thousand, polemicists such as Monbiot, Bakan or Klein have a far wider impact, but even they cannot compete with the audiences for *Wall Street* (1987) much less *Avatar* (2009). Admittedly, the impact of Hollywood blockbusters is likely to be shallow and transient but some popular media have had huge influence. For instance, the sitcom series of *Yes Minister* and *Yes Prime Minister* (1986–88) enthralled a generation and presented the British senior civil service as cynical, self-serving, manipulative and inefficient. The brilliant acting, writing and humour effectively concealed a vehicle for the ideas of the New Right and *Yes Minister* arguably hastened the subordination of the civil service to the political domination and the new public management discussed in Chapter 5 (see Randall, 2011: 274). Even as Sir Gus O'Donnell retired as Head of the Civil Service in 2011 the press coverage returned again and again to hackneyed comparisons with the cynical 'Sir Humphrey' figure of *Yes Minister* which had come to personify the senior official in the public mind.

How, then, has popular culture treated 'the corporation'? In a word, critically. In a review of business in English literature Blundell regrets that 'one is faced with a rather damning picture of prodigiously wasteful, yet Scrooge-like businessmen who are abnormal and antagonistic; corrupt, cunning and cynical; dishonest, disorderly, doltish, dumb and duplicitous; inhumane, insensitive and irresponsible; ruthless, unethical and unprincipled; and villainous to boot' (Blundell, 2000: 8). Dealing with a wider canvas, embracing Anglo-American literature and film, Parker observed that 'though there have been negative representations of management and corporations for some considerable time, it seems to me that they are almost becoming dominant' (Parker, 2002: 135). Thus, even as the power of the corporation in society is increasing, so this has generated a backlash with increased criticism of the corporation, its leaders and its managers. But although critical studies clearly dominate, popular culture also celebrates the corporate hero, especially in his buccaneering guise. Thus we see Pierce Brosnan playing the irresistibly glamorous and carelessly wealthy private equity banker in *The Thomas Crown Affair* (1998); Richard Gere playing the attractive and successful corporate raider, Edward Lewis, in *Pretty Woman* (1990); and Michael Douglas as the seductive, wealthy and unscrupulous corporate asset stripper, Gordon Gekko, in the totemic *Wall Street* (1987). These enviable heroes are examples of the financial wizards, the masters of the universe drawn from the world of financial engineering rather than from the giant managed organisations of the corporation. These are portrayals of a corporate world as a site of dangerous, high-octane glamour, but there are alternative, darker and more threatening portrayals of the corporation.

Novels and films increasingly feature the corporation as an actor or a location, or by abstracting some facet of corporate organisation or practice. Thus the fiction may feature the corporation as a workplace; as a location for romance, discrimination or creativity; or as an arena for the deployment of managerial techniques. Moreover, the industrial enterprise has been a subject of fictional presentation for hundreds of years. It features in Dickens' *Dombey and Son* (1848) or in Trollope's *The Way We Live Now* (1875) and Pollard (2000; 26) observes that Defoe's *Robinson Crusoe* (1719) 'can be read as a paean of praise to business activity'. It is therefore difficult to capture the range of representations of corporations but we can turn to cultural theorists who have provided summaries and insights. Thus Martin Parker sees a more critical approach to organisations from the early 1980s (Parker, 2002: 143) while Hassard and Holliday note that 'in recent times, Hollywood has produced a plethora of films concerned with the corporation' (1998: 64) and Corbett (1998: 204) provides an analysis of organisations in science fiction films drawn from a review of 118 films between 1970 and 1995. In a spirit of illustration, rather than rigour, we can draw out a range of well known, relatively recent and possibly influential examples arranged in the three themes of conventional morality; usurpation of government; and alternative futures.

Corporations can be visualised within a conventional, contemporary framework of morality in which their behaviour can be compared with prevailing expectation of law, ethics and responsible behaviour. In such contemporary settings novels and films can provide powerful, emotionally engaging critiques of a range of corporate misbehaviour. An example where the real world translates into film is *Erin Brokovich* (2000), based on actual events, in which the heroine, played by Julia Roberts, exposes the way in which West Coast Energy covered up cases of industrial poisoning. Similarly the many real world examples of bribery and corruption take on a vivid personal engagement through the book and subsequent film of *The Constant Gardener* (2005) in which John Le Carré presents callous drug experimentation on African populations by the Three Bees Corporation working for 'the multinational pharmaceutical giant Karel Vita Hudson of Basel'. The heroine begins to uncover the insidious nexus of influence between the British government and the corporation which is willing to murder to cover up its activities since, 'there'd be hell to pay in Africa if the story got out that Three Bees were poisoning people' (Le Carré, 2005: 549, 499). Unlike *Erin Brokovich* the book and the film end in tragedy, the calculating senior Foreign Office official joins the corporation and the decent, ethical constant gardener, played by Ralph Fiennes, is murdered on the last page. Corporate power, suggests Le Carré, is frighteningly, heartbreakingly, irresistible.

The more traditional, class-based critique of the corporation, centred on exploitation of the workforce, seems to feature less prominently in contemporary popular culture. Gritty industrial novels such as Alan Sillitoe's *Saturday Night and Sunday Morning* (1958, film 1960) conveyed the drudgery of the shop floor with echoes of the poverty portrayed in Orwell's (non-fiction) *The Road to Wigan Pier* (1937) but a focus on simple exploitation is perhaps less resonant in the post-1980s, post-industrial society. Instead, attention from the early 1980s turned to greed. The rise of the free market and the associated creation of the yuppie culture provoked books such as Martin Amis's *Money* (1984), with hypnotic accounts of overwhelming greed and the obsession with money as the measure of wealth and as the overwhelming purpose of human existence. This translated into corporate greed in *Wall Street* (1987), directed by Oliver Stone, in which the glamorous corporate raider Gordon Gekko, played by Michael Douglas, corrupts Adam Smith's invisible hand in his unforgettable 'greed is good' speech made at the annual general meeting of Teldar Paper in which he declares that, 'Greed, for lack of a better word, is good. Greed is right. Greed works. Greed clarifies, cuts through and captures, the essence of the entrepreneurial spirit . . . and greed, you mark my words, will not only save Teldar paper, but that other malfunctioning corporation called the USA'. His celebration of greed provided the motif for twenty years of turbo-capitalism and the triumph of high finance and market making, as conveyed in another film, this time shockingly biographical, as *The Smartest Guys in the Room* (2005) tells the story of the almost unbelievable arrogance and greed that created and then destroyed the Enron Corporation. There is a moral tale here. Gekko is outwitted and is incarcerated in a fictional prison (see the sequel, *Wall Street: Money Never Sleeps*, 2010). The Enron criminals, Jeff Skilling and Andrew Fastow, inhabit real prisons (in Skilling's case with a 24-year sentence) and Tom Wolfe's antihero, the millionaire bond trader Sherman McCoy, in *The Bonfire of the Vanities* (1987, and film 1990), is humiliated and destroyed.

The cultural indictments of greed thus seem preoccupied with the hubris of high finance rather than the managerial hierarchies of large corporations, and their attack is in any case ambiguous. Michael Douglas and Charlie Sheen, the stars of *Wall Street*, have commented that they still meet traders who went into Wall Street inspired by the film. Greed may bring moral censure but is also brings the ultimate consumer lifestyle and a cynical, macho, compelling glamour that has been termed 'sexy-greedy' (Hassard and Holliday, 2000: 13). Cultural critiques of the corporation can also perversely transmute into celebrations of the successful 'players'.

A final component of this theme of critiques based on conventional morality takes us from the glamour of Wall Street to the simply boring and oppressive – the 'mundane conspiracies' (Parker, 2002: 151) which accompany oppression in the corporate hierarchy. The tedious reality of managerialism in the lower echelons of the corporation is brilliantly captured in *The Office* (first broadcast, 2001). Set in the Slough office of the WernhamHogg Paper Co, the staff are exposed to the toe-curling embarrassment of regional manager David Brent's pitiful attempts at managerial leadership, with its implicit critique of those fashionable cultural management theories which stress engagement, participation and bonding with employees. Whether the actor Ricky Gervais intended his creation to capture the oppression of the workplace is unclear, but perhaps he achieves a condemnation of post-industrial, post-modern management more effectively than any scholarly study.

A second theme within popular critiques is provided by novels and films within which corporations usurp government either by creating alternative systems of governance, or by replacing government entirely. A brilliant example is provided by Max Barry's novel *Jennifer Government* (2003) in which nations are dominated by corporations and government itself has been privatised. Employees take on the names of their corporations, hence 'Jennifer Government' who is a field agent for the Australian government.

The book provides a weirdly logical vision of a future dominated by corporations and market principles. The central plot is of a marketing campaign in which John Nike, a Nike Vice President, contracts to have the first purchasers of their new Nike Mercuries trainers murdered, to emphasise how desperately they are in demand. To quote,

> 'We're going to shoot them', Vice President John said. 'We're going to kill anyone who buys a pair' ... 'We take out ten customers, make it look like ghetto kids, and we've got street cred coming out of our asses. I bet we shift our entire inventory within twenty-four hours.' (Barry, 2003: 6)

The story is compelling simply by virtue of the way in which it takes the calculations of marketing and profit maximisation to their logical conclusion. Another extrapolation of current investment strategies is provided by Richard Morgan in his book *Market Forces* (2004) in which the big money has moved from commodities to 'conflict investment'. In an apparently quasi-anarchistic world, hedge funds invest in conflicts anywhere in the world using tools and perspectives which would be familiar to today's political risk analysts. Morgan dedicates his novel 'to all those, globally, whose lives have been wrecked or snuffed out by the Great Neoliberal Drama and Slash-and-Burn Globalisation'. Like *Jennifer Government*, he portrays an impossible and soulless world, but one that is just sufficiently reflective of modern corporate strategies to prompt pause for thought.

An even more compelling narrative involving the perversion of the profit motive is Margaret Atwood's novel *Oryx and Crake* (2005) in which the Booker Prize-winning author portrays a future where genetic manipulation of animals and diseases threatens the destruction of mankind. The central character's father works for Helth Wyzer in a world where government seems to have faded away and order is provided by corporations, their security forces and secure compounds. Corporations manufacture diseases so that they can profit from marketing cures, thus 'the best diseases from a business point of view', says Crake, 'would be those that cause lingering illness. Ideally – that is, for maximum profit – the patient should either get well or die just before his or her money runs out. It's a fine calculation' (Atwood, 2005: 211). The cynical and morally perverted pursuit of profit has become the ultimately destructive mobilising principle in the world of *Oryx and Crake*, and there are evidently minimal public institutions or law enforcement agencies to protect the public interest and those outside the corporate embrace living in the 'pleeblands'. Atwood thus presents an indictment of corporate society and of the unregulated exploitation of technology and she does so with artistry, eloquence and the persuasive power of a celebrated novelist.

This ability to criticise whilst also to amuse, and to shock, is evident in the earlier classic war novel *Catch 22* (1961). One of the most compelling and admired novels of the 20th century, Joseph Heller's masterpiece also unveils the subterranean driving forces which propel the military machine towards increasing absurdity and murderous exploitation of its airmen. His irrepressible entrepreneurial puppet master is Milo Minderbinder, the mess officer, who runs a 'syndicate' engaged in worldwide profitable trading, regardless of its impact on the war effort or his fellow airmen. He sells ball bearings and petroleum to the Germans (Heller, 2004: 356), contracts with the enemy to bomb his own airfields, and has sold the painkilling morphine drugs from the first aid kits leaving a 'note that said "what's good for M&M Enterprises is good for the country"' (421). Heller's surreal tale is clearly unbelievable but it provokes a niggle of doubt and provides a parable of the moral bankruptcy of big business, willing to trade with the enemy and to put profits before patriotism and well ahead of heroism. In fact, of course, war is of great benefit to some businesses. Fortunes were made, products developed and the inheritors of Milo's legacy were the corporations that benefited from the US military–industrial complex (and from subsequent conflicts, such as Halliburton in Iraq; Klein, 2007: 292–3). The manipulative potential of corporations is similarly explored in the blockbuster world of James Bond whose adversary in *Tomorrow Never Dies* (1997) is the power-crazed Elliott Carver, the CEO of the Carver Media Group Network who intends to create conflict between the UK and China, only to be foiled by Pierce Brosnan's James Bond. Is Carver a veiled Rupert Murdoch? Certainly the viewer comes away with a reinforced image of the power of the global media corporation.

It is thus relatively easy to find popular culture reaching out to large audiences with portrayals of corporations conspiring with government and manipulating governments to exploit employees and the public. When they go further and replace governments the results are horrifying. Corporate rule brings a dystopia, a world of lying, manipulation, extreme inequality but also of an altered, corrupted society. The dystopian views are in the tradition of Aldous Huxley whose immensely influential *Brave New World* (1931) does not explicitly attack the corporation. On the other hand it is set in the 7th century AF 'After Ford', high rank earns the title of 'His Fordship' and there are hints that business has become the government (Jones, 2012). In any case we have a representation of a highly regimented, hierarchically organised society akin to a giant corporation. This body of literature and film offers us an interpretation of some of the corporate forces that may be dictating the overtly legitimate actions of government. It also serves as a visionary warning of what could go wrong if the steady deterioration in government capacity means that corporations are increasingly unchecked. The dystopian corporate futures carry a warning of systemic, structural threat. This is not the wrongdoing of individual CEOs or corporations, it is the entire society which has been subverted and perverted.

The literature and film which speculates on corporations replacing governments can be regarded as 'future fiction' but the third theme revolves more clearly around the specific genre of 'science fiction'. Science fiction books address a smaller audience although the films, as with *Avatar* (2009), may have a vast popular appeal. Scholars working within management studies have drawn on the science fiction canon to undertake subtle critiques of management and the corporation, and how we can visualise their trajectories, drawing on trends within contemporary society. They speculate about the impact of this media on the popular imagination and their argument that it is influential carries conviction. Images such as Mary Shelley's monster in *Frankenstein; or, the Modern Prometheus* (1818) provide a universally understood parable easily transferable to a corporate critique so that 'in these films, . . . the real enemy is no longer the individual Dr Frankenstein but the big corporations or states that sponsor them' (Parker, 2002: 145). These corporate enemies figure in contemporary science fiction.

By its very nature, science fiction explores future trajectories of current technology and speculates on how they may be driven or dictated by corporate strategies. Thus *Oryx and Crake* explores the future implications of genetic adaptation, and *I Robot* (2004) explores the implications of artificial intelligence, dealing with the classic issues defined by Isaac Asimov (1951) about how humankind can escape domination by its robotic creations. The hero, Del Spooner, played by Will Smith, uncovers a scheme for robots to take control of society, ostensibly, in echoes of Rousseau, to save humanity from itself. His efforts to foil the scheme are opposed by USR (US Robotics), the corporation which designed and manufactures the robots. USR is presented as a manipulative, secretive and murderous organisation which Spooner saves from itself after its CEO, Lawrence Robertson, is strangled by his own robots. In both cases it seems that the corporation's profit driven exploitation of its technology leads to the oppression of humanity and the potential destruction of civilisation.

We see the robotic theme also in one of the most influential science fiction films of the 1980s. *Blade Runner* (1982) is a film by Ridley Scott centred on the Tyrell Corporation which creates androids (replicants) which are virtually indistinguishable from humans. Rhodes and Westwood (2008: 76) capture the message, 'as the city decays and the earth's ecosystem is in ruins . . . Tyrell seems to be animated by only two things – doing business and realizing the potential of technology'. They go on to argue that '*Blade Runner* embodies an extreme distrust in the trajectory of capitalism' and that as 'a 2019 science fiction dystopia, *Blade Runner* exposes a vision of today's hard corporate realities. Realities when corporations seek to control not just business, but the very notion of what it might be to be human' (88, 91). In addition, therefore, to playing God by replicating a commercialised form of humanity, the Tyrell Corporation is complicit in global environmental destruction. Its cynical pursuit of profit echoes the string of four *Alien* films, also directed by Ridley Scott (and commercially more successful).

In the sinister *Alien* sequence (1972, 1985, 1992, 1997) Sigourney Weaver plays Ripley, a member of the crew of the Nostromo who 'work for a great interstellar corporation whose stated (initially secret) policy is that all other considerations are secondary to the return to earth of a living alien' (Corbett, 1998: 207). The alien is a commercial opportunity, sought for its potential to undertake profitable weapons research, and the viewers gradually begin to realise that the human crew are dispensable. In Corbett's dramatic summary, 'the unholy trinity of the monstrous phallic alien, Mother [the shipboard computer] and Ash [a traitorous robotic crew member] come to represent the imperialist company – patriarchal high technology capitalism at its most malevolent and rapacious' (1998: 208). It is doubtful that the mass of the viewing public came away from *Alien* with a revelation of the evils of 'patriarchal capitalism' but they surely would have had their instinctive distrust of corporate greed reinforced. In the simple black and white world of good and evil the corporation again becomes demonised, although here again its manipulations are exposed and confounded by the heroic, moral individual. Films, it seems, are ultimately more optimistic than books. The identification with the individual hero is, at least temporarily, more intense and there as a compulsion towards the happy ending. All these features are present in the last of these examples of a dangerous future in *Avatar* (2009).

Avatar provides a wonderful example of the critique of the corporation in popular culture simply because it was so popular. It was a box office sensation and the highest grossing film up to that time, taking the prize from *Titanic* (also directed by James Cameron). The plot of *Avatar* is a story of pure corporate greed. In the 22nd century the mining corporation RDA is in pursuit of a rare mineral, 'unobtainium' which is present in abundance on the planet Pandora. To mine the mineral the corporation has to remove the indigenous species, the humanoid Na'vi, and the film tells the story of failed attempts to relocate the indigenous civilisation followed by full-scale military assault by RDA security forces. The goal is clearly profit and the scruples of the management are over-ridden by the imperative to meet corporate goals. Ultimately the moral humans, including the human hybrid avatars, together with the collected tribes and the planet itself combine to defeat the corporation.

The RDA Corporation is a 'Vandal' in its original pejorative sense. In the name of greed it is willing to disdain and destroy an entire civilisation which, in many ways, is superior to its own. It can be compared to the pillage of Imperial Rome by the Vandals under their King Genseric in AD 455 (Gibbon, 1999: 706), and the audiences of *Avatar* are presented with an uncomplicated, simplistic parable condemning a philistine corporation, narrowly obsessed with huge profit, and willing to engage in an orgy of destructive exploitation with no apparent regime of accountability. But this message was obscured, and almost submerged, by the cinematic spectacle with extraordinary special effects, the highly successful 3-D format and the creation of the tall, blue humanoids with their beguiling religion, language and symbiosis with their environment. Commentary emphasised the commercial and technical success, with three Academy Awards for technical achievements.

In terms of its social and political message, *Avatar* was seen as a condemnation of US imperialism and the Iraq War. It was also interpreted as a 'clash of civilisations' film and as a celebration of pantheism. Some politicians praised it as a critique of capitalism and a defence of nature, but pundits also criticised its left-leaning stance and ideological bias. The great irony, of course, is that the film was made by Twentieth Century Fox, a subsidiary of News International and component of the Murdoch empire. It made profits for the very system it criticised, an element reinforced by its sponsorship by Coca Cola. In relation to the popular perception of the corporation *Avatar* is fascinating. Its plot is crude and obvious, its characterisations are one-dimensional, its victims are romanticised and, as a main stream blockbuster, it does not lend itself to the intense analysis and interpretation beloved of critical theorists. Yet its central villain is the corporation, its goal is profit, its (human) characters are trapped by corporate imperatives and the corporation is willing to use the most brutal means to secure its goals. But if the message is familiar, the audience is extraordinary. *Avatar* was the first film to gross over $2 billion and reached a global audience of at least 200 million. Did those 200 million viewers absorb the critique of the corporation? If only 10 per cent of them did then the film potentially influenced the cultural perceptions of 20 million people, many of them younger, more impressionable adults. It is clear that the message resonated with many opponents of corporate capitalism. In a surreal example of life imitating art the huge Vedanta Resources multinational mining corporation appeared to be behaving exactly like RDA in its attempts to mine bauxite from a mountain sacred to the God of the Dongria Kondh tribe in the Indian State of Orissa. The tribe had fought the plans and the Indian government for eight years, but the climax came at the AGM of Vedanta Resources in July 2010 when activists made up as Na'vi protested at the meeting and created substantial media coverage. The direct parallel with *Avatar* made for a powerful and extraordinarily topical indictment. In August 2010 the Indian government rejected the application for the mine and insisted that Vedanta clean up its smelter (see http://orissaconcerns.net, accessed 1 February 2012 and Xaxa, 2012).

This partial review of representations of the corporation in popular culture has picked out three discourses abstracted from the many interpretations and readings of recent film and literature. The discourse of conventional morality reflects the corporation behaving badly. It is all too believable, especially since it sometimes draws on actual cases, and it presents the audience with a vivid, engaging portrayal of how corporations can harm individuals, families and communities. The discourse of replacing government requires more of a leap of imagination, but it presents a disturbing extrapolation of where corporate strategies may lead if they are not checked, regulated and held accountable. Finally, the discourse of alternative futures paints a dystopian possibility, too awful to accept, too unreal to believe, but combining a prophecy and a warning. The audience leaves the cinema, closes the book, with a profound sense of relief that such a future is unlikely to ensue, but perhaps with a sense of unease that in order to avoid it, vigilance is to be recommended and corporations cannot be trusted. We can draw a series of conclusions from these discourses and cultural critiques which lead us back to consider their impact on corporate power, the corporate response and CSR.

First, the large corporation has consolidated its place as a constituent institution of modern society. It is natural, normal, part of the landscape and, just as films and books take aim at the government, the church, the army or the hospital, so too they confront the corporation. Second, despite its familiarity, the corporation often appears as a shadowy, intangible and sinister manipulator. Systematic presentations of the corporation as an organic whole are rare and instead 'it' is often a brooding presence, to be regarded with suspicion, but also misunderstood. Sympathetic portrayals are even rarer. Why is the corporation in popular culture so seldom a force for good? Third, academic studies of the corporation, and indeed of political power generally, are too dismissive of popular culture. Popular sentiments, popular prejudices, knee-jerk tabloid reactions may be regarded as irrelevant and outside the framework of elite understandings but they provide a context. Politicians must be aware of mass preferences. They tap into mass views through polls and focus groups and react through spin and the dynamics of the 'permanent campaign'. Those preferences are affected by popular literature and film to a greater extent than is recognised by intellectuals writing in learned journals. As Parker (2002: 134) acerbically puts it, 'an average popular film or book reaches more people than even the most hyped academic "best-seller". Most academic journals would be happy to reach a circulation of 1,000 . . . for most people, the latest blockbuster matters, whilst the latest critical management studies text doesn't even appear on the radar'. Films have impact, while academic writing too often pedantically pursues self-important ideas down arcane theoretical alleyways which elude colleagues, bore students and fail to engage with social improvement.

Fourth, and finally, popular critiques of the corporation help to create distrust of one of the central institutions of contemporary society. This worries some business people and most business organisations. In a thoughtful and unusually speculative study assessing the implications of the financial crisis the CBI identified five key drivers of business change over the next ten years. One of these was 'the decline in trust in business and markets' and the CBI points out that this matters for a range of reasons, including the likelihood that 'ultimately governments will intervene with tougher regulations and tighter control of business' (CBI, 2009: 10). Decline in trust will have a differential impact on corporations. Those in consumer-facing sectors and those identified in Chapter 2 as being exceptionally vulnerable to public contracting and regulation could be expected to regard declining trust as a major strategic risk. The risk lies in the fragility of the discursive power of business and it merges with the politics of austerity to reinforce challenges to business. The challenges have been especially evident in the financial sector and fuelled constant post-2008 demands for more restrictive regulation of executive rewards. It also emerged as an element in Labour Opposition attacks on the Coalition in the shape of Ed Miliband's identification of a cadre of 'predatory' companies (Miliband, 2011). These are not threats that intelligent business leaders can afford to ignore.

The CBI points out that trust in business in the UK and across Europe has been on a declining trend for some years but it is unclear what role has been played by popular culture. Is it a motive force or simply a mirror to cultural trends? Trust has become a subject for serious research and survey work. The PR corporation, Edelman, undertakes a well regarded annual survey of trust in institutions. The results are intriguing. Their 'trust barometer' in Table 8.1 indicates, however, that trust in business is greater than trust in government for five leading economies. In the UK, trust in institutions is alarmingly and puzzlingly weak, the proximity to the figures for Russia indicates a probably overdeveloped level of scepticism, but the relative distrust of government is consistent with the UK trust data presented in Chapter 6. One other intriguing result is that CEOs are more

Table 8.1 Levels of trust in business and in government

Question: 'How much do you trust business/government to do what is right?'

	Business %	Government %	Pro-business margin
UK	44	43	1
USA	46	40	6
Japan	53	51	2
Germany	52	33	19
Russia	41	39	2
Brazil	81	88	−7

Source: Edelman (2011).

trusted than their corporations. The public apparently seek authoritative figures and trust academics/experts (70 per cent) and CEOs (50 per cent) over government officials (43 per cent). Predictably, Edelman stresses the value of trust and argues that corporations are increasingly engaging to build trust which is, they also argue, equally as important to consumers as product quality (Edelman, 2011: 5, 7). The argument presented in this chapter so far indicates that if corporations want to build trust they have quite a mountain to climb in the area of popular film and literature. In fact the corporate response to declining trust and to public perceptions is multi-dimensional and includes a substantial investment in 'corporate social responsibility'.

CONCLUSION: ACCOUNTABILITY TO A SUSPICIOUS PUBLIC

Going back to our opening discussion of accountability, it is clear that large corporations are highly visible, as part of the life world and as represented in popular entertainment. It is also plausible to argue that the public image of the corporation is as shadowy, self-interested, manipulative and not to be trusted. They are also likely to imagine it as formidably powerful with few sources of constraint and possessing hidden but irresistible powers of persuasion. That, at least, is the image projected by fiction and film which is almost universally critical of corporations. This means that there is a distinct problem of political accountability. A public suspicious of corporations will expect their political leaders to create and enforce modes of effective accountability. But how powerful are these expectations? To return again to the opening discussion how influential are the popular media and does the public really care?

In conveying negative images the entertainment media must be regarded as potentially very influential. The messages they convey are undemanding, they are absorbed rather than imposed. Since they are seldom analysed by the audience they influence attitudes rather than overt opinions but they are able to mould attitudes far more effectively than reasoned argument. Depictions of corporate activities reveal the human dilemmas and cross-currents within the corporation. They illustrate more effectively than sober analysis that the corporation is indeed a contested and irrational arena within which policies are negotiated in complex processes. Popular depictions also capture the oppression of the corporate hierarchy and the domination of employees by procedures, instructions and self-evident expectations that brook no contradiction. Such depictions are not insights, rather they feed instinctive suspicions of authority, they fuel a visceral scepticism about corporate altruism and they therefore present a challenge to the discursive power of the corporation.

It might be expected that this negative atmosphere would worry business generally, and in particular the large corporations that are politically active. Corporations are concerned to project a good image to consumers and to employees. Reputations are important, especially since negative sentiments towards corporations and their senior management empower politicians and increase the chances of unfavourable regulation. It is not, therefore, surprising that as corporations have become more aware of popular pressures for political accountability they have responded by developing strategies to project themselves as responsible members of society. Those strategies have blossomed since the late 1990s and comprise a whole new area of corporate political activity, welcome to the world of corporate social responsibility, to which we turn in Chapter 9.

9. How persuasive is corporate social responsibility?

THE EMERGENCE OF CORPORATE SOCIAL RESPONSIBILITY

The increased attention to the idea of corporate social responsibility (CSR), its inclusion in corporate strategies, and the growth of the CSR 'industry' has been remarkable. In the UK an idea that was regarded as marginal, eccentric and largely dismissed by both proponents and critics of corporate capitalism became respectable from the early 1980s and is now firmly mainstream. The rise of CSR can only be explained in the context of other major changes in society, the economy and political ideology. Among those changes are the increased criticism of the corporation already outlined Chapter 8 but, of course, CSR is reflective of much more profound changes. Indeed, the CSR phenomenon illustrates, and provides evidence for, many of the themes explored in this book including, paradoxically, corporate political power.

Every mention of corporate social responsibility is simultaneously an affirmation of market power and hence a recognition that perfectly competitive markets are an illusion. Unless it is recognised that corporations have economic power, which can be translated into social and political power, then CSR is, by definition, nonsense. In a world of perfect markets CSR is impossible. In that world there is no surplus available to fund non-productive activities, there is no room for managerial discretion, and the diversion of resources to CSR brings bankruptcy. As a business concept CSR has been created by and for larger corporations. To this extent Friedman was quite right. His argument was that in a free economy, 'there is one and only one social responsibility of business – to use resources and engage in activities designed to increase its profits so long as it stays within the rules of the game, which is to say, engages in open and free competition, without deception or fraud' (Friedman, 1982: 133). The Friedmanite doctrine has permeated debate about CSR. It is simple, parsimonious and draws its authority from Adam Smith. Through the invisible hand the pursuit of profit enhances welfare but, and it is a huge 'but', only if markets are perfectly competitive. This book has argued that markets are only partially competitive. They are organised, regulated and substantially controlled by large corporations. Oligopoly is the norm and in that setting CSR makes perfect sense. CSR is 'the visible hand' of market power and managerial discretion. As corporate power has grown, so CSR has become more relevant and more important. CSR is the human face of the New Corporate State and it is a recognition that corporate power could be used to benefit individuals, communities and society at large. But, before drawing conclusions about the merits of CSR we should plot its rise, map its scale and explore the motives for corporations to include it in their strategies and their governance.

The term 'corporate social responsibility' is so vague and slippery that it could not be regarded as a 'concept'. Ougaard (2006: 228) calls it 'a movement' whilst van Oosterhaut and Heugens (2008: 198) argue that it is so conceptually flawed 'that the notion of CSR is better dispensed with altogether'. Yet it is clearly here to stay. It has become so ubiquitous and so institutionalised that it is better regarded as a 'management discourse' which seeks to attach meaning to corporate behaviour and strategies. A blunt political interpretation would be to regard CSR as 'privatisation of regulation', whilst an equally blunt managerial interpretation could be expressed as 'reputation management'. But perhaps these sweeping characterisations fail to do justice to the leverage of the term and we should examine more closely the by now vast range of literature that expresses the CSR discourse.

In his rigorous examination of corporate responsibility in a legal setting Parkinson (1993: 260) defined corporate social responsibility as 'incurring uncompensable costs for socially desirable but not legally mandated action'. He emphasised the voluntary element and the social focus. Among the many other competing definitions, one offered by Jones in 1980 elaborates both these elements and uses the loaded term 'obligations', hence 'corporate social responsibility is the notion that corporations have obligations to constituent groups in society other than stockholders' (cited in Carroll, 2008: 34). Jones also emphasises the broad scale of social obligations and the extensive range of stakeholders who could be affected. In the years since he wrote, the scale and scope of CSR has expanded to the point that the entire universe of social and environmental goods, from clean water to effective government, have come into play. Ougaard observes that 'few if any areas of human concern, in principle, are completely outside the scope of CSR' (2006: 233). The key point, however, is that the pursuit of this range of goals and public goods is voluntary. CSR is about self-regulation, it is about corporations choosing to operate to benefit other groups within society without any direct compulsion from government. Hence the frequent references to corporate philanthropy or corporate altruism.

It could be said that there is nothing new in CSR. The discussion in Chapter 2 of 'the license to operate' expressed the idea that incorporation and limited liability implied obligations for corporations to operate in the public interest. CSR re-affirms these original expectations which are, in fact, still part of the corporate culture in more solidaristic countries such as Germany and Japan. There is also, of course, a venerable and admirable tradition of business altruism. It is expressed in Christian doctrine, especially in the non-conformism of the Quakers and the Methodists (Kurtz, 2008: 254), and it inspired the various model communities created by 19th-century industrialists at Saltaire (Sir Titus Salt), Port Sunlight (Lever Brothers), Bournville (George Cadbury) and New Lanark (Robert Owen). Most of these early initiatives were undertaken by enlightened individuals rather than corporations and the history of contemporary, managerially focussed, CSR is usually dated back to the 1950s but modern CSR is much more recent, dating from serious debate in the 1980s, with a build up in the 1990s and fuller maturation in the 2000s.

There have been distinct national variations in the conception and adoption of CSR. It has been taken much more seriously throughout the 20th century in the USA, mainly because the private sector has always been more important in the delivery of public goods. Government has been non-interventionist, and there has been no socialist alternative operating, for instance, through nationalised industries (see Moon and Vogel, 2008: 306). It is logical, therefore, that as governments across Europe adopted neoliberal policies from the 1980s, so CSR gained greater centrality. As government retreated, so corporations grew in importance, but in the early 1980s CSR was not emphasised in boardrooms. Instead the growing influence of New Right policies generated over-confidence, as seen in corporate responsibility reporting, hence 'the dawn of the 1980s heralded a sharp decline in voluntary corporate social and environmental reporting' (Owen and O'Dwyer, 2008: 388). The renewed interest in CSR was more defensive, in response to crises, public criticism and threats to reputation (see Lee and Carroll, 2011:117 and Grafström and Windell, 2011: 228–9). Corporate responsibility acquired greater priority in the 1990s and analysis of UK coverage in the *Financial Times* and the *Guardian* shows a huge increase in references to CSR up to 2002 followed by a sustained coverage throughout the 2000s (Grafström and Windell, 2011: 225). By the late 2000s CSR had become an industry in its own right.

The CSR industry encompasses awards, league tables, codes of conduct, NGOs, specialist divisions of management consultants and auditors, government sponsored initiatives and, in the academic world, specialist journals and core topics in undergraduate and postgraduate business school courses. Levy and Kaplan (2008: 438) remark that 'the rapidity with which large corporations have adopted various standards and reporting mechanisms ... is quite astonishing, given the absence of financial inducements or regulatory coercion'. It is not practicable to itemise this landscape of initiatives but here we can mention two important international organisations. A significant initiative is the UN Global Compact launched in 2000 as a set of benchmarks for human rights, labour rights and environmental responsibility (Rasche and Kell, 2010; Hale, 2011). It operates through a corporate membership engaged with a series of learning networks and, although voluntary, it allows corporations to establish an authenticated standard of corporate responsibility with the associated reputational advantages. It has been criticised as superficial, poorly policed and with little real impact on corporate behaviour (see May, 2006: 278–9; Baccaro and Mele, 2011) but its real significance is perhaps in demonstrating that even the pre-eminent international political body, the United Nations, cannot regulate global corporations, but seeks to bolster self-regulation. It is therefore one of the first instances of a global body accepting the political and cultural power of the corporation.

A second ambitious and potentially significant body is the increasingly visible Global Reporting Initiative. For some time it had been argued that corporate social *performance* provided a more rigorous, transparent and accountable expression of corporate responsibility than the vague phrase 'CSR'. The focus on performance prompted the creation in 1997 of the Global Reporting Initiative (GRI) as an independent, non-governmental body providing guidelines for corporations to produce 'sustainability reports'. In 2002 it was formally affiliated as a UN collaborating centre. It has a Secretariat based in Amsterdam and has produced guidelines that aspire to be the sustainability equivalent to International Accounting Standards. Measured by visibility, productivity and reputation, it has been remarkably successful. The standards are widely used in corporate sustainability reports but the ambitions to create a vehicle of multi-stakeholder global governance have not been realised. Increasingly the GRI has become orientated towards the large corporations and business consultancies that fund its activities (Brown, 2011: 287) and it illustrates the tendency for CSR activities to be managed by corporations as a reputational tool rather than as a real driver of responsible behaviour.

At some point in the 2000s CSR came of age and the corporate social responsibility discourse became so influential that corporations were virtually required to engage, in the words of KPMG (2011: 6), 'corporate responsibility reporting has become a fundamental imperative for business ... It now seems to have become virtually mandatory for most multinational companies'. This observation comes from KPMG's triennial Survey of Corporate Social Responsibility Reporting which was launched in 1993 and has become a respected source of data. Their 2011 Report covered the world's 250 largest corporations (drawn from the *Fortune Global 500*) plus the 100 largest corporations from each of 34 countries, including China. By 2011 95 per cent of the largest 250 corporations produced reports on corporate responsibility and 64 per cent of the 3,400 large corporations. The growth in G250 reporting is startling, up from 35 per cent in 1999 and 64 per cent in 2005. The UK and Japan boasted 100 per cent reporting with the USA lagging at 83 per cent but China making rapid progress at 60 per cent (KPMG, 2011: 9–10). The Survey also noted a higher standard of reporting with 80 per cent of the G250 following the GRI global standard and with more corporations having their reports audited and integrated into their annual reports. There has, it seems, been something of a revolution in 'responsibility reporting' and, since reporting requires processes for defining and measuring, in addition to something to measure, the assumption is that some degree of active responsibility is becoming 'core business' for the world's largest corporations. We are seeing, says KPMG (2011: 22) 'the birth of a new era of "sincere" CR reporting'.

MOTIVATIONS FOR CORPORATIONS TO UNDERTAKE CSR

Assessing the rationale for CSR is an important component in answering the more central question, which is whether CSR involves corporations taking on political or governmental functions. In order to assess the rationale it is necessary to explore corporate motivations which can be examined under the four categories of enhanced profitability, risk management, regulatory frameworks, and CEO leadership. The most basic and obvious motive for engaging in CSR is that it protects profits, brings financial benefits or, in the clichés of shareholder value theory, it 'adds value'. This argument has become known as 'the business case' and it has dominated debate and research on CSR. Kurucz et al. (2008) itemise the potential for CSR to add value through cost reduction, competitive advantage, brand enhancement and synergistic value creation harnessing the economic benefits of social capital. If there is a business case, corporations would be perverse not to engage in CSR and it becomes self-justifying. Unfortunately, and quite predictably, there is no unambiguous body of research that proves that CSR always adds value. It obviously does in some cases with regard to certain types of corporation, sectors or contexts but it is impossible to generalise.

Risk management provides a second motivation for corporations to engage in CSR. It is not entirely separable from 'the business case', in fact all arguments in favour of CSR can ultimately be reduced to some form of the business case since they all seek to contribute to the survival of the business. Nevertheless, risk management is concerned with trust, popular perceptions and reputation and its benefits are less tangible and longer term. CSR can contribute to reduction of risk by establishing links with internal stakeholders (such as employees and investors) and with external stakeholders such as consumers, creditors, communities, suppliers and NGOs. Stakeholder management is a core component of CSR and has evolved as a specialism in its own right (see Friedman and Miles, 2006). Stakeholder engagement rests on the idealised principle that everyone affected by the activities of the corporation has a 'stake' in those activities and that stake should be recognised. In early formulations a stakeholder was a person or organisation whose actions affected the success of the corporation but that rapidly expanded to encompass all people affected by the corporation and further expanded to include for instance, the environment and future generations (Friedman and Miles, 2006: 14).

Whilst the idealised extremes of stakeholder aspirations appear simply as pious moralising the core idea is sound. It makes sense that those substantially affected by a corporation should be consulted, have their views heard and contribute towards the formulation of strategies. Many stakeholders already have a contractual relationship with their corporation and it would be perfectly possible to adapt company law to require managers to consult with, and to be influenced by, a wider group of stakeholders. In the UK this idea enjoyed a brief popularity in the mid-1990s when 'stakeholder capitalism' was widely debated and endorsed by New Labour (see Chapter 10). Political support for legislation faded away as New Labour turned instead to more business-friendly policies but voluntary stakeholder engagement matured as an approach favoured by management precisely because it is vague and malleable. It provides a plausible and seductive rhetoric with which to reach out to people and organisations who could materially damage corporate performance. Through CSR initiatives, partnerships and reporting, corporations present themselves as responsible and caring, as an antidote to the criticisms reviewed in Chapter 8 (Moon and Vogel, 2008: 306). If commercial partners, investors, consumers, employees and the myriad organisations within society with whom a corporation deals regard it as responsible and trustworthy, that provides substantial benefits. And corporations can be very effective in packaging their activities, managing their image and aligning corporate interests with societal interests. Examples are legion and available by visiting the website of any large corporation or looking at the awards and league tables provided in the UK by BITC (Business in the Community). This marketing serves as an antidote to the negative representations of the corporation examined earlier in Chapter 8. For every Margaret Atwood or Max Barry there are hundreds of positive, optimistic, reassuring messages from Diageo, Monsanto, Shell or PepsiCo.

CSR has, of course, progressed well beyond a simple projection of reassuring messages on corporate websites. The more creative corporations have developed CSR strategies which consciously build social capital through networks, codes of conduct, transparency initiatives and, increasingly, endorsement from NGOs (see Yaziji and Doh, 2009). This enables the corporation to assess and to anticipate risks and to adapt corporate strategies. To give two examples: first, engagement with consumers can assess the extent of 'ethical consumerism' in markets. This might allow better product development and marketing (Smith, 2008: 298) but it might also allow the corporation to anticipate and to mitigate consumer boycotts. Whilst ethical consumerism has limited purchase in most markets, a wildfire consumer boycott can seriously damage a corporation, as we saw with the Nike sweatshop campaign or the response to the BP Deepwater Horizon pollution catastrophe. In the UK, campaigns against Topshop and other tax avoiders mobilised by the 'UK Uncut' protesters had the side effect of putting the questionable ethics of tax avoidance squarely on the political agenda. The public protests helped to provoke the highly critical investigation by the PAC which concluded that 'we have serious concerns that large companies are treated more favourably by the Department (HMRC) than other taxpayers' (PAC, 2011: 4). A second example involves engagement with suppliers. A corporation might not own its suppliers and have no formal responsibility for their actions but a growing doctrine of 'social connectedness' (Scherer and Palazzo, 2011: 914) holds that corporations should be held complicit for abuses in their supply chains. An early model for supply chain monitoring is provided by the well regarded chemical industry Responsible Care Programme which was fuelled by the Bhopal poisoning tragedy (Fuchs, 2007: 123) and the whole question of supply chain responsibility has become a specialism within CSR (Tencati, 2011).

A third motive for corporations to invest in CSR is to respond to governmental preferences and to pre-empt undesirable regulation. The basic premise is, of course, that if corporations behave responsibly they will not need to be regulated, but it is misleading to conceive regulation as an either/or distinction between formal government regulation or self-regulation. In practice, as Stigler observed in 1971 (see Murphy, 2004: 10–11), many large corporations welcome regulation and the prevailing system in the advanced economies is one of 'regulatory capitalism' in which governments and corporations work in partnership to regulate markets. In this setting, persuasive CSR is useful, less to avoid regulation than to engage in regulatory dialogue with government from a position of legitimacy and strength. This might happen at the national level, as with measures by supermarkets to improve food quality and discourage obesity. Or it might happen at the international level such as the remarkably successful cooperative measures to ban the production and sale of CFCs which depleted the ozone layer. The Montreal Protocol of 1987 phased out the production of CFCs based on agreement between 24 major countries but with the active support of the two dominant corporations, DuPont and Allied Signal (see Murphy, 2004: 126)

As part of the redefinition of the relationship between government and the private sector, as outlined in Chapter 6, government has explicitly encouraged the growth of CSR. Moon and Vogel (2008: 302) outline the international trend for government support of CSR and they identify a variety of modes which they classify as exhortation, facilitation and partnering. In the UK the Department for Business Innovation and Skills (BIS) has maintained the practice of making a minister responsible for CSR and it encourages UK businesses to engage with initiatives such as GRI reporting and the UN Global Compact. In its periodic reports on CSR government has sought to present a coherent package of encouragement including government procurement and modest adaptation of company law which now requires directors to pursue 'enlightened' shareholder value (DBIS, 2008). The UK government has also consistently supported the voluntary charitable body Business in the Community (BITC) which was created in 1992 in the wake of the urban riots. BITC is regarded as the UK's leading CSR organisation with 845 members including 64 of the FTSE 100 (BITC, 2011) and, since 2002, it has prepared a corporate responsibility index. In 2010 145 corporations competed for a place in the index and 111 were ranked as displaying outstanding social and environmental performance. Among that 111 were many of the UK's largest corporations (*Financial Times*, 8 June 2011). Their awards provide independent confirmation of some level of corporate responsibility which could be used to legitimise their activities with government as well as with other stakeholders. Ten of the award winners were consultants or accountants for whom the promotion of corporate responsibility is a straightforward business opportunity, 14 were support services corporations and a further 20 utilities corporations (including transport). As discussed in Chapter 2, these are corporations who are committed political actors, whose commercial success rests on good relations with government. Those with the highest level of accreditation (Platinum Plus) could bask in peer approval, expressed at a Gala Dinner attended by Prince Charles as the patron of BITC. Despite the twee public relations fluff of 'platinum plus' and 'Big Ticks', which would make a primary school teacher blush, the corporations will have strengthened their positions as partners to government.

A fourth pressure emerges from the increased salience of the CSR discourse itself. It stimulates initiatives by CEOs, which may be expressions of egotistical aggrandisement, but also reflect a real imperative for the corporate elite to exercise political leadership. It was argued in Chapter 4 that the British corporate elite has a well developed sense of coherence, and that its engagement with government rests on a commitment to shared values. Central to those values is that corporations can provide leadership, are often superior at solving problems, and should be considered as at least equal partners with government. This requires corporate leaders to lead in social, environmental and political issues, as well as in commercial and economic fields. There is an elite or class interest in sustaining corporate legitimacy through CSR, and corporate 'statesmen' regard this as an intrinsic obligation of elite membership, whether in international gatherings (such as Davos), representative organisations (such as the CBI), or simply as expressing the commitment of their own corporation. There are many prominent examples. In 2012 one could look, for instance, to Sir Andrew Witty, the CEO of GlaxoSmithKline, who has articulated a benign vision for his corporation, and more widely, captured in the title of a speech: 'It's good for business for business to be good' (Witty, 2012).

HOW TO ASSESS THE CSR MOVEMENT?

This review of the motivations for corporations to engage in CSR is not reassuring. It suggests that the 'business case' remains highly influential and that CSR will only be genuinely pursued if it enhances shareholder value. CSR also has a role in avoiding reputational risk and in enhancing the autonomy of the corporation by keeping government at arm's length and bolstering corporate strengths in negotiations over regulatory frameworks. The argument about the rise of a 'CSR discourse', with associated pressures for reporting and corporate leadership is more hopeful but more difficult to assess. But even if it represents a deeper seated and more sincere effort to build CSR into business models it still does so under terms dictated by corporations and the corporate elite. As noted at the beginning of this chapter, CSR emerges from the three structural forces of a growth in the influence of large corporations; a reduction of government intervention in the economy; and globalisation, with its attendant diminution of public authority. CSR is an expression of a more substantial societal role for the corporation in the New Corporate State and therefore offers itself as a progressive movement. And there are many positives within the CSR movement. As noted in Chapter 7, many corporate leaders do share a genuine concern for longer-term societal threats such as poverty, resource scarcity, loss of biodiversity and environmental degradation which threaten the longer-term prospects for their corporations as well as their societies. Curiously, corporations are prone to plan for the longer term, a point emphasised by Galbraith (1967: 33) and conceded by Sklair (2001: 282) in his discussion of visionary CEOs. Accordingly, they often have a longer time horizon than governments. Within corporations employees are potentially a progressive force whether as concerned citizens, compliance professionals, or the well-educated, scientifically literate professionals who are essential for the success of knowledge-based corporations. There is, therefore, a progressive potential in CSR but at present it is inhibited by key flaws in the model.

The first major flaw is that CSR is almost entirely voluntary. If a corporation chooses not to pursue social or environmental goals, or to do so fraudulently, then there is no regulatory breach, no sanction other than that of the market (Vogel, 2005). The second flaw follows from the first, and involves limited accountability. The codes and reports that corporations comply with may be authenticated by bodies such as the GRI, by corporate auditors, or by NGOs but these are all malleable bodies without policing powers or recognised legitimacy (Gourevitch and Lake, 2012). Vogel (2010: 473) has asserted the influence of 'civil regulation' in controlling corporations, drawing on social and economic penalties rather than legal sanctions, but this sort of soft law can only be expected to have a contextual effect on corporate strategies. Voluntary self-regulation within a regime of weak accountability offers little reassurance.

A third flaw in the operation of CSR is the inescapable focus of the corporation on its financial health in a competitive environment. Corporations have to make profits, generate cash, pay dividends and increase shareholder value. They may have substantial market power but they have to recognise competitive challenges posed by existing competitors or new entrants. Especially in stock market capitalist economies, corporations are vulnerable to hostile takeovers, subsidiaries are closed, occasionally CEOs are removed. Compared with such fundamental threats to their integrity, we can hardly expect corporations to prioritise CSR. An anecdotal example is provided by the visionary CEO of PepsiCo, Indira Nooyi. By February 2012 she was coming under intense criticism, why? Simply because PepsiCo's stock had fallen, the corporation had failed to meet profit targets and was losing market share to Coke in the key US soft drinks market. As *Fortune Management* (13 February 2012) observed, 'irate investors have been calling . . . for Nooyi to step down'. Suddenly her CSR vision looked fragile, a liability rather than an asset, a lesson that other CEOs would not be slow to absorb.

The fourth flaw also follows from the recognition that the corporation is, under current law and expectations, essentially an economic institution. As such it suffers from a democratic black hole when it comes to CSR, or perhaps a public interest black hole would be a better expression. Even if we accepted that corporations were sincerely committed to programmes of CSR, and further accepted that they had surplus resources which they could properly commit to these programmes, how would they formulate their priorities and design the programmes? Unlike a government they have no set of ideological principles to define how to improve well-being, they have no political principles of justice, social contracts with citizens, or criteria of public interest and, above all, they have no popular mandate. They have not explained their priorities and programmes to the potential beneficiaries who can therefore neither judge their suitability, nor hold the corporation to account if they do not materialise. Further, what levels of competence and judgement do corporate executives bring to social and environmental programmes? They have not engaged in public debate like politicians, nor accepted principles of integrity and public service like civil servants. At best they are likely to be technically competent; at worst they may be careless, paternalistic, even neo-colonialist. There is something profoundly disturbing about corporations purporting to deliver the same social benefits as governments with complete disregard for the standards, processes, accountability and legal safeguards which in the governmental sphere are regarded as essential. This sense of unease is magnified in evaluating CSR undertaken by corporations whose core business raises ethical concerns. Thus PepsiCo, already mentioned, has a core business implicated in childhood obesity and one of the impressive, and commercially risky, aspects of Indira Nooyi's vision was to move Pepsi towards more healthy products. Starker examples are provided by BAT and Imperial Tobacco, both with 'Gold Awards' under the 2011 BITC Index. Is it consistent to create health problems for the community with one hand, and offer to aid it with the other? Similar contradictions, or hypocrisies, are seen with corporate taxation. Corporations employ shrewd tax advisers to reduce their tax liabilities, often by controversial means (see Beetham, 2011), thus denying governments resources to address exactly the sorts of issues that they target in CSR campaigns.

In short, the field of CSR, as currently constituted, with voluntary self-regulation by shareholder value-driven corporations, without a public interest mandate, is unsatisfactory. The flaws outlined above are seldom confronted by the CSR industry of scholars and professionals but the voices of sceptics can sometimes be heard (Sternberg, 2011). For Devinney

(2009: 44) 'the notion of a socially responsible corporation is potentially an oxymoron' and it is exactly the contradictory implications of corporate purpose that have to be confronted if CSR is to be a plausible way of meeting societal needs. These contradictions apply primarily, of course, to the Anglo-Saxon model of corporations. Outside this corporate world of largely English-speaking countries, pursuing 'stock market capitalism', corporations may still be regarded as 'responsible' but with other means of requiring responsibility. As explored in Chapter 10, the alternative means of securing corporate responsibility may involve legal obligations, discipline through membership of collective organisations, more inclusive modes of corporate governance, or responsiveness to governmental priorities. In these cases there is less of a need for voluntaristic exercises in corporate altruism because corporations outside the Anglo-Saxon world are already constrained by institutional or societal pressures.

Constraints on corporate autonomy outside stock market capitalist economies arise from the diversity of corporate ownership and corporate governance, discussed in more depth in Chapter 10. This diversity was examined in a trail-blazing study by Gourevitch and Shinn who analysed patterns in the ownership of corporations. They calculated a concentration ratio in which the US had a concentration ratio of 15, indicating that 15 per cent of corporations were controlled by a single shareholder (control being defined at 20 per cent shareholding). At the other end of the scale was Chile, where 90 per cent of corporations were controlled by a single shareholder. The 'Anglo-Saxon' countries all had concentration ratios below 30 per cent and were labelled the 'shareholder model' in which shareholding is very diffuse. The more concentrated economies included Germany and France, both at 65 per cent, these were termed the 'blockholder model' (Gourevitch and Shinn, 2005: 17–19). In blockholder countries the block of shares might be held by pension funds or banks, by families, or by the state, but the key point is that blockholders have direct control over managers. This provides a crucial corrective to the CSR preoccupation with the shareholder model, which proves to be the exception, 'most of the world operates through the blockholder model. It exists in Germany and Japan ... The diffuse shareholder model found in the United States is relatively unusual' (Gourevitch and Shinn, 2005: 5). The scope for managers to exercise discretion in pursuing CSR is much more constrained in blockholder systems where the exercise of corporate responsibility falls to owners who typically have a close and longstanding involvement with government.

In many societies in which blockholding is the norm, the corporation is viewed as part of a national community. As Donaldson (2008: 545) expresses it, 'in countries such as France and Germany where share ownership is far less dispersed among the public than in the United States, the citizenry views the main issue of corporate governance not to be the rights of shareholders, but the rights of the community in relation to the corporation'. Corporations that are embedded in the community will behave more responsibly towards their employees, society, and even the environment without seeking to assert their virtues through programmes of CSR. This behaviour will be embodied in legal or institutional arrangements such as employee co-determination and corporatist bargaining in Germany, state intervention in France, state ownership in China or social monitoring in Japan. The Japanese case is especially important, and we come back to examine it in Chapter 10, but it is worth emphasising here that the front rank Japanese corporation pays very little attention to its shareholders and attaches huge importance to its employees. Such corporations operate as social organisations (see Learmount, 2002: 113) within a system that has been celebrated as 'welfare capitalism' (Dore, 2000). Thus the large Japanese corporation displays a strong commitment to its workforce, to the communities within which it operates and, through a close relationship with the state bureaucracy, to Japanese national interests. Further, large Japanese corporations do appear inclined to adopt a longer-term perspective and to be prepared to anticipate and to ameliorate longer-term social and environmental threats. Mikler (2009), for instance, finds that Toyota and Honda have been the leaders among world automotive manufacturers attempting to respond to environmental pollution and global warming. The corporate social responsibility movement, which regards CSR essentially as corporate self-regulation, therefore emerged in the United States and takes on a different colouration and significance in other countries. Its growth parallels the increased influence of international financial markets and the decreased influence of government, but outside the United States it becomes more an expression of public purpose. Thus Moon et al. (2010: 525) note that 'Western Europe CSR is much more closely aligned with government policies, both as objects of government policy and as partners with government'. For Asian economies, Korea, Japan, and especially China, US-style CSR is far less relevant. Instead CSR is a corporate obligation enforced by society, employees and, especially in China, by the state.

This picture of comparative CSR has stressed the influence of the US model in the West and alternatives to the US model in Asian countries but, as with corporate power more broadly, CSR escapes the confines of the nation state when deployed globally by MNCs. Chapter 7 outlined the way in which corporations have become partners in global governance. Corporate statements on social and environmental responsibility are validated by their actions, measured against codes of conduct, and policed by NGOs and international organisations such as the GRI and the UN Global Compact. For weaker, smaller and developing countries these are the most significant pressures on corporations to behave responsibly. This evolving system of private authority or 'soft law' provides legitimacy and authority for MNCs and helps them to sustain the regulatory autonomy which Chapter 7 suggested they pursue. To a large extent they have been successful. Serious observers such as Bull (2010); Ougaard (2006) and Warhurst (2011: 78) investigate elaborate and effective partnerships in global governance which enhance corporate agendas. This growing dimension of corporate power is discussed by Fuchs (2007) in terms both of discursive power (presenting a positive image) and structural power (emphasising codes of conduct). In fact she is optimistic about the potential concluding that:

> Rules and standards developed and controlled by business do hold a significant promise... If standards with sufficiently stringent regulations for environmental and social conduct were to become the de facto norm for business practice, footloose capital could no longer avoid them. In this case, international governmental regulation would indeed be unnecessary. (Fuchs, 2007: 133)

Whether or not such optimism is justified, in the international arena we are seeing major transformation of global governance. To return to one of our key themes, in the international arena CSR is enhancing the authority of corporations who have transcended lobbying, unilateral action or non-compliance to become the sources of regulation. In the words of Levy and Kaplan (2008: 445–6), 'CSR is an emergent form of governance that can redeem, to some degree, the governance deficit that exists in the international arena... CSR is thus not just a struggle over practices, but one over the *locus* of governance authority'. These are bold claims that apply far more at the international level than at the level of the nation state, although the two levels must influence one another. This makes it even more essential to take stock of CSR and to determine whether it has the potential to contribute to a stable, accountable and effective mode of governance able to earn popular legitimacy.

THE PROMISE AND PITFALLS OF CORPORATE CITIZENSHIP

Earlier sections of this chapter outlined the expansion of CSR, initially as a response to criticism and potential threats, later as a deeper-seated discourse. A central question of this book is whether corporations and the corporate elite can be made politically accountable. CSR is also centrally concerned with this question and appears to offer a way forward. Is CSR a force for good? Does it have the potential to improve societal wellbeing or is it damaging? Might it damage the corporations themselves (the Friedmanite critique); might it actually damage societal cohesion or ecological sustainability; might it simply reinforce the influence of the corporate elite; and might it become deeply damaging by deterring or pre-empting necessary governmental regulation? The arguments presented above give critical answers to many of these questions. CSR in its present form is deeply flawed. Does this mean that it should be resisted, or should its potential be welcomed and measures taken to improve it? We turn now to two promising avenues for improvement.

Reinforcement of CSR could evolve through internal application of stakeholder theory as seen in Christine Parker's *The Open Corporation*, which emerges from the Australian School of responsive regulation. She mounts a passionate argument in favour of corporate self-regulation maintaining that 'corporate self-regulation is necessary to democracy' and that 'effective self-regulation therefore means putting 'stakeholders' in a position where they can inform corporate management' (Parker, 2002: 292 and x). Her marriage between management, democracy and law calls for a reconceptualization of the corporation as a responsive, participative arena welcoming to stakeholders. This seems idealistic but the research findings on responsive regulation indicate that the idealistic goals are capable of at least partial achievement and the 'open corporation' model is promising.

A second avenue addresses one of the basic flaws of CSR, the voluntary principle. In his analysis of the legal potential for securing greater corporate social responsibility Parkinson (1993: 346) consistently and subtly demonstrated the opportunities to place less emphasis on profit maximisation, and more emphasis on empowering stakeholders. The proposed reform of UK company law, which was widely debated in the mid-1990s, did not exploit this potential but company law reform remains a promising avenue. In the UK the 2006 Companies Act took a very small step in this direction by widening directors' duties and requiring them to address environmental, employee, social and community matters in the mandatory Business Review. Of course, this relies on action by the national state but some markets, and especially the European market, are so important that even huge multinationals could be expected to comply with national regulations. Corporations have lobbied hard and successfully against mandatory CSR requirements but it is possible that CSR has become in practice so necessary that some formal legal recognition would be accepted. Horn's (2012) study of European initiatives to reform and align European law is not encouraging – she paints a picture of resistance by corporations and neoliberal governments, but reform of company law remains an obvious avenue.

These embryonic notions of reform are important but they are overshadowed by a far more ambitious attempt to reconstruct the concept of the corporation by giving it an extra dimension in the form of 'corporate citizenship'. The idea of reconceptualising the corporation as a 'corporate citizen' is appealing to corporate executives, to management theorists and to legal scholars. More importantly, it is appealing to students of politics, and potentially to government, since it mobilises one of the most powerful sets of concepts in democratic theory and one of the most fundamental principles of political accountability. Like democracy itself, citizenship is an imprecise and normatively loaded term. Whilst to be 'a good citizen' wins unambiguous approval, people's definition of good citizenship will vary widely. We can, however, bring together some of the main, generally debated, characteristics of citizenship to present a model against which to judge claims for corporate citizenship. In the tradition of Athenian citizenship the main context is the community, or the collectivity, as opposed to more liberal approaches to citizenship, which stress individual rights to be protected from an overbearing state. Community-based conceptions of citizenship can be termed 'civic republicanism', and in simple terms embrace status, privileges, responsibilities and normative expectations.

Citizenship status is usually expressed in legal terms, although eligibility for citizenship may be based on ethnicity, nationality, parentage, class or geographic location. It is valuable to gain the legal standing of German, US or UK 'citizenship' but, other than obeying the law of the political unit, this says little about constraints over activities. Citizenship confers certain privileges enshrined in law and in the traditions and norms of society. Ideally privileges will include equality before the law, domestic and military security, political rights including voting, consultation and opportunities to participate in government, and participation in the benefits of a welfare state. In return citizenship implies a series of responsibilities which could also be termed duties or obligations. These obligations are over and above simple compliance with the law. They would demonstrate consideration for others in the community and concern for the common good of the collectivity.

Citizenship obligations would therefore include social obligations of participation, neighbourliness, volunteering and avoiding actions that others might find objectionable. The sense of service to the community is part of a civic ideal, or a civic culture, which creates a society far richer, cohesive and supportive than simply a collection of law-abiding individuals. The same set of expectations applies beyond social relationships and into environmental responsibilities. Citizenship would require a commitment to conservation or sustainability. It would militate towards responsible exploitation of natural resources in recognition that they are assets that belong to the community as a whole and to future generations. Thus far, the obligations associated with citizenship are comparable to those emphasised by exponents of CSR. But citizenship goes further. It extends into political obligations which, for the corporation, have profound implications. Citizenship pre-eminently carries responsibilities to support good government, through political actions such as voting, joining parties or engaging in debate. It may go further by joining governance through committees, standing for office or working with parties or pressure groups. The process would involve engaging in mature deliberations from a community rather than a selfish perspective. This is the ideal of deliberative democracy whereby issues of common concern are debated in impartial processes, without any element of coercion, and by reference to facts and expertise. Decisions of benefit to the community, but suboptimal to the individual, are accepted through respect for fair processes and generalised well-being. In this regard citizenship becomes a deeply normative set of concerns. It expresses the merits of what Marquand (2004) calls 'the public domain' and it addresses one of the great flaws in the notion of CSR outlined above. The flaw is, of course, the lack of a coherent, consistent and publicly accountable set of expectations about what CSR would actually deliver (see also Crane et al., 2008a: 44). The idea of citizenship might be vague but it is clearer and more demanding than the very partial purchase provided by CSR.

Given this background is it realistic to talk of 'corporate citizenship', and is it potentially productive? On the first question it probably is realistic to see corporations as having some of the attributes of citizens. They enjoy legal status by virtue of incorporation, which gives them various privileges of corporate 'personhood' as outlined in Chapter 1. Moreover, in some important regimes, such as the United States, they enjoy constitutional rights (see Crane et al., 2008a: 26; Monks, 2008: 50) which come close to human rights. Their legal status delivers a range of privileges similar to those enjoyed by human beings and extending to certain political privileges. In pluralist democracies it is usual for corporations to engage in the political process as interest groups. The more opaque areas are the responsibilities (or obligations) of corporations and the normative expectations about good citizenship. But it would have to be accepted that these aspects of good citizenship are also imperfectly observed by human citizens. Very few individuals live up to the ideals of citizen participation and altruism that proponents of the public domain advocate. Parker (2002: 39) in particular articulates an ideal of corporate citizenship and explores ways in which corporations can become genuine participants in deliberative democracy. For Crane et al. (2008a) the ideal is still some way off. In their extended study of corporate citizenship they explore multiple conceptions of corporations as citizens. They suggest that corporations are 'quasi-citizens' and, although they retain reservations, they emphasise repeatedly the political role of the large corporation arguing that 'ultimately, corporations are transformative in and of political arenas' (202) and, as part of that transformation, corporations, their associations and advisers are projecting themselves as corporate citizens.

We have seen that CSR has deep historical origins but that it began to mature as a core feature of corporate strategies during the 1990s. As the decade progressed, the language and symbolism of corporate citizenship became more pronounced and established itself within the CSR discourse. It appeared to be particularly attractive to large multinationals. In his study of the transnational capitalist class Sklair (2001) devotes two chapters to 'global corporate citizenship'. His treatment is intriguing. Although he writes from a critical perspective, he takes corporate citizenship very seriously. He analyses the employee relations, community support, philanthropic programmes and environmental engagement strategies of large corporations and picks out progressive, as well as cynical, examples (see Chapter 7). Sklair's case studies identify sincere and caring programmes; they also identify a genuine convergence of societal, environmental and corporate goals. Multinationals plan decades ahead and have a clear interest in creating affluent consumers and avoiding environmental catastrophes. A good example is provided by Diageo, the large international alcoholic beverages group. Sklair notes that it built up an impressive range of CSR initiatives from the late 1980s when it decided to adopt a strategy of globalisation. From the late 1990s its CSR Report was presented as a Corporate Citizenship Report. The 2010 version is a model of good practice and includes a section on compliance with CSR codes (such as the UN Global Compact) and details of supply chain compliance programmes actually called 'licence to operate', thus invoking that basic premise that corporations depend on societal (and perhaps governmental) approval (Diageo, 2011: 12). The Report is introduced on the website by the CEO, Paul Walsh, who declares in a video that 'we want to be good corporate citizens' and who places endearing emphasis on the long term: 'we want to be around for hundreds of years' (Diageo, 2011). With controversial products in the shape of high profile alcohol brands (including Guinness and Johnny Walker) the corporation clearly finds it necessary to supplement its 'responsible use of alcohol' policy with a wider programme of good citizenship. Diageo provides one example of the huge range of CSR and corporate citizenship practices which are reviewed in a wide academic literature including specialist management journals (such as *Business Ethics*

Quarterly and even *The Journal of Corporate Citizenship*). Corporate citizenship is thus rapidly evolving but, to return to the theme of this section, if corporate citizenship has much promise, what are the pitfalls?

Corporate citizenship is, of course, a Trojan horse. Its hidden forces capture governments, capture agendas and capture frameworks of meaning. There is something decidedly weird about a classic liberal organisation – in this case the utility-maximising market actor – now claiming a simultaneous identity as a community-regarding citizen, embracing a set of non-economic obligations. This paradox can only be resolved, as rehearsed in the opening paragraphs of this chapter, by accepting the corporation as relatively unconstrained by profit maximisation or the market. This has allowed the corporation to extend from the market into society; and from the private sector into the public sector. The way in which corporate citizenship extends and legitimises the corporation's political activities suggests almost a 'quadruple' bottom line, adding political responsibility to the classic trio of economic, social and environmental (see Maclean and Crouch, 2011: 5). The fatigue of government and the decline of the public sphere have opened the door to the corporation. David Marquand (2004) has bemoaned the 'marketisation' of the public sphere based on a neoliberal programme enforced through populist centralism. Does corporate citizenship constitute a mirror image, with the 'citizenisation' of the corporate sphere based on a programme of corporate social responsibility enforced by reputational risk? If only. We have reviewed the incoherent, voluntary and non-accountable nature of corporate citizenship. It would be hard to argue that this movement has transformed the nature of the corporation and instead we are seeing the colonisation of the public sphere extended. The corporate partnership with government explored in earlier chapters now rests more firmly on an ingeniously created foundation of corporate citizenship.

CONCLUSION: IMAGES OF THE CORPORATION

Chapters 8 and 9 have presented two dramatically opposed images of the corporation: the negative portrayal of the rapacious corporation in popular culture as against the positive portrayal of the caring corporation in CSR reporting. It is tempting to suggest that we are contrasting two genres of fiction: on the one hand the critique in popular culture with a foundation of fact but exploring malign potential with evil outcomes, and presented frankly as fiction in novels and films; and on the other hand the defence of the corporation in multiple CSR media, also based on a foundation of fact, but with a seductive presentation of benign potential for social and environmental well-being. Of course, many CSR professionals would reject the characterisation of CSR as 'marketing', much less as 'fiction', and the two fictions hardly have equal impact. CSR, or corporate citizenship, has become a core discourse underpinned by huge resources, dedicated organisations, and with support from governments and NGOs.

As noted above, commitment to CSR has become the norm for large corporations, and the pretensions towards corporate citizenship are taken seriously. Alongside this maturation of CSR we can consider the arguments advanced in earlier chapters about the corporation as a political actor at the international and at the national level – an actor that is steadily gaining political influence in partnership with government and benefiting from the marketization of public services and the commodification of activities within a consumer society. CSR can be seen as a structural consequence of increased power. It is employed by corporations to legitimise their influence and is demanded by society in a tacit acceptance of that political power. With power comes expectations of responsibility but is CSR, or even corporate citizenship, a sufficient guarantee of 'real' responsibility? The argument above suggests that it is not but it also leads into a debate about whether corporate citizenship can be reformed in ways that will increase real responsibility.

We can end this discussion with a paradox and a dialectical speculation. The paradox lies in the unforeseen strengthening of corporate social responsibility. It began as a smokescreen; a rather cynical presentation of good intentions and philanthropic gestures designed to divert the criticism of corporate behaviour. But the movement has taken on substance; it has spawned organisations, processes, a body of specialists and a set of societal expectations. A means of evading social control has arguably become a real constraint which is beginning to impact on core corporate strategies. The paradox would be of corporations becoming prisoners of their own rhetoric. The dialectical speculation rests on the resolution of the tension between the critical forces of popular critique and the protestations of CSR. If we can see the critique of the corporation in popular culture as the thesis; and the conscious development of programmes of CSR as the antithesis; what is the nature of the synthesis? The synthesis is still inchoate but must involve a revised vision of capitalism itself, leading into a revised vision of the corporation as an institution, and a revised theory of the firm as an actor with multiple responsibilities – a vision that rejects the orthodox views of the corporation as a profit-maximising market actor, pursuing the financial interests of its owners, blind to its wider impact on society at large. This vision leads us, in Chapter 10, to a consideration of how that synthesis is being obstructed by practices of corporate governance.

10. The explosion of interest in corporate governance

CORPORATE GOVERNANCE AS THE CONSTITUTION OF THE CORPORATION

The words 'corporate governance' are bland, unthreatening and moderately arcane. The issues with which it deals share nothing of those characteristics. Corporate governance deals with possibly the single most important social relationship in modern society, how the historically unprecedented wealth created by 21st-century corporations is controlled and distributed. Despite its importance the debate over corporate governance has been narrow and shockingly impoverished. The issues involved did not begin to attract serious attention until the early 1990s and the whole area was captured by the financial community, which created a dominant discourse focused on the rights of shareholders.

In the UK, and to a large extent internationally, corporate governance has become obsessed with the rights of shareholders, expressed in financial terms through the concept of shareholder value. The focus of concern is, quite rightly, senior management and the CEO who, as Berle and Means pointed out 80 years ago, have effectively taken control of the majority of large Anglo-American corporations. Conventional corporate governance therefore seeks to ensure that management will pursue the interests of shareholders. This is the 'principal–agent' problem which strives to ensure that managers will not countenance fraud, will avoid excessive risk taking, will keep shareholders informed, will pursue profits rather than growth or vanity, will prioritise a high share price and generous dividends and, especially nowadays, will not plunder the corporation through excessive remuneration. The main vehicle for establishing control over managers is the board of directors together with various mechanisms for seeking to align the interests of management and shareholders, and for protecting the rights of minority shareholders. The remarkable feature of this framework is that it treats the corporation as operating solely for the benefit of its shareholders. This is very odd. As we have seen from Chapter 1 onwards, the corporation is integrated into society and needs to justify a 'license to operate'. In practice many groups within society are dependent on corporations, most obviously employees but also all the other 'stakeholders' from bondholders to suppliers. As Mayer (2013: 12–13) points out, 'the interests of these other parties should at least rank alongside those of shareholders and, depending on the degree and extent of their commitment, potentially ahead of shareholders'. The alignment of management incentives with the interests of shareholders thus potentially de-aligns incentives with the interests of employees, suppliers, consumers and society at large. The case for privileging shareholders is normative and derives from their property rights even if, as Parkinson (1993: 40) maintains, shareholders cannot be shown to have a moral right over the control of corporate property. But the conventional view is that shareholders 'own' the corporation and that principle is also defended in efficiency terms. Since shareholders are interested in maximising their returns, they can be expected to pursue the greatest levels of efficiency, a convenient argument which travels badly. As we see below, German and Japanese corporations manage to achieve superior levels of efficiency without the spur of shareholder hunger.

In the UK, shareholder primacy continues to be embedded in company law which gives directors a 'fiduciary duty' to protect the interests of shareholders and, despite much discussion of the stakeholder corporation, the 2006 Companies Act reinforced shareholder rights (Mallin, 2010: 33). But governments have been hesitant about creating legal frameworks for corporate governance and instead have encouraged 'soft law' regulation through codes of conduct. Thus we have *The UK Corporate Governance Code* (FRC, 2010a), the early versions of which inspired the *OECD Principles of Corporate Governance Code*, first issued in 1999, and an epidemic of later codes so that now every country in the EU has some sort of code in place. These codes rarely make the headlines and appear as technical, rather dreary provisions which are voluntary in the UK and apply only to companies quoted on the London Stock Exchange.

The political debate around corporate governance in the UK has been muted and largely been confined within parameters created by the financial community. Occasionally the issues do generate controversy and creative debate as with the considerations in the UK in the late 1990s around the reform of company law. And, of course, scandals regularly provoke re-examination of corporate governance and heart-searching over reform. Enron in particular sparked a passionate debate about the very viability of US corporate capitalism and created a legal structure in the shape of the 2002 Sarbanes–Oxley Act, which greatly strengthened audit control and has an extra-territorial reach since it applies to any corporation quoted on Wall Street. More recently the financial crisis has again raised classic corporate governance issues but, with each episode of introspection, the reflex has been to define the response in terms of managerial shirking and as a principal–agent problem. The impulse to strengthen the principals leads again to attempts to increase the powers of shareholders, to make them more activist and more engaged, and therefore to sidestep the more important political consideration of a wider responsibility to a range of stakeholders.

The narrow, technical and pragmatic discussion around corporate governance seems also to have deterred political scientists. With some honourable exceptions (see Parkinson et al., 2000) corporate governance was, until very recently, virtually ignored by political science. The two trailblazing projects which have recognised the political gravity of corporate governance are the ambitious book by Gourevitch and Shinn (2005) and the series of publications emerging from the Amsterdam Research Centre (Overbeek et al., 2007; van Apeldoorn and Horn, 2007; Horn, 2012). Both projects affirm the pure politics of resource allocation within and by corporations: 'corporate governance – the authority structure of the firm – lies at the heart of the most important issues of society' (Gourevitch and Shinn, 2005: 3). Corporate governance should provide a means of political accountability but before embarking on an examination of the practice of contemporary corporate governance we should recall the criteria by which it should be evaluated.

Earlier chapters have pointed to the history of limited liability and the way in which corporations were licensed by the state with expectations of serving the public good as well as private gain. It has been argued that the increased strength and salience of corporations transformed the largest of them into governing institutions and, since the late 1980s, their governing role has increased as part of the New Corporate State. In this setting it is inescapable to apply to corporations similar criteria of good governance that we would apply to the governments of liberal-democratic states. This approach echo's Dahl's bemused observation that Americans fought prolonged and all-consuming battles to secure political rights in a democratic state, yet have tolerated autocracy and subordination in the workplace. 'Thus a system of government Americans view as intolerable in governing the state has come to be accepted as desirable in governing economic enterprises' (Dahl, 1985: 162). He asks if any country can truly regard itself as democratic when its major economic institutions exclude basic political rights of expression, representation and accountability. What, then, are the flaws in corporate governance measured against norms of liberal democracy?

We can compare the governance of a large corporation with those of a liberal democracy (the UK) using standard categories of political institutions as seen in Table 10.1. The system of government practised in the

Table 10.1 Comparing national and corporate governance

	UK government	UK corporate governance	German corporate governance
Political function			
Head of State	Queen	Chairman	Chairman of supervisory board
Constitution	Public law	Company law	Company and labour law
Executive	Cabinet	Board	Supervisory and management boards
Leader	PM	CEO	Collective
Government	Civil service	Managers	Managers and works council
Legislature	Parliament	Board	Supervisory board
Citizens	Voters	Shareholders	Shareholders, employees, banks
Accountability	Elections Parliament	Board AGM Market for CC	Supervisory board Elections to board
Institutional authority	State	Corporation	Corporation

Note: CC = corporate control.

UK is far from perfect in securing political freedoms but, even measured against this imperfect standard, conventional corporate governance exhibits three democratic shortcomings. First, there is an extraordinary concentration of power in the board of directors. It acts as the executive, setting policies and developing strategies, but it is also the legislature, setting rules for the organisation. Further, whoever controls the board controls the corporation and this is often the CEO who becomes comparable to a presidential prime minister, or elected dictator. Second, the electorate is narrow, comprising only shareholders, so that all other stakeholders, and especially employees, are disenfranchised. Third, accountability is weak. Instead of general elections there are ritualised annual general meetings manipulated by boards and dominated by proxy votes. Instead of parliamentary scrutiny there is the compliant auditor, the opinion of the financial markets, but also the market for corporate control and the risk of hostile takeover, the corporate equivalent of a coup. These incongruities between democratic political expectations and their lack of purchase in the corporate world should be glaringly obvious but in Britain are veiled behind a taboo against challenging shareholder supremacy, possibly as misleading a concept as consumer supremacy. In the words of Charkham, a member of the seminal 1992 Cadbury Committee:

it is one of the more curious features of the UK's arrangements that accountability, which has been so great a consideration in the political sphere, counts for so little in the economic. This is a subject worthy of deep study, for it may be to blame for many of the UK's problems. (Charkham, 1994: 257)

Corporate governance thus provides the equivalent of a 'constitution' for quoted corporations. In the following sections we examine in more detail the flawed Anglo-American constitutional model, analyse the German and Japanese alternatives, and come back to the position of the stakeholder. The chapter concludes with an evaluation of the current orthodoxy and the need for the creation of a more responsible, more accountable corporate system.

THE CURIOUSLY QUARANTINED UK MODEL

The neglect of corporate governance in postwar British politics is little short of astonishing. For 30 years it was ignored within political debate and for 20 years up to 2012 it was effectively quarantined by the City and the accountancy profession so that there was never serious public debate about the rights of corporate boards to control and direct 'their' corporations in the ostensible interests of shareholders. Instead the dominant theme has been the separation of ownership and control with a diffusion of shareholding and the inability of shareholders to control (or even appoint) the directors who have operational control over their investments.

This is a peculiarly Anglo-American obsession. In most countries shareholding is concentrated in the hands of 'blockholders' and the preoccupation has been how to protect the financial interests of minority shareholders and employees. For the UK, however, the divorce of ownership and control is virtually complete and, in his scrupulous study of the pattern of ownership in Britain, Cheffins sees little prospect of change, concluding that 'in the UK, the outsider/arm's-length system of ownership and control that first emerged with the railway companies in the 19th century and became predominant during the second half of the 20th century should survive well into the 21st century'. This finding is important in confirming the maintenance of board and managerial autonomy although, as we see below, managers are induced by the financial sector to bias their strategies towards short-term shareholder gains. Whether this can be interpreted as the exertion of control by 'owners' is very doubtful, especially since the beneficiaries are financial intermediaries, traders, and 'owners' whose shareholdings are transient and involve no commitment to the long term success of the corporation. Why did this managerial dominance go unchallenged?

For the Conservatives, the right to manage and the right to invest were basic components of the post-war settlement and were elements to be protected, not challenged. Moreover, some of the company directors and all the City firms who benefited from the permissive regime were part of the Establishment; important and powerful components of the traditional elite. The Conservatives had no inclination to challenge or reform the system of company law that placed minimal obligations on the organisation of companies, gave extensive powers to directors and licensed a system of autonomous business self-regulation. This passive, permissive orthodoxy which regarded the corporation as a private association was enshrined in 'the legal model' (Parkinson, 1993: 76) and it was a model taken for granted by the unions and the Labour Party which took virtually no interest in the control of the corporation or the reform of company law. Clift et al. (2000: 81) examined this puzzling myopia and concluded that it was due to 'deep-rooted adversarial conceptions of the company within the Labour movement, which were expressed in the commitment to nationalisation to secure the public interest and the commitment to trade union independence'. In other words, Labour was opposed to capitalism in principle and not inspired by reforms which could make it work more effectively. The main exception was the debate over industrial democracy in the 1970s which was prompted by the EU draft fifth directive on company law issued in 1972 with proposals for two-tier boards. The British debate centred on the 1977 Bullock Report which advocated equal worker representation on the boards of large companies (Clift et al., 2000: 77). The proposals were rejected, which allowed Gamble and Kelly (2000: 42) to observe that 'the regulatory framework for companies in Britain has shown remarkably little change since it was set in place between 1844 and 1865', going on to add that 'the Thatcher government elected in 1979 . . . was not interested in reorganising the way companies were run'. Hence the traditional system of corporate governance was consolidated within the New Corporate State, and maintained even in the face of the challenges arising from the 2008 financial crisis. Paradoxically, as we see below, shareholder-orientated corporate governance was if anything strengthened by post-crisis reforms. We can turn now to the details of that corporate governance system and to the gestation of the *UK Corporate Governance Code*, sheltered in a quarantined atmosphere, and nursed by City interests and the accountancy profession.

Pressures to reform the governance of large quoted corporations mounted at the end of the 1980s. They arose from doubts about damaging takeovers and management buyouts and were reinforced by corporate scandals. In particular the fraud by Robert Maxwell and the collapse of the Maxwell Group in 1991 had a huge impact on financial opinion and a critical report by the Securities and Investment Board prompted the *Financial Times* to observe 'in a sense, we are in the last chance saloon for self-regulation' (cited in Grant, 1993: 154). Still, the Conservative government of John Major proved reluctant to legislate and into this vacuum stepped the City financial establishment under the colourless leadership of the accountants. In 1988 a Financial Reporting Council (FRC) had been created as a self-regulatory body, supported by the government, but with no legislative basis, in order to improve standards of financial reporting. In 1991 it set up a Committee on the Financial Aspects of Corporate Governance chaired by Sir Adrian Cadbury and known colloquially as the Cadbury Committee. Its report and its 'Code of Best Practice' has proved extraordinarily influential in the UK and internationally. Cadbury proposed a system of self-regulation for British quoted companies. They would be required to pay attention to the Code of Best Practice as part of the London Stock Exchange listing rules, but their compliance with the Code would be voluntary. The principle to be applied would be 'comply or explain'. In other words, non-compliance with the Code would be acceptable provided the company explained why it had chosen not to comply. The Code was avowedly flexible. It allowed discretion in interpretation and covered organisation, duties and processes focussed on the composition and conduct of the board of directors. So, for instance, it suggested that the roles of the Chairman and the CEO should be separated, it pressed for independent non-executive directors (NEDs), and for an audit committee. The rationale was to strengthen oversight over the CEO, the Board, and the corporation itself, in order to protect the interests of shareholders. It consolidated the operation of the traditional 'legal model' but, paradoxically, it had no legal basis. Neither chairmen, NEDs, CEOs nor audit committees were (or still are) specified in British company law.

The Cadbury Code and its successors provide the constitution for the large corporation operating in the UK. In an odd parallel with the UK's 'unwritten' constitution it relies on custom, expectations and voluntary compliance (see also Hutton 1996: 295). It is primarily about organisation. It does contain norms in relation, for instance, to transparency, independence and conflicts of interest, but it is value-free. It does not articulate goals such as equality, freedom or even efficiency, and it makes no reference to employees, stakeholders or society at large. It is, in fact, an impoverished document that fails to engage with the vast majority of the issues of corporate power and responsibility rehearsed in this book. But that is not surprising. The Cadbury Report was only ever intended as a stopgap to pre-empt or influence legislation in the UK or in Europe and, more particularly, to protect auditors. As Freedman (1993: 293) pointed out, 'the influence of the accountancy profession in instigating the (Cadbury) process is very clear'. She went on to argue that:

> essentially this was a defensive move. Blame was being directed at auditors for corporate failure in a fashion which the accountancy profession considered unfair ... The Committee's emphasis in its report and Code of Best Practice on the responsibility of directors for the governance of their companies was intended to correct the balance and direct blame where it belongs.

In this light, virtually all interested parties expected government legislation through a comprehensive review of company law. Thus Charkham noted that corporate accountability 'should be prescribed by law. The UK is now faced with a further period of evasion and prevarication' (1994: 333). And indeed, consideration of company law reform was set in motion. There was wide agitation for reform which would move corporate governance towards 'stakeholder capitalism' (see Parkinson, 1993; Hutton, 1996, ch. 12; Kelly et al., 1997) but the Company Law Review, established by the Labour government in 2002, laboured to produce a mouse. It set the agenda for the 2006 Companies Act which was a substantial consolidating Act but essentially confirmed the status quo as regards corporate governance. It made limited improvements to shareholders' rights but confirmed a corporate commitment to 'enlightened shareholder value' that fell far short of the aspirations of the social democrat reformers. Thus, section 172 on director's 'duty to promote the success of the company' requires directors to act:

> for the benefit of its members as a whole, and in doing so have regard (among other matters) to:
> a) the likely consequences of any decision in the long term
> b) the interests of the company's employees
> c) the need to foster the company's business relationships with suppliers, customers and others
> d) the impact of the company's operations on the community and the environment
> e) the desirability of the company maintaining a reputation for high standards of business conduct, and
> f) the need to act fairly between members of the company
> (Companies Act, 2006, s.172(1))

The 'having regard to' formula leaves discretion with senior managers and board members whose primary concern remains with shareholders. It certainly fails to provide any mandatory rights for stakeholders although there is at least a token recognition of their importance. More importantly, the issues of board organisation and behaviour are not altered and effectively left to the self-regulatory regime policed by the FRC and the *UK Corporate Governance Code.*

The continued disinterest of the Labour government in systematic reform of corporate governance was demonstrated by Tony Blair who 'just after his 2005 general election victory ... was prepared to criticise the Sarbanes–Oxley Act in the United States ... Blair believed the measures had been too draconian' (Taylor, 2005: 193). The Chancellor, Gordon Brown, went even further. One of the most progressive elements of the Company Law Review had been the requirement, included in the 2005 Companies Act, to produce an 'Operating and Financial Review' (OFR) for every listed corporation. The OFR would have outlined the corporation's strategy including social, environmental and community engagement, and would have provided indicators of performance against the strategic goals. The OFR had a statutory basis, would have been overseen by the FRC, and was due to come into effect in March 2006. In an extraordinary stroke of opportunistic vandalism Brown announced, in a speech to the CBI in November 2005, that the OFR would be abandoned. This deregulatory gesture was greeted with dismay by corporate governance reformers, by the accountancy profession, and by industry itself (Eaglesham and Timmins, 2005; Villiers, 2005: 205). Many corporations were already producing OFR-type reports and were geared up for the requirement which had been debated for ten years. Friends of the Earth went so far as to challenge Brown's decision through judicial review but the repeal was sustained and Britain's powerful Chancellor, and presumptive prime minister, sent a clear signal to industry that corporate governance remained a private matter between management and shareholders. To return to the quarantine theme, accountants again stepped into the vacuum and 'the Accounting Standards Board publish(ed) almost all of the planned OFR as its "statement of best practice" for narrative reporting' (Tomorrow's Company, 2007: 4). Corporate governance hence continued as a process sub-contracted to City accountants.

The voluntary 'code of best practice' thus remains the framework within which British corporate governance is regulated. The Cadbury provisions have been adapted on the basis of a procession of further insider reports (such as Hampel and Higgs, see Mallin, 2010: 26–32) to become a 'Combined Code' evolving into *The UK Corporate Governance Code* issued by the FRC in 2010. It remains concise with only two pages of principles and 17 pages of elaboration. It expands moderately on the Cadbury requirements in areas such as a nominations committee, tests of independence for NEDs, and a controversial requirement for annual re-election of directors. Above all it remains voluntary. The Listing Rules are policed by the FSA but the Code itself is not even part of the listing rules which simply require that a listed company should state how it has applied the Code principles and give reasons for any non-compliance. The Code continues to be developed and publicised by the FRC which has acquired statutory powers to regulate auditors but still has a voluntary role with regard to corporate governance. Ever since 1991, therefore, and against early expectations, UK corporate governance has operated through what appears an outdated model of self-regulation, insulated from legislative intervention, and steered safely away from radical reforms by a cosy combination of accountants and investors. In 1993 Freedman warned that 'the danger is that the Cadbury Report will be seen as an end and not the beginning of the debate' (Freedman, 1993: 294). She was remarkably prescient and went on to observe that 'the self-congratulatory, self-reinforcing, merry-go-round indicates the hold the accountancy profession has on the reform process' (295). Here we see in practice the limitations on political choice discussed in Chapter 7, specifically the restriction of choice by accountants who, as part of the corporate elite, maintain control over corporate governance as a foundation of the New Corporate State.

As a closing assessment of the UK system, three flaws deserve emphasis. First is the suitability of self-regulation. In essence the UK Corporate Governance Code is ludicrous. It prescribes an organisation chart for the governance of listed companies only, and even for this set of corporations compliance is voluntary and partial. In 2003 only 34 per cent of corporations were fully compliant; by 2011 this had increased to 50 per cent of the FTSE350 but 16 per cent were non-compliant with only minimal explanation (MacNeil and Li, 2006: 486; Grant Thornton, 2011: 6). The 'comply or explain' provision enters an Alice in Wonderland world. There are no provisions as to what form explanation for non-compliance should take, no guidelines for acceptable explanations, and no sanctions. The assumption has been that corporations will be induced to comply by reputational damage which will lower the share price. Hence Adrian Cadbury observed that self-regulation 'should more accurately be called market regulation' (Cadbury, 2002: 10), but there is no clear evidence that even these assumed market pressures are effective, in fact for some periods the reverse is the case with non-complying corporations having above average share price increases (MacNeil and Li, 2006: 490). This 'comply or explain' phrase was not even used in the original Cadbury Report (Committee on the Financial Aspects of Corporate Governance, 1992) but it has been elevated to a dogma which acts as a facade concealing something close to licensed arrogance on the part of corporate boards, or at least a continuation of cosy 'club government' in which the indulged NEDs of the largest corporations, as core members of the corporate elite, have become the notables of the New Corporate State (Froud et al., 2008: 176).

The second flaw is the almost exclusive focus on shareholders as the beneficiaries of corporate governance. We have seen how this emerges from theories of principal–agent relations and from the traditional British legal model. The quite intentional effect of this emphasis is to subordinate control of corporations to financial markets, to engage in what Horn (2012: 148) calls 'the marketization of corporate control' which is the logical outcome of shareholder value maximisation. Thus the corporate governance provisions in the UK, and most other countries, apply only to corporations quoted on the stock exchange. A more logical approach, which was advanced by the Final Report of the UK Company Law Review, was to identify 'companies with significant economic power' – over a certain size threshold, to which the OFR would have applied (Villiers, 2005: 206). As it is, all those unquoted corporations identified in Chapter 4 as part of the corporate elite escape the corporate governance requirements. For quoted companies the onus has been placed on shareholders to monitor and to engage with boards. This is despite perennial confirmation that shareholders are mainly interested in short-term returns and not in long-term engagement. The problem of 'short-termism' has been recognised for decades and was yet again reviewed by John Kay during 2012 (Kay, 2012). There are two additional problems with shareholder activism. First is that the vast majority of share investors have neither the time nor the inclination to monitor, to engage and to seek to influence boards. Such is the obsession that they should do so that the FRC developed a 'Stewardship Code' (FRC, 2010b) which exhorted institutional investors to be more active. Roach (2011: 493) was very sceptical about the design of the Code (effectively written by fund managers) or its likely effect on the relationship between shareholders and boards, which is just as well. The second problem is that increased shareholder activism by the finance industry is deeply harmful and the last thing the responsible corporation should be exposed to.

In order to create productive, responsible corporations, the Anglo-American imperative to empower shareholders is precisely the wrong policy. This argument has been articulated by Colin Mayer, an authority on corporate finance, who regrets the way in which 'the driving force behind the firm is the creation of shareholder value. It is the purpose of the corporation, its moral imperative and its director's primary obligation' (Mayer, 2012: 34). But, he argues, shareholders have become irresponsible owners. They are interested in share price manipulation, in speculative interventions, in short-term gains and in predatory takeovers. For Mayer, 'the corporation is a rent extraction vehicle for the shortest-term shareholders. By threatening interventions such as takeovers and hedge fund activities, they can hold all other shareholders, including longer-term shareholders to ransom' (Mayer, 2012: 135). A final absurdity of attempts at shareholder empowerment arises simply from the identity of the shareholders. By 2010 41 per cent of UK shares were owned overseas, over half by US investors (ONS, 2012). Why, we might wonder, should we seek to entrust control of the UK corporate economy to overseas investors and encourage them to ignore the interests of UK employees, consumers, communities and the UK public interest?

The third flaw in the British model is the obverse of the privileging of shareholder interests; it is the failure to enfranchise stakeholders. The case for recognising the interests of stakeholders has been rehearsed at many points in this book. It also forms part of Mayer's analysis expressed as a 'stakeholder obligation' to those who have a commitment to the firm. That obligation has a moral dimension but it also has a functional dimension in building trust by stakeholders which persuades them to intensify their commitment to the corporation. A similar stakeholder obligation was expressed in political terms earlier in this chapter through the democratic logic that those governed by an institution should have some representation in its decision-making.

UK corporate governance fails entirely to recognise this stakeholder obligation and the quarantining of the corporate governance debate has kept stakeholder interests off the agenda. This is an example of the operation of structural power, the 'second face of power', which restricts the consideration of options to those that will be tolerated by structurally powerful interests, in this case City investors, corporate leaders and accountancy professionals. With the complicity of government, the accounting elite defined corporate governance narrowly in terms of financial reporting and, with the support of the finance industry, they also narrowed the central concern to the consideration of shareholder interests. This narrowing of the agenda can be demonstrated by the composition of the Cadbury Committee and the makeup of the FRC. The Cadbury Committee comprised 12 men: four accountants, four financial market specialists, three industrialists and one lawyer. The Secretariat was from the DTI and they consulted 14 institutions and over 70 companies and individuals drawn almost wholly from the world of accountancy and City finance with no stakeholder (and no employee) representatives. This pattern of capture by accountants and investors was perpetuated in the FRC which has been drawn from the accountancy and City investor establishment. The way in which the FRC has continued to dominate the evolution of corporate governance in the UK is remarkable, and its ability to avoid or divert major reform proposals has been little short of brilliant. In this it has been helped by the complexity of corporate governance issues and, frankly, by the dull technical nature of the discourse which they generate. Great excitement can be whipped up about autocratic CEOs or executive remuneration rewards for failure, but as soon as attention turns to audit committees or proxy votes in AGMs the headlines evaporate. The importance of depoliticising the issues around corporate governance has been emphasised by Culpepper (2011) in his discussion of the way in which 'quiet politics' allows managers to secure their preferred outcomes. In the UK case, however, it is not just managers but a broader managerial and financial elite that has captured the debate.

We should end this discussion of UK corporate governance with some conclusions about who controls corporations and whose interests they serve. The central question is straightforward, as Cheffins (2008) concludes, corporations are controlled by their managers although, of course, that squeezes analysis down to a more detailed consideration of categories of managers, differentiating between CEOs, board executives, senior non-board managers, and NEDs. The 'in whose interests' question is more complex. In their comparative study, Gourevitch and Shinn (2005: 205) categorise the UK as an example of 'managerism' in which we see 'the alignment of owners and workers versus managers, in which governance outcomes favour managers', although they accept that there are high levels of minority shareholder protection. Their other examples of managerism are France and the United States, although they accept a contested balance of power between owners and managers in the USA as in the UK. Thus, whilst we might accept that managers are in effective control of corporations, it is also clear that they have to respond to the pressures exerted by shareholders. Those varied shareholders may actively intervene through votes or takeovers, or they may passively exert influence simply through selling their shares. Some, especially employee pension funds (such as Hermes) will be very active, some, such as investment banks may be completely passive.

In order to secure a clearer insight into how UK corporate governance affects corporate power and the distribution of benefits we can recall the role of governance as a 'political constitution'. This approach also draws on the characterisation of the corporation in Chapter 2 as a policy maker with internal decision-making and policy-making processes. Those processes are structured by the system of corporate governance. In public policy making we see policy options elaborated in civil service networks, presented to Cabinet Ministers and the prime minister, decided upon, legislated in the light of voter preferences and implemented. In the corporation, policy options are elaborated by managers in dialogue with external networks, presented to the senior management and the CEO, ratified and legislated by the board in the light of shareholder preferences and implemented. What corporate governance does is to identify the corporate decision-makers, the processes and the internal power structures. These structural factors will influence how policies are developed and in whose interests they are likely to operate. They allow observers to anticipate outcomes but the detailed policy choices, as with government, are contingent on the circumstances and the relative influence and determination of the various internal actors. We can anticipate that management will pursue their own self interest as well as the corporate good; and that they will be concerned with, and will justify their policies with reference to, short-term shareholder value but, as with politics itself, policies will be the outcome of negotiation and power relations within corporate policy-making structures. Thus the British principle of shareholder primacy leads to the demand for high financial returns but, as Rebérioux argues, shareholders and their representatives, including auditors and NEDs, are external to managerial decision-making and lack the knowledge and access directly to influence outputs. Managers deliver high rewards but they do so on their own terms. For Rebérioux (2007: 69):

> capital markets have increased their ability to obtain results (in terms of financial return) but they are structurally limited in their ability to appreciate the way these requirements are met. This contributes to make managerial power less accountable: financial irregularities multiply and executive remunerations explode. Shareholder primacy fails exactly where it strives to succeed: it reinforces the discretionary power of managers rather than limiting it.

Thus the unanticipated consequences of the shareholder value focus of British corporate governance leads to an increase in corporate and systemic crises. Astute investors may be able to anticipate such crises, and even profit from them, but the malign effects on the wider set of stakeholders, and on society at large, are less avoidable.

THE ALTERNATIVES AND THE SEDUCTIVE GERMAN MODEL

The identification and evaluation of different models of capitalism has become a central concern of comparative politics and political economy since the fall of the Berlin Wall. Attention turned to the now striking contrasts between different types of capitalism which proliferated as formerly socialist or communist states, from India to China, Brazil to Russia, began to develop their own distinctive variants on the capitalist theme (see Chapter 2). As part of the process of comparison, corporate governance emerged as an important element in capitalist models. The centrality of corporate governance was emphasised in an early, influential and passionate polemic by a French businessman, Michel Albert, whose *Capitalisme contre Capitalisme* published in French in 1991 contrasted the cut-throat Anglo-American capitalism with the more caring continental Rhine model 'which sees the company as a social institution and an enduring community deserving of the loyalty and affection of its members, who can expect a measure of company care and protection in return' (Albert, 1993: 146). The confrontation between the two (or in reality several, see Schmidt, 2002, 2009) variants of European capitalism has been a constant source of tension as corporate governance has evolved and as the European Commission has moved to support a more Anglo-American system in its attempts to harmonise corporate governance across Europe. The Anglo-American/Rhineland contrast places corporate governance in context as part of an integrated capitalist system and it therefore provides a wider canvas than the contrast between 'shareholder' and 'blockholder' systems outlined in Chapter 8. More to the point, the Rhineland alternative provides the revelation that there are alternatives to the UK legal model of shareholder primacy. The three flaws of the UK model identified above are not found in the German version of Rhenish capitalism, as indicated in Table 10.1. In the traditional German model, instead of self-regulation we see regulation structured by law; instead of a preoccupation with shareholder value we see principles of public interest and the corporation as a stakeholder entity; instead of stakeholder exclusion we see a dense network of formal and informal provisions which recognise stakeholder interests and (especially for employees) gives them a voice in corporate policy making.

The wider capitalist systems within which these corporate governance arrangements are embedded can be presented as national models. For the UK it was a 'mixed economy' until the late 1980s when, as discussed in Chapter 4, elite circulation transformed it into the New Corporate State. In Germany the postwar model has been of a self-conscious 'social market economy' which is more sceptical of the free market and accepts a supervisory role for government whilst simultaneously defending the freedom of the corporation in a model of 'organised capitalism' (Allen, 1989: 288–9). The central importance of corporations as defining features of these capitalist models was articulated by Hall and Soskice in their 'Varieties of Capitalism' (VoC) school of research introduced in Chapter 2. The Hall and Soskice approach to comparative political economy is actor-based with the assumption that actors (including corporations) seek to maximise goals through rational calculation. They emphasise the role of the corporation: 'this is a firm-centred political economy that regards corporations as the crucial actors in a capitalist economy' and they consider the relationships that corporations develop with other actors to argue that the success of a corporation rests on its ability 'to coordinate effectively with a wide range of actors' (Hall and Soskice, 2001: 6). The five key sets of relationships are: industrial relations; corporate governance; vocational training and education; inter-firm relations; and employee relations. LMEs coordinate them primarily through markets, whilst CMEs manage coordination through networks and negotiation structured by distinctive institutions (such as banks) and processes (such as interlocking directorships). They suggest that each capitalist model has assembled a portfolio of mutually supportive institutions, rules and processes that facilitate coordination and are 'complementary'. Thus UK corporate governance rests on a liquid stock market (to permit shareholder sanctions), a flexible labour market (to allow cost cutting) and generalised education (to permit labour mobility), whilst German corporate governance depends on 'patient' long-term capital provided by banks, a restricted labour market (to avoid poaching of workers) and specialised education (to allow the development of firm-specific skills). This diagnosis of complementarity has important implications for convergence of systems and we return to it below.

The VoC framework suggests that both models can be successful and each embody distinctive sources of comparative advantage. The central concern is to explain economic success measured in growth (hence the subtitle of the gospel: *The Institutional Foundations of Comparative Advantage*, Hall and Soskice, 2001), although the framework can be productively employed to address many related questions including more political issues such as equality (CMEs could be expected to display greater income equality) and security (again, CMEs are likely to offer more job security and welfare benefits). The framework has proved so creative that it has 'revolutionised the study of contemporary political economy' (Hancké et al., 2007: 36) and in the process it has generated extensive criticism and adaptation (see Hancké et al., 2007: 5–8; Jackson and Deeg, 2008: 686; Thelen, 2012). Critics point out that the two models appear to be stylised accounts of the USA and Germany but, for our purposes, the models can be used to help explain power relations and to set the scene for more explicitly normative analysis.

The German model of capitalism involves less uncritical faith in the market, it is more inclusive, more strategic and frankly more nationalistic than the UK model. It sees corporations as stakeholder, or even as social, organisations with obligations to the community, and it is no surprise that this model has long been an inspiration to British social democrats. A high point of advocacy and reformist zeal came in the mid-1990s as expressed in Will Hutton's influential *The State We're In* which analysed capitalist models and reflected that 'almost every economic and social indicator shows that Germany continues to perform either as well as Britain or better' Hutton, 1996: xvii). He went on to advocate 'stakeholder capitalism' as noted above, but the high hopes that New Labour would endorse a Germanic stakeholder approach were soon dashed. At the Treasury Brown was far more interested in competition and markets whilst Blair was building bridges with business and the CBI (see Chapter 5). Taylor notes that, 'the most substantial achievement of the tacit Blair–CBI understanding came in the Prime Minister's active willingness to block any attempt by the European Commission to introduce a legally binding European Union directive that would require all companies . . . to create information and consultative committees' (Taylor, 2001: 262). Before exploring Labour's rejection of Rhineland reforms in favour of an intensification of the UK's LME model we should spell out in more detail what German corporate governance involves.

German corporate governance rests on two main foundations. The first is distinctively German and involves the organised representation of labour and its incorporation into decision-making through the mechanisms of 'co-determination'. German company law requires that corporations have a dual board comprising a supervisory board (*Aufsichtrat*) and a management board (*Vorstand*). The supervisory board appoints the management board and approves major corporate strategies. The extraordinary feature, which seems almost inconceivable to an Anglo-Saxon audience, is that for corporations employing over 500 people one third of the supervisory board must be employee representatives, and for over 2,000 employees one half must be from the employees' side. Further, co-determination goes down to the shop floor. The works council laws provide for a manager–worker council in every plant or facility with rights including information and consultation. The works councils are, in practice, more important and effective than supervisory boards and have allowed workers to protect their interests in negotiation with management.

The second foundation is committed long-term share ownership through a dense network of cross-shareholding, bank shareholding, and a constrained market for shares. Thus Vitols (2001: 342) noted that, in 1995, 53 per cent of German shares were held by other enterprises or banks who constituted a group of share blockholders and, even by 2006, Culpepper shows that for a sample of 40 quoted German corporations the average stable shareholder held 45 per cent of the shares (as against 12 per cent in the UK). The banks lie at the heart of this blockholder control. They include public banks as well as the big private banks and, for the 1990s, Callaghan (2009: 742) noted that a study of the top 100 listed corporations showed that 'banks controlled an average of 84 per cent of voting rights': 23 per cent by direct ownership and 61 per cent through proxy votes based on the traditional German practice of shareholders granting proxy votes to the corporation's main bank (the *Hausbank*). Extraordinarily, she also notes that in 1996 the hugely powerful Deutsche Bank chaired 29 per cent of the boards of the 100 largest corporations. The long-term patient funding provided by banks means that the German stock market has been far less important as a source of capital for most corporations and a far smaller proportion of corporations are listed than in other OECD countries (742 corporations in 2012 compared with 2,864 in London and 1,110 in Paris: World Federation of Exchanges, 2012). Meanwhile, and consistent with blockholding and a less liquid market in shares, there are fewer mergers and almost no hostile takeovers. Between 1990 and 2007 there were only three successful hostile takeovers in Germany as against 45 in the UK (Culpepper, 2011: 33).

German corporate governance thus offers an alternative and successful model to the shareholder-dominated Anglo-American variant. But to capture the essence of Rhineland capitalism it is necessary to look beyond the formal and informal rules to take account of the other institutional components of norms and cognitive frameworks. The norms of German corporate governance are deep-seated and carefully nurtured. Donnelly et al. (2001: 18) trace the origins of co-determination back to the middle of the 19th century. They build on concepts of collective interest and mutual respect which expresses itself in a search for consensus. It is an approach to leadership and decision-making that balances the interests of shareholders, managers and employee representatives over the long term. The combination of patient capital, managerial planning and employee job security requires strategies conceived over a much longer time horizon than the next quarterly profit figures. These norms of consensus, long-termism and security allow the system to function effectively avoiding the confrontations or the calculations of immediate self-interest that would be expected in an Anglo-American setting.

The German model provides a context or cognitive framework within which corporate governance is embedded and in which certain understandings are taken for granted. First, since the stock market is not considered especially important there is less of a preoccupation with share price, the views of shareholders or 'the market' (Charkham, 2005: 31). Rather than a financial calculus, German governance tends to emphasise product development, technical excellence and market share. The German model creates corporations that excel in traditional industries characterised by incremental innovation: cars and machine tools rather than software and entertainment. Second, the German system is an explicit 'stakeholder' model. The Stock Corporation Act of 1937 defined the corporation as a stakeholder entity (Barker, 2010: 247) and Donnelly et al. (2001: 40) note that 'German corporate law recognises a general obligation of companies to consider the public interest . . . (this) . . . has led to a greater internalisation of public interest issues into corporate governance'. Corporate decision makers hence consider community, sectoral and German national interests as a matter of course when reviewing strategic options.

Despite its attractions, the prevailing view amongst academics as well as practitioners is that it would be impractical to export the German model beyond its Northern European heartland where variants operate in Austria, Sweden and Denmark. The VoC school emphasises national institutional complementarities (Hancké et al., 2007: 11) arguing that it would be difficult to introduce German-style co-determination without also changing industrial relations, vocational education, longer-term capital markets and activist banks. Without those complementary institutions co-determination would be a fish out of water, impractical and unattainable (see also Soskice, 1997: 125). But this rather defeatist interpretation seems not to operate in the reverse direction and over the past 15 years there have been predictions of a transformation of the German model towards 'good' corporate governance on the Anglo-American model and a degree of change has taken place impelled by a combination of forces. The pressures for a move towards a more shareholder-orientated system in Germany were reinforced by domestic governance failures (Barker, 2010: 243) but have deeper-seated structural roots. A key incentive has been the desire to access global financial markets and for large German corporations to seek listings in London and Wall Street. This requires minority shareholder protections and conformity with corporate governance codes which should increase the availability and decrease the cost of equity capital. Such market opportunities have formed the basis for a series of pressures and reform proposals from the European Commission which has become a proponent of market liberalisation and had effectively operated as a champion of minority shareholder interests and the Anglo-American model (Barker, 2010: 9).

An intense debate has been underway for a decade over the regulation and control of the corporation in Europe. It embraces law reform, with proposals for a European company statute; and competition policy, with measures to restrict European champions and facilitate takeovers and the market for corporate control. But the key element is corporate governance, with the expectation across much of corporate Europe, and certainly in the UK, that convergence on the Anglo-American model is desirable and inevitable. There is a rather weary *Economist*-type assumption that history, economic logic and financial efficiency are all on the side of shareholder value and that, ultimately, the obstinate Europeans will have to bow to the inevitable. But it is very far from certain that the

Anglo-American model is indeed inevitable and even less certain that it is desirable. Indeed, the 2008 financial crisis could have been expected to have discredited the shareholder value model. Shareholders clearly failed in exercising adequate control of risk and in fact encouraged excessively risky, income-maximising strategies in financial institutions. Yet, perversely, the regulatory reaction has been further to reinforce shareholder focus, a point we come back to in the concluding section. The battle in Europe over the design of corporate governance has received surprisingly little attention from students of politics, with the striking exception of the Amsterdam research group. Van Apeldoorn and Horn (2007: 94) mount a passionate critique of the efforts by the European Commission to facilitate the creation of 'European shareholder capitalism' which they characterise as 'the marketization of corporate control'. By this they mean the growth in control of corporations by stock markets and the financial players which dominate them. Their neo-Marxist approach has succeeded in identifying key problems and helped to shift the debate. Thus Horn (2012: 63) detects a reconsideration of shareholder primacy within the European Commission, although the Commission's Green Paper issued in 2011 was remorselessly Anglo-Saxon in its approach and could have been written by the UK's FRC (European Commission, 2011).

Global financial markets, abetted by the European Commission, have brought pressure to bear on the German model, but the pressures have been mediated by domestic actors. The internal threats to the system have come from surprising sources – the banks and the SPD ; the very institutions that appeared to be the beneficiaries of the national regime. The three big private universal banks, Deutsche, Commerzbank and Dresdner Bank (which was taken over by Commerzbank in 2008) bought into the Anglo-Saxon financial casino with 'a switch of business strategy towards more lucrative investment banking' (Barker, 2010: 236). They downgraded their lending to domestic corporations, used European competition policy to attack the state guarantee privileges enjoyed by the German public savings banks (Wilks, 2005: 124), and made a policy decision to surrender the chairmanships of supervisory boards (Barker, 2010: 238). The effect of this surrender was to remove the broad stabilising perspective provided by the *Hausbank* so that, 'today more chairpersons of the supervisory board of large corporations are former CEOs of the same company . . . and former top managers are systematically replacing bankers as board members. These facts suggest that the power of managers is increasing' (Hackenthal et al., 2005: 405). The German banks paid the price of speculation and shared the pain of the financial crash but are unlikely to return to traditional practices. In any case, the regulatory system has itself changed

Table 10.2 Major reforms to German corporate governance

Date	Party	Content	Effect
1998	CDU/FDP	Corporate Sector Supervision and Transparency Act (KonTraG)	Abolish unequal voting rights, limit proxy votes
1998	SPD/Green	Raising of Capital Act	Endorse international accounting standards
2000	SPD/Green	Tax Reduction Act (change to income tax)	Remove penalty on sale of cross-shareholding
2001	SPD/Green	Corporate Governance Code (Cromme Code)	OECD model
2002	SPD/Green	Transparency and Disclosure Act	Mandated Cromme
2001	SPD/Green	Takeover Law	Limited liberalisation

Sources: Höpner (2007), Gourevitch and Shinn (2005), Barker (2010).

as a result of the paradoxical policy stance adopted by the SPD (Social Democratic Party).

Despite the orthodox assumption that the German stakeholder model works to favour the interests of organised labour, the SPD, the party of labour, supported a series of liberal, pro-shareholder reforms between 1998 and 2002. The major developments are outlined in Table 10.2.

As a brief summary of these measures, the KonTraG contained a variety of provisions to facilitate minority shareholder protection, including abolition of the unequal voting rights often used by blockholders (especially families) to retain control. It also increased transparency and limited proxy voting by banks. It was championed by the FDP (Free Democratic Party) in the coalition which, as a liberal party, was to be expected, but it was also supported by the SPD (Höpner, 2007: 406) which was less predictable. After the October 1998 SDP/Green coalition victory the liberalisation measures included endorsement of Anglo-Saxon accounting standards and a key change in the income tax rules allowing banks to sell their cross shareholdings without a tax penalty. The coalition also set up the Cromme Commission on corporate governance which produced a code modelled on OECD principles and the government legislated to require all public companies to 'comply or explain', thus actually going further than the UK Code in coverage and enforcement (Barker, 2010: 251). Finally, after the EU Takeover Directive was abandoned, a German takeover law was enacted which facilitated takeovers (although it retained the right to take defensive measures). These reforms were driven forward by the SPD with Gerhard Schröder as its modernising Chancellor. Observers reflected on the curiosity of a social democratic government apparently unravelling the most social democratic regime in Europe in favour of a shareholder model with neoliberal connotations. What was going on? Höpner (2007: 410) puts the emphasis on the historical revulsion of the trade unions against support provided by blockholders, in the shape of cartels and trusts, to the Nazi regime. But he also suggests that there was an alliance between 'core' workers and shareholders to improve profitability from which they could both benefit (2007: 414). Hence we may see the influence of a labour elite, highly unionised and protected by co-determination in the larger corporations. In any event, Höpner (2007: 415) concludes that 'corporate governance reform strengthened the supervisory boards vis-à-vis managers, resulting in an institutional gain for employee's co-determination'. That conclusion sits oddly with Culpepper's (2011: 3) thesis that managers are the dominant actors in the design of corporate governance, but perhaps the two interpretations are consistent if we consider the position of finance.

The SPD reforms of corporate governance were targeted directly at bank or blockholder dominance, co-determination was never a candidate for abolition. Höpner points out that, since 1963, 'trade unions called out for ... above all, the reduction in the power of the banks' (2007: 410). They achieved this whilst also enhancing corporate transparency and reinforcing the institution of co-determination. Meanwhile, management accepted the reality of co-determination but strengthened their own position by reducing the influence of bank blockholders and replacing bank nominees on supervisory boards. This was an exercise in downgrading the influence of finance. Culpepper (2011: 65) observes that 'the proportion of large blockholdings held by *non*financial firms remained stable' and it was nonfinancial management that was driving the reforms. 'The German peak association, the BDI, was dominated by industrial managers ... The BDI excludes many of the financial sector companies that favoured the liberalization of German markets for corporate control' (Culpepper, 2011: 54). They used their influence to moderate the liberalisation of takeovers so that the German law was less stringent than the European proposals.

The net effect of these changes was to create an apparatus of minority shareholder protection and a simulacrum of shareholder-led corporate governance whist retaining a stakeholder regime. Virtually all commentators share the view that change has been gradual and certainly does not amount to the creation of shareholder capitalism (see Barker, 2010: 254: Culpepper, 2011: 49; Vitols, 2005: 395). Hackenthal et al. (2005: 404) go so far as to say 'no fundamental change has occurred ... Stakeholder orientation has not been replaced'. Instead we have seen a reduction in the influence of the private banking sector and an increase in the influence of employees and non-financial management. The 'marketisation of corporate control' which has progressed substantially in the UK and in France, and which is being promoted at the EU level, has been stopped in its tracks in Germany. The German model of corporate governance remains a striking and distinctive alternative to the Anglo-American orthodoxy.

What conclusions can we draw from this examination of the German model? Perhaps the most important is that it emphasises that there are successful alternatives to the Anglo-American model. The German corporate economy is the most impressive in Europe, and in some respects the world. And it is not unique. The German model has similarities in Northern Europe and in Japan. The CME economies are equally as successful as the LMEs and are regaining prestige in the wake of the 2008 financial crisis. The German model has evolved, it has taken on a more hybrid form with greater elements of minority shareholder protection, but it remains seductive. Jonathan Charkham posed the question 'which system is the best?'. He praised the Japanese model but concluded that 'the Germans make their system work more consistently' (Charkham, 1994: 364). Twenty years later the German model again appears attractive in terms of economic efficiency and accountability and, for our purposes, addresses with more honesty the question of corporate power.

It is clear that a degree of internal democracy exists within the corporation in Germany, even if it does not meet the standards of self-government advocated by Dahl (1985, see also Ch. 2). Donnelly et al. suggest instead that the idea of 'constitutionalisation' is more appropriate than that of democracy. Hence, 'while related to political democracy co-determination did not institute pure democratic principles into capitalist enterprise but "constitutionalised" the relationship between stakeholders in a regime of participation that implies a sharing of responsibility and mutual obligations' (Donnelly et al., 2001: 23). The German corporate constitution, as outlined in Table 10.1, applies most clearly to employees, but networks, cross-shareholdings and board membership also give a voice to suppliers, creditors and communities. German corporate law requires directors to take account of these stakeholders in addition to shareholders but this has a subtler cognitive or cultural dimension which Charkham (2005: 30) expresses as 'a genuine sense of obligation to the community'. The consensus decision-making within German corporations therefore balances interests and constrains autocratic managers and egotistical CEOs. The fairness and mutual accommodation that internal democracy can bring should also increase trust and deliver the greater commitment to the corporation which sets up a virtuous circle of success (see Mayer, 2013: 59). The German corporate policy making system is thus typically more pluralist that the dominant executive model typical of Anglo-American corporations and internally power is negotiated, held accountable and exercised collectively. What about the deployment of corporate power within society at large?

Big corporations and the corporate elite are powerful within German society. The German post-war sense of achievement is based on economic success, technical excellence and a self-sacrificing contribution to European integration. The corporations have been central to these achievements and have earned prestige and influence. It is important, of course, not to be starry-eyed about German corporations. They are guilty of all the malpractices that exist in other economies. They exploit workers, export jobs, damage the environment, form cartels, bribe foreign governments, subvert their own works councils and pay their executives inflated salaries. The truly striking feature of German corporate power is that it is recognised within society and held to account by laws, social institutions and corporate governance. Germany recognises corporations as governing institutions and rejects the Anglo-American public/private hypocrisy with its pretence that the 'private' world of property and contract should be immune from governmental intervention and that the corporation is simply a private association. If Germany can see through the illusion and operate a mature, consensual system of stakeholder corporate governance, whilst delivering industrial success, then so can other regimes. Mrs Thatcher used to invoke TINA (there is no alternative) in defence of her economic policies. Germany demonstrates that TINA is a false goddess in the field of corporate governance.

ASIAN ALTERNATIVES

The range of corporate governance alternatives to the Anglo-Saxon shareholder model extends to a number of important Asian models which appear irrational and endangered to a British audience. The alternatives include those of Japan, South Korea and China. The corporations governed through those models are household names or, in the case of China, becoming so. Corporations such as the Japanese NTT, Hitachi or Toyota; the Korean Samsung, LG or Hyundai; the Chinese Sinopec, China National Petroleum or China Mobile Communication (all in the Fortune Global 100) are successful in their own right and representative of vibrant successful economies which nonetheless prosper with regimes very different to the expectations of shareholder corporate governance.

Each of these three systems is distinctive, embedded in very different economies with deep historical roots. Generalisation is therefore dangerous and each system deserves a more extensive treatment but, from the narrow perspective of corporate governance, there are some common features in relation to markets, motives and corporate power. All of these societies are sceptical about the allegedly benign workings of free markets. They all are, or have been, 'developmental states' where economic development has been given absolute priority as a matter of state policy so that the state has structured society to accelerate industrial development by privileging corporations and suppressing workers, savers and consumers. The reflex norms built into Anglo-American economic institutions of a benign market, and market solutions as a default setting, is not shared in these Asian economies. The default setting is far more likely to be state guidance. Of course these economies utilise markets very effectively, but they do not trust them. For Japan Dore has classically pointed to an inability on the part of the Japanese to accept Adam Smith; they 'have never managed actually to believe in the invisible hand. They have always insisted ... that the butcher, the baker, and the brewer need to be benevolent as well as self-interested' (Dore, cited in Whittaker and Deakin, 2009: 269). Accordingly, arguments resting on the proposition that markets, including stock markets, are benign and efficient meet an immediate scepticism.

Secondly, conventional Western models of economic behaviour are typically less valid in these Asian settings. Models based on the assumption of rational (economic) utility maximisation which underpin principal–agent approaches and which infuse all western discussion of corporate governance have far less purchase in the more collectivist societies of Japan, Korea and China. There is no need to adopt cultural determinism, which explains economic behaviour by reference to consensus, groupism or even *wa* (harmony), but there is a need to accept that institutions in these societies incorporate different norms and cognitive frameworks. Investors, managers and workers will be influenced by peer pressure and by a concern with the corporation, the community and the nation as much as by market signals and financial gain. Managers within corporations, and corporations within society, can be expected to act more like the 'corporate citizens' discussed in Chapter 9 and hence with a recognition of duties and obligations which constrain self-interested pursuit of economic gain. Again, Western assumptions about corporate governance, posited on a narrow economistic picture of human motivation, will find much Asian corporate governance puzzling (see also Learmount, 2002: 160).

Thirdly, each of these societies is more open in recognising the political as well as the economic power of large corporations. Japan and Korea are CMEs (coordinated market economies) and regard large corporations as essential partners in securing societal goals. Historically, of course, and still in China, corporate power pre-dated democratic politics and these countries are less liable to concede the pluralist conceit (see Chapter 2) that corporations are simply one more interest group within a democratic pluralist system of government. In none of these societies would corporations be visualised simply as private associations of individuals, as they are in the Anglo-American legal model. It follows that the proposition that the corporation is owned by, and should be operated for the benefit of, shareholders, or at least minority shareholders, would be regarded as absurd. Blockholder shareholders are a different proposition, be they banks, families or the Communist Party, but they are dealt with through explicit political alliances, not through mechanisms of corporate governance.

The social context within which modes of corporate governance have developed in Japan, Korea and China is therefore unwelcoming to the preoccupations and prescriptions offered by Anglo-American corporate reformers. These countries share the dominance of the corporate form in their economies as part of the global convergence noted in chapters 1 and 3; their corporations are vehicles of national wealth and national pride. They led the Japanese post-war growth miracle; they took Korea from starvation to prosperity in one astonishing generation; and they are the locomotive of the stunning Chinese corporate revolution in wealth generation. As such, the status and power of these large corporations is not in doubt, but their influence on policy and individual well-being also deserves emphasis. None of these societies have substantial welfare states so that the importance of employment and fringe benefits provided by corporations becomes even more valuable. The centrality of corporations means that they are more clearly recognised as partners in governance and their senior managers are integrated into ruling elites. This could take the form of the close relationships between corporate leaders, politicians and bureaucrats seen in Japan, or the inclusion of corporate leaders into communist cadres in China, or the involvement of *chaebol* families with the military and now with politicians in Korea. President Lee Myung-Bak, Korean President from 2008 to 2013 was a former CEO of Hyundai Engineering and Construction. In these three Asian countries attempts have been made to persuade governments to conform to Anglo-American patterns of corporate governance in order to access international equity capital, although after the 2008 financial crisis, the Anglo-American model must appear less attractive, if not actually toxic.

JAPAN: A STAKEHOLDER SOCIETY

Japan remains one of the world's most successful economies; huge (in 2010 the third largest economy), wealthy (with GDP per capita higher that the UK, France or Germany), innovative, egalitarian and stable. It presents an enviable model of political economy which is both fascinating and elusive. Fascinating because it contradicts virtually every assumption underpinning conventional Anglo-American corporate governance; elusive because Japanese political economy is replete with paradox, enduringly opaque and appears so culturally distinct that its dynamics seem impossible to emulate. The large Japanese corporation enjoys substantial autonomy from shareholder pressure but experiences many other pressures from a highly networked society in which it is deeply embedded. The way in which corporations are constrained, channelled and made accountable by societal norms leads them to be regarded as 'a public institution' or as a 'community firm' (Keidanren, cited in Deakin and Whittaker, 2009: 18, 22). To understand the nature of corporate governance in this distinctive capitalist model it is necessary to pick out some of the key features of Japanese political economy beginning with the blockholder effects of corporate alliances.

Japan's corporate structure developed over the post-war period into a hierarchy dominated by large first-rank corporations typically organised into coherent conglomerate groupings, the *keiretsu*. The three largest are familiar names, Mitsui, Mitsubishi and Sumitomo but there were a variety of groups, often organised around banks, in a dense network of alliances analysed by Gerlach in his *Alliance Capitalism* (1992). The system rested on stable, long-term cross-shareholdings in which a controlling proportion of shares were held by sister corporations in the same group. Shares were held as much as a gesture of commitment rather than as a source of income and control. Capital was sourced from banks or retained earnings so that equity capital was an irrelevance, share dealing was regarded as mildly disreputable, and 'senior management of Japanese firms had virtually no interest in the share price and other benchmarks of performance in which shareholders might have an interest' (Olcott, 2009: 204). Through cross-shareholding, 'Japanese managers had, in effect, created a set of synthetic blockholders' (Gourevitch and Shinn, 2005: 170) so that, as late as 1994, 45 per cent of shares in Japanese listed corporations were held by 'stable shareholders' (Miyajima and Kuroki, 2007: 81). There was no market for corporate control and managers enjoyed absolute autonomy from shareholders.

A second core feature is the principle of lifetime employment for (mainly) male employees in large firms, a weak external labour market and firm-specific skills. About 70 per cent of Japanese employees enjoy strong job security (2007 figures, Araki, 2009: 228) and expect to pursue careers within the corporate group. Managers and board members are recruited internally and 'the external market for CEOs is still to all intents and purposes non-existent' (Olcott, 2009: 218). Again, this appears extraordinary when compared with Anglo-American fluid labour markets. The contrast is emphasised by the Japanese worker's loyalty to the firm and to fellow employees that is so intense that workers will put the firm ahead of the family – indeed, in some respects, the corporation is the family. In order to safeguard employment corporations tend to pursue growth, rather than profits, and plan for long-term stable survival.

The third feature follows from the privileging of employees over shareholders. The large Japanese corporation is a stakeholder institution in which the beneficiaries are the employees and the managers. Learmount describes it as 'a community of employees' rather than just a production mechanism and he notes that corporations he studied 'seemed to echo the notion of the company as a social organisation above all else' (Learmount, 2002: 97, 113). This appears a paternalistic relationship, far more so than with German co-determination. Japanese workers are not organised through the sort of forceful industry unions seen in Germany, and the expectation is that they will work hard and make sacrifices for the sake of the corporation. The stakeholder web extends beyond employees to banks, sister corporations and suppliers. Corporations work hard to establish relationships of trust with commercial partners and rely on trust and good long-term relations, rather than on law and contracts, in what has been termed 'relational contracting' (Dore, 1983). The exclusion of shareholders and the compliant workforce means that managers control the Japanese corporation and that collective management, represented in bodies such as *Keidanren* (the Japanese Federation of Business Organizations), are the most powerful actors in domestic politics.

The supportive political system comprises the fourth key feature of the Japanese capitalist model. The system has been described as corporatist, as a CME, and historically as a developmental state, all terms which seek to capture the close cooperation between industry and the state. The post-war consensus on economic development, as a necessity to respond to the physical and emotional devastation of defeat, underpinned policies favourable to industrial investment and a political system which favoured business interests. Democratic politics was dominated by the Liberal Democratic Party (LDP) which held office continuously until 1993 and predominately since. The LDP is conservative, nationalist and firmly in favour of manufacturing industry, but the key engagement with corporations has come through the bureaucracy. There has been a 30-year debate about the degree to which Japan's economic success has been due to an enlightened, powerful and supremely confident bureaucracy which has consistently tailored macro and micro-economic policy in corporate interests. The debate was inspired by Chalmers Johnson's *MITI and the Japanese Miracle* (1982) and, on the whole, subsequent research modifies his celebration of bureaucratic leadership. But what is beyond doubt is the partnership between the administrative elite, business leaders and, more episodically, assertive politicians working together to create an industrial machine which, by the late 1980s, appeared the most impressive in the world.

The fifth feature of Japan's corporate governance displays some similarities with the UK in that the legal basis of the board of directors is vague but Anglo-American in its formal provisions. The Japanese Commercial Code was revised under the Occupation in 1950 reflecting US company law to stipulate that the ultimate governing body is the shareholders but that the board of directors is vested with executive authority (Deakin and Whittaker, 2009: 4). Traditionally Japanese boards were huge with 30–40 members, all of whom came from within the group. The most senior post is the President (or CEO) who will select executive directors and in practice decisions would be made by a small inner group and ratified by the board (Charkham, 2005: 131–3). This sort of board appears ceremonial and impossibly unwieldy, but of course the board does not represent shareholders, instead members act to build and sustain networks within the corporation and in the wider corporate community. Directors have been described as the 'elders of the corporate community' who maintain dialogue and build a strong sense of mutual responsibility between the corporation and its many stakeholders (see Learmount, 2002: ch. 7).

To many Anglo-American students of corporate governance, and to most leaders of financial institutions, the Japanese system appears economically inefficient and 'deviant' (Dore, 2005). But in true varieties of capitalism fashion it is well integrated into the institutions of the Japanese CME model and has worked effectively. It privileges long-term productive industry and managers, rather than short-term financial industry and shareholders, and it reverses the flaws in the UK system outlined above. It remains, like the UK system, essentially a model based on self-regulation. But whilst UK boards pay more attention to shareholders and marginalise other stakeholders, the Japanese regime provides a mirror image. Stakeholders receive the attention and the benefits whilst shareholders are marginalised. From a perspective of corporate social responsibility this appears defensible. Corporations act responsibly towards employees, trading partners and local communities, and they give serious attention to the national interest. Whilst social democratic reformers of the 1990s never treated Japan with the approval that they gave to the German model, there was widespread admiration of the Japanese corporate system (Hutton, 1996: 274) qualified by fear of Japan's formidable corporate machine and the competitive challenge it presented.

There is, of course, a danger in romanticising the community dimension of Japanese corporate governance which also has a darker side with respect to excluded employees, domestic inefficiency and political corruption. As regards employees, 'lifetime employment remains a norm for 70–85 per cent of listed companies' (Jackson, 2007: 285), but lifetime employment is not available for many workers in smaller firms or for 'nonregular' employees who tend to be young or female. These non-regular workers accounted for about 34 per cent of the workforce in 2007. They are excluded not only from lifetime employment but also from union protection. Japan's enterprise unions tend only to represent regular (lifetime) employees and, in any case, union membership had fallen to 18 per cent by 2007 (Araki, 2009: 227, 239). Thus 'nonregular employees have endured less protection and have been treated as "shock absorbers" to maintain the security of employment for regular employees' (Araki, 2009: 249). Lifetime employment therefore carries a price of serious exploitation for a significant minority of the workforce.

As regards domestic inefficiency, in many respects Japan operates a dual economy. As Porter (1990: 394) pointed out, in internationally traded, highly competitive sectors such as automobiles and consumer electronics, Japanese firms are remarkably efficient and, as with the Toyota system of lean production, they have redefined manufacturing excellence. But in domestic fields such as construction, retailing and utilities, the competitive pressures are absent, regulatory protection operates, and corporations can be hugely inefficient (Porter et al., 2000: 5). There are often social or political bargains at work (such as support for 'Mom and Pop' stores) but also a toleration of monopolies and cartels. Tokyo Electric Power (TepCo) provides an example of a monopolist which relied on political connections and political funding to sustain a shockingly inefficient electricity monopoly. The corporation was only exposed when the 2011 tsunami and mismanagement of its nuclear safety crisis revealed its inadequacies, which eventually resulted in nationalisation (*The Economist*, 11 May 2012).

A third objectionable dimension of Japan's corporate governance is seen in political corruption through corporate funding of politicians. It is an unfortunate similarity that politics in Japan, like politics in the United States, is 'money politics' in which individual politicians, factions and parties require large campaigns funds to succeed. Partly this is structural. Japan has multi-member electoral constituencies in which members of the same party (mainly the LDP) will compete against each other using financial influence and generosity rather than ideology, policy or charisma. Money also lubricates the networks of favours and obligations that dynamise Japanese politics and the source of money is business. Political funding in Japan has complex dimensions (see Babb, 2001: ch. 4) but, broadly speaking, corporations contribute large sums of money to individual politicians and faction leaders. They contribute individually, or though trade associations or, often, under the counter in informal ways which ingeniously evade the laws to control political funding. The true scale of funding streams is difficult to estimate but it continues to allow business influence over policy making, thus Hamada (2010: 336) notes that 'Japanese business interests can buy political influence'. Whilst a tolerant attitude would accept arm's-length, transparent funding of political parties, the Japanese picture extends to scandals, outright bribery, pork-barrel subsidies and governmental favouritism which undermines the credibility of democratic politics.

The discussion so far has examined traditional Japanese corporate governance and emphasised its social, stakeholder orientation whilst also recognising its closed, elitist character and integration into party and bureaucratic politics. The most influential actors are managers, partly operating as senior corporate executives but also in senior positions in business associations. Japan appears as a highly coordinated economy in which corporations have much prestige, and often more effective power that politicians. In terms of elite configurations it can be seen as a 'corporate state' but one far more nationalistic, and far less dominated by finance, than the UK's New Corporate State. But this was the traditional regime and many pundits expected radical change towards the Anglo-American shareholder model.

The pressure for change in Japanese corporate governance intensified in the mid-1990s and precipitated change from 1997 onwards when the LDP lost its governing majority. The pressures were fourfold. First, the collapse in Japanese growth in the 'lost decade' of the 1990s prompted agitation from the managers of large productive corporations for measures to enable restructuring. Second, the stagnation obliged corporations to begin to wind-back cross-shareholdings which also allowed foreign investors dramatically to increase their holdings of Japanese equities. Overseas holdings went from 5 per cent in 1990 to 14 per cent in 1998 and 28 per cent in 2008. Third, banks became less reliable sources of capital and corporations turned to financial markets creating the temptation to enter into Tiberghien's 'golden bargain' in which 'global investors offer domestic politicians a deal whereby abundant and cheap capital flows come in exchange for corporate reforms that guarantee the rights of minority shareholders and a high return on investment through the facilitation of corporate restructuring' (Tiberghien, 2007: xii). He argues that this bargain was substantially accepted by politicians in France and Korea, less so by those in Japan. Fourth, many commentators have detected a normative shift towards acceptance of a shareholder framework. The most influential articulation of this trend comes from one of the most respected external authorities on Japanese political economy, Ron Dore, a defender of the Japanese community firm. In a book published in Japanese in 2006 Dore identifies a 'silent shareholder revolution' (Inagami, 2009: 176) which was developing into a fashionable new orthodoxy in the media, among politicians, and in the offices of METI (the Ministry of Economy, Trade and Industry, formerly MITI). He saw shareholder value as becoming respectable, along with support for a market for corporate control, thus, 'a few managers may mutter their dissatisfaction, but after less than two decades of missionary activity, the conversion of Japan to the theology of shareholder sovereignty seems complete' (Dore, 2009: 161). For Dore, therefore, these pressures for change have proved successful. Others are not so sure.

Reform of Japanese corporate governance has attracted considerable attention. Studies deal with the reconfiguration of cross-shareholdings, change in lifetime employment, revision of the Commercial Code, changes in the structure and composition of boards, shareholder activism and the market for corporate control. Space prohibits extended discussion of these developments which are rehearsed in a series of excellent publications (Jackson and Moerke, 2005; Aoki et al., 2007: Tiberghien, 2007; Whittaker and Deakin, 2009; Culpepper, 2011). The broad conclusion of all these commentators is of the resilience of the Japanese system of stakeholder corporate governance. As with Germany, there have been reforms but the state 'has not transformed the core of corporate governance' (Tiberghien, 2007: 212). Concentrating more narrowly on hostile takeovers, Culpepper (2011: 142) concluded that after 2005, managers initially in favour of liberalisation became more sceptical and 'mobilised to adopt a system of hostile takeover protection'. His study is interesting in its emphasis on managerial preferences which he sees as the determining force in corporate governance outcomes in France and Germany as well as in Japan. Aoki also identified limited change and concluded that Japan is moving to a hybrid system in which stock market evaluations come to supplement managerial choices and stakeholder interests (Aoki, 2007: 428).

In their exceptionally rich study Whittaker and Deakin and their contributors tell a story of continuity which outlines significant changes which have responded to pressures but have been crafted to produce 'a renewal of the postwar model of the large Japanese corporation . . . not in spite of the legal, institutional, and competitive changes of the early 2000s, but, paradoxically, because of them' (Deakin and Whittaker, 2009: 2). They also see a hybrid form of corporate governance emerging in which boards mediate between different stakeholder groups instead of representing shareholders, as in the UK model, or passively protecting core employees, as in the traditional Japanese model (ibid.: 22). This picture of creative adaptation shows some similarities with Germany, inasmuch as gestures have been made to the shareholder model but there has not been a rejection of the principles of coordination or the goals which it serves. The Japanese model, like the German model, appears to have emerged from the period of challenge and reform unchanged is essence and arguably in fact strengthened.

Expectations of convergence on an Anglo-American shareholder model of corporate governance were naïve. Japan has a long history of resisting outside pressure (*gaiatsu*) and of retaining key institutional powers such as managerial autonomy. For instance, the decline in cross-shareholding has for some corporations been compensated for by share buybacks. But these shares are not retired, they are retained as treasury stock so that 'at the end of March 2008, 156 companies were their own largest shareholder, including Toyota Motor' (Inagami, 2009: 180) – a remarkable, but apparently legal, gesture of managerial defiance. More generally, the resilience of the Japanese model would appear to confirm the VoC theory of institutional complementarities: states are unlikely to engage in transformation of key institutions which are inconsistent with their prevailing mode of coordination. Instead outside pressures can be employed to secure desirable adaptation of existing models. In this case it seems that corporate governance pressures helped to enhance central decision-making capacity, they facilitated corporate restructuring and strengthened managerial autonomy. In Japan, as in Germany, the broad group that has benefited from corporate governance adaptation is management.

CONCLUSION: THE NEED FOR REINVENTION OF CORPORATE GOVERNANCE

The simple conclusion to this review of existing theories and practices is that corporate governance is too important to be left to shareholders. Corporate governance has gone from a rather specialised concern of company law to become an aspect of our political systems. This transition is evident in the UK but, as we have seen, corporate governance has been kept off the agenda of electoral politics and it is perhaps no coincidence that the self-regulatory regime emerged in the early 1990s, in parallel with the emergence of the New Corporate State. The discussion presented above conveys a deep dissatisfaction with UK governance, and sought to demythologise the shareholder theories on which current regulatory practices are based. It was argued that the property rights justification for shareholder ownership of the corporation is flawed and that there is no moral basis for shareholder dominance. The shareholder value focus is based on a deception. The internal governance of the corporation in Britain is seen to fail against standards of democratic practice and key stakeholders are unrecognised or excluded. Moreover, the system is dysfunctional in terms of productive success and economic efficiency. Responding to short-term financial pressures and incentives, top management have financially re-engineered their corporations and arguably reduced the productive capacity of the whole economy. There is much evidence to support this position which has been eloquently assembled by Colin Mayer (2013).

This critique is reinforced through comparison with Germany and Japan who function more successfully than the UK with different regimes of corporate governance. They do not display the weaknesses of the UK regime and they underline the viability of alternatives which might appear preferable on the grounds of democratic principles, stakeholder engagement and simple productive efficiency. The comparisons are valuable in helping to understand the strategies and political actions of Japanese and German corporations, but it is doubtful that those models could be reproduced in other economies. They rest on specific national-level political bargains and reflect the political and economic history of the states in which they are embedded. How do they impact on multinational corporations who enjoy the additional powers explored in Chapter 7? As discussed above in relation to European reforms, the globalisation of markets makes it difficult to sustain stakeholder regimes and the model which is consistently advocated as appropriate for a globalised economy is the Anglo-American shareholder model. This presents a challenge for global governance.

Given the lack of purchase of existing theoretical approaches, and the absence of a compelling model to operate at either the national or the global level, it is not easy to define options for reform. The starting point for a discussion of how corporate governance should be redefined and reformed is to recognise that the corporation is a self-contained entity, separate from its owners. As such it is an amoral institution, licensed by society, with a constitution provided by law and regulations of corporate governance but capable of pursuing a variety of goals. But this is just a starting point. The more demanding task of examining how corporate governance should be reformed to contribute towards a productive redefinition of the corporation and its role in society is taken up in Chapter 11.

11. Conclusion: fairy-tales, facts, foci and futures

The business corporation is a work of genius. It has harnessed material resources, technology and organisation, mobilised by human imagination and innovation, to create wealth and mass prosperity unimaginable to earlier generations. In the process it has unleashed less attractive aspects of human ambition including greed, dominance and a lust for status, but at least these baser impulses have operated through peaceful commerce. Its sheer success means that it has become a constituent feature of contemporary political life, omnipresent, often unremarked, but powerful enough to dictate political choices. The opening chapter concluded that we do not have adequate theories or frameworks to assess the influence of the corporation over contemporary politics. In response to that lack, the book argues that we should regard the large corporation as a governing institution which has become part of the governance of society and which therefore affects democratic process, political choice and the design and implementation of public policy. Until recently the power of the corporation was held in balance. Since the late 1980s that balance has been overturned; an argument that has been made in various settings in earlier pages. During the time this book has been researched and written, the extent of the contemporary imbalance has become clearer and more worrying. The benign aspects of business success have perversely created a creature capable of doing immense damage and there is a risk that the corporation is becoming malignant. An initial concern has therefore evolved with this book to become more active unease, verging on foreboding. Reforms are imperative if we are not to allow this governing institution to evolve into a source of oppression, exercising one-dimensional enslavement. This closing chapter therefore presents a critical evaluation of the corporation in contemporary politics. It is not measured or judicious, it is contentious, provocative and with a polemical edge; but let us start with a more sober positioning of the argument.

The institutional approach taken in this book is outlined in Chapter 1. Institutions are the means by which societies organise relationships. They embody the mix of rules, conventions and expectations by which individuals make sense of the world around them and they are, by definition, intangible. Thus 'the market' is an institution and so is 'the corporation'. By this we mean the authority of the large business corporation in the abstract. It is not suggested that every individual corporation joins in governance or deploys political power, but its institutional authority mandates a corporation to engage in governance and the way in which an individual corporation chooses to exploit that mandate within the political system is a matter for individual political analysis. An instructive parallel can be drawn with the institution of 'the law'. The law is constituted by a set of rules (legislation and the constitution); it involves a set of tacit norms (rule of law, trial by peers); and it is embedded in cultural assumptions (justice, law abiding, legality). Not all lawyers, judges or courts live up to these principles, but they all draw authority from them. Similarly, not all corporations benefit from the rules, observe the norms, or meet cultural expectations. Corporations have discretion within that framework of authority and their role as individual political actors is both constrained and empowered by this institutional setting.

To accept that 'the corporation' is an institution should be commonplace; to argue that it is 'governing' is more adventurous. It was argued in Chapter 1 that the corporation is 'political' in that it takes part in the classic political role of the allocation of values for society. Its political salience has been affirmed again and again throughout the book and illustrated, in particular, in the characterisation of the UK as a New Corporate State in which the corporation shares in government. The 'governing' proposition therefore states what should perhaps be obvious, namely that corporations are integrated into political processes, at the global level they act as de facto governments through private regulation, and at the national level they make public policy, as chapters 4, 5 and 6 on the UK demonstrated.

Now to the central problem. Institutions have a moral core; they earn authority by fulfilling definitive human needs. These are: for the family, unconditional love and loyalty; for the law, justice and the peaceful resolution of disputes; for the market, cooperative exchange and economic welfare; for the church, helping one's fellow man and spiritual inspiration. Even the monarchy has a code of public service. What is the equivalent for the corporation? Efficiency? Technical progress? Peaceful commerce? Wealth? Self-interest? Or even greed? As explored extensively in this book, the involvement of the corporation in government is not legitimised by any democratic process, only shareholders elect CEOs. If, in addition to a lack of popular consent, corporations also have no moral standing, if they are amoral, then should society accept their role in government? This is crisis territory. It is a crisis that sits at the heart of the market states that constitute the next generation of nation-states.

Conclusion: fairy-tales, facts, foci and futures 253

The illegitimacy of corporate colonisation of government merges with the sheer scale of damage that ever-larger corporations can wreak to pose a threat to contemporary society. It is a risk to set alongside the risks posed by terrorism, nuclear war or epidemics. It is a risk amply demonstrated by the 2008 financial crash, in which large financial corporations were the main culprits, but environmental crises are equally as threatening. The horrors of BP's Deep Water Horizon, or TepCo's nuclear meltdowns are a harbinger of yet unimagined disasters capable of affecting whole countries and hundreds of millions of people. The problem of how to make corporations accountable, how to attach to them adequate legitimacy, is one of the most fundamental facing 21st-century society. It is imperative to reinvent the corporation, to re-evaluate its role in society and to reconsider its license to operate. Before looking to futures of reform, however, we should finalise the diagnosis and draw together the insights from earlier chapters. The conclusions are presented under the three headings of fairy-tales, facts and theoretical foci before going on to touch on some future possibilities.

FAIRY-TALES

There are a range of orthodox views about corporations and their powers which are severely mistaken. By 'orthodox views' is meant the standard assumptions that inform the competitiveness agenda, public policy and journalistic comment in English-speaking countries. This section seeks to debunk or demythologise seven of these myths.

First, the business corporation is a publicly licensed organisation, it is not an autonomous private body. This is the single most important message of this book. We need to draw the large business corporation into the realm of democratic accountability and in order to do so we must explode the traditional British liberal myth that the corporation has a separate, private existence insulated from political control by transcendent property rights. The corporation is a legal creature, constituted by the state, with a public origin and a purpose to serve society. To assert otherwise is an Anglo-American disease that other societies should protect against.

Second, shareholders do not own corporations. The corporation is a legal person which owns its own assets and engages in independent decision-making. The very principle of limited liability underlines the semi-detached relationship between shareholders and the corporation in which they invest. Neither can shareholders claim some moral right of ownership as the suppliers of risk capital. In one of the most impressive treatments of corporate power Parkinson (1993: 40) concludes that shareholders 'cannot be shown to have an antecedent moral right of control over corporate property' and hence that 'the property rights justification must fail, and with it the project of explaining companies as private shareholder domains'. This perspective is receiving increasing recognition. An FT columnist observed that 'the first step to restoring management to its proper stewardship role is to abandon the myth of shareholder ownership' (Caulkin, 2012: 12). But on this myth, of course, rests the whole superstructure of UK corporate governance.

Third, corporate social responsibility is a dead-end. At best it is an honest misconception, at worst a fraud, on stakeholders and the public. The flaws analysed in Chapter 8 are simply too profound for CSR to address societal and environmental issues without transformative change in the conception of the corporation. CSR may actually do more harm than good by engaging the energies and enthusiasm of committed employees and pre-empting more effective processes of accountability. Corporations seeking to be socially responsible should pay their fair share of taxes and treat their stakeholders with generosity. The stakeholder concept, on the other hand, is much more worthwhile, as is the idea of corporate citizenship.

Fourth, orthodox understanding of 'the market' is deeply deceptive. Advocacy of the market, and especially of the free market, is arguably the most powerful mobilising force in modern society. Pursuit of the benefits of the market have transformed public policies, reconfigured entire states and generated an impassioned debate around 'neoliberalism' as the dominant contemporary model of capitalism. But the market is not free and the idea of neoliberalism can be a distraction when it confronts the operation of market forces at the macro-level of the state or the global economy, but fails to recognise that those forces are controlled at the meso or sectoral level by corporations. As argued in Chapter 1, and repeatedly throughout this book, markets are constituted by government regulation in partnership with corporations and the great majority of modern markets are oligopolies. A small number of large corporations exert market power and substitute hierarchy and collusion for open markets and competition. The market discourse is a very effective project of deception, often self-deception, which conceals a reality of market intervention by corporations through corporate strategies and through their influence over government agencies. Neoliberalism is only part of the threat, corporate greed perverts markets.

Fifth, corporations have more influence within the democratic process than do voters. The design and implementation of public policy caters to corporate interests to a greater extent than to popular interests expressed in public opinion. The New Corporate State, outlined for the UK in chapters 4 and 5, involves a shrinking of democratic choice, or more correctly of voter choice. Agendas are set by politicians and government officials in dialogue with corporations or their intermediaries (such as management consultants), manifestos are directed at business interests as much as at voters. Whilst some policy issues retain huge public support and are democratic totems – such as the NHS, land use planning or the state pension – others, from unemployment benefit and immigration to sporting sponsorship and internet access are decided by reference to corporate preferences. Democratic choice therefore shrinks both in terms of those policy options treated as viable, and in terms of key areas of public policy excluded from political debate. Whole swathes of issues of public concern in areas such as monetary policy, competition policy and utility regulation are now managed by independent regulators insulated from political influence and tasked to maintain profitable corporations in managed markets. In these fields citizens have become consumers; as voters, like elected politicians, they are self-righteously kept at arm's-length.

The sixth source of orthodox misapprehension is pluralism: the political theory that all interests have a voice, all voices are equally heard by a government that is independent of interests, and that governments select policies on the basis of a reasoned assessment of policy preferences in pursuit of the public interest (see Chapter 2). In this highly idealised form the theory is clearly unrealistic, but it is important as the default option which informs much journalistic comment, governmental procedures and popular ethical judgements of public life. Pluralism provides a misleading interpretation of how corporate interests are imposed on the contemporary state, and provides an even less useful model of how corporations should be held to account. Chapter 6 outlined corporate goals in the UK and argued that they dominate the policy agenda. Other interests are marginalised, government itself is colonised by business in the model of partnership working, and policy decisions are taken as much in the corporate interest as in the public interest. In this New Corporate State, reforms informed by a pluralist agenda – such as regulating lobbying or controlling donations to political parties – are futile, tinkering at the edges of corporate power.

The seventh fairy-tale involves the false friend TINA and applies more particularly to what Gamble (2009b: 17) calls the 'Anglosphere', the UK and the USA. The idea that 'There Is No Alternative' is very powerful in the Anglosphere and we encountered the dominance of Anglo-American, or plain American, perspectives in Chapter 1 on the norm of the corporate form, Chapter 7 on the organisation of multinationals, and in Chapter 10 on models of corporate governance. In truth there are several actual or theoretical alternative ways of structuring the corporate form, encouraging convergence with the public interest and ensuring that corporations are accountable. In Chapter 10 we looked at Japanese and German alternatives, at the end of this chapter we touch on theoretical alternatives. The key point is that the model of autonomous corporations, motivated by shareholder value and answerable only to stock markets and financial markets, must be seen as only one possible institutional model, and one that is far from the best.

These seven propositions have been discussed in earlier chapters in a number of settings and especially in relation to the UK. The myths that they seek to discredit are mutually supportive and comprise a dominant or 'hegemonic' discourse which rests on hallowed pillars of contemporary liberal society, namely the sanctity of a private sphere insulated from the state; the moral and wealth-creating benefits of markets; and the superiority of democracy within a liberal democratic state. Who could deny the value of these achievements of western civilisation? Yet each of these achievements has been used as a veil behind which a more objectionable deployment of corporate power has taken place. The fairy-tales need to be recognised as such in order to expose a discourse that legitimises corporate power, skews democratic politics, and delivers huge benefits to a narrow elite. The discussion hence moves from fairy-tales to 'facts'.

FACTS

The seven 'facts' advanced below emerge from clear bodies of evidence discussed in earlier chapters, or are so much a feature of contemporary societies that they should be regarded as relatively unambiguous. The claim is that they are proven hypotheses which provide propositions upon which to build subsequent theories. The first fact is the proposition, advanced in Chapter 1, that the corporate form has become a global norm. At the broadest level this appears uncontroversial. Across the post-communist countries the apparatus of state-organised production has been dismantled in favour of corporate entities. The discussion of privatisation in Chapter 6 also pointed to a transformation in capitalist economies with large state-owned enterprises becoming shareholder corporations. The *Fortune Global 500* is no longer dominated by the United States. The 2012 listing shows that the world's largest corporations are drawn from 34 states and, even when the state retains a shareholding, they conform to global expectations in their legal constitution, their adherence to accounting conventions and, as discussed in chapter 10, in their adoption of common features of corporate governance. The shareholder corporation has displaced the organisation of economic activity by state bureaucracies, nationalised industries and also by partnerships and cooperatives. The fact that the business corporation has become the dominant organisation in most national, and in global, economies is evident. It is less clear whether it has nurtured a global corporate elite and whether its organisational form is converging on an Anglo-American model rather than the Japanese, the German or some alternative model. The discussion of China in Chapter 3 indicated the continuing influence of the US corporate model.

Second, the large corporation is 'political' in a number of senses. Internally it operates as a political system with an internal hierarchy but with variable governance arrangements that may have elements of democracy (as in large German corporations). Externally it operates as a political actor in order to forward its interests in business associations or by negotiating directly with government agencies. Its most significant political role, however, lies in its ability to generate and distribute wealth and associated benefits. This is the classic political role of the authoritative allocation of values for society. This transmutation of market power into political power has been evident in most mature market economies and must rank as a 'fact' of contemporary political economy. The interesting question is whether the increased power, global reach and institutional authority of these political actors, combined with the post-liberal shrinkage of the state, has produced a new settlement – a new but stable political relationship akin to corporate citizenship.

Third, new settlements accommodating corporate power within established liberal democracies are emerging in many contemporary societies, and especially in the UK. As outlined in chapters 4 and 5, the Labour Party and the civil service have undergone a transformation from hostility and scepticism to an acceptance of, and support for, the financial and corporate sector. These transformations are common ground, although the exact nature of the state in which they operate remains controversial. Chapter 7 argued that the new settlement in the UK has served as a model for transformations in other states and for modes of structuring global governance.

Fourth, in some ways the UK clearly is a model for new modes of engagement with corporations, either as an innovator or as a confirmation that American-style delegation of governance to corporations can also work in Europe. The UK has moved to a significant level of 'government by corporation', most obviously in the swathe of services now delivered by privatised corporations, but more importantly in the growth of the public services industry. The contracting out of public services to corporations is a long-established mode of policy implementation, but it has been taken to extremes in the UK. Corporations have taken responsibility for a range of sensitive and politically controversial public policy goals in areas like front-line policing and care for the elderly. The growth of the public services sector outlined in Chapter 6 is another 'fact' of corporate influence in society. Clearly a partnership has become necessary between government bodies and corporations involved in service delivery. The more disconcerting aspect relates to the reductions in governmental capability. In a number of sectors UK government is now incapable of meeting many public policy objectives without the cooperation of corporations. Government now pursues policy goals by seeking to regulate corporate behaviour, which attaches a greatly increased salience to the politics of regulation.

Fifth, it is important for corporations to create a good reputation, and in the quest for legitimacy Chapter 9 demonstrated that corporations are investing huge resources. The growth in corporate social responsibility reporting is remarkable and is reaping dividends. Following the 2007–08 financial crisis bankers became hate figures but the level of trust in non-financial corporations and their CEOs remained respectable. Polls in the UK showed only moderate trust in business but ministers and politicians did even worse (see Chapter 5). Internationally, trust in corporations is substantial, which provides evidence of their improving status as one of the most respected institutions in many emergent societies. The improvement in corporate respectability is a fact that should not come as a surprise. It is a natural effect of the greater support for capitalism and admiration for the market as explored in Chapter 7. The implications are important. Despite critiques of the corporation from the left, from the Greens, from the Occupy movement and in popular culture, as reviewed in Chapter 8, the corporation can draw on wellsprings of legitimacy that provide it with a basis on which to enter into a partnership with elected governments. Democratic legitimacy, which we argued was lacking at the beginning of this chapter, appears to be emerging from 'brand legitimacy'.

Sixth, there is a fact which poses a threat to corporate legitimacy but provides a testament to corporate power: the fact of increasing inequality. Since the late 1980s income inequality has increased rapidly and the share of the richest 1 per cent has doubled in the USA and the UK (see Chapter 5). This is a well-documented global pattern (although it is less marked in continental Europe) which can be used to emphasise the scale of rewards going to senior managers in corporations and financial organisations. It was used in Chapter 5 also to provide evidence of the power of a corporate elite comprising a much smaller group, perhaps 0.01 per cent of the income distribution. Whilst some inequality is inevitable there is something very near to a consensus that the level of inequality has become excessive, with harmful consequences for the economy, society and democracy itself (Barry, 2005: 180).

Seventh is the fact, explored in chapters 3 and 7, that corporations participate as partners in global governance. Their participation is very wide-ranging, it is often technical, often dependent on soft law, codes and agreements, but it is widely recognised and widely encouraged. In some areas corporations become the only source of international order and for some developing countries also a source of national order. The degree to which international corporate power enjoyed by multinationals can be translated into dealings with national governments in developed states is less clear.

FOCI

The central purpose of this book has not been to argue that large business corporations possess political power. That is obvious, and anyone who maintains otherwise is peculiarly blinkered. Instead the book has sought to delineate the origins and exercise of corporate power in order to explore the potential for integrating the corporation into the mix of political institutions as a means of improving its accountability. The project is therefore to 'normalise' our understanding of corporate influence, to embark on 'the emancipation of belief' (Galbraith, 1975: 241). This book seeks to confirm that the exercise of corporate power is an everyday feature of life in advanced industrial societies and not exceptional, not necessarily improper, and certainly not confined simply to economic transactions. The evaluation of corporate power, and its relationship to democracy, remains immature partly because the global triumph of the corporate form is very recent. Outside the United States corporations historically operated within a constrained political environment, but they have been unleashed by a combination of political doctrine, the collapse of communism, globalisation and the sheer wealth-creating genius of the corporation. The triumph of the corporation has been almost accidental. Massive political movements have sought to secure market freedoms and democratic freedoms; corporate freedoms have hitched a ride and corporations have become the locomotive of economic progress acquiring status, respectability and power along the way. It has been a revolution without flags, a silent revolution; for critics a silent surrender.

The fairy-tales and facts already rehearsed in this chapter indicate that societies are currently addressing the business corporation with a set of concepts and expectations that are naïve, tendentious and verging on delusional. What then to put in in their place? The argument presented in earlier chapters revolves around the three concepts of the governing institution, the corporate elite and the New Corporate State. It can be encapsulated as follows.

As an abstract concept the business corporation has been presented as an institution. This simple idea, rehearsed in several different forms in earlier chapters, is of huge importance. It provides the corporation with authority and legitimacy which operates as an asset for individual corporations as actors. Crucially, it has also been presented as a governing institution. Not all individual corporations engage in governing which is a quality of business representatives and a narrower group of influential corporations. The influential corporations could be defined by size, market power or the political salience of their activities. These are the corporations with the potential to benefit or harm society and for whom the license to operate should be made explicit. As carriers of institutional authority these corporations could be expected to shoulder responsibility for their own and more general corporate conduct – not superficial corporate social responsibility, but substantive corporate citizenship with the moral expectations and the obligations which are the reciprocal of citizenship rights. This question of affirming moral foundations for elite corporations is of the essence, the myth that they are simply amoral economic bodies is the original sin of corporate capitalism.

Which brings us to elites. It is argued that elite approaches can be used effectively to identify the coherence, goals and stability of corporate leadership. Large corporations provide the foundation for a managerial elite of corporate executives and supporting intermediaries. These are the people who direct and to a large extent control large corporations and wield corporate power. They are not a class, but they are a coherent elite who share advanced managerial skills, attitudes and huge rewards. These leaders of the corporate world experience personal power and too often also a set of incentives and opportunities which militate towards personal gain rather than social or environmental responsibility. The prevailing norms of managerialism are deeply embedded within the elite and lead to a calculative, often cynical and dangerously arrogant exercise of leadership. The ideas of the stewardship of the corporation, or the principle of acting as a trustee for stakeholders, may be articulated but are not enforced. The lack of moral principle evident in the corporate form is mirrored by weak pressures towards personal responsibility within the corporate elite itself. Just as influential corporations should earn a license to operate, so corporate elite might be expected to display responsible leadership. The idea that only a 'fit and proper person' should serve as a director of a large corporation has not yet become a societal expectation.

The rise of the corporation and the associated corporate elite is part of a transformation in governance both nationally and globally. The global dissemination of capitalism from the mid-1980s onwards has led to new political bargains, to the redesign of systems of governance and a reconfiguration of political economy that in the West has gone under the misleading label of neoliberalism. A transformation suggests a qualitative change to a new political order in which large corporations are central actors within an institutional order that could be termed a market state, but for this book would be termed a corporate state. It is hardly a revelation that this new order poses a threat to democracy at the national level and impedes the creation of viable democratic institutions at the global level. The whole cycle of democratic choice is subverted by systemic corporate involvement in governance. Societies have less choice over their political leaders, those leaders are less powerful, vital policy areas are excluded from democratic influence, democratic choice in other areas is constrained and policies are implemented in ways that enhance profits, not accountability. But instead of railing against this diminution of democratic choice and discrediting of liberal democracy, the challenge is first to recognise the realities of the transformed political order and then to pursue further measures of redesign which will make corporations accountable and harness their potential for meeting societal ends rather than their own. The final section on futures explores possible avenues; this section ends with a warning of what the future holds if we accept unrestrained corporate power – it deals with the UK as a parable.

In the UK the transformation to a corporate state is complete. The large business corporation has displaced other institutions, including the civil service, and a corporate and financial elite has emerged as a governing cadre. The political elite has compromised with corporate power and negotiated a new settlement described in Chapter 4 as the New Corporate State. The characteristic politics within the new state is a relationship of partnership in policy making and implementation between political and corporate elites. The democratic integrity of the British state has therefore become even more fragile. Corporate elites have penetrated government, public policies are skewed by privileged corporate participation in policy making, and the overriding purpose of the state is increasingly to serve corporate interests. In some ways this settlement is a rational reaction to the new realities of the global economy. The disadvantages of the New Corporate State were masked by the long boom which generated sufficient additional resources to benefit most sections of society and hence inspire tolerance of a startling increase in economic inequality. With the end of the long boom, the state rescue of the banking system, and the socialisation of the costs of recession, the New Corporate State appears much less benign, although still stable. There remains the question, however, of whether this is a state constituted in a national economy and reflecting particular national politics, or whether it is a national expression of a global governance. The UK corporate elite is significantly 'denationalised'. The influential corporations are highly multinational and many important corporations are subsidiaries of overseas-based multinationals. The financial elite operates in global markets and the intermediaries such as lawyers and consultants are also internationalised. In Chapter 7 this complex relationship between national and global governance regimes was explored. To a degree the UK has become a model for global relationships, but it is also exposed to global corporate strategies to a greater extent than any other large Western country. The UK hence continues in its role as a laboratory for innovative changes in political economy. It illustrates in this case how global economic and political regimes may affect nation-states and, simultaneously, what choices for global governance are offered by the UK model. It is a model which emerges from earlier chapters as deeply objectionable, in which corporate political power creates individual policy fiascos and collective decline. We are already seeing a return to the declinism of the early 1980s (Elliott and Atkinson, 2012), with a depressing future for the mass of the population underscored by the continued prosperity of a narrow elite. But the extent to which the British state has become a hostage to global corporate power is substantial and disturbing for those seeking to challenge the New Corporate State and to reinvent the corporation, so what can be said about future prospects?

FUTURES

It would be delightful to end this story of foreboding with some straightforward account of proposed reforms or some theoretical visions for reinventing a corporate system that has become a threat to the very civilisation that it has created. In the early aftermath of the 2008 financial crisis there was a widespread feeling that things would never be the same again, that having teetered on the edge of an economic catastrophe, a Depression to put the 1920s into the shade, that revolutionary change was inevitable. Unfortunately that change has not emerged. Why? Perhaps because of a failure of vision, a lack of viable alternatives or, for the Occupy movement, a suppression of viable alternatives. There has been a welcome intellectual self-examination amongst economists which has questioned the great god growth (see Hutton, 2010; Coyle, 2011; Skidelsky and Skidelsky, 2012; Stiglitz, 2012) and there have been abundant critiques, some of which have expressed similar concerns to those advanced in this book (see especially

Crouch, 2011). There is, however, little consensus among academics, observers or political parties, at least in the UK, about which options for reform are most promising. We therefore end instead with a brief review of a spectrum of possibilities for reform, for making the corporation as a governing institution more accountable, less destructive, and better able to contribute towards human fulfilment. The spectrum stretches from modest and relatively easy reforms at one end, to revolutionary change at the other. We consider first incremental policy changes and go on to review systemic change; revolutionary change at the national level; and end with the imperative for institutional change.

Incremental Change: Reinventing the Corporation

There is an appetite for change in the way in which corporations are regulated to redefine their role in society. A Conservative MP lambasts the current system as 'crony capitalism' (Norman, 2011; 4); the economics correspondent of *The Times* opines that 'the need for a new model of capitalism is almost universally acknowledged' (Kaletsky, 2010: xiii); Ed Miliband's attack on predatory capitalism is applauded by a Conservative commentator (Mount, 2012: 211). Regulatory change is in the air and reform may involve a reassertion of the power of the state operating through new regulatory agencies with enhanced powers. This is certainly happening. In the UK financial regulation has been reconfigured and banking regulation is a focus of hyperactivity in the UK, at the European level and globally. But these are aimed at controlling the shareholder corporation, in the footsteps of Sarbanes–Oxley. A more productive route is to redefine the very concept of the corporation which involves changes in company law and in corporate governance. So the founder editor of *Corporate Governance* calls for a 'reinvention' of the corporation but he reverts to traditional measures to reassert shareholder influence, albeit with proposals for 'stakeholder liaison groups' (Tricker, 2011: 391). The theme of 'redefinition' of the corporation is taken up by Crane et al. (2008a: 202) who, like this book, insist that corporations are political actors. They would redefine the corporation from a citizenship perspective with associated obligations and responsibilities, but what exactly that means in practice is left rather vague. For concrete proposals we could look back to the debates on stakeholder capitalism and the fertile but ultimately neutered proposals for company law reform (see Chapter 10). A more recent and persuasive manifesto for reform is offered by Colin Mayer in an analysis that emerges from his lightheartedly deadly evisceration of shareholder capitalism.

Most critics of corporate capitalism nonetheless accept the potential merits of the large corporation (for instance: Sklair, 2002: 63; Barber,

2007: 316; Crouch, 2011: 101). The inclination is not to look to the state to control corporations but to redesign the corporation itself and its role within national and global society. This is also Mayer's preference: 'we should look to the corporation itself to take the lead in rectifying its own defects. Stop relying on government' (2013: 142). His solution is to transform corporate governance and to recreate the corporation as a 'trust firm'. 'A trust firm is a corporation that has a board of trustees who are the guardians of the firm's stated values and principles' (2013: 112). Trust firms would be flexible in the nature and appointment of their trustees and in their articulation of their values. They would answer to their wider body of stakeholders and would accept guidance only from committed long-term shareholders. The corporation would be managed in the longer-term interests of all stakeholders and the values could extend to public and charitable goals. This is a radical proposal for the ethical reinvention of the corporation. It would require major changes in company law creating a new mode of corporate governance, and it would need a degree of international acceptance. It would earn its legitimacy from its performance and its conformity to company law enacted by elected governments, not through its own democratic standing. It provides a viable blueprint for reform which could be adopted by UK political parties, although there would be determined opposition from the financial elite. It is a promising agenda.

Systemic Change: a New National Variant of Capitalism

There are several well developed and successful alternatives to the Anglo-American model of stock market capitalism. They offer a set of possibilities for reforms that would address a range of existing institutional features of British capitalism moving beyond corporate governance. The essential core of such reforms must involve a reduction in the size and influence of the financial sector and the framework of pressures and expectations it places on quoted corporations. Stock markets across Northern Europe are smaller, more functional, longer-term in their approach and offer an attractive model. In Japan stock markets are of minor relevance yet the corporate system operates successfully. This set of possibilities therefore takes us back to the debates around stakeholder capitalism and the contrasts between the Rhineland and the Anglo-Saxon models that were alive during the 1990s. The merits of alternative CME-type models were firmly discredited by the long boom but the financial crash and the prolonged recession will once again highlight, in particular, the merits of German institutions as that resilient economy recovers.

The most important Rhineland-type reforms, from the point of view of corporate power, are those which redirect the purpose of the large corporation towards the sort of community commitment and stakeholder awareness discussed in Chapter 10. Corporate management would remain powerful but it would not be primarily responsive to the principles of shareholder ownership and shareholder value policed by financial institutions and the market for corporate control. The stock and bond markets would become once again simply a source of investment capital rather than a speculative arena rendered obscene as well as absurd by the antics of derivatives traders and high intensity computerised trading. The financial elements of the corporate elite would need to shrink in size and influence as part of the elimination of City dominance. There is popular support for a radical reappraisal of banking and the financial industry, and not only from the Occupy movement and the Green movement. There is a deep vein of popular anger from a public contemplating a decade of banker-induced austerity and a surge of regulatory reappraisal generating the sort of sober analysis found in the Vickers and Kay Reports. What is less evident is visionary leadership either from the Labour Party or from the European Commission. Ed Miliband has spoken critically of predatory corporations but neither in the Party or in social democratic think tanks is there yet a blueprint for change. The Commission meanwhile is buried under the Eurozone crisis and necessarily obsessed with managing financial markets rather than transcending them. Financialisation of the UK and European economies remains dominant five years after the onset of crisis. In the UK the New Corporate State remains in place.

If a remodelling of the UK economy inspired by foreign models still appears unlikely then there remains the possibility that domestic evolution will redesign a new, improved version of the British capitalist model. This is the theme of Kaletsky's (2010) *Capitalism 4.0* which seeks to forecast and define a new version of capitalism identified as a fourth model, the three previous models being defined in part by their relationship with government. Kaletsky's analysis anticipates incremental rather than revolutionary change and it is intriguing partly because it is attuned to the reality of gradual policy change (as might be expected from this respected economic journalist), and partly because it extrapolates from the 'partnership' model which has featured in earlier pages. In effect it therefore examines whether the New Corporate State can be improved through a recalibrated relationship between business and government. He anticipates a continuation of the pattern in which government does less directly, continuing to provide services through the private sector, but he sees a larger role for government in macroeconomic management and financial regulation. More directly relevant to corporate power he concludes, rather optimistically, that 'the free market ideal of shareholder control was buried a year after the crisis' (298). Corporations thus need to embark on 'a deep reconsideration of the relationships between corporate managements, shareholders, and governments ... Businesses will have to acknowledge wider definitions of their objectives than maximising their company's share price. (314)'. He therefore anticipates even closer working relations between governments and corporations marked by pragmatism and tolerance on both sides rather than a doctrinaire market fundamentalism that kept them in separate spheres. This is a vision of continued but more benign partnership consistent with the 'Big Society' message of David Cameron. It is a reassuring prospect but implausible unless shareholder value is genuinely abandoned in favour of real stakeholder engagement.

Revolutionary Change: Transcend Capitalism

This book is aimed at reform not revolution. The achievements of capitalism are too impressive, and its political victory too complete, to justify an alternative system or to believe that revolutionary change could succeed. But of course there are many variants of capitalism and they are all in constant motion. There are many sources of change and options for improvement all of which should be subject to serious debate and deliberation. A part of that debate is to consider fundamental critiques of capitalism as a system and a consideration of alternatives as a source of challenge. Those alternatives are nowadays far less likely to be idealised socialist or communist models but rather based on principles of co-operation, feminism, environmentalism or communitarianism. The green critique has become the most compelling as the scale of climate change and the tragedies of species extinction and environmental devastation become undeniable. The growth and consumption that fuels capitalism and energises the large corporation is leading remorselessly into natural disasters that risk the extinction of human civilisation. But there also remains a place for classic Marxist critiques. In relation to the financial crisis, notes a member of the UK Coalition Cabinet, 'Karl Marx produced a remarkably prescient description of where we are now' (Cable, 2009: 8) and as the global economy entered another crisis of capitalism Marx's analysis of the laws of capitalism took on a whole new relevance (Gamble, 2009b: 48).

An explicitly Marxist analysis of corporate power is provided by Susanne Soederberg. She focuses on corporate governance and her aim is to 'repoliticize' corporate power. She presents the corporation as an expression of class domination and, in common with many Marxist analyses, she therefore rejects theories of managerial control in favour of the underlying dominance of owners (Soederberg, 2010: 13). By implication she presses for radical change in the United States but her prime aim is similar to this book, to expose the realities of corporate power rather than to provide a manifesto for change. The challenge of defining an alternative system, again from a Marxist perspective, is enthusiastically taken up by David Schweickart. He is one of the latest in a long tradition of left-wing evangelists of alternative models of political economy and his work is eloquent, vibrant and full of challenging insights. He is a proponent of a democratic transition to a successor system which would keep a market economy but abolish private ownership and wage labour. His vision is of market socialism based on a model of economic democracy. At the heart of the model is a carefully considered and elaborated system of workplace democracy, hence 'a firm under Economic Democracy is regarded not as a thing to be bought or sold (as it is under capitalism) but as a community. When you join a firm, you receive the rights of full citizenship, that is, full voting rights' (Schweickart, 2011: 50). The cooperative firm is placed within a transformed institutional landscape with abolition of financial markets in favour of a social investment fund, a role for the state as employer of last resort and as a defender of national interests through fair trade rather than free trade. In short, all the key institutions defining a particular variety of capitalism would be reformed. This transformation is, of course, justified on the basis of a critique of the economic, social and environmental defects of existing US-type capitalism. Within his critique is the assertion that contemporary liberal democracy falls short of 'real' democracy because of the capitalist class (or, in the language of this book, the corporate elite). This brings us full circle to the discussion in Chapter 1 of the paradox of highly valued political democracy co-existing with the barely questioned economic oppression of an absence of economic democracy. Schweickart's vision addresses exactly this source of oppression.

Like many idealist architects of left wing alternatives to capitalism Schweickart's vision will be ridiculed as outdated, unworkable and impoverishing. But in the wake of the financial crisis the scope for debate has been widened. Such socialist alternatives are unlikely to receive serious support from contemporary political parties and would encounter fierce opposition from every entrenched capitalist institution and especially from large corporations and the corporate elite, but there are elements which have greater purchase. The idea of worker management and ownership, for instance, appears as an increasingly attractive route for reform and has received serious attention, especially from Liberal Democrats in Britain.

The Imperative of Institutional Reform

This has been a book about political institutions so we should end where we started, with the transformation of the corporation into a governing institution. There is a desperate need for institutional reform. The right institutions provide the key to national success and to a prosperous, contented society (an old argument recently reaffirmed by Acemoglu and Robinson, 2012). More pessimistically, a failure to move away from dynamics of exponential growth in a finite world will produce environmental catastrophe (Jackson, 2009). The institution of the corporation has become an institution of governance which poses the classic political dilemma of how to make governments responsive to those they rule. The history of civilisation is punctuated by the rise of democratic movements and by revolutions; modern societies now need to call corporate autocracies and corporate elites into a framework of responsibility. This requires a revolution of understanding which exposes the ideas which serve as vehicles for elite domination and power (Schmidt, 2011). The arguments advanced in this book seek to contribute to a process of institutional change simply because the biggest obstacle to reform is denial. Large corporations must accept that their responsibility extends into government, and so must the rest of society and its politicians. There is a current of scholarly opinion to that effect evident in a series of studies from Galbraith to Parkinson; Parker; Crane, Matten and Moon; Schweikart; Horn; and Mayer. But the task of compelling the elites of the New Corporate State to concede that large corporations should accept real responsibility has to overcome the fairy-tales, and affirm the facts outlined in the earlier sections of this chapter.

Perhaps the best hope for enlightenment is the possibility of a rupture between political and corporate elites based on the recessionary collapse in growth. Without growth there is a politics of austerity which jeopardises the influence of structural dependency. If corporations can no longer deliver prosperity then they can no longer keep incumbents in power, and during 2012 we have seen incumbent governments losing elections across Europe. Political elites may then regard corporate privileges as less valuable and less defensible to a public buffeted by austerity and indignant about inequality. Under these circumstances the opposition by the financial elite to stakeholder reforms of corporate governance may be less effective, the self-serving rhetoric of shareholder value may be revealed as illusory, corporate leaders may form a more genuine commitment to corporate citizenship. At present, at least in the UK, elite partnership is sustained by some breathtakingly ludicrous narratives. If this book can go some small way to expose those narratives to discerning students and a deceived public it will amply have justified its writing.

Bibliography

Abbott, P. (2008), 'Our 21st Top Consulting Firms Survey', *Accountancy Age*, 9 October.

Acemoglu, D. and J. Robinson (2012), *Why Nations Fail: The Origins of Power, Prosperity, and Poverty*, London: Profile.

Acoba (Advisory Committee on Business Appointments) (2010), *Appointments taken up by Crown Servants since 1 April 2009*, http://acoba.independent.gov.uk (accessed 8 November 2010).

Adelstein, R. (1989), '"Islands of Conscious Power": Louis D. Brandeis and the Modern Corporation', *Business History Review*, **63** (Autumn), 614–56.

Albert, M. (1993), *Capitalism Against Capitalism*, London: Whurr.

Allen, C. (1989), 'The Underdevelopment of Keynesianism in the Federal Republic of Germany', in P. Hall (ed.), *The Political Power of Economic Ideas: Keynesianism Across Nations*, Princeton: Princeton University Press, pp. 263–89.

Amis, M. (1984), *Money: A Suicide Note*, London: Jonathan Cape.

Amoore, L. (2006), 'Making the Modern Multinational', in C. May (ed.), *Global Corporate Power*, London: Lynne Rienner, pp. 47–64.

Annan, N. (1990), *Our Age: The Generation That Made Post-war Britain*, London: Weidenfeld and Nicolson.

Aoki, M. (2007), 'Conclusion: Whither Japan's Corporate Governance?', in M. Aoki, G. Jackson and H. Miyajima (eds), *Corporate Governance in Japan: Institutional Change and Organizational Diversity*, Oxford: Oxford University Press, pp. 427–48.

Aoki, M., G. Jackson and H. Miyajima (eds) (2007), *Corporate Governance in Japan: Institutional Change and Organizational Diversity*, Oxford: Oxford University Press.

Apostolides, N. and R. Boden (2005), 'Cedric the Pig: Annual General Meetings and Corporate Governance in the UK', *Social Responsibility Journal*, **1** (1), 53–62.

Araki, T. (2009), 'Changes in Japan's Practice-Dependent Stakeholder Model and Employee-Centred Corporate Governance', in H. Whittaker and S. Deakin (eds), *Corporate Governance and Managerial Reform in Japan*, Oxford: Oxford University Press, pp. 222–53.

Asenova, D. and M. Beck (2010), 'Crucial Silences: When Accountability Met PFI and Finance Capital', *Critical Perspectives on Accounting*, **21** (1), 1–13.

Asimov, I. (1951), *I, Robot*, Gnome Press.

ATKearney (2009), 'New Concerns in an Uncertain World: The 2007 A.T.Kearney FDI Confidence Index', www.atkearney.com (accessed 4 August 2009).

Atkinson, A.B. (2007), 'The Distribution of Top Incomes in the United Kingdom 1908–2000', in A.B. Atkinson and T. Pikety (eds), *Top Incomes Over the Twentieth Century*, Oxford: Oxford University Press, pp. 82–140.

Atwood, M. (2003), *Oryx and Crake*, New York: Doubleday.

Babb, J. (2001), *Business and Politics in Japan*, Manchester: Manchester University Press.

Baccaro, L. and V. Mele (2011), 'For Lack of Anything Better? International Organizations and Global Corporate Codes', *Public Administration*, **89** (2), 451–70.

Bakan, J. (2004), *The Corporation: The Pathological Pursuit of Profit and Power*, revised edn, London: Constable.

Ball, S. (1994), 'The National and Regional Party Structure', in A. Seldon and S. Ball (eds), *Conservative Century: The Conservative Party since 1900*, Oxford: Oxford University Press.

Barber, B. (2001), *Jihad vs McWorld*, New York: Ballantine, first published 1995.

Barber, B. (2007), *Consumed: How Markets Corrupt Children, Infantalize Adults, and Swallow Citizens Whole*, New York: W.W. Norton.

Barber, M. (2007), *Instruction to Deliver: Tony Blair, Public Services and the Challenge of Achieving Targets*, London: Politico's.

Barker, R. (2010), *Corporate Governance, Competition, and Political Parties: Explaining Corporate Governance Change in Europe*, Oxford: Oxford University Press.

Barnett, C. (1986), *The Audit of War: The Illusion and Reality of Britain as a Great Nation*, London: Macmillan.

Barry, B. (2005), *Why Social Justice Matters*, Cambridge: Polity

Barry, M, (2003), *Jennifer Government*, London: Abacus.

Beetham, D. (2011), *Unelected Oligarchy: Corporate and Financial Dominance in Britain's Democracy*, Liverpool: Democratic Audit.

Béland, D. (2010), 'The Idea of Power and the Role of Ideas', *Political Studies Review*, **8** (2), 145–54.

Benedict, R. (1948), *The Chrysanthemum and the Sword: Patterns of Japanese Culture*, Boston: Houghton Mifflin.

Beresford, P. (2010), 'Rising from the rubble', *Sunday Times Rich List 2010*, 25 April, 4–7.

Berle, A. and G. Means (1932), The *Modern Corporation and Private Property*, New York: Commerce Clearing House, revised edn, 1967.
Bernhagen, P. (2007), *The Political Power of Business: Structure and Information in Public Policymaking*, London: Routledge.
BERR (2008), *Public Services Industry Review: Understanding the Public Services Industry: How Big, How Good, Where Next?* a review by DeAnne Julius, London: Department for Business Enterprise and Regulatory Reform.
Bexell, M., J. Tallberg and A. Uhlin (2010), 'Democracy in Global Governance: The Promises and Pitfalls of Transnational Actors', *Global Governance*, **16** (1), 81–101.
Binham, C. (2012), 'Six Law Firms have Clout for FTSE 100', *Financial Times*, 27 February.
BITC (2011), *Annual Report 2011: Transforming Business, Transforming Communities*, Business in the Community, available at www.bitc.org.uk/resources (accessed 16 March 2012).
Blair, T. (2010), *A Journey*, London: Hutchinson.
Bloomberg New Energy Finance (2012), *UK Big 6 Utility Investment Trends: A Report for Greenpeace UK on the Generation Investments of the Big 6 Utilities*, available at www.bnef.com/WhitePapers/download/70 (accessed 12 August 2012).
Blundell, J. (2000), 'Forward', in A. Pollard (ed.), *The Representation of Business and English Literature*, Indianapolis: Liberty Fund.
Blyth, M. (2002), *Great Transformations: Economic Ideas and Institutional change in the Twentieth Century*, Cambridge: Cambridge University Press.
Bobbitt, P. (2002), *The Shield of Achilles: War, Peace and the Course of History*, London: Penguin.
Boswell, J. and J. Peters (1997), *Capitalism in Contention: Business Leaders and Political Economy in Modern Britain*, Cambridge: Cambridge University Press.
Bovaird, T. (2006), 'Developing New Forms of Partnership with "the Market" in the Procurement of Public Services', *Public Administration*, **84** (1), 81–102.
Bower, T. (2007), *Gordon Brown: Prime Minister*, London: Harper Perennial, revised edn.
Braithwaite, J. (2008), *Regulatory Capitalism: How it Works, Ideas for Making it Work Better*, Cheltenham, UK and Northampton, MA, USA: Edward Elgar.
Braithwaite, J. and P. Drahos (2000), *Global Business Regulation*, Cambridge: Cambridge University Press.

Bremmer, I. and P. Keat (2009), *The Fat Tail: The Power of Political Knowledge for Strategic Investing*, Oxford: Oxford University Press.

Brown, H. S. (2011), 'Global Reporting Initiative', in T. Hale and D. Held (eds), *Handbook of Transnational Governance: Institutions and Innovations*, Cambridge: Polity, pp. 281–9.

Bull, B. (2010), 'Rethinking Multilateralism: Global Governance and Public–Private Partnerships with the UN', in M. Ougaard and A. Leander (eds), *Business and Global Governance*, Abingdon: Routledge, pp. 181–99.

Burnham, J. and R. Pyper (2008), *Britain's Modernised Civil Service*, Houndmills: Palgrave Macmillan.

Büthe, T. and W. Mattli (2011), *The New Global Rulers: The Privatization of Regulation in the World Economy*, Princeton: Princeton University Press.

Cabinet Office (2010), 'Top Suppliers Asked to Contribute to Government's Efficiency Drive', News Release, 8 July.

Cable, V. (2009), *The Storm: The World Economic Crisis and What it Means*, London: Atlantic.

Cadbury, A. (2002), *Corporate Governance and Chairmanship: A Personal View*, Oxford: Oxford University Press.

Cairncross, F. (2002), *The Company of the Future: Meeting the Management Challenges of the Communications Revolution*, London: Profile.

Callaghan, H. (2009), 'Insiders, Outsiders, and the Politics of Corporate Governance: How Ownership Structure Shapes Party Positions in Britain, Germany, and France', *Comparative Political Studies*, **42** (6), 733–62.

Campbell, A. and R. Scott (eds) (2007), *The Blair Years: Extracts from the Alastair Campbell Diaries*, London: Hutchinson.

Campbell, C. and G. Wilson (1995), *The End of Whitehall: Death of a Paradigm?*, Oxford: Blackwell.

Capling, A. and R. Higgott (2009), 'Introduction: The Future of the Multilateral Trade System – What Role for the World Trade Organization?', *Global Governance*, **15**, 313–25.

Carroll, A. (2008), 'A History of Corporate Social Responsibility: Concepts and Practices', in A. Crane et al. (eds), *The Oxford Handbook of Corporate Social Responsibility*, Oxford: Oxford University Press, pp. 19–46.

Cass, D. (2005), *The Constitutionalization of the World Trade Organization: Legitimacy, Democracy and Community in the International Trading System*, Oxford: Oxford University Press.

Caulkin, S. (2012), 'Losing their grip', *Business Education Supplement, Financial Times*, 14 May.

Cawson, A., K. Morgan, D. Webber, P. Holmes and A. Stevens (1990), *Hostile Brothers: Competition and Closure in the European Electronics Industry*, Oxford: Clarendon.
CBI (2007), *Going Global: The World of Public–Private Partnerships*, London: CBI.
CBI (2009), *The Shape of Business: The Next 10 Years*, London: CBI.
CBI (2010a), *Leaner and Fitter: Boosting Productivity in Public Services*, London: CBI.
CBI (2010b), *Creative Ideas for Challenging Times: A CBI Public Services Board 2009 Campaign Review*, London: CBI.
Cerny, P. (1997), 'Paradoxes of the Competition State: The Dynamics of Political Globalization', *Government and Opposition*, 251–74.
Cerny, P. (2000), 'Political Globalization and the Competition State', in R. Stubbs and G. Underhill (eds), *Political Economy and the Changing Global Order*, Oxford: Oxford University Press.
Cerny, P. (2010), 'The Competition State Today: From Raison D'Etat to Raison du Monde', *Policy Studies*, **31** (1), 5–21.
Chandler, A. (1990), *Scale and Scope: The Dynamics of Industrial Capitalism*, Cambridge, MA: Belknap Press.
Chandler, A. and B. Mazlish (eds) (2005), *Leviathans: Multinational Corporations and the New Global History*, Cambridge: Cambridge University Press.
Charkham, J. (1994), *Keeping Good Company: A Study of Corporate Governance in Five Countries*, Oxford: Clarendon.
Charkham, J. (2005), *Keeping Better Company: Corporate Governance Ten Years On*, Oxford: Oxford University Press.
Cheffins, B. (2003),'Will Executive Pay Globalise Along American Lines?', *Corporate Governance*, **11** (1), 8–24.
Cheffins, B. (2008), *Corporate Ownership and Control: British Business Transformed*, Oxford: Oxford University Press.
Chen, J., X. Liu and W. Li (2010), 'The Effect of Insider Control and Global Benchmarks on Chinese Executive Compensation', *Corporate Governance*, **18** (2), 107–23.
Childs, S. (2006), *Political Parties and Party Systems*, in P. Dunleavy, R. Heffernan, P. Cowley and C. Hay (eds), *Developments in British Politics 8*, Houndmills: Palgrave Macmillan, pp. 56–76.
Chorev, N. and S. Babb (2009), 'The Crisis of Neoliberalism and the Future of International Institutions: A Comparison of the IMF and the WTO', *Theory and Society*, **38** (5), 459–84.
Chhotray, V. and G. Stoker (2009), *Governance Theory and Practice: A Cross-Disciplinary Approach*, Houndmills: Palgrave Macmillan.
Clift, B., A. Gamble and M. Harris, (2000), 'The Labour Party and the

Company', in J. Parkinson, A. Gamble and G. Kelly (eds), *The Political Economy of the Company*, Oxford, Hart: pp. 52–81.

Clifton, J., F. Comín and D. Díaz (2006), 'Privatizing Public Enterprises in the European Union 1960–2002: Ideological, Pragmatic, Inevitable?', *Journal of European Public Policy*, **13** (5), 736–56.

Coase, R. (1937), 'The Nature of the Firm', *Economica*, **4** (November), 386–405.

Coen, D. (2009), 'Business Lobbying in the European Union', in D. Coen and J. Richardson (eds), *Lobbying the European Union: Institutions, Actors and Issues*, Oxford: Oxford University Press, pp. 145–68.

Coen, D. and J. Richardson (eds), (2009), *Lobbying the European Union: Institutions, Actors and Issues*, Oxford: Oxford University Press.

Coen, D., W. Grant and G. Wilson (eds) (2010), *The Oxford Handbook of Business and Government*, Oxford: Oxford University Press.

Committee on the Financial Aspects of Corporate Governance (Cadbury Committee), (1992), London.

Cook, P. (1998), 'Privatisation in the UK: Policy and Performance', in D. Parker (ed.), *Privatisation in the European Union: Theory and Policy Perspectives*, London: Routledge.

Corbett, J.M. (1998), 'Sublime Technologies and Future Organization in Science Fiction Film, 1970–95', in J. Hassard and R. Holliday (eds), *Organization – Representation: Work and Organization in Popular Culture*, London: Sage, pp. 247–58.

Cowley, P. (2011), 'Political Parties and the British Party System', in R. Heffernan, P. Cowley and C. Hay (eds), *Developments in British Politics 9*, Houndmills: Palgrave Macmillan, pp. 91–112.

Coyle, D. (2011), *The Economics of Enough: How to Run the Economy As If the Future Matters*, Princeton: Princeton University Press.

Craig, D. (2006), *Plundering the Public Sector: How New Labour are Letting Consultants Run Off with £70 Billion of our Money*, London: Constable.

Crane, A., D. Matten and J. Moon (2008), *Corporations and Citizenship*, Cambridge: Cambridge University Press.

Crane, A., A. McWilliams, D. Matten, J. Moon and D. Siegel (eds) (2008), *The Oxford Handbook of Corporate Social Responsibility*, Oxford: Oxford University Press.

Crouch, C. (2004), *Post-Democracy*, Cambridge: Polity.

Crouch, C. (2011), *The Strange Non-Death of Neoliberalism*, Cambridge: Polity.

Culpepper, P. (2011), *Quiet Politics and Business Power: Corporate Control in Europe and Japan*, Cambridge: Cambridge University Press.

Cutler, C. (2006), 'Transnational Business Civilization, Corporations, and the Privatization of Global Governance', in C. May (ed.), *Global Corporate Power*, London: Lynne Reiner, pp. 199–225.

Cutler, C. (2010), 'Unthinking the GATS: A Radical Political Economy Critique of Private Transnational Governance', in M. Ougaard and A. Leander (eds), *Business and Global Governance*, London: Routledge, pp. 78–96.

Dahl, R. (1985), *A Preface to Economic Democracy*, Berkeley: University of California Press.

Damodaran, H. (2008), *India's New Capitalists: Caste, Business and Industry in a Modern Nation*, Ranikhet: Permanent Black.

Davies, S. (2007), 'UK Municipal Waste Management: From a Public Service to a Globalised Industry', *Competition and Change*, **11** (1), 39–57.

Davis, D. (2012), 'Crony Capitalism', *Prospect*, March, 24–26.

DBIS (2008), *Corporate Responsibility Report*, London: Department for Business, Innovation and Skills.

Deakin, S. and H. Whittaker (2009), 'On a Different Path? The Managerial Reshaping of Japanese Corporate Governance', in H. Whittaker and S. Deakin (eds), *Corporate Governance and Managerial Reform in Japan*, Oxford: Oxford University Press, pp. 1–27.

Defoe, D. (1719), *Robinson Crusoe*, London, Penguin Classics, 2003

De Grauwe, P. and F. Camerman, (2003), 'Are Multinationals Really Bigger Than Nations?', *World Economics*, **4** (2), 23–37.

Democratic Audit (2012), *How Democratic is the UK? The 2012 Audit: Executive Summary*, available at www.democraticaudit.com (accessed 19 March 2012).

Devinney, T. (2009), 'Is the Socially Responsible Corporation a Myth? The Good, the Bad, and the Ugly of Corporate Social Responsibility', *Academy of Management Perspectives*, **23**, 44–56.

Diageo (2011), *Corporate Citizenship Report 2010*, available at http://www.diageo.com/Lists/Resources/Attachments/1342/2012%20SRR_FINAL.pdf (accessed 26 April 2012).

Dickins, C. (1848), *Dombey and Son*, London: Bradbury and Evans.

Dickson, B. (2008), *Wealth into Power: The Communist Party's Embrace of China's Private Sector*, Cambridge: Cambridge University Press.

Dieter, H. (2009), 'The Multilateral Trading System and Preferential Trade Agreements: Can the Negative Effects be Minimized?', *Global Governance*, **15**, 393–408.

DiMaggio, P. and W. Powell (1991), 'The Iron Cage Revisited: Institutional Isomorphism and Collective Rationality', in W. Powell and P. DiMaggio (eds), *The New Institutionalism in Organizational Analysis*, Chicago: University of Chicago Press, pp. 63–82.

Djelic, M.-L. (1998), *Exporting the American Model: The Postwar Transformation of European Business*, Oxford: Oxford University Press.

Donaldson, T. (2008), 'The Transatlantic Paradox: How Outdated Concepts Confuse the American/European Debate about Corporate Governance', in A. Crane, A. McWilliams, D. Matten, J. Moon and D. Siegel (eds), *The Oxford Handbook of Corporate Social Responsibility*, Oxford: Oxford University Press, pp. 543–51.

Donnelly, S., A. Gamble, G. Jackson and J. Parkinson (2001), *The Public Interest and the Company in Germany and Britain*, London: Anglo-German Foundation for the Study of Industrial Society.

Dore, R. (1983), 'Goodwill and the Spirit of Market Capitalism', *British Journal of Sociology*, **34** (iv), 459–82.

Dore, R. (2000), *Stock Market Capitalism: Welfare Capitalism: Japan and Germany versus the Anglo-Saxons*, Oxford: Oxford University Press.

Dore, R. (2005), 'Deviant or Different? Corporate Governance in Japan and Germany', *Corporate Governance*, **13** (3), 437–46.

Dore, R. (2009), 'Japan's Conversion to Investor Capitalism', in H. Whittaker and S. Deakin (eds), *Corporate Governance and Managerial Reform in Japan*, Oxford: Oxford University Press, pp. 134–62.

Dowding, K. (1995), *The Civil Service*, London: Routledge.

Drucker, P. (1993), *Post-Capitalist Society*, New York: HarperCollins.

Dryzek, J. (1996), *Democracy in Capitalist Times: Ideals, Limits and Struggles*, Oxford: Oxford University Press.

Dryzek, J. and P. Dunleavy (2009), *Theories of the Democratic State*, Houndmills: Palgrave Macmillan.

DTI (1994), *Competitiveness: Helping Business to Win*, Cmnd 2563, London: HMSO.

du Gay, P. (2008), 'Keyser Süze Elites: Market Populism and the Politics of Institutional Change', in M. Savage and K. Williams (eds), *Remembering Elites*, Oxford: Blackwell.

Dunning, J. (1993), *Multinational Enterprises and the Global Economy*, Wokingham: Addison Wesley.

Dunning, J. (1997), *Alliance Capitalism and Global Business*, London: Routledge.

Eaglesham, J. and N. Timmins (2005), 'Brown Criticised for Abolishing Operating and Financial Review', *Financial Times*, 5 December.

Economist, The (2012a), 'Special Report: State Capitalism', 21 January.

Economist, The (2012b), 'Tepco's Nationalisation: State Power', 11 May.

Edelman (2011), *Edelman Trust Barometer 2011: Annual Global Opinion Leader Study*, available at www.edelman.com/trust/2011 (accessed 17 March 2012).

Edwards, C. (2010), 'Oral Evidence to the Select Committee on Economic Affairs by Allyson Pollack and Chris Edwards', *Private Finance Projects and Off-Balance Sheet Debt*, Volume II: Evidence, 1st Report of Session 2009–10, House of Lords, HL 63-II, March, pp. 143–51.

Elliott, L. and D. Atkinson (2012), *Going South: Why Britain Will Have a Third World Economy by 2014*, Houndmills: Palgrave Macmillan.

Engelen, E., I. Ertürk, J. Froud, S. Johal, A. Leaver, M. Moran, A. Nilson and K. Williams (2011), *After the Great Complacence: Financial Crisis and the Politics of Reform*, Oxford: Oxford University Press.

Ertürk, I., J. Froud, S. Johal and K. Williams (2005), 'Pay for Corporate Performance or Pay as Social Division? Rethinking the Problem of Top Management Pay in Giant Corporations', *Competition and Change*, **9** (1), 49–94.

Ertürk, I., J. Froud, S. Johal, J. Law, A. Leaver, M. Moran and K. Williams (2012), *Deep Stall? The Eurozone Crisis, Banking Reform and Politics*, Manchester: CRESC Working Paper, 110.

Esty, D. (2002), 'The World Trade Organization's Legitimacy Crisis', *World Trade Review*, **1** (1), 7–22.

Etzioni, A. (2001), *The Monochrome Society*, Princeton: Princeton University Press.

European Commission (2011), *Green Paper: The EU Corporate Governance Framework*, Brussels, COM(2011) 164.

Evans, M. (2006), 'Elitism', in C. Hay, M. Lister and D. Marsh (eds), *The State: Theories and Issues*, Houndmills: Palgrave Macmillan, pp. 39–58.

Evans, M. (2010), 'Cameron's Competition State', *Policy Studies*, **31** (1), 95–115.

Faucher-King, F. and P. Le Galès (2010), *The New Labour Experiment*, Stanford: Stanford University Press.

Feigenbaum, H., J. Henig and C. Hamnett (1998), *Shrinking the State: The Political Underpinnings of Privatization*, Cambridge: Cambridge University Press.

Fielding, S. (2011), 'Fiction and Politics: Towards an Imagined Political Capital?', *Parliamentary Affairs*, **64** (2), 223–32.

Financial Times (2010), *FT Global 500 2010*, London: *Financial Times*, available at www.ft.com.

Financial Times (2011), *Responsible Business: Special Report*, 8 June 2011.

Financial Times (2012), *UK 500*, analysed by industrial sector, available at: http://media.ft.com/cms/a6e7a5e8-ca80-11e1-89f8-00144feabdc0.pdf.

Flinders, M. (2005), 'The Politics of Public–Private Partnerships', *The British Journal of Politics and International Relations*, **7** (2), 215–39.

Flohr, A., L. Rieth, S. Schwindenhammer and K.D. Wolf (2010), 'Variations in Corporate Norm-Entrepreneurship: Why the Home State

Matters', in M. Ougaard and A. Leander (eds), *Business and Global Governance*, London: Routledge, pp. 235–56.

Forbes, (2012), William D Green profile, available at http://www.forbes.com/profile/william-green-2/ (accessed 30 August 2012).

Fortune Management (2012), 'Pepsi's CEO faces her biggest challenge', available at http://management.fortune.cnn.com/2012/02/13 (accessed 22 May 2012).

Foster, C. (2005), *British Government in Crisis*, Oxford: Hart.

Frank, T. (2001), *One Market Under God: Extreme Capitalism, Market Populism and the End of Economic Democracy*, London: Secker & Warburg.

Fraser, S. (2005), *Wall Street: A Cultural History*, London: Faber & Faber.

FRC (2010a), *The UK Corporate Governance Code*, London: Financial Reporting Council, available at www.frc.org.uk.

FRC (2010b), *The UK Stewardship Code*, London: Financial Reporting Council, available at www.frc.org.uk.

Freedman, J. (1993), 'Accountants and Corporate Governance: Filling a Legal Vacuum?', *The Political Quarterly*, 285–97.

Freyer, T. (1992), *Regulating Big Business: Antitrust in Great Britain and America, 1880–1990*, Cambridge: Cambridge University Press.

Freyer, T. (2006), *Antitrust and Global Capitalism, 1930–2004*, Cambridge: Cambridge University Press.

Friedman, A. and S. Miles (2006), *Stakeholders: Theory and Practice*, Oxford: Oxford University Press.

Friedman, M. (1982), *Capitalism and Freedom*, Chicago: University of Chicago Press (first published, 1962).

Froud, J. and K. Williams (2007), 'Private Equity and the Culture of Value Extraction', *New Political Economy*, **12** (3), 405–20.

Froud, J., A. Leaver, G. Tampubolon and K. Williams (2008), 'Everything for Sale: How Non-executive Directors Make a Difference', in M. Savage and K. Williams (eds), *Remembering Elites*, Oxford: Blackwell, pp. 162–86.

Fuchs, D. (2007), *Business Power in Global Governance*, London: Lynne Reinner.

Fukuyama, F. (1992), *The End of History and the Last Man*, New York: Free Press.

Galanter, M. and S. Roberts (2008), 'From Kinship to Magic Circle: The London Commercial Law Firm in the Twentieth Century', *International Journal of the Legal Profession*, **15** (3), 143–78.

Galbraith, J. K. (1952), *American Capitalism: The Concept of Countervailing Power*, Boston: Houghton Mifflin.

Galbraith, J. K. (1967), *The New Industrial State*, London: Hamish Hamilton.
Galbraith, J. K. (1975), *Economics and the Public Purpose*, Harmondsworth: Penguin, first published 1973.
Galbraith, J. (2009), *The Predator State: How Conservatives Abandoned the Free Market and Why Liberals Should Too*, New York: Free Press, paperback edition.
Gamble, A. (1994) *The Free Economy and the Strong State: The Politics of Thatcherism*, second edn, London: Macmillan.
Gamble, A. (2003), *Between Europe and America: The Future of British Politics*, Houndmills: Palgrave Macmillan.
Gamble, A. (2009a), 'The Western Ideology', *Government and Opposition*, **14** (1), 1–19.
Gamble, A. (2009b), *The Spectre at the Feast: Capitalist Crisis and the Politics of Recession*, Houndmills: Palgrave Macmillan.
Gamble, A. and G. Kelly (2000), 'The Politics of the Company', in J. Parkinson, A. Gamble and G. Kelly (eds), *The Political Economy of the Company*, Oxford: Hart, pp. 21–49.
Gates, L. (2009), 'Theorizing Business Power in the Semi-periphery: Mexico 1970–2000', *Theory and Society*, **38** (1), 57–95.
Geppert, M. and C. Dörrenbächer (2011), 'Politics and Power in the Multinational Corporation: An Introduction', in C. Dörrenbächer and M. Geppert (eds), *Politics and Power in the Multinational Corporation: The Role of Institutions, Interests and Identities*, Cambridge: Cambridge University Press, pp. 3–38.
Gerlach, M. (1992), *Alliance Capitalism: The Social Organisation of Japanese Business*, Berkeley CA: University of California Press.
Germain, R. (2010), *Global Politics and Financial Governance*, Houndmills: Palgrave Macmillan.
Gibbon, E. (1999), *The Decline and Fall of the Roman Empire*, BCA (first published between 1776 and 1788).
Gibson, O. (2012), 'Olympics CEO Paul Deighton to Take On Treasury Role', *The Guardian*, 5 May.
Giddens, A. (1974), 'Elites in the British Class Structure', in P. Stanworth and A. Giddens (eds), *Elites and Power in British Society*, Cambridge: Cambridge University Press, pp. 1–21.
Gill, S. (2002), 'Constitutionalizing Inequality and the Clash of Globalizations', *International Studies Review*, **4** (2), 47–65.
Gilpin, R. (2000), *The Challenge of Global Capitalism*, Princeton, NJ: Princeton University Press.
Goldman, I. and R. Palan (2006), 'Corporate Citizenship', in Christopher May (ed.), *Global Corporate Power*, London: Lynne Reiner, pp. 181–97.

Goldstein, A. (2007), *Multinational Corporations From Emerging Economies: Composition, Conceptualization and Direction in the Global Economy*, Houndmills: Palgrave Macmillan.

Gourevitch, P. and J. Shinn (2005), *Political Power and Corporate Control: The New Global Politics of Corporate Governance*, Princeton, NJ: Princeton University Press.

Gourevitch, P. and D. Lake (2012), 'Beyond Virtue: Evaluating and Enhancing the Credibility of Non-Governmental Organizations', in P. Gourevitch, D. Lake and J. Stein (eds), *The Credibility of Transnational NGOs*, Cambridge: Cambridge University Press.

Gowan, P. (1987), 'The Origins of the Administrative Elite', *New Left Review*, **162** (Mar/April), 4–34.

Grafström, M. and K. Windell (2011), 'The Role of Infomediaries: CSR in the Business Press During 2000–2009', *Journal of Business Ethics*, **103**, 221–37.

Grant, A. (2005), 'Party and Election Finance in Britain and America: A Comparative Analysis', *Parliamentary Affairs*, **56** (1), 71–88.

Grant Thornton (2011), *Corporate Governance Review 2011*, London: Grant Thornton, available at http://grant-thornton.co.uk/eu/publications/2011.

Grant, W. (1993), *Business and Politics in Britain*, second edn, Houndmills: Macmillan.

Grant, W. and D. Marsh (1977), *The Confederation of British Industry*, London: Hodder and Stoughton.

Greve, C. (2010), 'Public–Private Partnerships in Business and Government', in W. Grant, D. Coen and G. Wilson (eds), *The Oxford Handbook of Business and Politics*, Oxford: Oxford University Press, pp. 585–99.

Grey, C. (1999), '"We are all Managers Now": "We Always Were": On the Development and Demise of Management', *Journal of Management Studies*, **36** (5), 561–85.

Grey, C. (2009), 'Speed', in P. Hancock and A. Spicer (eds), *Understanding Corporate Life*, London: Sage, pp. 27–45.

Grote, J. (2008), 'Persistent Divergence? Chemical Business Associations in Britain and Germany', in J. Grote, A. Lang and V. Schneider (eds), *Organized Business Interests in Changing Environments: The Complexity of Adaptation*, Houndmills: Palgrave Macmillan, pp. 65–87.

Grote, J., A. Lang and V. Schneider (eds) (2008), *Organized Business Interests in Changing Environments: The Complexity of Adaptation*, Houndmills: Palgrave Macmillan.

Guttsman, W.L. (1963), *The British Political Elite*, London: Macgibbon & Kee.

Habermas, J. (1976), *Legitimation Crisis*, London: Heinemann.

Hackenthal, A., R. Schmidt and M. Tyrell (2005), 'Banks and German Corporate Governance: On the Way to a Capital Market-Based System?', *Corporate Governance*, **13** (3), 397–407.

Haigh, G. (2004), *Bad Company: The Strange Cult of the CEO*, London: Aurum.

Hale, T. (2011), 'United Nations Global Compact', in T. Hale and D. Held (eds), *Handbook of Transnational Governance: Institutions and Innovations*, Cambridge: Polity, pp. 350–56.

Hale, T. and D. Held (2011), 'Editor's Introduction: Mapping Changes in Transnational Governance', in T. Hale and D. Held (eds), *Handbook of Transnational Governance: Institutions and Innovations*, Cambridge: Polity, pp. 1–36.

Hall, P. and D. Soskice (2001), 'An Introduction to Varieties of Capitalism', in P. Hall and D. Soskice (eds), *Varieties of Capitalism: The Institutional Foundations of Comparative Advantage*, Oxford: Oxford University Press, pp. 1–68.

Hamada, Y. (2010), 'Japanese Business–Government Relations', in D. Coen, W. Grant and G. Wilson (eds), *The Oxford Handbook of Business and Government*, Oxford: Oxford University Press, pp. 330–45.

Hanahoe, T. (2003), *America Rules: US Foreign Policy, Globalization and Corporate USA*, Dingle: Brandon.

Hancké, B. (2001), 'Revisiting the French Model: Coordination and Restructuring in French Industry', in P. Hall and D. Soskice (eds), *Varieties of Capitalism: The Institutional Foundations of Comparative Advantage*, Oxford: Oxford University Press, pp. 307–34.

Hancké, B., M. Rhodes and M. Thatcher (2007), 'Introduction: Beyond Varieties of Capitalism', in B. Hancké, M. Rhodes and M. Thatcher (eds), *Beyond Varieties of Capitalism: Conflict, Contradictions and Complementarities in the European Economy*, Oxford: Oxford University Press, pp. 3–38.

Hannah, L. (2007), 'The "Divorce" of Ownership from Control from 1990 Onwards: Re-calibrating Imagined Global Trends', *Business History*, **49** (4), 404–38.

Harrod, J. (2006), 'The Century of the Corporation', in C. May (ed.), *Global Corporate Power*, London: Lynne Reiner, pp. 23–46.

Haseler, S. (2000), *The Super-Rich: The Unjust New World of Global Capitalism*, Houndmills: Macmillan.

Hassard, J. and R. Holliday (1998), 'Introduction', in J. Hassard and R. Holliday (eds), *Organization – Representation: Work and Organization in Popular Culture*, London: Sage, pp. 1–15.

Hatcher, M. (2003), 'Public Affairs Challenges for Multinational

Corporations', in S. John and S. Thomson (eds), *New Activism and the Corporate Response*, Houndmills: Palgrave Macmillan, pp. 97–113.

Haufler, V. (2006), 'Global Governance and the Private Sector', in C. May (ed.), *Global Corporate Power*, London: Lynne Reiner, pp. 85–103.

Hay, C. (1999), *The Political Economy of New Labour: Labouring Under False Pretences?*, Manchester: Manchester University Press.

Hay, C. (2002), 'New Labour and the "Third Way" Political Economy: Paving the European Road to Washington?', in M. Bevir and F. Trentmann (eds), *Critiques of Capital in Modern Britain and America: Transatlantic Exchanges 1800 to the Present Day*, Houndmills: Palgrave Macmillan, pp. 195–219.

Hay, C. (2004), 'Re-Stating Politics, Re-Politicising the State: Neo-Liberalism, Economic Imperatives and the Rise of the Competition State', *Political Quarterly*, **75** (Supplement, August), 38–50.

Hay, C. (2006), 'Constructivist Institutionalism', in R.A.W. Rhodes, S. Binder and B. Rockman (eds), *The Oxford Handbook of Political Institutions*, Oxford: Oxford University Press, pp. 56–74.

Hay, C. (2007), *Why We Hate Politics*, Cambridge: Polity

Hayward, J. (1995), *Industrial Enterprise and Economic Integration: From National to International Champions in Western Europe*, Oxford: Oxford University Press.

Heffernan, R. (2007), 'Tony Blair as Party Leader', in A. Seldon (ed.), *Blair's Britain 1997–2007*, Cambridge: Cambridge University Press.

Heffernan, R. (2011), 'Labour's New Labour Legacy: Politics after Blair and Brown', *Political Studies Review*, **9** (2), 163–77.

Held, D. (2004), *Global Covenant: The Social Democratic Alternative to the Washington Consensus*, Cambridge: Polity.

Held, D. and M. Koenig-Archibugi (eds) (2005), *Global Governance and Public Accountability*, Oxford: Blackwell.

Held, D. and A. McGrew (2002), *Globalization/Anti-Globalization*, Cambridge: Polity.

Held, D., A. McGrew, D. Goldblatt and J. Perraton (1999), *Global Transformations: Politics, Economics and Culture*, Cambridge: Polity.

Heller, J. (2004), *Catch-22*, London: The Folio Society, first published, 1955.

Helm, D. (2004), *Energy, the State and the Market: British Energy Policy since 1979*, revised paperback edn, Oxford: Oxford University Press.

Hennessy, P. (1989), *Whitehall*, London: Secker & Warburg.

Héritier, A., A.K. Müller-Debus and C. Thauer (2011), 'The Responsible Corporation: Regulating the Supply Chain', in C. Crouch and C. Maclean (eds), *The Responsible Corporation in a Global Economy*, Oxford: Oxford University Press, pp. 119–39.

Hertz, N. (2001), *The Silent Takeover: Global Capitalism and the Death of Democracy*, London: Arrow.
Hibou, B (ed.) (1999), *Privatising the State*, London: Hurst.
High Pay Commission (2011a), *Interim Report*, London: Compass.
High Pay Commission (2011b), *Final Report*, London: Compass.
Hills, J. (2004), *Inequality and the State*, Oxford: Oxford University Press.
Hirschman, A. (1986), *Rival Views of Market Society: and Other Recent Essays*, New York: Viking.
Holland, S. (1975), *The Socialist Challenge*, London: Quartet.
Hood, C. (1994), *Explaining Economic Policy Reversals*, Buckingham: Open University Press.
Höpner, M. (2007), 'Corporate Governance Reform and the German Party Paradox', *Comparative Politics*, **39** (4), 401–19.
Horn, L. (2012), *Regulating Corporate Governance in the EU: Towards a Marketization of Corporate Control*, Houndmills: Palgrave Macmillan.
Horsfall, D. (2010), 'From Competition State to Competition States?', *Policy Studies*, **31** (1), 57–76.
HSBC (2011), 'Right-to-Buy Sales Continue at Low Levels', HSBC Personal Finance Newsroom, 5 October, available at www.newsroom.hsbc.co.uk (accessed 10 August 2012).
Hsueh, R. (2011), *China's Regulatory State: A New Strategy for Globalization*, Ithaca: Cornell University Press.
Huisman, W. (2012), *Schwarzbuch WWF: Dunkle Geschäfte im Zeichen des Panda*, Munich: Gutersloher Verlaghaus (Black Book WWF: Shady deals under the sign of the Panda).
Hutton, W. (1996), *The State We're In*, revised edn, London: Vintage.
Hutton, W. (2010), *Them and Us: Changing Britain – Why We Need a Fair Society*, London: Little Brown.
Huxley, A. (1932), *Brave New World*, London: Chatto & Windus.
Hyde, M. (2012), 'London 2012; Will Nick Buckles Pass the Baton of Blame?', *The Guardian*, 17 July.
IFS (2010), *Poverty and Inequality in UK: 2010*, London: Institute for Fiscal Studies.
IFSL Research (2009), *PFI in the UK & PPP in Europe 2009*, London: International Financial Services London.
IMD (2010), *IMD World Competitiveness Yearbook 2010*, IMD Business School, available at www.imd.ch.
Inagami, T. (2009), 'Managers and Corporate Governance Reform in Japan: Restoring Self-Confidence or Shareholder Revolution?' in H. Whittaker and S. Deakin (eds), *Corporate Governance and Managerial Reform in Japan*, Oxford: Oxford University Press, pp. 163–91.

Ingham, G. (1984), *Capitalism Divided? The City and Industry in British Social Development*, Houndmills: Macmillan.

Ireland, P. (2000), 'Defending the *Rentier*: Corporate Theory and the Reprivatization of the Public Company', in J. Parkinson, A. Gamble and G. Kelly (eds), *The Political Economy of the Company*, Oxford: Hart.

Jabko, N. (2006), *Playing the Market: A Political Strategy for Uniting Europe, 1985–2005*, Ithaca: Cornell University Press.

Jackson, G. (2007), 'Employment Adjustment and Distributional Conflict in Japanese Firms', in M. Aoki, G. Jackson and H. Miyajima (eds), *Corporate Governance in Japan: Institutional Change and Organizational Diversity*, Oxford: Oxford University Press, pp. 282–309.

Jackson, G. and R. Deeg (2008), 'From Comparing Capitalisms to the Politics of Institutional Change', *Review of International Political Economy*, **15** (4), 680–709.

Jackson, G. and A. Moerke (2005), 'Continuity and Change in Corporate Governance: Comparing Germany and Japan', *Corporate Governance*, **13** (3), 351–61.

Jackson, T. (2009), *Prosperity Without Growth: Economics for a Finite Planet*, London: Earthscan.

Jagger, S. (2010), 'Call for Crackdown on Rich Tax-dodgers "Poisoning Society"', *The Times*, 13 September.

James, O. (2001), 'Business Models and the Transfer of Businesslike Central Government Agencies', *Governance*, **14** (2), 233–52.

Jenkins, S. (2007), *Thatcher and Sons*, revised edn, London: Penguin.

Johnson, C. (1982), *MITI and the Japanese Miracle: The Growth of Industrial Policy, 1925–1975*, Stanford CA: Stanford University Press.

Johnson, S. and J. Kwak (2010), *13 Bankers: The Wall Street Takeover and the Next Financial Meltdown*, New York: Pantheon Books.

Jones, G. (2005a), *Multinationals and Global Capitalism: From the Nineteenth to the Twenty-First Century*, Oxford: Oxford University Press.

Jones, G. (2005b), *Renewing Unilever: Transformation and Tradition*, Oxford: Oxford University Press.

Jones, G. (2010), *Multinational Strategies and Developing Countries in Historical Perspective*, Harvard Business School, Working Paper 10-076.

Jones, P. (2012), 'Reading the Dystopian: A Critical Reading of the Utopianism in Contemporary Management', PhD thesis, University of Warwick.

Jordan, G. and L. Stevenson, (2003), 'Beyond Win–Lose Processes? The Potential of Group Co-operation Strategies', in S. John and S. Thomson (eds), *New Activism and the Corporate Response*, Houndmills: Palgrave Macmillan, pp. 31–48.

Kaletsky, A. (2010), *Capitalism 4.0*, London: Bloomsbury.
Kay, J. (2011), 'A Good Crisis Gone to Waste', *Prospect*, September, 22–7.
Kay, J. (2012), *The Kay Review of UK Equity Markets and Long Term Decision Making: Final Report*, July, London: BIS.
Kelly, G., D. Kelly and A. Gamble (eds) (1997), *Stakeholder Capitalism*, Houndmills: Macmillan.
Klein, N. (2002), *No Logo*, revised edition, New York: Picador.
Klein, N. (2007), *The Shock Doctrine: The Rise of Disaster Capitalism*, London: Allen Lane.
Kozinets, R. (2002), 'Can Consumers Escape the Market? Emancipatory Illuminations from Burning Man', *Journal of Consumer Research*, **29** (1), 20–38.
KPMG (2011), *KPMG International Survey of Corporate Responsibility Reporting 2011*, KPMG International Cooperative, available at http://www.kpmg.com/UK (accessed 22 May 2012).
Kuhn, R. (2007), 'Media Management', in A. Seldon (ed.), *Blair's Britain 1997–2007*, Cambridge: Cambridge University Press, pp. 123–42.
Kurucz, E., B. Colbert and D. Wheeler (2008), 'The Business Case for Corporate Social Responsibility', in A. Crane, A. McWilliams, D. Matten, J. Moon and D. Siegel (eds), *The Oxford Handbook of Corporate Social Responsibility*, Oxford: Oxford University Press, pp. 83–112.
Kurtz, L. (2008), 'Socially Responsible Investment and Shareholder Activism', in A. Crane, A. McWilliams, D. Matten, J. Moon and D. Siegel (eds), *The Oxford Handbook of Corporate Social Responsibility*, Oxford: Oxford University Press, pp. 249–80.
Lambert, Sir R. (2010), 'Does business have a role as a force for good?' Speech to the RSA, 30 March.
Lang, A., R. Karsten and V. Schneider (2008), 'From Simple to Complex: An Evolutionary Sketch of Theories of Business Association', in J. Grote et al. (eds), *Organized Business Interests in Changing Environments*, Houndmills: Palgrave Macmillan, pp. 17–41.
Lazonick, W. (1991), *Business Organization and the Myth of the Market Economy*, Cambridge: Cambridge University Press.
Lazonick, W. and M. O'Sullivan (2004), 'Maximising Shareholder Value: A New Ideology for Corporate Governance', in T. Clarke (ed.), *Theories of Corporate Governance: The Philosophical Foundations of Corporate Governance*, London: Routledge, pp. 289–303 (first published 2000).
Learmount, S. (2002), *Corporate Governance: What can be learned from Japan?* Oxford: Oxford University Press.
Le Carré, J. (2005), *The Constant Gardener*, London: Hodder and Stoughton (first published 2001).

Lee, S.Y. and C. Carroll (2011), 'The Emergence, Variation, and Evolution of Corporate Social Responsibility in the Public Sphere, 1980–2004: The Exposure of Firms to Public Debate', *Journal of Business Ethics*, **104**, 115–31.

Levy, D. and R. Kaplan, 2008, 'Corporate Social Responsibility and Theories of Global Governance: Strategic Contestation in Global Issue Areas', in A. Crane, A. McWilliams, D. Matten, J. Moon and D. Siegel (eds), *The Oxford Handbook of Corporate Social Responsibility*, Oxford: Oxford University Press, pp. 432–51.

Leys, C. (2001), *Market-Driven Politics: Neoliberal Democracy and the Public Interest*, London: Verso.

Lilley, S. and A. McKinley (2009), 'Editorial: Matters of Fact/Matters of Fiction: Imagining and Implementing Institutional Change', *Culture and Organization*, **15** (2), 129–33.

Li, J. and Y. Tang (2010), 'CEO Hubris and Firm Risk-Taking in China: The Moderating Role of Managerial Discretion', *Academy of Management Journal*, **53** (1), 45–68.

Lijphart, A. (1999), *Patterns of Democracy: Governmental Forms and Performance in Thirty Six Countries*, New Haven: Yale University Press.

Lindblom, C. (1977), *Politics and Markets: The World's Political–Economic Systems*, New York: Basic Books.

Lloyd, R. (2008), 'Promoting Global Accountability: The Experiences of the Global Accountability Project', *Global Governance*, **14**, (3), 273–81.

Locke, R. and J.-C Spender (2011), *Confronting Managerialism: How the Business Elite and Their Schools Threw Our Lives Out of Balance*, London: Zed.

LOCOG (2011), *London Organising Committee of the Olympic Games and Paralympic Games Ltd: Annual Report 2010/11*, available at http://www.london2012.com (accessed, 14 August 2012).

Lukes, S. (2005), *Power: A Radical View*, second edn, Houndmills: Macmillan.

Lunt, N. (2010), 'Winning Hearts and Minds for the Competition State', *Policy Studies*, **31** (1), 23–37.

Maclean, C. and C. Crouch (2011), 'Introduction: The Economic, Political, and Ethical Challenges of Corporate Social Responsibility', in C. Crouch and C. Maclean (eds), *The Responsible Corporation in a Global Economy*, Oxford: Oxford University Press, pp. 1–28.

Maclean, M., C. Harvey and J. Press (2006), *Business Elites and Corporate Governance in France and the UK*, Houndmills: Palgrave Macmillan.

Maclean, M., C. Harvey and R. Chia (2010), 'Dominant Corporate Agents and the Power Elite in France and Britain', *Organization Studies*, **31** (3), 327–48.

MacNeil, I. and X. Li (2006), '"Comply or Explain": Market Discipline and Non-Compliance with the Combined Code', *Corporate Governance*, **14** (5), 486–96.
Mallin, C. (2010), *Corporate Governance*, third edn, Oxford: Oxford University Press.
Mandelson, P. (2010), *The Third Man*, London: Harper Collins.
Marangos, J. (2008), 'The Evolution of the Anti-Washington Consensus Debate: From "Post-Washington Consensus" to "After the Washington Consensus"', *Competition and Change*, **12** (3), 227–44.
March, J. (1962), 'The Business Firm as a Political Coalition', *Journal of Politics*, **24** (4), 662–78.
March, J. and J. Olsen (1989), *Rediscovering Institutions: The Organizational Basis of Politics*, New York: The Free Press.
Marcuse, H. (1964), *One Dimensional Man: Studies in the Ideology of Advanced Industrial Society*, Boston: Beacon.
Marlow, B. (2012), 'Man Utd's World Stock Market Tour Ends on Wall Street', *The Sunday Times*, 8 July.
Marquand, D. (2004), *Decline of the Public: The Hollowing-out of Citizenship*, Cambridge: Polity.
May, C. (2006a), 'Introduction', in C. May (ed.), *Global Corporate Power*, London: Lynne Reinner, pp. 1–22.
May, C. (2006b), 'Global Corporate Power and the UN Global Compact', in C. May (ed.), *Global Corporate Power*, London: Lynne Reinner, pp. 273–82.
May, C. (ed.) (2006), *Global Corporate Power*, London: Lynne Reinner.
Mayer, C. (2013), *Firm Commitment: Why the Corporation is Failing Us and How to Restore Trust in It*, Oxford: Oxford University Press.
McCluskey, J. and J. Swinner (2010), 'Media Economics and the Political Economy of Information', in D. Coen, W. Grant and G. Wilson (eds), *The Oxford Handbook of Business and Government*, Oxford: Oxford University Press, pp. 643–62.
McGregor, R. 2010, *The Party: The Secret World of China's Communist Rulers*, London: Allen Lane.
McLean, I. (2004), 'The History of Regulation in the United Kingdom: Three Case Studies in Search of a Theory', in J. Jordana and D. Levi-Faur (eds), *The Politics of Regulation*, Cheltenham, UK and Northampton, MA, USA: Edward Elgar, pp. 45–66.
Megginson, W. and N. Sutter (2006), 'Privatization in Developing Countries', *Corporate Governance*, **14** (4), 234–65.
Micklethwait, J. and A. Wooldridge (2003), *The Company: A Short History of a Revolutionary Idea*, London: Wiedenfeld & Nicholson.

Middlemas, K. (1986), *Power, Competition and the State: Vol 1 Britain in Search of Balance, 1940–61*, Houndmills: Macmillan.

Middlemas, K. (1991), *Power, Competition and the State: Vol 3 The End of the Postwar Era: Britain since 1974*, Houndmills: Macmillan.

Mikler, J. (2009), *Greening the Car Industry: Varieties of Capitalism and Climate Change*, Cheltenham, UK and Northampton, MA, USA: Edward Elgar.

Miliband, E. (2011), Speech to the Labour Party Conference, Liverpool, 27 September, available at, http://www.telegraph.co.uk/news/politics/ed-miliband/8791870/Labour-Party-Conference-Ed-Milibands-speech-in-full (accessed 12 March 2012).

Mills, C.W. (1956), *The Power Elite*, New York: Oxford University Press.

Minister for Government Policy (2011), *Open Public Services White Paper*, Cm 8145, London: TSO.

Miyajima, H. and F. Kuroki (2007), 'The Unwinding of Cross-Shareholding in Japan: Causes, Effects, and Implications', in M. Aoki, G. Jackson and H. Miyajima (eds), *Corporate Governance in Japan: Institutional Change and Organizational Diversity*, Oxford: Oxford University Press, pp. 79–124.

Monbiot, G. (2000), *Captive State: The Corporate Takeover of Britain*, London: Macmillan.

Monks, R. (2008), *Corpocracy: How CEOs and the Business Roundtable Hijacked the World's Greatest Wealth Machine – And How to Get It Back*, Hoboken, NJ: Wiley.

Monks, R. and N. Minow (2004), *Corporate Governance*, third edn, Oxford: Blackwell.

Moon J. and D. Vogel (2008), 'Corporate Social Responsibility, Government and Civil Society', in A. Crane, A. McWilliams, D. Matten, J. Moon and D. Siegel (eds), (2008), *The Oxford Handbook of Corporate Social Responsibility*, Oxford: Oxford University Press, pp. 303–23.

Moon, J., N. Kang and J.-P. Gond (2010), 'Corporate Social Responsibility and Government', in D. Coen, W. Grant and G. Wilson (eds), *The Oxford Handbook of Business and Government*, Oxford, Oxford University Press, pp. 512–43.

Moran, M. (2003), *The British Regulatory State: High Modernisation and Hyper-Innovation*, Oxford: Oxford University Press.

Moran, M. (2006), 'The Company of Strangers: Defending the Power of Business in Britain, 1975–2005', *New Political Economy*, **11** (4), 453–77.

Moran, M. (2008), 'Representing the Corporate Elite in Britain: Capitalist Solidarity and Capitalist Legitimacy', in M. Savage and K. Williams (eds), *Remembering Elites*, Oxford: Blackwell, pp. 64–79.

Moran, M. (2009), *Business, Politics and Society: An Anglo-American Comparison*, Oxford: Oxford University Press.

Morgan, G. and S. Quack (2005), *Institutional Legacies and Firm Dynamics: The Internationalisation of British and German Law Firms*, Warwick: CSGR Working Paper, 169/05.

Morgan, R. (2004), *Market Forces*, London: Gollancz

Mosley, L. (2003), *Global Capital and National Governments*, Cambridge: Cambridge University Press.

Mount, F. (2012), *The New Few or A Very British Oligarchy*, London: Simon & Schuster.

Mueller, D. (2003), *The Corporation: Investment, Mergers and Growth*, London: Routledge.

Murphy, D. (2004), *The Structure of Regulatory Competition: Corporations and Public Policies in a Global Economy*, Oxford: Oxford University Press.

Nace, T. (2003), *Gangs of America: The Rise of Corporate Power and the Disabling of Democracy*, San Francisco: Berrett-Koehler.

NAO (2010a), 'Memorandum by the National Audit Office, written evidence to Select Committee on Economic Affairs', *Private Finance Projects and Off-Balance Sheet Debt, Volume II: Evidence*, 1st Report of session 2009–10, House of Lords, HL 63-II, London: TSO, pp. 78–113.

NAO (2010b), *Central Government's Use of Consultants and Interims*, HC 488, session 2010–11, London: TSO.

NEF (2009), *The Cuts Won't Work: Second Report of the Green New Deal Group*, London: New Economics Foundation.

Nölke, A. and H. Taylor (2010), 'Non-Triad Multinationals and Global Governance: Still a North–South Conflict?', in M. Ougaard and A. Leander (eds), *Business and Global Governance*, London: Routledge, pp. 156–77.

Norman, J. (2011), 'Conservative Free Markets, and the Case for Real Capitalism', available at www.jessenorman.com (accessed 8 August 2012).

North, D. (1990), *Institutions, Institutional Change and Economic Performance*, Cambridge: Cambridge University Press.

Oborne, P. (2008), *The Triumph of the Political Class*, revised edn, London: Pocket Books.

Olcott, G. (2009), 'Whose Company Is It? Changing CEO Ideology in Japan', in H. Whittaker and S. Deakin (eds), *Corporate Governance and Managerial Reform in Japan*, Oxford: Oxford University Press, pp. 192–221.

ONS (2009), *Wealth in Great Britain: Main Results from the Wealth and*

Assets Survey 2006/08, edited by Chris Duffin, London: Office for National Statistics.
ONS (2010), 'Share Ownership Survey, 2008', *Statistical Bulletin*, London: Office for National Statistics, January.
ONS (2012), 'Ownership of UK Quoted Shares 2010', *Statistical Bulletin*, London: Office for National Statistics, February.
Orwell, G. (1937), *The Road to Wigan Pier*, London: Gollancz.
O'Shea, J. and C. Madigan (1999), *Dangerous Company: The Consulting Powerhouses and the Businesses They Save and Ruin*, London: Nicholas Brealey.
Osler, D. (2002), *Labour Party PLC: New Labour as a Party of Business*, Edinburgh: Mainstream.
Ougaard, M. (2006), 'Instituting the Power to do Good?' in C. May (ed.), *Global Corporate Power*, London: Lynne Reinner, pp. 227–47.
Ougaard, M. (2008), 'Private Institutions and Business Power in Global Governance', *Global Governance*, **14** (3), 387–403.
Ougaard, M. (2010), 'Introducing Business and Global Governance', in M. Ougaard and A. Leander (eds), *Business and Global Governance*, London: Routledge, pp. 1–36.
Ougaard, M. and A. Leander (eds) (2010), *Business and Global Governance*, London: Routledge.
Overbeek, H., B. van Apeldoorn and A. Nölke (eds) (2007), *The Transnational Politics of Corporate Governance Regulation*, Abingdon: Routledge.
Owen, D. and B. O'Dwyer (2008), 'Corporate Social Responsibility: The Reporting and Assurance Dimension', in A. Crane, A. McWilliams, D. Matten, J. Moon and D. Siegel (eds), *The Oxford Handbook of Corporate Social Responsibility*, Oxford: Oxford University Press, pp. 384–409.
PAC (2010), *Central Government's Use of Consultants and Interims*, Public Accounts Committee, HC610, London: TSO.
PAC (2011), *HM Revenue & Customs 2010–11 Accounts: Tax Disputes*, Public Accounts Committee, HC1531, London TSO.
Padgett, S. and P. John (2010), 'How do Political Parties Shape Public Opinion? Britain in a European Perspective', in A. Park et al. (eds), *British Social Attitudes Survey*, London: Sage, pp. 39–61.
Painter, A. (2009), 'The Washington Consensus is Dead', *The Guardian*, 10 April.
Palan, R. (2010), *Tax Havens: How Globalization Really Works*, Ithaca: Cornell University Press.
Park, A. et al. (eds) (2010), *British Social Attitudes Survey*, London: Sage.
Parker, C. (2002), *The Open Corporation: Effective Self-regulation and Democracy*, Cambridge: Cambridge University Press.

Parker, D. (1998), 'Privatisation in the European Union: An Overview', in D. Parker (ed.), *Privatisation in the European Union: Theory and Policy Perspectives*, London: Routledge.

Parker, D. (2009), *The Official History of Privatization: Volume I: The Formative Years, 1979–1987*, London: Routledge.

Parker, D. (2012), *The Official History of Privatization: Volume II: Popular Capitalism, 1987–1997*, London: Routledge.

Parker, M. (2002), *Against Management: Organization in the Age of Managerialism*, Cambridge: Polity.

Parkinson, J. (1993), *Corporate Power and Responsibility: Issues in the Theory of Company Law*, Oxford: Clarendon.

Parkinson, J., A. Gamble and G. Kelly (eds) (2000), *The Political Economy of the Company*, Oxford: Hart.

PASC (2009), *Lobbying: Access and Influence in Whitehall*, Public Administration Select Committee, HC36-I, London: TSO.

PASC (2010), *Outsiders and Insiders: External Appointments to the Senior Civil Service*, Public Administration Select Committee, HC241, London: TSO.

Pattberg, P. (2007), *Private Institutions and Global Governance: The New Politics of Environmental Sustainability*, Cheltenham, UK and Northampton, MA, USA: Edward Elgar.

Perrow, C. (2009), 'Modeling Firms in the Global Economy', *Theory and Society*, **38** (3), 217–43.

Peston, R. (2005), *Brown's Britain*, London: Short Books.

Peston, R. (2008), *Who Runs Britain?*, London: Hodder & Stoughton.

Picciotto, S. (2011), *Regulating Global Corporate Capitalism*, Cambridge: Cambridge University Press.

Plant, R. (2003), 'A Public Service Ethic and Political Accountability', *Parliamentary Affairs*, **56** (4), 560–79.

Polanyi, K. (1944), *The Great Transformation: The Political and Economic Origins of Our Time*, New York: Rinehart.

Pollard, A. (2000), 'Introduction', in A. Pollard (ed.), *The Representation of Business and English Literature*, Indianapolis: Liberty Fund.

Pollard, S. (1984), *The Wasting of the British Economy*, 2nd edn, London: Croom Helm.

Porter, M. (1990), *The Competitive Advantage of Nations*, London: Macmillan.

Porter, M., H. Takeuchi and M. Sakibara (2000), *Can Japan Compete?*, Houndmills: Palgrave Macmillan.

Prabhakar, R. (2004), 'Do Public Interest Companies Form a Third Way Within Public Services?', *British Journal of Politics and International Relations*, **6** (3), 353–69.

Prais, S. (1976), *The Evolution of Giant Firms in Britain: A Study of the Growth of Concentration in Manufacturing Industry in Britain 1909–70*, Cambridge: Cambridge University Press.
Privatization Barometer (2009), 'The PB Report 2009', available at www.privatizationbarometer.net (accessed 22 March 2012).
Przeworski, A. and M. Wallerstein (1988), 'Structural Dependence of the State on Capital', *American Political Science Review*, **82** (1), 11–30.
PWC (2010), 'Law Firms' Survey', available at www.pwcco.uk/lawfirms (accessed 23 August 2011).
Randall, N.J. (2011), 'Imagining the Polity: Cinema and Television Fictions as Vernacular Theories of British Politics', *Parliamentary Affairs*, **64** (2), 263–80.
Rasche, A. and G. Kell (eds) (2010), *The United Nations Global Compact: Achievements, Trends and Challenges*, Cambridge: Cambridge University Press.
Rebérioux, A. (2007), 'The Paradoxical Nature of Shareholder Primacy: A Re-Consideration of the Enron-Era Scandals in the US and the EU', in H. Overbeek, B. van Apeldoorn and A. Nölke (eds), *The Transnational Politics of Corporate Governance Regulation*, Abingdon: Routledge, pp. 59–74.
Redding, G. and M. Witt (2007), *The Future of Chinese Capitalism: Choices and Chances*, Oxford: Oxford University Press.
Reich. R. (2009), *Supercapitalism: The Battle for Democracy in an Age of Big Business*, London: Icon (first published 2007).
Rhodes, C. and R. Westwood (2008), *Critical Representations of Work and Organization in Popular Culture*, London: Routledge.
Richardson, J. and D. Coen (2009), 'Institutionalizing and Managing Intermediation in the EU', in D. Coen and J. Richardson (eds), *Lobbying the European Union: Institutions, Actors and Issues*, Oxford: Oxford University Press, pp. 337–50.
Rimington, J. (2008), 'The Value of the Remuneration of High Civil Servants in Britain in the 20th Century and its Implications', *Public Administration*, **86** (4), 1107–25.
Ritzer, G. (1996), *The McDonaldization of Society*, revised edition, Thousand Oaks, CA: Pine Forge.
Roach, B. (2005), 'A Primer on Multinational Corporations', in Alfred Chandler and Bruce Mazlish (eds), *Leviathans: Multinational Corporations and the New Global History*, Cambridge: Cambridge University Press, pp. 19–44.
Roach, L. (2011), 'The UK Stewardship Code', *Journal of Comparative Law Studies*, **11** (2), 463–93.

Rugman, A.M. (2005), *The Regional Multinationals: MNEs and 'Global' Strategic Management*, Cambridge: Cambridge University Press.
Rugman, A. and J. D'Cruz (2000), *Multinationals as Flagship Firms*, Oxford: Oxford University Press.
Sampson, A. (1962), *The Anatomy of Britain*, London: Hodder & Stoughton.
Sampson, A. (1992), *The Essential Anatomy of Britain: Democracy in Crisis*, London: Hodder & Stoughton.
Sampson, A. (1995), *Company Man: The Rise and Fall of Corporate Life*, London: HarperCollins.
Sandel, M. (1996), *Democracy's Discontents*, Cambridge: Harvard University Press.
Sandel, M. (2012), *What Money Can't Buy*, London: Allen Lane.
Savage, M. and K. Williams (2008), 'Elites Remembered in Capitalism and Forgotten by Social Sciences', in M. Savage and K. Williams (eds), *Remembering Elites*, Oxford: Blackwell, pp. 1–24.
Schäferhoff, M., S. Campe and C. Kaan (2009), 'Transnational Public–Private Partnerships in International Relations: Making Sense of Concepts, Research Frameworks, and Results', *International Studies Review*, **11** (3), 451–74.
Scherer, A. and G. Palazzo (2011), 'The New Political Role of Business in a Globalized World: A Review of a New Perspective on CSR and its Implications for the Firm, Governance, and Democracy', *Journal of Management Studies*, **48** (4), 899–931.
Schmidt, V. (2002), *The Futures of European Capitalism*, Oxford: Oxford University Press.
Schmidt, V. (2006), 'Institutionalism', in C. Hay, M. Lister and D. Marsh (eds), *The State: Theories and Issues*, Houndmills: Palgrave Macmillan, pp. 98–117.
Schmidt, V. (2009), 'Putting the Political Back into Political Economy by Bringing the State Back in Yet Again', *World Politics*, **61** (3), 516–46.
Schmidt, V. (2011), 'Discursive Institutionalism: Scope, Dynamics and Philosophical Underpinnings', in F. Fischer and J. Forester (eds), *The Argumentative Turn Revised: Public Policy as Communicative Practice*, Durham, NC: Duke University Press.
Schmidt, V. and C. Radaelli (2004), 'Policy Change and Discourse in Europe: Conceptual and Methodological Issues', *West European Politics*, **27** (2), 183–210.
Schmitter, P. (2010), 'Business and Neo-corporatism', in D. Coen, W. Grant and G. Wilson (eds), *The Oxford Handbook of Business and Government*, Oxford: Oxford University Press, pp. 248–58.

Schneider, V. and F. Häge (2008), 'Europeanization and the Retreat of the State', *Journal of European Public Policy*, **15** (1), 1–19.

Schweickart, D. (2011), *After Capitalism*, 2nd edn, Lanham: Rowan and Littlefield.

Scott, J. (1984), *Directors of Industry: The British Corporate Network 1904–76*, Cambridge: Polity.

Scott, J. (1997), *Corporate Business and Capitalist Classes*, Oxford: Oxford University Press.

Scott, J. (2008), 'Modes of Power and the Re-Conceptualization of Elites', in M. Savage and K. Wiliams (eds), *Remembering Elites*, Oxford: Blackwell, pp. 27–43.

Scott, W.R. (1995), *Institutions and Organizations*, London: Sage.

Scott, W.R. (2008), 'Approaching Adulthood: The Maturing of Institutional Theory', *Theory and Society*, **37** (5), 427–42.

Seldon, A. (2004), *Blair*, London: The Free Press

Select Committee on Economic Affairs (2010), *Private Finance Projects and Off-Balance Sheet Debt, Volume I: Report*, House of Lords, HL 63-I, London: TSO.

Select Committee on Economic Affairs (2011), *Auditors: Market Concentration and Their Role*, House of Lords, HL 119-I, London: TSO.

Sell, S. (2000), 'Big Business and the New Trade Agreements: The Future of the WTO?', in R. Stubbs and G. Underhill (eds), *Political Economy and the Changing Global Order*, Oxford: Oxford University Press, pp. 174–83.

Sengupta, M. (2009), 'Making the State Change Its Mind – the IMF, the World Bank and the Politics of India's Market Reforms', *New Political Economy*, **14** (2), 181–210.

Shaoul, J. (2005), 'A Critical Financial Analysis of the Private Finance Initiative: Selecting a Financial Method or Allocating Economic Wealth?', *Critical Perspectives on Accounting*, **16**, 441–71.

Shelley, M. (1818), *Frankenstein: or the Modern Prometheus*, London: Lacking, Hughes, Harding, Mavor and Jones.

Sherman, J. (2010), 'Private Sector Chiefs will have Power to Sack Whitehall Mandarins'. *The Times*, 16 December.

Sherman, J. (2011), 'Rethink Over "Unpalatable" Privatisation of Public Services', *The Times*, 4 May.

Shonfield, A. (1965), *Modern Capitalism: The Changing Balance of Public and Private Power*, Oxford: Oxford University Press.

Sillitoe, A. (1958), *Saturday Night and Sunday Morning*, London: Allen.

Simmons, B., F. Dobbin and G. Garrett (2006), 'Introduction: The International Diffusion of Liberalism', *International Organization*, **60** (4), 781–810.

Simon, H. (1957), *Administrative Behaviour*, 2nd edn, New York: Macmillan.
Singh, R. (2011), 'Do Partners Have Fee Income Pulling Power?', *Accountancy Age*, 14 September.
Skidelsky, R. and E. Skidelsky (2012), *How Much is Enough? The Love of Money and the Case for the Good Life*, London: Penguin, Allen Lane.
Skinner, Q. (1999), 'Hobbes and the Purely Artificial Person of the State', *The Journal of Political Philosophy*, **7** (1), 1–29.
Sklair, L. (2001), *The Transnational Capitalist Class*, Oxford: Blackwell.
Sklair, L. (2002), *Globalization: Capitalism and its Alternatives*, Oxford: Oxford University Press.
Sklair, L. (2009), 'The Emancipatory Potential of Generic Globalization', *Globalizations*, **6** (4), 525–39.
Smith, Adam (1776), *An Inquiry into the Nature and Causes of the Wealth of Nations*, London: W. Strahan and T. Cadell; edition cited, *The Wealth of Nations*, NewYork: Modern Library, 1937.
Smith, C. (2008), 'Consumers as Drivers of Corporate Social Responsibility', in A. Crane, A. McWilliams, D. Matten, J. Moon and D. Siegel (eds), *The Oxford Handbook of Corporate Social Responsibility*, Oxford: Oxford University Press, pp. 281–302.
Soederberg, S. (2010), *Corporate Power and Ownership in Contemporary Capitalism: The Politics of Resistance and Domination*, London: Routledge.
Stern S. and E. Seligmann (2004), *The Partnership Principle: New Forms of Governance in the 21st Century*, London: Archetype.
Sternberg, E. (2011), 'How Serious is CSR: A Critical Perspective', in C. Crouch and C. Maclean (eds), *The Responsible Corporation in a Global Economy*, Oxford: Oxford University Press, pp. 29–54.
Stiff, P. (2010), 'Bart Becht Collects More Than £90 m as Shares Rise in Reckitt Benckiser', *The Times*, 8 April.
Stigler, G. (1971), 'The Theory of Economic Regulation', *Bell Journal of Economics and Management Science*, Spring, 114–41.
Stiglitz, J. (2002), *Globalization and Its Discontents*, London: Penguin.
Stiglitz, J. (2012), *The Price of Inequality*, London: Penguin, Allen Lane.
Stopford, J. and S. Strange (1991), *Rival States, Rival Firms: Competition for World Market Shares*, Cambridge: Cambridge University Press.
Story, J. (2010), 'China and the Multinational Experience', in D. Coen, W. Grant and G. Wilson (eds), *The Oxford Handbook of Business and Government*, Oxford: Oxford University Press, pp. 346–80.
Strange, S. (1994), 'Wake up Krasner! The World *Has* Changed', *Review of International Political Economy*, **1** (2), 209–19.

Strange, S. (1996), *The Retreat of the State: The Diffusion of Power in the World Economy*, Cambridge: Cambridge University Press.

Streeck, W. (1997), 'German Capitalism: Does it Exist? Can it Survive?', in C. Crouch and W. Streeck (eds), *Political Economy of Modern Capitalism: Mapping Convergence and Diversity*, London: Sage.

Strum, P. (1993), *Brandeis: Beyond Progressivism*, Lawrence: University Press of Kansas.

Sunday Times (2012), *Sunday Times Rich List 2012*, London: Times Newspapers.

Swank, D. (2006), 'Tax Policy in an Era of Internationalization: Explaining the Spread of Neoliberalism', *International Organization*, **60** (4), 847–82.

Taylor, R. (2001), 'Employment Relations Policy', in A. Seldon (ed.), *The Blair Effect: The Blair Government 1997–2001*, London: Little Brown, pp. 245–69.

Taylor, R. (2005), 'Mr Blair's British Business Model – Capital and Labour in Flexible Markets', in A. Seldon and D. Kavanagh (eds), *The Blair Effect 2001–5*, Cambridge: Cambridge University Press, pp. 184–206.

Taylor, R. (2007), 'New Labour: New Capitalism', in A. Seldon (ed.), *Blair's Britain, 1997–2007*, Cambridge: Cambridge University Press, pp. 214–40.

Tenbücken, M. (2008), 'Business Interest Associations and Corporate Lobbying: Which Role for Brussels?', in J. Grote, A. Lang and V. Schneider (eds), *Organized Business Interests in Changing Environments: The Complexity of Adaptation*, Houndmills: Palgrave Macmillan, pp. 200–220.

Tencati, A. (2011), 'The Governance of Global Supply Chains', in C. Crouch and C. Maclean (eds), *The Responsible Corporation in a Global Economy*, Oxford, Oxford University Press, pp. 157–74.

Thatcher, M. (2007), *Internationalisation and Economic Institutions: Comparing European Experiences*, Oxford: Oxford University Press.

Thelen, K. (2012), 'Varieties of Capitalism: Trajectories of Liberalization and the New Politics of Social Solidarity', *Annual Review of Political Science*, **15** (1), 137–59.

Tiberghien, Y. (2007), *Entrepreneurial States: Reforming Corporate Governance in France, Japan and Korea*, Ithaca: Cornell University Press.

Tivey, L. (1978), *The Politics of the Firm*, Oxford: Martin Robertson.

Tomorrow's Company (2007), 'The Future of Corporate Reporting: State of Play – February 2007' available at http://www.tomorrowscompany.com/publications.aspx (accessed 22 March 2012).

Toynbee, P. and D. Walker (2008), *Unjust Rewards: Exposing Greed and Inequality in Britain Today*, London: Granta.

Treasury (2004), *Releasing Resources to the Front Line: Independent Review of Public Sector Efficiency* (Gershon Review), London: HMSO.

Tricker, B. (2011), 'Re-inventing the Limited Liability Company', *Corporate Governance*, **19** (4), 384–93.

Trollope, A. (1875), *The Way We Live Now*, London: Chapman and Hall.

Turner, A. (2009), *The Turner Review: A Regulatory Response to the Global Banking Crisis*, London: Financial Services Authority.

UNCTAD (2006), *World Investment Report: FDI from Developing and Transition Economies: Implications for Development*, New York: United Nations Conference on Trade and Development.

UNCTAD (2008), *World Investment Report: Transnational Corporations and the Infrastructure Challenge*, New York: United Nations Conference on Trade and Development.

UNCTAD (2009), *World Investment Report: Transnational Corporations, Agricultural Production and Development*, New York: United Nations Conference on Trade and Development.

UNCTAD (2012), *World Investment Report: Towards a New Generation of Investment Policies*, New York: United Nations Conference on Trade and Development.

UNISON (2008), *The Rise of the 'Public Services Industry': A Report for UNISON by Paul Gosling*, London: UNISON.

Useem, M. (1984), *The Inner Circle: Large Corporations and the Rise of Business Political Activity in the U.S. and U.K.*, Oxford: Oxford University Press.

Valente M. and A. Crane (2010), 'Public Responsibility and Private Enterprise in Developing Countries', *California Review of Management*, **62** (3), 52–78.

Van Apeldoorn, B. (2000), 'Transnational Class Agency and European Governance: The Case of the European Round Table of Industrialists', *New Political Economy*, **5** (2), 157–81.

Van Apeldoorn, B. and L. Horn (2007), 'The Transformation of Corporate Governance Regulation in the EU: from Harmonization to Marketization', in H. Overbeek, B. van Apeldoorn and A. Nölke (eds), *The Transnational Politics of Corporate Governance Regulation*, Abingdon: Routledge, pp. 77–97.

Van Der Wal, Z., G. De Graaf and K. Lasthuizen (2008), 'What's Valued Most? Similarities and Differences between the Organizational Values of the Public and Private Sector', *Public Administration*, **86** (2), 465–82.

Van Oosterhout, H. and P. Heugens (2008), 'Much Ado About Nothing: A Conceptual Critique of Corporate Social Responsibility', in A. Crane, A. McWilliams, D. Matten, J. Moon and D. Siegel (eds), *The Oxford Handbook of Corporate Social Responsibility*, Oxford: Oxford University Press, pp. 197–223.

Veblen, T. (1899), *The Theory of the Leisure Class: An Economic Study of Institutions*, New York: Macmillan.

Vernon, R. (1971), *Sovereignty at Bay: The Multinational Spread of US Enterprises*, Harmondsworth: Pelican.

Villiers, C. (2005), *Corporate Reporting and Company Law*, Cambridge Books Online, http://ebooks.cambridge.org.

Vitols, S. (2001), 'Varieties of Corporate Governance: Comparing Germany and the UK', in P. Hall and D. Soskice (eds), *Varieties of Capitalism*, Oxford: Oxford University Press.

Vogel, D. (1989), *Fluctuating Fortunes: The Political Power of Business in America*, New York: Basic Books.

Vogel, D. (2005), *The Market for Virtue: The Potential and Limits of Corporate Social Responsibility*, Washington, DC: The Brookings Institution.

Vogel, D. (2008), 'Private Global Business Regulation', *Annual Review of Political Science*, 11 (1), 261–82.

Vogel, D. (2010), 'Taming Globalization? Civil Regulation and Corporate Capitalism', in D. Coen, W. Grant and G. Wilson (eds), *The Oxford Handbook of Business and Government*, Oxford: Oxford University Press.

Wade, R. (2007), 'Should We Worry About Income Inequality?', in D. Held and A. Kaya (eds), *Global Inequality: Patterns and Explanations*, Cambridge: Polity, pp. 104–31.

Warhurst, A. (2011) 'Past, Present and Future Corporate Responsibility: Achievements and Aspirations', in C. Crouch and C. Maclean (eds), *The Responsible Corporation in a Global Economy*, Oxford: Oxford University Press, pp. 55–83.

WEF (2002), *The 2001–02 Global Competitiveness Index*, Davos: World Economic Forum.

WEF (2009), *The Global Competitiveness Report 2009–10*, Davos: World Economic Forum, available at http://www.weforum.org/issues/global-competitiveness/index.html (accessed 15 August 2012).

WEF (2011), *The Global Competitiveness Report 2011–12*, Davos: World Economic Forum, available at http://www.weforum.org/issues/global-competitiveness/index.html (accessed 15 August 2012).

Weiss, L. (1997), *The Myth of the Powerless State: Governing the Economy in a Global Era*, Cambridge: Polity.

Wendt, A. (2004), 'The State as a Person in International Theory', *Review of International Studies*, 30 (2), 289–316.
WFE (2012), 'World Federation of Exchanges', *Statistics Reports*, available at: http://www.world-exchanges.org/statistics.
Whitley, R. (1974), 'The City and Industry: The Directors of Large Companies, Their Characteristics and Connections', in P. Stanworth and A. Giddens (eds), *Elites and Power in British Society*, Cambridge: Cambridge University Press, pp. 65–80.
Whitley, R. (1999), *Divergent Capitalisms: The Social Structuring and Change of Business Systems*, Oxford: Oxford University Press.
Whitley, R. (2001), 'How and Why are International Firms Different? The Consequences of Cross-Border Managerial Coordination for Firm Characteristics and Behaviour', in G. Morgan, P.H. Kristensen and R. Whitley (eds), *The Multinational Firm: Organizing Across Institutional and National Divides*, Oxford: Oxford University Press, pp. 27–68.
Whitley, R. (2005), 'How National are Business Systems? The Role of States and Complementary Institutions in Standardizing Systems of Economic Coordination and Control at the National Level', in G. Morgan, R. Whitley and E. Moen (eds), *Changing Capitalisms? Internationalization, Institutional Change, and Systems of Economic Organization*, Oxford: Oxford University Press, pp. 190–231.
Whittaker, H. and S. Deakin (2009), 'Corporate Governance, Institutions, and the Spirits of Capitalism', in H. Whittaker and S. Deakin (eds), *Corporate Governance and Managerial Reform in Japan*, Oxford: Oxford University Press, pp. 266–91.
Whittington, R. and M. Mayer (2000), *The European Corporation: Strategy, Structure and Social Science*, Oxford: Oxford University Press.
Wiener, M. (1981), *English Culture and the Decline of the Industrial Spirit 1850–1980*, Cambridge: Cambridge University Press.
Wilks, S. (1981), 'Planning Agreements: The Making of a Paper Tiger', *Public Administration*, **59**, 399–419.
Wilks, S. (1988), *Industrial Policy and the Motor Industry*, revised edn, Manchester: Manchester University Press.
Wilks, S. (1997), 'The Amoral Corporation and British Utility Regulation', *New Political Economy*, **2** (2), 279–98.
Wilks, S. (2005), 'Competition Policy: Challenge and Reform', in H. Wallace, W. Wallace and M. Pollack (eds), *Policy-Making in the European Union*, 5th edn, Oxford: Oxford University Press, pp. 113–39.
Wilks, S. (2007), 'Boardization and Corporate Governance in the UK as a Response to Depoliticization and Failing Accountability', *Public Policy and Administration*, **22** (4), 443–60.

Wilks, S. (2008), 'Board Management of Performance in British Central Government', in *Holy Grail or Achievable Quest? International Perspectives on Public Sector Performance Management*, Toronto: KPMG International, pp. 125–38.

Wilks, S. (2010), 'Competition Policy', in D. Coen, W. Grant and G. Wilson (eds), *The Oxford Handbook of Business and Government*, Oxford: Oxford University Press, pp. 730–56.

Wilks, S. (2013), 'The National Identity of Global Companies', in J. Mikler (ed.), *The Handbook of Global Companies*, Oxford, Wiley-Blackwell, forthcoming.

Wilks, S. and M. Wright (eds) (1987), *Comparative Government–Industry Relations: Western Europe, the United States, and Japan*, Oxford: Clarendon.

Williams, I. and H. Shearer (2011), 'Appraising Public Value: Past, Present and Futures', *Public Administration*, **89** (4), 1367–84.

Williamson, O. (1981), 'The Modern Corporation: Origins, Evolution, Attributes', *Journal of Economic Literature*, **19**, 1537–68.

Wilson, J.R. and A. Thomson (2006), *The Making of Modern Management: British Management in Historical Perspective*, Oxford: Oxford University Press.

Wintour, P. and N. Davies (2011), 'Coulson Quits as Hacking Scandal Rocks Downing St.', *The Guardian*, 22 January.

Witty, Sir A. (2012), 'It's Good for Business for Business to be Good', keynote speech at Cranfield School of Management, 18 January.

Wolfe, T. (1987), *The Bonfire of the Vanities*, New York: Farrar Strauss Giroux.

Woods, N. (2006), *The Globalizers: The IMF, the World Bank and Their Borrowers*, Ithaca: Cornell University Press.

World Bank (2009), *World Development Report 2009: Reshaping Economic Geography*, Washington DC: The International Bank for Reconstruction and Development.

Wring, D. (2006), 'The News Media and the Public Relations State', in P. Dunleavy, R. Heffernan and C. Hay (eds), *Developments in British Politics 8*, Houndmills: Palgrave Macmillan, pp. 231–50.

Xaxa, V. (2012), 'Identity, Power, and Development: The Kondhs in Orissa, India', in S. Sawyer and E. Gomez (eds), *The Politics of Resource Extraction: Indigenous Peoples, Multinational Corporations and the State*, Basingstoke, Palgrave Macmillan.

Yaziji, M. and J. Doh (2009), *NGOs and Corporations: Conflict and Collaboration*, Cambridge: Cambridge University Press.

Young S. with S. Lowe (1974), *Intervention in the Mixed Economy*, London: Croom Helm.

Zhu, J.-M. and E. Morss (2005), 'The Financial Revolutions of the Twentieth Century', in A. Chandler and B. Mazlish (eds), *Leviathans: Multinational Corporations and the New Global History*, Cambridge: Cambridge University Press, pp. 203–18.

Index

Abbott, P. 83
Accenture 83
accountability
 areas of 177–8
 to a suspicious public 195–6
accountancy elite 79, 80–82, 84, 167, 204, 225–6, 228–9
Acemoglu, D. 268
Addleshaw Goddard 82
Adelstein, R. 5
administrative elite 77–9
 subordination of 100–105
Advisory Committee on Business Appointments 78
Albert, M. 231
Alien (1972) 191
Allen, C. 231
Allen & Overy 82
alternative futures 190–93
Amoore, L. 46, 50, 172
Amsterdam Research Centre 219, 236
Anglo-Saxon corporation model 9–15, 217–30
 alternatives to 230–43, 264–6
 export of 148–50, 235–9
anti-capitalist/anti-globalisation activism 36, 153–4
antitrust 2, 4, 36, 121, 153
Aoki, M. 248
Apostolides, N. 129
Araki, T. 244, 246
ArcelorMittall 56
Asenova, D. 133, 141–2
Ashurst 82
Asia, corporate governance models 240–43
Asimov, Isaac 190
associational involvement 39
ATKearney 'FDI Confidence Index' 47
Atkinson, A.B. 90–91

Atkinson, D. 262
Atwood, M. 188
audit committees 223, 228–9
authority, political parties 96–100
autonomy
 constraints on 14, 208
 global regime 153–8
 MNCs 48, 54, 59–61, 243
Avatar (2009) 184, 190, 191–3

Babb, S. 151
Bakan, J. 11, 22
Ball, S. 96
Bank of England 107
banks
 bonuses 92–3
 elite activities 75–6
 Germany 233–4, 236–7
 role in capitalism 106–8
 support for reform of 265
Barber, B. 170–71
Barber, M. 102, 103
Barker, R. 234–5, 236, 237
Barry, B. 90, 259
Barry, M. 187–8
Beck, M. 133, 141–2
Beetham, D. 90
Benedict, R. 11
Beresford, P. 90
Berle, A. 4, 12, 179, 217
Bernhagen, P. 24
'big bang' deregulation 69, 81, 108
bilateral trade agreements 153, 154
Binham, C. 81
Blade Runner (1982) 190–91
Blair, Tony 70–71, 98, 99, 102, 103, 107, 133, 225, 233
'blockholder model' 13, 208–9, 221, 231, 233–4, 238, 242, 243
Blundell, J. 184–5
Blyth, M. 68, 121, 122, 174, 179

boards of directors
  Germany 233, 236, 238
  Japan 245
  UK 220, 223, 225–6, 233, 236, 238
Bobbitt, P. 103, 113–14, 116, 148
Boden, R. 129
Bonfire of the Vanities (1987) 187
Boswell, J. 67, 110, 111, 118, 121
Bovaird, T. 134
Bower, T. 71
Braithwaite, J. 73, 164
brand image 11, 22, 50–51, 108, 143, 154, 156, 170–72
Brandeis, Louis 36
Brave New World (1931) 189–90
Bremmer, I. 163
BRIC economies 5–6, 45, 46, 54, 55, 166
  see also China
Brown, Gordon 70–71, 99, 104, 107, 153, 225
Brown, H.S. 107, 200
'buddy' system 79
Bullock Report (1977) 222
bureaucracy, Japan 244–5
Burnham, J. 102
business advisers 40, 97–8, 101, 104–5, 138–9
business associations 24–5, 30, 34, 39, 60, 109, 118–20, 238, 247
  see also Confederation of British Industry (CBI)
business case, CSR 201–2, 205
Business in the Community (BITC) 202, 204–5
business representation 105–13
Büthe, T. 157, 173

Cable, V. 266
Cadbury Committee (1992) 220–21, 223–6, 228
Cairncross, F. 50
Callaghan, H. 233–4
Camerman, F. 6
Cameron, David 72, 79, 85, 103, 140, 266
Campbell, A. 85
Campbell, C. 101
Capgemini 83
Capita 26, 134–5, 137, 140–41

capitalism
  new national variant of 264–6
  transcending 266–7
Capling, A. 153
career politicians 96–100, 101
Carroll, A. 198
Cass, D. 152
Catch 22 (1961) 189
Caulkin, S. 254
Cawson, A. 25, 26
Centrica 130
CEOs 22, 59–60, 75–6, 79, 92, 102, 104, 112, 194–5, 205, 206–7, 220, 229, 244
Cerny, P. 29, 112, 148, 159, 165–6
Chalmers Johnson 245
Chandler, A. 4, 12
Charkham, J. 220–21, 224, 234, 239, 245
Cheffins, B. 92, 221, 229
Chen, J. 59
Chhotray, V. 42
China
  corporate governance model 240–43
  MNCs 56, 57–61
Chinese Communist Party (CCP) 58, 60
Chorev, N. 151
civic consumerism 170
civic republicanism 212–13
civil regulation 156–7, 206
civil service
  critique of 184
  modernisation 100–105
  post-political careers 78, 99, 139–40
  as supporting bureaucrats 77–9
Clifford Chance 82
Clift, B. 222
Clifton, J. 127
co-determination 209, 233–5, 238, 239, 244
co-regulation 156, 157
Coalition government 29, 79, 98–9, 103, 107, 131, 141, 194
Coase, R. 9
codes of conduct 155–7, 206, 210, 218, 223–6, 259
Coen, D. 24, 25, 108–9
collective representation, shift from 108–10

Commercial Code, Japan 245, 248
commodification 171, 172, 216
'community model' 208–9
Companies Act (2006), UK 211, 218, 224–5
Company Law Review (2002) 224–5, 227
company law 211–12
  reform of 218–19, 222–6, 237–8
comparative democracy 16
comparative perspective 29–31
competition policy 112, 125, 149, 152–3, 164, 177–8, 235, 236–7
'competition state' 29, 112, 118–19, 148, 159, 165–6
competitiveness league tables 160–63
concentration of power 50, 63, 90, 220
Confederation of British Industry (CBI) 67, 107, 110, 118, 135–6, 137–8, 140, 194, 225, 233
Conservative Party 29, 37, 66, 68, 69, 71–2, 79, 95–100, 122–6, 222–3
Constant Gardener (2005) 186
consumer society 168–73, 180–81, 266
conventional morality 186–7, 193
Cook, P. 122
coordinated market economies (CMEs) 30, 165, 232, 239, 241, 243, 247, 264
Corbett, J.M. 185, 191
corporate appointments, ex-civil servants 78, 99, 139–40
corporate bias and shrinking democratic choice 113–16
corporate citizenship 20, 32, 44, 166–7, 171, 175–6, 178, 241, 254, 257, 260, 268
  promise and pitfalls 210–15
corporate elite 32–7
  assessing political power 37–40
  circulation in UK 66–70
  composition of 73–86
  definition and identification 37
  organising of 105–13
  and power and equality 87–93
  rupture with political elite 268
corporate executives as elite 74–7
corporate form
  alternative ways of structuring 255–6
  as global norm 256–7

corporate governance
  Asian models 240–43
  alternatives to UK model and German model 230–40
  as constitution of the corporation 217–21
  Japanese model 243–9
  need for reinvention 249–50
  UK model 221–30
Corporate Governance Code
  Germany 237
  UK 218, 222, 225–6
corporate hero 182, 185
corporate policy preferences 22–3, 38–9, 117–21
corporate power
  and corporate elite 87–93
  and democratic settlements 64–5
  from international operations 45–54
  implications of energy privatisation 129–32
  institutional foundations 15–19
  normalising 40–41
  origins, exercise and control of 19–20
  political analysis of 23–32
corporate rationality, nature of 21–3
Corporate Sector Supervision and Transparency Act (1998), Germany 237
corporate size 4–8, 38, 126–7
corporate social responsibility (CSR) 258
  comparative assessment 205–10
  emergence 197–201
  as misconception/fraud 254
  motivations to undertake 201–5
  as response to anti-capitalism 154
corporations, appraising 1–3
council housing privatisation 124
Coyle, D. 180
Craig, D. 140
Crane, A. 173, 214, 263
'crony communism' 60
cross-shareholding 34, 233, 243, 247, 237, 248, 249
Crouch, C. 8, 53, 73, 116, 121
Culpepper, P. 14, 229, 233–4, 238, 248
cultural corporate positioning 178–83

cultural corporate representations 184–95
cultural–cognitive dimension 18–19
cultures favouring MNCs 168–73
Cutler, C. 44, 167, 174

D'Cruz, J. 47
Dahl, R. 219, 239
Damodaran, H. 59
Davies, N. 85
Davies, S. 137
Davis, D. 79
De Grauwe, P. 6
Deakin, S. 241, 243, 245, 248–9
debt 75–6, 107, 160, 180–81
Deeg, R. 51
deliberative democracy 213–14
delivery, emphasis on 102–3, 133
Deloitte 80–81, 83
democratic choice, subversion of 113–16, 254–5, 260–61
democratic settlements
  and corporate power 64–5
  see also Post-war Settlement
Department for Business Innovation and Skills (BIS), UK 204
Department of Energy and Climate Change (DECC) 131
developmental states 241, 243, 244
deverticalisation, MNCs 49–50
Devinney, T. 207–8
Diageo 214–15
Dickson, B. 57, 58, 60, 164
Dieter, H. 154
DiMaggio, P. 57
discursive institutionalism 17–18
discursive power 53, 63, 80, 163, 166, 183, 194, 196, 210
distributive business interests 118, 119–20
Djelic, M.-L. 155
Doh, J. 156
Dombey & Son (1848) 185
Donaldson, T. 208–9
Donnelly, S.A. 234–5, 239
Dore, R. 209, 244, 245, 248
Dörrenbächer, C. 51
Dowding, K. 78
Drucker, P. 13
Dryzek, J. 16

du Gay, P. 99, 105
Dunning, J. 43, 46, 50, 51

E.ON UK 130, 131
'eclectic paradigm' 51
economic accountability 177–8
economic advantage indicators 87–8
economic decline 67–8
economic elite 34, 58, 60, 65, 69–70, 88
economic growth norm 165–6, 268
economic policy 48, 52, 104, 107, 112, 121–2, 159–66, 245
economic prosperity 25, 128, 129, 46
economic scale, MNCs 6–7, 48
Edelman trust survey 194–5
EDF Energy 130, 131
Edwards, C. 142
efficiency
  Japan 246
  privatisation 128–9
  public–private partnerships 132–8, 140–42
'efficient markets' theory 14
electoral rationale 28–9
elite circulation 65–70, 139–40, 231
elite coherence 33–4, 110–13
Elliott, L. 262
emergent country multinational corporations (EMNCs) 45, 46, 54–61
employee accountability 178
employees as stakeholders 218, 231, 233, 234, 238, 239, 243–4, 246
Employment White Paper (1944) 66
employment, importance of 180
energy sector, implications of privatisation 129–32
Engelen, E. 115
enhanced corporate power and international operations 45–51
'enlightened shareholder value' 204, 224–5
entertainment media, influence of 193–4, 196
environmental responsibilities 22, 32, 119–20, 156, 167, 175–6, 209–10, 212–13
Erin Brokovich (2000) 186
Ernst & Young 80–81
Ertürk, I. 92, 160

Establishment 65, 66, 70, 76, 95–6, 99–101, 222
Esty, D. 153
'ethical consumerism' 203
EU-level lobbying 108–9
Europe
  export of shareholder model 148–50, 235–9
  privatisation 127
  public–private partnerships 135
European Commission 127, 231, 233, 235–6, 265
Eurozone crisis 160, 265
Evans, M. 29, 33

facts 256–9
fairy-tales 73, 164, 253–6
family-owned businesses 10, 12, 56, 59, 86, 172
Faucher-King, F. 68, 103
favourable public policy 38–9
Federation of German Industry (BDI) 238
Feigenbaum, H. 123–4, 126, 128–9
'fiduciary duty' 14, 218
finance
  political parties 96–7
  role in capitalism 106–8
finance capital 141–2
financial accountability 177–8
financial crisis (2008) 72, 75, 76, 88, 107–8, 153, 158, 159–60, 180, 183, 236, 253, 262, 266
financial elite 69–70, 72, 75–6, 92–3, 108, 114, 228–9, 261–2, 264
financial health, focus on 206–7
financial markets, rules and protocols 158–63
Financial Reporting Council (FRC)
  Code of Best Practice 223–8, 236
  Stewardship Code 227
financial sector
  business interests 120
  remuneration 92–3
  support for reform of 265
Financial Services Authority (FSA) 92, 107, 225–6
financialisation 120, 265
fiscal gain from privatisation 124
Flinders, M. 134, 137

Flohr, A. 149, 166
foci 259–62
foreign direct investment (FDI) 46–7, 54–6, 161–3
foreign takeovers 69, 108
Fortune 500 37
Fortune Global 500 5, 7, 35, 37, 256
Foster, C. 101, 102, 103
Fourteenth Amendment 11
fractional business interests 118, 120
France, shift to market capitalism 159
Frankenstein (1818) 3, 190
free market orthodoxy 67, 68, 69, 95, 120–21, 150, 151–2, 164, 254
Freedman, J. 224, 226
Freshfields 82
Freyer, T. 36
Friedman, A. 197, 202
Froud, J. 226
FT 100 37, 74–6, 80–82, 83, 88, 92, 204
FT 350 80, 88, 226
FT Global 500 5, 7, 35, 37, 126–7, 256–7
Fuchs, D. 17, 43, 51, 53, 63, 156, 163, 183, 203, 210
Fukuyama, F. 7
futures 189–90, 262–8

G4S 142–3
Galanter, M. 82
Galbraith, J.K. 4, 5, 36, 70, 115, 121, 157, 169, 206, 259
Gamble, A. 3, 10, 68, 95–6, 164, 222, 255, 266
Gates, L. 152
Geppert, M. 51
Gerlach, M. 243
Germain, R. 148
Germany, corporate governance 220, 230–40
Gibbon, E. 192
Gibson, O. 140
Giddens, A. 66
Gill, S. 152
Gilpin, R. 43
global corporate power 147–50
global cultures 168–73
global diffusion, multinational corporate form 54–61

global governance partnership
global constitution for corporate partnership 173–6
global cultures favouring MNCs 168–73
global norms favouring MNCs 163–8
global rules favouring MNCs 150–63
from national to global corporate power 147–50
'global law firm' model 82
global market norms 163–8
global reach 38
global regime, stability and autonomy 153–8
Global Reporting Initiative (GRI) 200, 201, 206, 210
global rules, enforcing 158–63
globalisation 46–51, 69
'globalizing professionals' as elite 79–85
Goldman, I. 44, 53, 151
Goldstein, A. 56
Gourevitch, P. 12–13, 30–31, 60, 79, 206, 208, 219, 229, 237, 243
governing institutions 1–2, 3, 16–17, 24, 27, 43, 45, 52, 53–4, 109, 219, 260
government preferences, response to 203–4
Gowan, P. 100
Grafström, M. 199
Grant, W. 25, 67, 105, 106, 223
greed 14, 93, 123–4, 172, 186–7, 191–3, 254
Greve, C. 135
Grey, C. 182
Grote, J. 109
Guttsman, W.L. 97

Hackenthal, A. 236, 238–9
Häge, F. 127
Haigh, G. 22
Hale, T. 43, 53
Hall, P. 29–30, 231–2
Hamada, Y. 247
Hanahoe, T. 111, 154, 155
Hancké, B. 159, 232, 235
Hannah, L. 12
Harrod, J. 2, 6, 44

Haseler, S. 90
Hassard, J. 183, 185, 187
Hatcher, M. 154
Haufler, V. 156, 157
Hay, C. 28–9, 68, 71, 97, 159, 166
Hayward, J. 166
Hayward, Tony 113
Heffernan, R. 96, 97
hegemonic power 3, 7, 17, 111–12, 122, 148–9, 154–5, 171, 183, 256
Held, D. 43, 53, 159, 164
Heller, J. 189
Helm, D. 129
Hennessy, P. 102
Herbert Smith 82
Hertz, N. 154
Heugens, P. 198
Higgott, R. 153
High Pay Commission 92
Hills, J. 89, 90
Hirschman, A. 61
Holland, S. 36–7
Holliday, R. 183, 185, 187
Hood, C. 125, 126
Höpner, M. 237, 238
Horn, L. 211–12, 227, 236
Horsfall, D. 118
hostile takeovers 206, 220, 222–3, 227–8, 234, 248
Hsueh, R. 57
Huisman, W. 156
Hutton, W. 85, 86, 107, 232–3, 246
Huxley, A. 189
hybrid forms of governance 157, 239, 248–9
Hyde, M. 143

I Robot (2004) 190
IBM Business Consulting 83
ideological convergence 72
image management 202–3
Inagami, T. 248, 249
incremental change 263–4, 265–6
individual firm lobbying, shift to 108–10
inequality
  growth of 258–9
  and power 87–93
  tolerance of 69–70
Ingham, G. 107

institutional foundations of corporate power 15–19
institutional order, components of 18–19
institutional reform, imperative of 267–8
instrumental power 53
interlocking directorships 34–5, 76, 111, 232
international executive labour market 61
International Monetary Fund (IMF) 67, 151, 152, 160
international perspective 31–2
international political economy (IPE) 31, 43–4, 51–4, 174
investment regulation 152–3, 158–63
invisible hand 48, 186, 197, 241
Ireland, P. 11, 15
isomorphism 57–8

Jackson, G. 51, 246
Jackson, T. 170, 268
Jagger, S. 91
James, O. 8
Japan
  corporate governance model 240–49
  corporate social responsibility 209
Jenkins, S. 99
Jennifer Government (2003) 187–8
John, P. 72
Johnson, S. 76, 108
Joint Stock Companies Act (1856), UK 10
joint stock companies 48, 57
  and pursuit of wealth 8–15
Jones, G. 23, 46, 47, 50, 59, 154
Jones, P. 189
Jordan, G. 156
Julius Review (2008) 133, 134, 135–6, 138–9

Kaletsky, A. 93, 263, 265–6
Kaplan, R. 199–200, 210
Kay, J. 227
Keat, P. 163
Keidanren 39, 244
keiretsu 50, 243
Kelly, G. 3, 10, 222

Klein, N. 50, 154, 155, 170
Kozinets, R. 180
KPMG 78, 80–81, 99
  Survey of Corporate Social Responsibility Reporting 200–201
Kurecz, E. 201
Kuroki, F. 243
Kurtz, L. 199
Kwak, J. 76, 108

labour elite 238
Labour Party 36–7, 66–8, 222
  undermining support for 122–5
  see also New Labour
Lake, D. 206
Lambert, R. 113
Lang, A. 25
large corporations, norm of 4–8
Lazonick, W. 9, 14
Le Carré 186
Le Galès, P. 68, 103
Learmount, S. 244
legal accountability 177–8
legal elite 81–2
legal model 14, 222, 223, 227, 231, 242
'legal personality' 9, 10–11, 15, 21–3, 213, 253
Levy, D. 199–200, 210
Leys, C. 46, 125, 147–8
Li, J. 59
Li, X. 226
liberal democracy, government constraints posed by 27–9, 88
liberal democratic equilibrium 16
Liberal Democratic Party, Japan 244–5, 246–7
Liberal Democrats, UK 96, 267
liberal market economies (LMEs) 30, 232, 233, 239
'liberationism' 111–12, 118
'license to operate' 3, 15, 110, 175, 199, 217, 219, 253, 260
lifetime employment 243–4, 245, 248
Lijphart, A. 16, 65
Lilley, S. 184
limited liability 3, 9–10, 15, 57, 62, 199, 219, 253
Lindblom, C. 27–8
Linklaters 82

Lloyd, R. 156
lobbying 24–5, 39, 67, 105–6, 108–10, 135, 137–8, 183
Locke, R.169, 181
LOCOG (London Organising Committee of the Olympic Games) 140
London Olympics 140, 142–3
London Stock Exchange (LSE) 74, 75, 218, 223
long-term share ownership 72, 227, 232, 233–4, 243, 264
Lowe, S. 122

McGrew, A. 164
McKinley, A. 184
McLean, I. 124
Maclean, C. 34, 53, 74, 77, 88, 108, 111, 115
MacNeil, I. 226
Madigan, C. 83, 84
Mallin, C. 218
management boards 78–9, 104, 220, 233
management buyouts 141, 222–3
management consultancy elite 78, 79, 80, 83–4, 105, 172, 182
management culture 172–3
managerial capitalism 12–13, 31
managerial control 1, 9, 11–13, 15, 33, 35, 59–60, 221–2, 266–7
'managerialism' 1, 20, 101–4, 169, 181–3, 187, 229–30, 260
Mandelson, P. 85
manipulation 85, 110, 169–70, 180, 184, 189
manufacturing sector 107, 120
Marangos, J. 121
March, J. 18, 168, 178–9
Marcuse, H. 170
market discourse
  deception of 254
  dominance of 120–21
market failure 9, 129, 142–3, 158, 224
Market Forces (2004) 188
market norm 164
market power 5, 6, 21, 38, 137, 152–3, 177, 197–8, 254
market share, energy sector 129–31
market socialism 267

'market state' 53, 103, 113–14, 148, 166, 252, 260
market system, government constraints posed by 27–9
marketisation 7–8, 26–7, 46, 171–2, 215
markets, embedding 125–6
Marlow, B. 172
Marquand, D. 213, 215
Marsh, D. 67, 106, 107
Marx/Marxism 25, 27–8, 35, 76, 88, 120, 266–7
Mattli, W. 157, 173
May, C. 31
Mayer, C. 218, 227–8, 250, 263, 264
Mayer, M. 37
Means, G. 4, 12, 179, 217
media elite 85–6
membership, political parties 96–7
mergers and acquisitions 47, 82, 84, 234
Micklethwait, J. 8
Middlemas, K. 66, 67–8
Mikler, J. 209
Miles, S. 202
Miliband, Ed 131, 194, 263, 265
Mills, C.W. 34
minority shareholder protection 59–60, 217, 221, 229, 235, 237, 238–9, 247–8
Minow, N. 22
'mixed economy' 8, 66, 121–2, 231
Miyajima, H. 243
model communities 199
'modernity' 168–9
Monbiot, G. 5, 110
Money (1984) 186
Monks, R. 11, 22
monopoly power 38, 124, 128–9, 177, 246
Moon, J. 202, 204, 209
Moore, Michael 36
morality 10–11, 19, 185–9, 191–3, 252–4, 260
Moran, M. 25, 67, 72, 97, 106, 109, 146
Morgan, G. 82
Morgan, R. 188
Mosley, L. 160
'most favoured nation' principle 150–51, 152

motivation indicators 38–9
Mount, F. 93, 263
Mueller, D. 4, 12
multi-divisional (M-form) organisational form 12, 104
multilateral trade agreements 151, 154
multinational corporations 31–2
  economic scale 6–7
  enhanced power of 45–51
  global constitution for corporate partnership 173–6
  global cultures favouring 168–73
  global norms favouring 163–8
  global rules favouring 150–63
  perspectives on power of 51–4
  transcending the nation-state 42–5
Murdoch, Rupert 85–6, 192
Murphy, D. 53, 159, 203–4

Nace, T. 10, 11
nation-states
  comparison of economic size of multinationals and 6–7
  corporations transcending 42–5
National Audit Office (NAO) 78, 141, 142–3
'national champions' 69, 130, 166
national corporate power 147–50
national distribution, large corporations 5
national governance, compared to corporate governance 219–21
national origins, MNCs 47–9
'national treatment' principle 150–51, 152
neo-corporatism 26, 34, 110, 117
neoliberalism 68, 69, 72–3, 111, 120–21, 127, 148, 158–66, 254
New Corporate State 70–73, 257–8, 261–2
  civil service 'modernization' 100–105
  corporate bias and democratic choice 113–16
  organising and corporate elite 105–13
  partnership and new public services industry 132–44
  policy options of corporations 117–21
  political elite and transformed party system 95–100
  privatisation 121–32
'new economy' thesis 49–51
new institutional capitalism 34
new interest groups, creation of 126
New Labour 28–9, 68, 70–72, 77, 90, 96–100, 103–4, 125, 132, 134, 137–8, 224–5, 233
new market opening 151–2, 154
'new public management' 8, 26–7, 101–4, 132, 184
News International 85–6, 192
Nölke, A. 54
Non-Executive Directors (NEDs) 79, 159, 223, 225, 226, 229, 230
non-profit delivery modes 74, 143
non-regular workers, Japan 246
non-Western MNCs, convergence with Western corporate forms 56–9
Nooyi, Indira 206–7
Norfolk and Norwich Hospital Trust 142
norm entrepreneurs 149
Norman, J. 263
norms 18, 163–8
Northcote–Trevelyan Report (1854) 100–101

O'Donnell, Gus 84, 102, 184
O'Dwyer, B. 199
O'Shea, J. 83, 84
O'Sullivan, M. 14
Oborne, P. 98, 99
Office (2001) 187
offshore markets 159
Olcott, G. 243, 244
oligopoly 4–5, 21, 36, 72–3, 81, 121, 254
Olsen, J. 18, 168, 179
'open corporation' model 211
'Operating and Financial Review (OFR) 225, 227
opportunity indicators 39–40
Organization for Economic Cooperation and Development (OECD), Guidelines for Multinational Corporations 155
Oryx and Crake (2005) 188, 190
Ougaard, M. 155, 198, 210

output-based commissioning 136
Owen, D. 199
ownership, separation from control 11–13, 208, 217

Padgett, S. 72
Painter, A. 153
Palan, R. 44, 53, 151
Palazzo, G. 203
Park, A. 69
Parker, C. 211, 213–14
Parker, D. 122, 123, 124, 128
Parker, M. 179, 181, 185, 187, 190, 194
Parkinson, J. 14, 198, 211, 218, 222, 254
partnership perspective 7–8, 26–7, 43–4, 132–5, 150, 261
pension funds 13
PepsiCo 206–7
perfectly competitive markets 197–8
Perrow, C. 50
Peston, R. 71, 75
Peters, J. 67, 110, 111, 118, 121
Picciotto, S. 151
Plant, R. 133
pluralism 24–6, 34, 41, 66–70, 106, 109
  as fairy-tale 255
Polanyi, K. 15, 172
policy advice, downgrading 101–4
policy failure 101, 105, 115, 122, 158
political accountability 143, 178, 195–6, 212, 219, 220–21
political analysis of corporate power
  comparative perspective 29–31
  international perspective 31–2
  partnership perspective 26–7
  pluralist conceit 24–6
  structural perspectives 27–9
political donations 96–7, 246–7
political elite 34, 66–70
  rupture with corporate elite 268
  and transformed party system 95–100
political freedoms 15–16
political party system, transformation of 95–100
political power
  assessment of 37–40
  definition of 17–19

political process, corporations as subordinate to 25–6
political project, privatisation as 122–5, 127–8
political risk analysis 160–63
politically vulnerable sectors 75, 76
Pollard, A. 185
'popular capitalism' 123–4
popular culture, critique of corporations in 184–95
popular images of corporations 178–83
Porter, M. 67, 165, 246
Post-war Settlement 66–8, 77, 96, 100–101, 105–6, 113, 222
Powell, W. 57
power sharing 26–7, 42–4
Pretty Woman (1990) 185
PriceWaterhouseCoopers (PWC) 80–81, 83
principal–agent relations 12, 217, 219, 227, 241
Private Finance Initiative (PFI) 26, 39, 133, 134, 135–6, 141–2
private sector appointees, civil service 77–8, 99, 139–40
privatisation 7–8, 37, 121–32, 152–3, 172
Privatization Barometer 126–7
pro-business cultural framework 169–70
professional service organisations 79–85
profitability, public–private partnerships 140–42
property rights 15, 62, 125, 154, 218, 250, 253–4
Przeworski, A. 28
public interest companies (PICs) 138, 143
public interest mandate, CSR 207
public obligations 7–8, 26–7, 109–10
public perceptions
  corporations/government 97–8, 153–4, 194–5, 258
  private service provision 143–4
  privatisation 129, 132
public service ethos 140, 143
public service industry (PSI) 132–44, 257–8

public services industry, components of 134–5
public–private partnerships (PPPs) 26–7, 39, 44, 132–44, 257–8
Pyper, R. 102

Quack, S. 82

Radaelli, C. 17
railway companies 4, 10, 221
Raising of Capital Act (1998), Germany 237
Randall, N.J. 184
Rebérioux, A. 230
Redding, G. 59
regulated products/markets 38
'regulatory capitalism' 73, 114, 203–4
regulatory dialogue, bolstering corporate legitimacy/strength in 203–5
'regulatory state' 114, 136–7
relational contracting 141, 244
remuneration 83, 87, 91–3, 102, 112–13
reporting standards 200, 201
reputation 40, 196, 198, 200–203, 205, 215, 226
reputational intermediaries 79–85
resources indicators 38
revolutionary change 266–7
Rhine model 231–40, 264–5
Rhodes, C. 182, 190
Richardson, J. 25
Ridley Scott 190–91
Rimington, J. 102
risk assessment 160–63
risk management 201–3
risk transfer 50, 136, 142–3
Ritzer, G. 170, 180
Roach, L. 227
Road to Wigan Pier (1937) 186
Roberts, S. 82
Robinson Crusoe (1719) 185
Robinson, J. 268
Rugman, A.M. 47
rule system 18, 150–63
RWE npower 130, 131

Sampson, A. 66
Sarbanes–Oxley Act (2002) 218, 225, 263

Saturday Night and Sunday Morning (1958) 186
Schäferhoff, M. 44, 157
Scherer, A. 203
Schmidt, V. 17, 159, 173, 268
Schmitter, P. 117
Schneider, V. 127
Schweickart, D. 154, 267
Scott, J. 33, 35
Scott, R. 18–19, 85
Scott, W.R. 168
Scottish Power 130
Seldon, A. 70–71
self-interest 69–70, 112–13, 115, 172
self-regulation 155–7, 198, 200, 203–4, 209, 211, 223–6, 245
Sell, S. 151
Sengupta, M. 152
Serco 26–7, 134–5, 139, 142
Shaoul, J. 133
share ownership, changing composition of 13, 228
shared power 26–7, 42–4
shareholder activism 227–8, 229, 248
'shareholder model' 13–15, 208, 217–30, 249, 250
    export to Europe 235–9
shareholder ownership myth 253–4
shareholder value 13–15, 104, 118, 201, 205, 207–8, 217, 227, 235–6, 248, 250
Sherman Act (1890) 4, 36
Sherman, J. 79, 103
Shinn, J. 12–13, 30–31, 60, 79, 208, 219, 229, 237, 243
Shonfield, A. 29
'short termism' 93, 221–2, 227–8, 230
Simmons, B. 164
Simon, H. 23
Singh, R. 80
Single European Act 127
single shareholder control 208
Skinner, Q. 21
Sklair, L. 32, 35, 53, 73, 77, 79, 88, 113, 167, 170–71, 175, 206, 214
Slaughter & May 82
small firms 4, 21, 59, 119, 128
Smartest Guys in the Room (2005) 187
Smith, A. 10, 186, 197, 241
Smith, C. 203

Social Democratic Party (SPD), Germany 236–8
social organisations 26, 33, 209, 231–40, 244
Soederberg, S. 35, 266–7
'soft law' 155–6, 206, 210, 218, 223–6, 259
Soskice, D. 29–30, 231–2
South Korea, corporate governance model 240–43
sovereignty debate 31, 42–3, 52–3
Spender, J.-C. 169, 181
SSE (Scottish and Southern) 130
stability, global regime 153–8
'stakeholder capitalism' 110, 202, 224, 233, 263, 264
stakeholder engagement 202–3, 211, 266
stakeholder model 234–40, 243–9
stakeholder obligation 228
stakeholder regulation 155–6, 157
state capitalism 56, 60, 165, 224
state-owned companies 36–7, 56, 57–8, 59, 66–7, 126–7, 129, 131–2, 222, 256
Steria 83
Sternberg, E. 207
Stevenson, L. 156
Stiff, P. 92
Stigler, G. 114, 203
Stiglitz, J. 88, 151
Stock Corporation Act (1937), Germany 234–5
Stoker, G. 42
Stopford, J. 31, 61
Story, J. 57
Strange, S. 31, 52–3, 61
Streeck, W. 26
structural dependency 28–9, 32, 41, 71, 114, 268
structural perspectives 27–9
structural power 28, 38, 53, 63, 156, 210, 228
'super rich' 90
supervisory boards 220, 233, 236, 238
supply chains 50, 84, 203, 214
sustainability norm 165, 167, 200, 213
Swank, D. 159
systemic change 264–6
systemic ideology 111–12

Takeover Law (2001), Germany 237–8
Tang, Y. 59
Tax Reduction Act (2000), Germany 237
taxation 48, 89–90, 91–2, 108, 159, 203, 207
Taylor, H. 54
Taylor, R. 71, 225, 233
Tenbücken, M. 109
Tencati, A. 203
Thatcherism 29, 37, 68, 69, 77, 95–6, 99–100, 101, 122–5, 130, 132, 148, 155, 240
'Third Way' 68, 134, 137
Thomas Crown Affair (1998) 185
Tiberghien, Y. 248
Tivey, L. 13
Tomorrow Never Dies (1997) 189
Toynbee, P. 92
traditional regulation 157
transnational capitalist class (TCC) 32, 35, 73–86
transnational corporations 47–8, 49
Transparency and Disclosure Act (2002), Germany 237
Treasury 104, 107, 233
Tricker, B. 263
'trust firms' 264
trust, corporations/government 97–8, 194–5, 258
Turnbull, Andrew 102
Turner, A. 71, 107, 158

UK
  circulation of elites 66–70
  composition of corporate elite 73–86
  control of corporate elite 36–7
  corporate elite, power and inequality 87–93
  corporate governance model 217–30
  corporate social responsibility 204–5, 211–12
  democratic settlements and corporate power 64–5
  see also New Corporate State
UK Uncut 203
United Nations (UN)
  Centre on Transnational Corporations 155

Global Compact 60–61, 156, 200, 210
Transnationality Index 48–9
World Investment Report 55–6
unions 66–7, 96, 97–8, 100, 122–3, 139, 178, 222, 238
unquoted corporations 227
US
  control of corporate elite 36
  corporate governance 218–19
  corporate social responsibility 199
  hegemony of 153, 154–5
  neoliberalism 68
Useem, M. 34, 74
usurpation of government 187–90, 193

Valente, M. 173
'value skimming' 92–3
van Apeldoorn, B. 43, 111, 236
Van Oosterhaut, H. 198
varieties of capitalism (VoC) 2, 29–30, 53, 165, 231–2, 235, 245, 249
Veblen, T. 170
Vernon, R. 31, 37, 61
Villiers, C. 227
Vitols, S. 233
Vogel, D. 4, 25, 156, 202, 204, 206
voluntary principle, CSR 211–12

Walker, D. 92
Wall Street (1987) 184, 185, 186–7
Wallerstein, M. 28
Washington Consensus 64, 128, 148, 151–2, 153, 155
waste management services 136–7
Watmore, Ian 84
Way We Live Now (1875) 185

wealth
  pursuit of 8–15
  redistribution of 69, 88–9, 90
Weiss, L. 52
'welfare capitalism' 166, 209
welfare gains, privatisation 128–9
welfare state 66, 88, 89, 113, 166, 212, 242
Wendt, A. 21
Westwood, R. 182, 190
Whitley, R. 29, 46, 76
Whittaker, H. 241, 243, 245, 248–9
Whittington, R. 37
Wilks, S. 11, 29, 37, 79, 102, 122, 153, 177, 236
Williamson, O. 9
Wilson, G. 101
Windell, K. 199
Wintour, P. 85
Witt, M. 59
Witty, A. 205
Woods, N. 151–2
Wooldridge, A. 8
worker representation 209, 222, 233–5, 238, 239, 244
World Bank 128, 151, 152
World Economic Forum, Global Competitiveness Index 161–2
World Trade Organisation (WTO) 57, 58, 61, 150–52, 153–4
Wright, M. 29

Yaziji, M. 156
Yes Minister/Yes Prime Minister (1986–88) 184
Young, S. 122